Price-Based Investment Strategies

Adam Zaremba • Jacob "Koby" Shemer

Price-Based Investment Strategies

How Research Discoveries Reinvented Technical Analysis

palgrave
macmillan

Adam Zaremba
Poznan University of Economics
and Business, Poznan, Poland

Jacob "Koby" Shemer
AlphaBeta
Tel Aviv, Israel

ISBN 978-3-030-08267-3 ISBN 978-3-319-91530-2 (eBook)
https://doi.org/10.1007/978-3-319-91530-2

Cover design by Ran Shauli

Printed on acid-free paper

This Palgrave Macmillan imprint is published by the registered company Springer Nature Switzerland AG
The registered company address is: Gewerbestrasse 11, 6330 Cham, Switzerland

To my daughters, Alice and Suzie, who continually provided me requisite breaks from writing this book.
Adam Zaremba

Praise Page

"Zaremba and Shemer have written the seminal book on research-based technical analysis. They discuss the theoretical basis, implementation details, and performance results of strategies based on stock price movement. These include traditional momentum, trend following, reversals, acceleration, skewness, volatility, and seasonality. They do this not only individually but by blending these together creating remarkable results. I whole-heartedly recommend this book to all portfolio managers and asset allocators receptive to price-based investing."

—Gary Antonacci, *Author of Dual Momentum Investing: An Innovative Strategy for Higher Returns with Lower Risk*

"This is an excellent book which challenges the status quo. Just over fifty years ago two future Nobel Laureates, Samuelson and Fama, pointed out if stock prices were random then 'the work of the chartist, like the astrologer, is of no real value in stock market analysis' (Fama, 1965). With that, technical analysis was dismissed, being regarded as voodoo art. The authors, however, build on the well-known momentum anomaly as a price-based anomaly and show this is but one of many. They argue that contrary to the generally accepted view, there is indeed a place for price-based analysis, thus rehabilitating technical analysis. The book is well worth reading."

—Christo Auret, *Head of Finance Division, School of Economic and Business Sciences, University of the Witwatersrand, and Editor-in-chief, Investment Analysts Journal; and Robert Vivian, Professor of Insurance and Finance, School of Economic and Business Sciences, University of the Witwatersrand*, and Editor, *Investment Analysts Journal*

"This book is an accessible and adept exposition of the pivotal role played by stock return predictors in financial markets and portfolio design. Adam Zaremba and Jacob Shemer present a thorough review of the most important empirical techniques used in asset allocation strategies. Given its easy-to understand language, the book is a valuable resource for academics, students, and market professionals."

—Turan Bali, *Robert Parker Chair Professor of Finance, McDonough School of Business, Georgetown University, USA*

"Zaremba and Shemer expertly present, assess, and unify the new academic research on price-based strategies in comparison to the old perspective on technical analysis, making it available in one place and accessible to a practitioner audience. The strategies presented have in common that they work, are easy to implement (using past price information only), and for that reason can be implemented and adjusted on a daily basis, in contrast to fundamental strategies."

—Ronald Balvers, *DeGroote School of Business, McMaster University*

"Zaremba and Shemer collect all of the price-based investment strategies in one place. This comprehensive, yet approachable work may serve as a practical guidebook for both researchers and investors."

—Nusret Cakici, *Gabelli School of Business, Fordham University, USA*

"There is plenty of evidence to suggest that fund managers that manage their portfolios using their discretion tend to produce disappointing long-term performance for their investors. In sharp contrast, there is now a wealth of academic evidence that suggests that simple, rules-based investing can produce very attractive returns for investors – particularly when these rules are based upon securities prices. For anyone looking for an alternative to the active fund management industry Dr Zaremba's book provides an excellent review and analysis of the possible benefits of rules-based investing."

—Andrew Clare, *Chair in Asset Management, Cass Business School*

"The latest book by Zaremba and Schemer presents a panoply of price-based investment strategies that has something new and interesting to offer to both the experienced practitioner as well as the curious academic. The authors use a disciplined and focused approach dispelling the scepticism about investment strategies based on technical analysis. A thoroughly researched monograph contributing to the chipping away of the market efficiency dogma central to finance academia for the past half a century."

—Paskalis Glabadanidis, *Department of Accounting and Finance, Business School, University of Adelaide*

"*Price-Based Investment Strategies* does an excellent job summarizing the power of prices when it comes to building investment strategies. The book will serve as a great reference for professionals and sophisticated individual investors. Read it."

—Wesley R. Gray, PhD, *CEO of Alpha Architect and Co-author of Quantitative Momentum*

"Zaremba and Shemer have compiled a comprehensive overview of the research on price-based investment strategies. This book effectively elucidates the extensive knowledge accumulated over the last three decades. The theoretical review and empirical analyses provide the necessary foundation for both practitioners looking to implement technical trading strategies and academics whose research aims to understand the drivers of these strategies' profits. It is a must-read for both groups."

—Scott Murray, *Assistant Professor of Finance,* J. Mack Robinson *College of Business, Georgia State University*

"All finance professionals, irrespective of their views on technical and fundamental analyses, will find a lot in this book to rekindle their interest. In particular, if you have always been puzzled by momentum strategies, the evidence gathered in this book will unravel the ambiguities. As someone involved in the development of students, "Price-based investment strategies…" is my go-to guide on the subject. Zaremba and Shemer have assembled the best research on the subject and variety of data and turned it into an important resource for investors and academics which I have recommended to my colleagues and graduate students."

—Isaac Otchere, *Sprott School of Business, Carleton University*

"This book provides a thorough presentation of investment strategies that have made a large impact on how professional investors trade, relying on decades of academic research. For example, the book shows how investors may benefit from price trends and subsequent mean-reversion. These ideas are formalized by the academic return factors such as momentum, time-series momentum, long-term reversal, and betting-against-beta. The book considers "price-based strategies", meaning investment strategies that only rely on knowing past prices — rather than also relying on such accounting information or macroeconomic data — which keeps the book focused on strategies that are relatively straightforward to implement, at least in principle."

—Lasse Heje Pedersen, *Principal at AQR Capital Management and Finance Professor at Copenhagen Business School and NYU*

"There is an on-going schism between the pure approach of financial economics and econometrics that tends to support overall the efficient market hypothesis on the one hand and the practitioners, active fund managers and traders, on the other hand, who continue to ignore these findings by and large and, for a fraction of them, provide superior performance. In this context, this book is a remarkable resource to reconcile these communities, proposing a modern informed survey of the main results on how so-called technical analyses of past prices and past returns can provide insights in future returns and risks. Both practitioners and academic will find it highly valuable to position their own approach and obtain inspiration."

—Didier Sornette, *Professor of Entrepreneurial Risks at ETH Zurich and Finance at the Swiss Finance Institute*

"A practical guide to modern technical analysis offering a fresh look at price-based investment strategies. Well-grounded both in theory and empirical studies may convince even biggest skeptics of technical analysis. As the book bridges top academic research with practical application it is undoubtedly valuable both for academicians and investors."

—Adam Szyszka, *Professor of Finance, Warsaw School of Economics, and Co-founder and Partner, AT INVEST Ltd.*

"This book provides an excellent review on the recent developments in price-based investment strategies shaping the contemporary technical analysis, especially used in international asset management. The intuition behind the quantitative strategies, the techniques of implementing these strategies, and evaluating their performance are explained clearly and competently. The book is a strong reference for portfolio managers and academicians interested in international asset allocation and is a valuable resource for introductory graduate courses in empirical asset pricing."

—Mehmet Umutlu, *Associate Professor of Finance and Head of the Department of International Trade and Finance, Yasar University*

"This book gives the reader insights into the growing body of literature on trend investing.

It also relates the trend investing with other documented and proven return factors."

—Pim van Vliet, PhD, *Portfolio Manager Conservative Equities at Robeco*

"This book is a must-read for those who want to improve their investment strategies. The recommendations of the book are based on well-established academic research. The book is easy to read. I highly recommend this book."

—Joseph Vu, *Associate Professor of Finance, DePaul University*

Preface

Technical and fundamental analyses are the two principal schools of thought in investment management. The crucial difference between the two lies in the type of information used by analysts. While technicians rely on historical price behavior and trading volume of securities, fundamental analysts pore over financial, industry, and economic factors to predict future returns. The rivalry between the schools is as old as the modern financial sector, and the winner in this horse race is yet to be seen.

Although technical analysis has always been appealing to investors, for a long time it was being ignored by the academic community. Primarily because the profitability of the technical analysis stood in stark contrast to the efficient market hypothesis (EMH), which dominated the thinking of the 1960s and 1970s. According to the EMH theory, in the informationally efficient market the prices always accurately reflect the available information. Especially in an economic downturn, all the information on past prices should be duly discounted. Why? Because if thousands of investors do their best to exploit technical opportunities, then any possible profits quickly dry up. In other words, there is no place for any abnormal returns to be earned through technical analysis. As Paul Samuelson (1965, p. 44) observed in his study, "There is no way of making an expected profit by extrapolating past changes in the future price, by chart or any other esoteric devices of magic or mathematics. The market quotation already contains in itself all that can be known about the future and in that sense has discounted future contingencies as much as it is humanly possible." How firmly the community believed in the EMH is well expressed by another quote from Michael Jensen (1978), who famously wrote, "I believe there is no other proposition in economics which has more solid empirical evidence supporting it than the Efficient Market Hypothesis."

From the academic standpoint, technical analysis was being frowned upon as a sort of trickery rather than a valid form of security analysis. The fundamental analysis and rigorous examination of both financial and economic information were held as the only proper means to forecast prices and formulate expectations about future returns. While the EMH was the dominating way of thinking, the early attempts to seek inefficiencies were predominantly focused on valuation and financial conditions. The numerous studies conducted in the 1980s provided convincing evidence that stocks with low capitalization, low price-to-fundamentals ratios, and good quality delivered abnormal returns.[1] These phenomena became so broadly acknowledged to be finally included in the most popular models used in financial markets (Fama and French 1992, 1993). While the fundamental analysis remained the approved school of thought exercised by both investors and academics, the technical analysis was dismissed as financial voodoo.

This situation continued until 1993 when Jegadeesh and Titman published their groundbreaking study on the so-called momentum effect. What is momentum? It is a well-established tendency for assets with good past performance to continue to outperform, while poor past performers continue to disappoint. Although individual momentum strategies may differ in the level of sophistication, sorting periods, predictive indicators, and more, their fundamental rule is surprisingly simple: stick to past winners and shy away from losers. As it has been coined and often repeated by market practitioners, "the trend is your friend."

Since its initial discovery, studies on momentum have widely proliferated making it one of the most pervasive and robust anomalies ever discovered. The momentum effect has been documented not only across numerous stock markets but also in various asset classes, including bonds, currencies, and commodities, and even investment styles (Asness et al. 2013; Avramov et al. 2016). It has been identified across more than two centuries, starting from the Victorian age and the first US equities market of 1800 (Chabot et al. 2008; Geczy and Samonov 2017)

[1] For example, Banz (1981), Basu (1983), Rosenberg et al. (1985), Bhandari (1988). For a comprehensive review, see Zaremba and Shemer (2016a).

Two decades since its discovery, momentum investing has proved to approximate the holy grail of the financial markets: the ideal investment strategy for any investor, combining the two most desirable traits of any investment strategy—robustness and simplicity. While the evidence for momentum is probably more pervasive and timeless than for any other investment technique, its implementation is astonishingly straightforward, requiring neither complex data nor sophisticated skills. Most surprisingly and in contrary to the other complicated and time-consuming fundamental approaches, a momentum-based strategy needs only a single data input, namely a stock price.

Interestingly, this is only the beginning of the story. The rediscovery of momentum investing coincided with a preponderance of other techniques also solely relying on the price behavior. A perfect example: volatility risk. Academicians have always believed in a link connecting risk and return in financial markets. The reality, however, turned out to surprise us all when in 2006, Ang, Chen, and Xing found that the volatility is negatively related to future returns. Simply speaking, the lower the past volatility, the higher the future returns! This phenomenon has been later confirmed across numerous markets and assets classes, including international equities, bonds, and even derivatives!

Not only pure volatility but also the shape of return distributions has been found meaningful. The skewness effect—as a perfect example—has stemmed from the mounting evidence proving that either positive or negative past extreme returns can be very informative of the future performance.[2] While the effect can be utilized through various technical approaches, even through a maximum daily return over the previous month (Bali et al. 2011), in the end, it always leads to the same conclusion: skewness does matter.

Having started with only a handful of pure price-based strategies—the momentum effect, volatility, and skewness—the list is growing rapidly. Short- and long-run reversals, seasonal effects, intraday patterns, downside and extreme risks, maximum yearly prices, liquidity are another return-predictive that have been attracting much interest in recent years. All the techniques share a simple yet important trait: they rely only on the stock price. Taken together they constitute a new body of modern technical analysis which is research based, covers numerous aspects of price behavior, and now is probably more profitable and convincing than ever before.

[2] See, for example, Bali et al. (2016) for review.

Nowadays, the price-based research techniques have imperceptibly entered the pantheon of investment techniques, perhaps even dethroning the art of fundamental analysis. The sole momentum effect is currently perhaps the most intensively investigated single topic in finance. In almost any volume of the top-tier finance journals, there is at least one paper on momentum. A quick search for the term "momentum" in the SSRN—a popular research preprint server—produces over a thousand papers written over the last three years only. Clearly, the price-based strategies are no longer rejected; they are the apple of the eye of the finance literature.

The price-based strategies are not only simple but also astonishingly efficient. Fundamental data, such as financial statements, is usually available, at best, quarterly, while price, daily (or even intraday), makes price-based strategies richer than the basic fundamental approach. Although they rely on much less data than the fundamental techniques, the strategies can yield even higher returns. This transpires not only from sophisticated research but even from analysts' performance. A recent study by Avramov et al. (2017) compared the performance of technical and fundamental recommendations, proving the technical approach to be much more successful.

The modern technical analysis has come full circle: from the voodoo art on the periphery of the legitimate investment practices to the pantheon of research-proven strategies being based on research, backed by strong academic evidence, and both surprisingly efficient and profitable.

The primary goal of this work is to create a practical guide to price-based investment techniques, covering the last two decades of rapid discoveries in asset pricing empirical research. Taken together, they constitute what might be called the modern art of technical analysis. We demonstrate how various aspects of the past price behavior could be translated into profitable money management strategies for international markets. This book lays out a range of state-of-the-art quantitative strategies, additionally describing their theoretical basis, implementation details, and performance over the recent decades.

The main aim of this book is to tell the story of this "price-based" revolution that took over investing. We take the reader on a journey leading through various investment techniques, showing how much information on the future returns is encapsulated in the price and how simply and efficiently it can be translated into profitable strategies. We demonstrate how the recent research discoveries have transformed the art of modern technical analysis.

This book includes both theoretical and empirical content. The evidence on price-based investing is currently scattered across various papers and subjects. Thus, we first review and systematize the existing studies on price-based investing. We present the major groups of price-driven strategies, which are based on momentum, trend following, reversal, skewness, price, volatility effects, and seasonalities. On the one hand, we depict the theoretical background of the presented strategies along with the existing empirical research. On the other hand, the book makes the case for an empirical investigation of all the described approaches to global financial markets. We reexamine the performance of multiple strategies using a comprehensive sample, conducting a wide-range comparison of performance data from the 24 major developed markets around the world ranging over the last 20 years. We construct practical portfolios and display their performance, depicting for investors their basic characteristics. This way, the book not only provides new insights for academicians but also provides a practical guide for stock market investors.

Alongside the replication and comparison of numerous price-based strategies, we show how these strategies can be combined to form an efficient portfolio. We intend to focus on two issues: strategic and tactical asset allocation.

In strategic allocation, we show how general investors can benefit from blending multiple price-based strategies. Thanks to low correlation among the strategies, the multi-strategy portfolios display lower volatility, and the individual strategies may constitute the building blocks of a solid portfolio the same way as individual stocks or bonds were used in the past.

Interestingly, there might be an even more efficient way to combine various price-based strategies as from time to time investors could try to tilt their portfolios and overweight some strategies. This is further discussed in the section on timing the price-based strategies. How can one time the strategies? A few of the most pervasive stock selection approaches—based on momentum, cross-sectional seasonality, or valuation—proved to work not only for individual securities but also for the entire strategies. Taking the momentum effect as an example, the strategies that performed best (worst) in the past tend to continue to outperform (underperform) in the future (Avramov et al. 2016). This book shows how these regularities could be capitalized on to the investor's advantage.

To sum up, the book you are holding in your hands aims to present a comprehensive review of the price-based investment strategies for stock market investors. It provides a guide for both academicians and investors, showing how the modern research has reinvented the technical analysis over the recent decades.

In order to examine the practical applicability of various strategies, we also test real data from equity markets. In particular, we examine a number of different price-based strategies to evaluate their performance both in individual countries and globally. Amassing a large sample of stocks, we employ a consistent methodology to form portfolios from sorts on various price-based variables, providing, thus, comprehensive and up-to-date evidence on the performance of numerous equity quantitative strategies.

The book is composed of eight chapters. We start with the review of different price-based strategies, considering both their theoretical explanation and empirical performance. For each strategy, we explain both the underlying concept and the theoretical grounding. We also present existing empirical evidence on the stock selection based on these strategies.

The first chapter shortly summarizes the methods and data employed in this study. We describe our data sources and preparation procedures. We also demonstrate how we form and evaluate the investment strategies.

Chapter 2 describes the well-established phenomenon of momentum, defined as the tendency of securities with good (poor) past performance to overperform (underperform) in the future. It is one of the most pervasive anomalies ever discovered with supportive evidence across numerous asset classes. The chapter presents various momentum techniques and their variations, along with potential improvements.

Chapter 3 is about long- and short-term reversal patterns. While the momentum strategy assumes continuation of the price movement, the reversal strategies rely on a contrary postulating that the price trend will revert. How can both phenomena coexist? The solution is the investment horizon. While the momentum effect is present in the mid-term (3–12 months), the reversal occurs either in the short term (1 month) or in the long term (3–5 years). This chapter will thoroughly discuss the sources and implementation of reversal strategies in financial markets.

Chapter 4 discusses one of the most puzzling anomalies—the low-risk phenomenon. Even in today's finance, the relationship between risk and return seems controversial. While crucial implication of the standard models states that a higher risk is followed by higher expected return, the empirical evidence seems to contradict this expectation. The recent evidence has supported the idea that the standard measures of realized risk, including volatility or systematic risk, negatively predict abnormal returns. Surprisingly, other risk measures related to extreme or downside risk prove to be positive predictors of performance. Importantly, all of these measures might potentially help investors to choose market outperformance. In Chap. 4, we carefully analyze this phenomenon.

Chapter 5 concentrates on the role of the return distribution. Some studies have shown that not only the volatility or past returns matter but also the shape of the return distributions. To some extent, investors treat stocks as lotteries which can make them rich. In consequence, the right-skewed distributions, with a large chance of exceptionally high returns, finally tend to disappoint. The impact of skewness can be measured in many ways: from very sophisticated measures, like co-skewness or idiosyncratic skewness, to plain and simple ones like maximum daily return over the previous month. All of these measures are interesting predictors of future returns.

Chapter 6 focuses on building cross-sectional strategies based on calendar anomalies. Seeking seasonal regularities in a stock market is as old as the art of investment analysis. January seasonality and "sell in May and go away" are patterns known to virtually any investor in the stock market. While popular, they are, at the same time, highly controversial. For a long time, the seasonal anomalies belonged to the most "magical" tools of technical analysis. Yet again, the recent research discoveries have painted a completely different picture. Many of the seasonal anomalies could be captured by the so-called cross-sectional seasonality—the foundation of all seasonal anomalies—namely a tendency of stocks which performed well (poorly) in the same calendar month in the past to continue to outperform (underperform). We demonstrate how investors can use this effect to their own benefit.

Chapter 7 attempts to pursue a slightly trickier question: can we predict returns based on raw prices? In other words, can the nominal price forecast future performance? Is it better to invest in low- or high-price stocks? We review all conflicting evidence and reexamine the nominal-price investing approach across multiple countries.

Chapter 8 focuses on a mata-level analysis. Could use return or price-based patterns to rotate across the different strategies? Is there momentum in strategy returns?

The book ends with our conclusions of the price-based strategies, also showing the potential directions for further research, which could shed more light on the investment techniques and help in developing new tools for international investors.

Poznan, Poland — Adam Zaremba
Tel Aviv, Israel — Jacob "Koby" Shemer

References

Asness, C. S., Moskowitz, T. J., & Pedersen, L. H. (2013). Value and momentum everywhere. *Journal of Finance, 68*(3), 929–985.

Avramov, D., Cheng, S., Schreiber, A., & Shemer, K. (2016, in press). Scaling up market anomalies. *Journal of Investing*. Available at SSRN: https://ssrn.com/abstract=2709178 or https://doi.org/10.2139/ssrn.2709178. Accessed 23 Oct 2017.

Avramov, D., Kaplanski, G., & Levy, H. (2017). *Talking numbers: Technical versus fundamental investment recommendations*. Available at SSRN: https://ssrn.com/abstract=2648292 or https://doi.org/10.2139/ssrn.2648292. Accessed 21 Oct 2017.

Bali, T., Cakici, N., & Whitelaw, R. F. (2011). Maxing out: Stocks as lotteries and the cross-section of expected returns. *Journal of Financial Economics, 99*(2), 427–446.

Bali, T. G., Engle, R. F., & Murray, S. (2016). *Empirical asset pricing: The cross section of stock returns*. Hoboken: Wiley.

Banz, R. W. (1981). The relationship between return and market value of common stocks. *Journal of Financial Economics, 9*, 3–18.

Basu, S. (1983). The relationship between earnings yield, market value and return for NYSE common stocks: Further evidence. *Journal of Financial Economics, 12*, 129–156.

Bhandari, L. C. (1988). Debt/equity ratio and expected common stock returns: Empirical evidence. *Journal of Finance, 43*(2), 507–528.

Chabot, B., Ghysels, E., & Jagannathan, R. (2008). *Price momentum in stocks: Insights from Victorian age* (NBER working paper No. 14500). Available at: http://www.nber.org/papers/w14500. Accessed 20 Oct 2015.

Fama, E. F., & French, K. R. (1992). The cross-section of expected returns. *Journal of Finance, 47*, 427–466.

Fama, E. F., & French, K. R. (1993). Common risk factors in the returns on stocks and bonds. *Journal of Financial Economics, 33*, 3–56. https://doi.org/10.1016/0304-405X(93)90023-5.

Geczy, C., & Samonov, M. (2016). Two centuries of price-return momentum. *Financial Analysts Journal, 72*(5), 32–56. https://doi.org/10.2469/faj.v72.n5.1.

Geczy, C., & Samonov, M. (2017). Two Centuries of Multi-Asset Momentum (Equities, Bonds, Currencies, Commodities, Sectors and Stocks). Available at SSRN: https://ssrn.com/abstract=2607730 or http://dx.doi.org/10.2139/ssrn.2607730.

Jensen, M. C. (1978). Some anomalous evidence regarding market efficiency. *Journal of Financial Economics, 6*(2–3), 95–101.

Rosenberg, B., Reid, K., & Lanstein, R. (1985). Persuasive evidence of market inefficiency. *Journal of Portfolio Management, 11*, 9–17.

Samuelson, P. A. (1965). Proof that properly anticipated prices fluctuate randomly. *Industrial Management Review*, *6*, 41–49.

Zaremba, A., & Shemer, J. (2016a). *Country asset allocation*. New York: Palgrave Macmillan.

Zaremba, A., & Shemer, J. (2016b). Is small beautiful? Size effect in stock markets. *Country Asset Allocation*, 67–79. https://doi.org/10.1057/978-1-137-59191-3_4.

Zaremba, A., & Shemer, J. (2016c). Momentum effect across countries. *Country Asset Allocation*, 161–181. New York: Palgrave Macmillan. https://doi.org/10.1057/978-1-137-59191-3_10.

Zaremba, A., & Shemer, J. (2016d). Value versus growth: Is buying cheap always a bargain? *Country Asset Allocation*, 9–38. New York: Palgrave Macmillan. https://doi.org/10.1057/978-1-137-59191-3_2.

Zaremba, A., & Shemer, K. (2016e). *What drives the momentum in factor premia? Evidence from international equity markets*. Paper presented at the 20th EBES Conferences, September 28–30, 2016, Vienna, Austria.

Zaremba, A., & Shemer, J. (2016f). Testing the country allocation strategies. *Country Asset Allocation*, 123–136. New York: Palgrave Macmillan. https://doi.org/10.1057/978-1-137-59191-3_7.

Acknowledgments

We would like to thank all the people who also contributed to the development of this book. In particular, our hats are off to Krzysztof Zaremba without whom this book could never have been completed. Special thanks to Bartłomiej Dzięciołowski, who helped us make this book a reality.

Adam Zaremba also especially thanks his wife, Patricia, for her continuous support and countless sacrifices she made to help him get to this point.

The research presented in this book was a part of project no. OPUS 2016/23/B/HS4/00731 financed by the National Science Centre of Poland. The views expressed in this book are those of the authors and not necessarily those of any affiliated institution.

Contents

List of Figures

List of Tables

CHAPTER 1

Data, Portfolios, and Performance: How We Test the Strategies

In this book, we demonstrate the performance of various strategies, which can require only a single input: historical prices. In this section, we will begin our journey to the world of price-based investing with a short description of how we both calculated and tested these strategies on real historical data. All the strategies have been implemented in a consistent and identical way so as to assure their comparability. Below, we describe three major aspects of our examinations: (1) the data we use, (2) the method we form the portfolios, and (3) the method we evaluate their performance.

What Data We Use?

Today's financial markets know almost no borders. Sitting in his living room in Berlin an investor can access equity markets in London, New York, or even Tokyo with a single mouse-click. The world of investing has become more interconnected and accessible than ever before. As a result, we do not test our strategies in a single market, even if it's as large as the American market, but instead, we test them in a robust sample of 24 developed countries with extensive and well-established stock markets—that is, Australia, Austria, Belgium, Canada, Denmark, Finland, France, Germany, Greece, Hong Kong, Ireland, Israel, Italy, Japan, the Netherlands, New Zealand, Norway, Portugal, Singapore, Spain, Sweden, Switzerland, the UK, and the USA. These markets span across

A. Zaremba, J. "Koby" Shemer, *Price-Based Investment Strategies*,
https://doi.org/10.1007/978-3-319-91530-2_1

many continents and cultures and account for the majority of capitalization in global equity markets. We have based our computations on the price data sourced from FactSet. Naturally, our tests could be further extended to include the emerging or frontier markets, but our focus on the developed economies guarantees the strategies to be accessible to most of the developed-market investors.

As we have focused on the period from January 1995 to June 2017, our sample is fresh and timely, reflecting the recent changes and developments in financial markets. We also used older data, for instance, when forming a strategy for January 1995 requires data from the earlier periods as, for example, a momentum strategy which relies on past performance. At times, the return data for some or all of the countries is available for the shorter periods, in which case we use them. We calculate all of the strategies separately for individual countries.

We collected the initial data in local currencies as comparisons based on various currencies could be misleading (Liew and Vassalou 2000; Bali et al. 2013). This is especially reasonable for countries where inflation and risk-free rates are very high and differ significantly across the markets. As most studies adopt the dollar-denominated approach (Waszczuk 2014a), we also denominated all the data in US dollars to obtain comparable results on an international scale.[1] For consistency, whenever we needed to use the risk-free rate (e.g., to calculate excess returns), we used the benchmark returns on the US three-month Treasury bills. Throughout the book, we have used gross returns, that is, returns unadjusted for tax (whether income taxes or taxes on dividends), and rely on monthly returns, which is probably most prevalent among such studies, although most of the accounting data would change only quarterly.[2]

[1] This approach was used in numerous studies of the cross-section of stock returns. Examples include Liu et al. (2011), Bekaert et al. (2007), Brown et al. (2008), Rouwenhorst (1999), Barry et al. (2002), Griffin (2002), Bali and Cakici (2010), Chui et al. (2010), Hou et al. (2011), de Groot et al. (2012b), de Moor and Sercu (2013a, b), and Cakici et al. (2013).

[2] Waszczuk (2014a, b) indicates that the discrete-time asset pricing theory provides no information on the relevant interval of expected returns (Fama 1998). Thus, we choose monthly intervals, which are also the most widely used in similar studies. The reasons are twofold. On the one hand, it offers a sufficient number of observations to ensure power of the conducted tests. On the other hand, monthly intervals avoid excessive exposure to the micro-structure issues (de Moor and Sercu 2013a). Lower frequency could be adequate for the estimation of capital cost but not for asset pricing tests, for which shorter time intervals markedly improve their quality. In practice, it is used rather rarely, mainly when the research additionally encompasses macroeconomic data. The paper by Avramov and Chordia (2006),

Finally, being aware that not all stocks in equity market are tradable, for example, stocks of companies with extremely low liquidity and market capitalization would be very difficult to trade freely, we applied a series of various static and dynamic filters to the common stocks within our calculations at the beginning of each month when forming the investment portfolio. We took account of only companies with the total stock market capitalization exceeding $100 million and the average daily trailing six-month turnover beyond $100,000. As a very low price may also lead to practical difficulties with trading, due to a wide bid-ask spread, we discarded stocks with the trading price below $1.00 at the beginning of a given month.[3]

Portfolios Structure

As in our study we have reviewed a lot of different strategies, to make them easily comparable, we investigated the strategies using portfolios designed in an identical fashion. To test various investment approaches, we applied the so-called one-way sorted portfolios by ranking all the stocks in our universe on a characteristic which in academia is called the "return-predictive variable" for it helps forecast future price changes. Naturally, for our purposes, we used price-based return-predictive variables. Having thus sorted the securities, we formed a long portfolio of stocks ranked with the highest predicted return and a short portfolio of securities with the lowest predicted returns.

In order to calculate returns in a given month, typically called month t, we sorted the stocks within the sample at the end of the previous month (month $t-1$) according to the investigated characteristic, for example,

who investigated the Consumption CAPM, may serve as an example. Some of the methods and their description in this book are analogous and sourced from Zaremba and Shemer (2017).

[3] The filters applied in this book are similar to plenty of asset pricing studies on international equities. For instance, de Moor and Sercu (2013a, b) set the minimum market value at $100 million on the international sample and additionally limit the examinations to stocks with monthly trading volume larger than $100,000, identically as in this book. Brown et al. (2008) include only equities belonging to the intersection of top 50% market liquidity and top 50% market capitalization. van der Hart et al. (2005) set the lower boundary for the firm capitalization at $100 million for the last month of the study sample and Burghof and Prothmann (2011) use the limit of GBP20 million. Considering the price of the stock, most of the studies rely on the SEC definition, implying that penny stocks priced below $5 (Jegadeesh and Titman 2001; Gutierrez and Kelley 2008; Bhootra 2011).

short-run return and long-run return. Having ranked the markets by the investigated characteristics, we then determined the 20th and 80th percentile breakpoints for each measure. In other words, by focusing only on the 20% of the securities with the highest expected returns and the 20% of the stocks with the lowest predicted future returns, we consequently arrived at two quintile subgroups.[4]

Subsequently, we weighted the respective equities from portfolios. For simplicity, we used a straightforward weighting method—equal weighting, under which each of the best (or worst) stocks from the top (or bottom) quintiles of the ranking was assigned the same weight, that is, a fraction of the portfolio. In other words, we divided the portfolio into equal parts and bought the same amount of every stock. In practice, many methods are used, and all of them has some pros and cons.

Equal Weighting Among various methods, this is perhaps the simplest way of weighting portfolio components, giving identical weights to all securities. Importantly, we are likely to rebalance such portfolio frequently as stock prices rise and fall every month, changing thus the share in the portfolio. To hold equal stocks, the investor needs to rebalance it on a systematic basis. The more frequent the rebalancing, the more frequent the trading. Whereas the more trades we do, the higher rise the total transaction costs. As a result, a frequently rebalanced equal-weighted portfolio might finally prove costly for investors. In contrast, for portfolios constructed from one-way sorts, the cost drag may not significantly exceed other types of weightings, for example, the value weighting as the portfolio turnover comes not only from rebalancing but mostly from stocks entering and leaving the portfolio, which is common across all weighting schemes. To its advantage, this approach generates no overweight of any type of stocks making equally weighted portfolios exhibit decent exposure to small companies, which tend to yield high anomaly returns.

[4] The type of quantile portfolios highly depends on the number of available constituents, and it is a trade-off between the number of assets available and the grid resolution (Waszczuk 2014b). The most widely considered alternatives are quintiles, for example, Banz (1981) and Chan et al. (1998), and deciles, for example, Jegadeesh and Titman (1993, 2001) and Lakonishok et al. (1994). We decided that 78 diversified index portfolios are sufficient for the 20th and 80th breakpoints but insufficient for the 10th and 90th breakpoints. Among alternative approaches, Bauman et al. (1998) considered quartile grouping, Achour et al. (1998) worked with tertile portfolios, and Brav et al. (2000) used the 50% cut-off. In our case, due to a relatively small number of assets in the portfolios, we mostly rely on tertile portfolios.

Capitalization Weighting Weighting on stock market capitalization, as an alternative to equal-weighting scheme, assigns bigger weights to stock market companies with large market values. As this approach concentrates in particular on large and liquid companies, it may result in lower trading costs (Novy-Marx and Velikov 2016; Zaremba and Nikorowski 2017), although the differences are moderate (Zaremba and Andreu Sánchez 2017), because a large part of the turnover stems from stocks entering and leaving the portfolio rather than from the rebalancing. To its disadvantage, capitalization weighting returns tend to appear the strongest in small caps and this type of portfolio formation underweights small caps diminishing the portfolio benefits from cross-sectional patterns.

Liquidity Weighting Liquidity weighting is a good candidate for an even more realistic approach to weighting portfolio constituents as it grants a higher share in the portfolio to the most liquid securities ranked by, for example, turnover; its unquestionable advantage is the low-trading cost: the investor concentrates on stocks that are highly liquid, which as a rule also display narrow bid-ask spreads. Unfortunately, such portfolios give also preference to the most efficient market segments, making the stocks less likely to display strong anomalous behavior.

Factor Weighting Following the factor-weighting approach, we weight the stocks neither according to their capitalization or liquidity but rather by their expected return proxied by an additional variable. For instance, when building a portfolio on the book-to-market ratio, you can weigh the components by the standardized book-to-market ratio; strictly speaking, the weights could be tied to either the raw variables (see, e.g., Zaremba and Umutlu 2018) or the ranking values (Asness et al. 2017).

This approach guarantees the portfolio share be closely linked to the expected performance. Unfortunately, the weights might also prove quite volatile, especially in the case of dynamic strategies, like momentum, leading to a high turnover and, in consequence, high trading costs.

Enhanced Indexing and Other Methods There are numerous other techniques of weighting the components of quantitatively managed portfolios. Some rely on sophisticated optimization algorithms while others are rule based (Narang 2013). One of the increasingly popular methods includes fundamental weighting based on weighting portfolio components on fundamental variables: for example, sales or the book-to-market ratio. This approach delivers decent returns at the level of both individual stocks and whole countries or indices.[5]

Evaluation of the Strategies

To present the performance of various strategies, we have facilitated an array of statistical data: mean returns, volatilities, or skewness, using the following both simple and popular ratios to assess the returns and strategy risk.

Sharpe Ratio The Sharpe ratio originates from William Sharpe, a Nobel Prize laureate, who in his research entitled "Mutual Fund Performance" (Sharpe 1966) formulated the index, which was later named after him. Undoubtedly, the ratio is still the most popular investment performance measurement tool, which accounts for not only profit but also risk.

Under the most traditional definition, the Sharpe ratio measures the excess rate of return per unit of risk taken by the investor (Sharpe 1966). The ratio is calculated by dividing the excess return and the risk understood as the volatility (standard deviation) of these excess returns.[6] By excess return, we mean the difference between the return on the investigated portfolio and the return of the risk-free instrument.[7] Throughout

[5] For stocks, see, Arnott et al. (2005), Tamura and Shimizu (2005), Hsu and Campolo (2006), Walkshausl and Lobe (2010), and Zaremba and Miziołek (2017a). For comprehensive literature surveys, see Chow et al. (2011), Amenc et al. (2012), and Bolognesi and Pividori (2016); for country equity indices, see Estrada (2008), Yan and Zhao (2013), and Zaremba and Miziołek (2017b).

[6] In the literature, by default the term *volatility* means a yearly *standard deviation* of returns. Both terms are used in this book in the same meaning.

[7] In financial studies, we have two main methods of converting prices to returns: the arithmetic (simple) and logarithmic return approach. The latter is usually preferred for three basic reasons: (1) better arithmetical properties (including compounding over time), (2) return distributions that represent a larger degree of normality than arithmetic returns, and (3) reduced heteroscedasticity in logarithmic returns series (Waszczuk 2014b). This type of returns are not fully additive over assets, but the bias is rather small, especially for the short time intervals; so they are also used in the cross-sectional studies (e.g., Liew and Vassalou [2000], Diacogiannis and Kyriazis [2007]). In the calculations used in this book, for the sake

this book, it is represented by benchmark returns on the US three-month Treasury bills.

The Sharpe ratio is a simple measure and could be expressed with the following formula:

$$SR = \frac{\overline{R}}{\sigma} \tag{1.1}$$

whereby $\overline{R}$ represents the mean excess return on the investigated portfolio over the examined period, and σ is its standard deviation of excess returns. The ratio is usually presented on an annual basis, that is, with yearly excess returns.[8] Although our computations are based on monthly intervals, we also adopted an annualized version of the ratio by simply multiplying the monthly Sharpe ratio by the square root of 12.

While an unquestionable virtue of the Sharpe ratio is its simplicity, it performs poorly in the environment of negative excess returns. For this reason, we facilitated the Sharpe ratio with the so-called Jensen's alpha.

Jensen's Alpha The Jensen's alpha is a measure derived from the capital asset pricing model (CAPM, Sharpe 1964).[9] The CAPM is a simple model that was invented by the famous researcher—William Sharpe—for three main purposes: to explain the reasons for portfolio diversification, to create a framework for valuating assets in a risky environment, and to explain differences in the long-term returns of various assets.[10] The CAPM laid

of simplicity, we use arithmetic returns. For further discussion on the return calculation for financial studies, see Roll (1984) or Vaihekoski (2004).

[8] The Sharpe ratio was later frequently revised and modified by many authors, including its inventor; across this book, however, we rely on the simplest and most intuitive definition described by Sharpe (1966). For more examples of the modifications and revisions of the Sharpe ratio, see Sharpe (1994), Vinod and Morey (1999), Dowd (2000), Israelsen (2005), or Le Sourd (2007).

[9] The detailed characteristics of the Sharpe model were extensively presented in a number of financial textbooks, for example, Francis (1990), Elton and Gruber (1995), Campbell et al. (1997), Cochrane (2005), or Wilmott (2008).

[10] Treynor (1961, 1962), Lintner (1965a, b) and Mossin (1966) developed a similar model at the same time, so all four—including Sharpe (1964)—are now considered to be the fathers of the CAPM model. See also French (2003).

the foundation for many other methods of performance evaluation in investment portfolio management.

The fundamental assumption of the model states that volatility of a financial instrument can be broken down into two parts: a systematic and specific risk. The systematic risk stems from general changes in the market conditions and relates to the volatility of the market portfolio, whereas the specific risk relates to volatility which is, however, driven not by the market but by the internal situation in the company. In other words, losses ensuing a market crash are rather of a systematic nature while losses due to an employee strike belong to the specific risk category.

The CAPM model bears some vital implications for both portfolio construction and diversification. When building a portfolio, systematic risks of individual stock simply add up; however, specific risks, not being correlated, set each other off. Therefore, in a well-diversified portfolio, the influence of the specific risk is generally negligible, and in a well-functioning market, a rational investor may ignore the specific risk and concentrate solely on the systematic part. After all, would the investor even consider the specific risk if it could be easily diversified away at no cost?

This important implication of the CAPM model—stating that the investors should be only compensated for the systematic risk because the specific risk can be easily eliminated—is

$$R_{i,t} = \alpha_i + R_{f,t} + \beta_{rm,i} \cdot \left(R_{mt} - R_{f,t}\right) + \varepsilon_{i,t}, \tag{1.2}$$

where $R_{i,t}$, $R_{m,t}$, and $R_{f,t}$ are returns on the analyzed security or portfolio; i, the market portfolio and risk-free returns at time t; and α_i and $\beta_{rm,i}$ are regression parameters. $\beta_{rm,i}$ is the measure of the systematic risk which tells us how aggressively the stock reacts to the price changes in the broad market. Fundamentally, the CAPM formula implies that the excess returns on the investigated security or portfolio should increase linearly with the systematic risk measured with beta: the higher the risk, the higher the expected return.

Finally, the α_i intercept measures the average abnormal return: the so-called Jensen's alpha. It is defined as the rate of return earned by the portfolio or a strategy in excess of the expected return from the CAPM model. The Eq. 1.3 could be easily rewritten to be used to evaluate past returns on a portfolio:

$$\alpha_i = \overline{R_i^E} - \beta_i \cdot \left(\overline{R_m^E}\right), \tag{1.3}$$

where α_i is the Jensen's alpha on the investigated portfolio, $\overline{R_i^E}$ is its mean excess return over the examined period, β_i is the market beta, and $\overline{R_m^E}$ is the mean excess return on the market portfolio.[11] Throughout the book, we have used the capitalization-weighted return as the proxy for the market portfolio, which we calculated based on either gross or the risk-free rate, consequently represented by the US three-month T-bills.[12] Importantly, as far as a zero-investment portfolio is concerned, there is no need to subtract any risk-free rate.

The decisive rule for the Jensen's alpha states that when alpha from the CAPM model turns negative, it signals the investment in the analyzed strategy, or portfolio, to become unreasonable as a higher return at a comparable risk level could be achieved via investments in the risk-free asset and market portfolio.

Statistical Significance One important challenge in examining investment strategies is to distinguish when seemingly abnormal returns are truly abnormal and when it is pure coincidence. If a trader earned 10% annually for five consecutive years, how can we tell whether he has followed a superior investment strategy or he just got lucky? For this purpose, whenever we reported any mean returns or alphas, we simultaneously reported their

[11] For simplicity, in the book we use the Jensen's alpha in its most basic form. Nonetheless, this performance measure has been frequently updated and modified over time (Zaremba 2015). For example, Black (1972) suggested using a portfolio with a beta coefficient equal to zero instead of a risk-free return. Brennan (1970), on the other hand, constructed a model taking into account taxes. Elton and Gruber (1995) suggested using a total risk instead of a systematic one. Many papers also suggested putting additional attention to the way the profit was earned and how the alpha coefficient was decomposed in respect of its origin (e.g., Treynor and Mazuy 1966, McDonald 1973, Pogue et al. 1974, Merton 1981, Henriksson and Merton 1981, Henriksson 1984, Grinblatt and Titman 1989). Furthermore, a substantial body of research attempts to improve the measure of systematic risk. There are several basic strands in this line of studies. The first uses conditional betas taking different values for growing and declining markets (Ferson and Schadt 1996; Christopherson et al. 1999). The second approach incorporates other risk factors and macroeconomic variables (e.g., Ross 1976; Fama and French 1996; Carhart 1997; Amenc and Le Sourd 2003). Example of different types of systematic risk could be found in the models of Connor and Korajczyk (1986), based on the arbitrage pricing theory, the index model by Elton et al. (1993), or the management style analysis according to Sharpe (1992).

[12] In particular, we source the market factor returns from Kenneth R. French's website: http://mba.tuck.dartmouth.edu/pages/faculty/ken.french/data_library.html.

statistical significance which at least to some extent helps us statistically differentiate real return patterns from mere luck. When some mean return, or alpha, exceeds zero at the 5% level, it indicates a 5% risk of no real pattern in the returns, even though we have identified it in the historical data. In other words, the returns could turn positive only in our specific sample, and this result may not be replicated in another sample. Thus, this 5% threshold could also be interpreted as the probability of the returns plunging below zero when implementing this strategy to another sample.

The statistical significance test may be one sided, that is, informing us whether the returns are significantly higher than zero, or two sided, that is, informing us whether the returns depart from zero (either below or above).

Throughout this book, we presented the significance of both the mean and abnormal returns of the tested strategies[13] aiming to provide a better view on how compelling the performance of the strategies really is. If the abnormal returns remain significant at the level of 1% or 5%, we can be fairly sure that the strategy is no random return pattern. At 10%, the evidence is still firm, but less convincing. Once the significance plunges below 10%, the probability that the abnormal returns result from pure chance is considerable, thus it would be risky to assume it would continue in the future.[14]

References

Achour, D., Harvey, C., Hopkins, G., & Lang, C. (1998). Stock selection in emerging markets: Portfolio strategies in Malaysia, Mexico, and South Africa. *Emerging Markets Quarterly, 2*, 38–91.

Aczel, A. D. (2012). *Complete business statistics* (8th ed.). Morristown: Wohl Publishing.

Amenc, N., Goltz, F., & Lodh, A. (2012). Choose your betas: Benchmarking alternative equity strategies. *Journal of Portfolio Management, 39*(1), 88–111.

[13] All the regression parameters in this book were estimated using the OLS method. This approach has been employed, among many others, by Fama and French (2012). Furthermore, all the *t*-statistics were estimated using the bootstrap standard errors to avoid any distributional assumptions. Under our null hypothesis, all of the intercepts equal zero whereas the alternative hypothesis assumes the contrary. The bootstrap simulations are performed with the use of 10,000 random draws. All the statistical analyses are performed in R.

[14] Further details could be found in basically any statistical textbook, for example, Aczel (2012).

Amenc, N., & Le Sourd, V. (2003). *Portfolio theory and performance analysis*. Hoboken: John Wiley & Sons.

Arnott, R. D., Hsu, J., & Moore, P. (2005). Fundamental indexation. *Financial Analyst Journal, 61*(2), 83–99.

Asness, C. S., Frazzini, A., & Pedersen, L. H. (2017). *Quality minus junk*. Available at SSRN: https://ssrn.com/abstract=2312432 or https://doi.org/10.2139/ssrn.2312432. Accessed 23 Oct 2017.

Avramov, D., & Chordia, T. (2006). Asset pricing models and financial market anomalies. *Review of Financial Studies, 19*(3), 1001–1040.

Bali, C., & Cakici, N. (2010). World market risk, country-specific risk and expected returns in international stock markets. *Journal of Banking and Finance, 34*, 1152–1165.

Bali, T. G., Cakici, N., & Fabozzi, F. J. (2013). Book-to-market and the cross-section of expected returns in international stock markets. *Journal of Portfolio Management, 39*(2), 101–115.

Banz, R. W. (1981). The relationship between return and market value of common stocks. *Journal of Financial Economics, 9*, 3–18.

Barry, C., Goldreyer, E., Lockwood, L., & Rodriguez, M. (2002). Robustness of size and value effects in emerging equity markets, 1985–2000. *Emerging Markets Review, 3*, 1–30.

Bauman, W. S., Conover, C. M., & Miller, R. E. (1998). Growth versus value and large-cap versus small-cap stocks in international markets. *Financial Analyst Journal, 54*(2), 75–89.

Bekaert, G., Harvey, C., & Lundblad, C. (2007). Liquidity and expected returns: Lessons from emerging markets. *Review of Financial Studies, 20*, 1783–1831.

Bhootra, A. (2011). Are momentum profits driven by the cross-sectional dispersion in expected stock returns? *Journal of Financial Markets, 14*, 494–513.

Black, F. (1972). Capital market equilibrium with restricted borrowing. *Journal of Business, 45*, 44–455.

Bolognesi, E., & Pividori, M. (2016). Fundamental indexation in Europe: New evidence. *Journal of Financial Management, Markets and Institutions, 4*(2), 103–128.

Brav, A., Geczy, C., & Gompers, P. (2000). Is the abnormal return following equity issuance anomalous. *Journal of Financial Economics, 56*, 209–249.

Brennan, M. J. (1970). Taxes, market valuation and corporate financial policy. *National Tax Journal, 25*, 417–427.

Brown, A., Du, D. Y., Rhee, S. G., & Zhang, L. (2008). The returns to value and momentum in Asian markets. *Emerging Markets Review, 9*, 79–88.

Burghof, H. P., & Prothmann, F. (2011). The 52-week high strategy and information uncertainty. *Financial Markets and Portfolio Management, 25*(4), 345–378.

Cakici, N., Fabozzi, F. J., & Tan, S. (2013). Size, value, and momentum in emerging market stock returns. *Emerging Markets Review, 16*, 46–65.

Campbell, J. Y., Lo, A. W., & MacKinlay, A. C. (1997). *The econometrics of financial markets*. Princeton: Princeton University Press.
Carhart, M. M. (1997). On persistence in mutual fund performance. *Journal of Finance, 52*(1), 57–82.
Chan, L., Karceski, J., & Lakonishok, J. (1998). The risk and return from factors. *Journal of Financial and Quantitative Analysis, 33*, 159–188.
Chow, T., Hsu, J. C., Kalesnik, V., & Little, B. (2011). A survey of alternative equity index strategies. *Financial Analysts Journal, 67*(5), 37–57.
Christopherson, J. A., Ferson, W. E., & Turner, A. L. (1999). Performance evaluation using conditional alphas and betas. *Journal of Portfolio Management, 26*(1), 59–72.
Chui, A. C. W., Titman, S., & Wei, J. K. C. (2010). Individualism and momentum around the world. *Journal of Finance, 65*(1), 361–392.
Cochrane, J. H. (2005). *Asset pricing*. Princeton: Princeton University Press.
Connor, G., & Korajczyk, R. (1986). Performance measurement with the arbitrage pricing theory: A new framework for analysis. *Journal of Financial Economics, 15*(3), 373–394.
de Groot, W., Pang, J., & Swinkels, L. A. P. (2012b). The cross-section of stock returns in frontier emerging markets. *Journal of Empirical Finance*, 19(5), 796–818.
De Moor, L., & Sercu, P. (2013a). The smallest stocks are not just smaller: Global evidence. *European Journal of Finance, 21*(2), 51–70.
De Moor, L., & Sercu, P. (2013b). The smallest firm effect: An international study. *Journal of International Money and Finance, 32*, 129–155.
Dowd, K. (2000). Adjusting for risk: An improved Sharpe ratio. *International Review of Economics and Finance, 9*(3), 209–222.
Elton, E. J., & Gruber, M. J. (1995). *Modern portfolio theory and investment analysis*. Hoboken: John Wiley & Sons.
Elton, E. J., Gruber, M. J., Das, S., & Hlavka, M. (1993). Efficiency with costly information: A reinterpretation of evidence from managed portfolios. *Review of Financial Studies, 6*(1), 1–22.
Estrada, J. (2008). Fundamental indexation and international diversification. *Journal of Portfolio Management, 34*(3), 93–109.
Fama, E. F. (1998). Market efficiency, long-term returns, and behavioral finance. *Journal of Financial Economics, 49*(3), 283–306.
Fama, E. F., & French, K. R. (1996). Multifactor explanations of asset pricing anomalies. *Journal of Finance, 51*(1), 55–84.
Fama, E. F., & French, K. R. (2012). Size, value, and momentum in international stock returns. *Journal of Financial Economics, 105*(3), 457–472.
Ferson, W. E., & Schadt, R. W. (1996). Measuring fund strategy and performance in changing economic conditions. *Journal of Finance, 51*(2), 425–461.
Francis, J. C. (1990). *Investments: Analysis and management*. New York: McGraw Hill Higher Education.

French, C. W. (2003). The treynor capital asset pricing model. *Journal of Investment Management, 1*(2), 60–72.

Griffin, J. M. (2002). Are the Fama and French factors global or country specific? *Review of Financial Studies, 15*, 783–803.

Grinblatt, M., & Titman, S. (1989). Portfolio performance evaluation: Old issues and new insights. *Review of Financial Studies, 2*, 393–421.

Gutierrez, R. C., Jr., & Kelly, E. K. (2008). The long-lasting momentum in weekly returns. *Journal of Finance, 63*(1), 415–447.

Henriksson, R. D. (1984). Market timing and mutual fund performance: An empirical investigation. *Journal of Business, 57*(1), 73–96.

Henriksson, R. D., & Merton, R. C. (1981). On market timing and investment performance II: Statistical procedures for evaluating forecasting skills. *Journal of Business, 54*(4), 513–533.

Hou, K., Karolyi, G. A., & Kho, B. C. (2011). What factors drive global stock returns? *Review of Financial Studies, 24*(8), 2527–2574. https://doi.org/10.1093/rfs/hhr013.

Hsu, J. C., & Campolo, C. (2006). New frontiers in index investing: An examination of fundamental indexation. *Journal of Indexes, 58*, 32–37.

Israelsen, C. L. (2005). A refinement to the Sharpe ratio and information ratio. *Journal of Asset Management, 5*(6), 423–427.

Jegadeesh, N., & Titman, S. (1993). Returns to buying winners and selling losers: Implications for stock market efficiency. *Journal of Finance, 48*, 65–91.

Jegadeesh, N., & Titman, S. (2001). Profitability of momentum strategies: An evaluation of alternative explanations. *Journal of Finance, 56*(2), 599–720.

Kyriazis, D., & Diacogiannis, G. (2007). Testing the performance of value strategies in the Athens Stock Exchange. *Applied Financial Economics, 17*(18), 1511–1528.

Lakonishok, J., Schleifer, A., & Vishny, R. W. (1994). Contrarian investment, extrapolation, and risk. *Journal of Finance, 49*(5), 1541–1578.

Le Sourd, V. (2007). *Performance measurement for traditional investments. Literature survey* (Research paper). DHEC Risk and Asset Management Research Centre. Available online: http://www.edhec-risk.com/performance_and_style_analysis/perf_measurement/index_html/attachments/EDHEC%20Publi%20performance%20measurement%20for%20traditional%20investment.pdf. Accessed 16 Oct 2017.

Liew, J., & Vassalou, M. (2000). Can book-to-market, size and momentum be risk factors that predict economic growth? *Journal of Financial Economics, 57*, 221–245.

Lintner, J. (1965a). The valuation of risk assets and the selection of risky investments in stock portfolios and capital budgets. *Review of Economics and Statistics, 47*(1), 13–37.

Lintner, J. (1965b). Security prices, risk and maximal gains from diversification. *Journal of Finance, 20*(4), 587–615.

Liu, M., Liu, Q., & Ma, T. (2011). The 52-week high momentum strategy in international stock markets. *Journal of International Money and Finance, 30*, 180–204.

McDonald, J. (1973). French mutual fund performance: Evaluation of internationally diversified portfolios. *Journal of Finance, 28*(5), 1161–1180.

Merton, R. C. (1981). On market timing and investment performance: An equilibrium theory of value for market forecasts. *Journal of Business, 54*(3), 363–406.

Mossin, J. (1966). Equilibrium in a capital asset market. *Econometrica, 35*(4), 768–783.

Narang, R. K. (2013). *Inside the black box: A simple guide to quantitative and high frequency trading*. Hoboken: Wiley.

Novy-Marx, R., & Velikov, M. (2016). A taxonomy of anomalies and their trading costs. *Review of Financial Studies, 29*(1), 104–147. https://doi.org/10.1093/rfs/hhv063.

Pogue, G., Solnik, B., & Rousselin, A. (1974). *International diversification: A study of the French mutual funds* (Working paper). Sloan School of Management. Available at http://dspace.mit.edu/handle/1721.1/48147. Accessed 17 Oct 2015.

Roll, R. (1984). A simple implicit measure of the effective bid-ask spread in an efficient market. *Journal of Finance, 39*, 1127–1139.

Ross, S. (1976). The arbitrage theory of capital asset pricing. *Journal of Economic Theory, 13*(3), 341–360.

Rouwenhorst, G. K. (1999). Local return factors and turnover in emerging stock markets. *Journal of Finance, 54*, 1439–1464.

Sharpe, W. F. (1964). Capital asset prices: A theory of market equilibrium under conditions of risk. *Journal of Finance, 19*(3), 425–442.

Sharpe, W. F. (1966). Mutual fund performance. *Journal of Business, 39* (January), 119–138.

Sharpe, W. F. (1992). Asset allocation: Management style and performance measurement. *Journal of Portfolio Management, 18*, 7–19.

Sharpe, W. F. (1994). The Sharpe ratio. *Journal of Portfolio Management, 21*(1), 49–58.

Tamura, H., & Shimizu, Y. (2005). *Fundamental indices. Do they outperform market-cap weighted indices on a global basis?* Tokyo: Global Quantitative Research, Nomura Securities.

Treynor, J. L. (1961). *Market value, time, and risk*. Available at SSRN: https://ssrn.com/abstract=2600356 or https://doi.org/10.2139/ssrn.2600356.

Treynor, J., & Mazuy, K. (1966). Can mutual funds outguess the market? *Harvard Business Review, 44*, 131–136.

Treynor, J. L (1962). *Toward a theory of market value of risky assets* (Unpublished manuscript). Final version in *Asset Pricing and Portfolio Performance* (pp. 15–22), 1999, Robert A. Korajczyk (ed.). London: Risk Books. Available also at SSRN: http://ssrn.com/abstract=628187 or https://doi.org/10.2139/ssrn.628187. Accessed 17 Oct 2015.

Vaihekoski, M. (2004). Portfolio construction for tests of asset pricing models. *Financial Markets, Institutions, and Instruments, 13*(1), 1–39.

van der Hart, J., de Zwart, G., & van Dijk, D. (2005). The success of stock selection strategies in emerging markets: Is it risk or behavioural bias? *Emerging Markets Review, 6*, 238–262.

Vinod, H. D., & Morey, M. R. (1999). *A double Sharpe ratio* (Working paper). Available at SSRN: http://papers.ssrn.com/sol3/papers.cfm?abstract_id=168748. Accessed 16 Oct 2017.

Walkshausl, C., & Lobe, S. (2010). Fundamental indexing around the world. *Review of Financial Economics, 19*(3), 117–127.

Waszczuk, A. (2014a). Assembling international equity datasets – Review of studies on the cross-section of returns. *Procedia Economics and Finance: Emerging Markets Queries in Finance and Business(EMQ 2013), 15*, 1603–1612.

Waszczuk, A. (2014b). *Diversity of empirical design – Review of studies on the cross-section of common stocks* (Working paper). Available at SSRN: http://ssrn.com/abstract=2428054 or https://doi.org/10.2139/ssrn.2428054. Accessed 11 Oct 2015.

Wilmott, P. (2008). *Paul Wilmott on quantitative finance*. Hoboken: John Wiley & Sons.

Yan, Z., & Zhao, Y. (2013). International diversification: Simple or optimization strategies? *International Journal of Finance, 25*(1), 1–33.

Zaremba, A. (2015). *The financialization of commodity markets: Investing during times of transition*. New York: Palgrave Macmillan.

Zaremba, A., & Andreu Sánchez, L. (2017). *Paper profits or real money? Trading costs and stock market anomalies in country equity indices*. Available at https://doi.org/10.2139/ssrn.3038514

Zaremba, A., & Miziołek, T. (2017a). Fundamental indexation in European emerging markets. *Romanian Journal of Economic Forecasting, 20*(1), 23–37.

Zaremba, A., & Miziołek, T. (2017b, in press). Nothing lasts forever (and everywhere): Fundamental indexation at the global level. *Journal of Index Investing, 8*(3), 6–20.

Zaremba, A., & Nikorowski, J. (2017). *Trading costs, short sale constraints, and the performance of stock market anomalies in Emerging Europe*. Available at SSRN: https://ssrn.com/abstract=2778063. Accessed 23 Oct 2017.

Zaremba, A., & Shemer, K. (2017, in press). Is there momentum in factor premia? Evidence from international equity markets. *Research in International Business and Finance*. https://doi.org/10.1016/j.ribaf.2017.12.002.

Zaremba, A., & Umutlu, M. (2018, in press). Less pain, more gain: Volatility-adjusted residual momentum in international equity markets. *Investment Analysts Journal*. https://doi.org/10.1080/10293523.2018.1469290.

CHAPTER 2

The Trend Is Your Friend: Momentum Investing

Momentum will be the start of our journey into the world of price-based strategies. Among hundreds of financial market anomalies so far discovered, the momentum strategy may be rightly called the queen of all anomalies. Like the holy grail of financial markets, it might be regarded as an ideal strategy for any investor, combining two essential characteristics: simplicity and robustness. On the one hand, its implementation is very straightforward and requires no sophisticated skills and data. On the other hand, it is perhaps one of the most pervasive and timeless return regularities ever discovered. It has been identified not only in equities but also in numerous other asset classes. It worked well a century ago. It has been delivering decent returns in recent years. These characteristics make momentum an attractive proposition for virtually any investor.

What Is Momentum?

Let us start by answering the most fundamental question: what is momentum? At a very high level, it is a well-established tendency of assets with good past performance to continue to overperform in the future and, analogously, for assets with poor past performance to continue to underperform. In other words, if a given stock, or bond, delivered good returns in the past, it is more likely than not that the trend will continue. There are many different momentum strategies which rely on various sorting techniques and predictive indicators, and differ greatly in sophistication.

A. Zaremba, J. "Koby" Shemer, *Price-Based Investment Strategies*,
https://doi.org/10.1007/978-3-319-91530-2_2

The most fundamental rule, however, remains always the same: stick to the winners and shy away from past losers. The trend is your friend, as market practitioners like to iterate.

While we now have a preponderance of momentum-related strategies, the most classical and common approach is relative momentum—which most frequently attributed to Jegadeesh and Titman (1993). This type of strategy ideally fits the practice of building portfolios based on sorting techniques. Under this approach, an outlook for a given security is predicted by its performance relative to other stocks in the markets. The strategy favors stocks with the highest past returns over the companies with the worst track record. Technically, the implementation is very simple: we rank stocks on their past returns. The return predictive signal used for ranking stocks might be thus as simple as:

$$RM_{i,t} = \frac{P_{i,t-1}}{P_{i,t-k}}, \tag{2.1}$$

where $RM_{i,\,t}$ is the momentum signal for stock i in month t is simply is price in the previous month ($P_{i,\,t-1}$) divided by its price some number of months (k) earlier ($P_{i,\,t-k}$). Plain and simple. You just sort stocks on their historical price changes: the bigger, the better. The only question remaining is, what is k. In other words, based on which past period we should sort the securities. In their seminal paper, Jegadeesh and Titman (1993) showed that the stocks that performed well over past 6–12 months continue to outperform in the next 3–12 months, that is, roughly speaking, a few months. Yet what is the optimal sorting and rebalancing period? Are there any alternatives? We will elaborate on these important nuances as soon as we present how the momentum strategy works.

Does Momentum Work?

The evidence on momentum performance is tremendously abundant, including both academic and anecdotal proofs.[1] The latter could be traced back to David Ricardo (Antonacci 2015), a well-respected classical economist who most probably first coined the famous momentum adage, "cut your losses, let your profits run," laying thus the foundation for the entire

[1] Antonacci (2015) provides an interesting survey on the early evidence on momentum.

trend-following philosophy. What's more, Ricardo had been very successful in translating his concept into real profits, he is said to retire at the age of 42 with a real fortune worth today US$65 million.

Momentum concepts also emerged in the finance literature of the early twentieth century. The famous book by Edwin Lefevre (2010) entitled *Reminiscences of a Stock Operator* may serve as a perfect example. This popular masterpiece unraveled the investment approach of Jesse Livermore, a well-known trader of the previous century, who recommended buying shares at their new heights, which vividly resembles a popular trend-following strategy based on price breakouts (Jaffarian 2009). The famous maxim of Livermore that "prices are never too high to begin buying or too low to begin selling" perfectly encapsulates the trend-following concept.

The trend-following approach was, perhaps, the most common approach among pre-World War II gurus and legendary speculators of the time, including Richard Wyckoff (1924); George Seamans (1939); Arnold Bernhard, the founder of the Value Line Investment Survey (Antonacci 2015, p. 14); and Robert Rhea, the Dow theorist (Rhea 1932; Gartley 1935, 1945). It was not until the research by Alfred Cowles III and Herbert E. Jones (1937) that momentum became a subject of scientific research.

Looking back, the work of Cowles and Jones (1937) does seem most impressive, given that their painstaking computations were conducted with no assistance of a computer or even a calculator. Cowles and Jones collected data on stock prices and dividends from the years 1920 to 1935, a great accomplishment in its own right, and discovered probably the first scientific proof of momentum. In their manuscript they noted, "[T]aking one year as the unit of measurement for the period 1920 to 1935, the tendency is very pronounce for stocks which have exceeded the median in one year to exceed it also in the year following." Hence, high performance over the previous year is a promising sign of good returns in the future. In other words, momentum works.

The post-war era brought an even higher interest and popularity of momentum strategies. Its simplicity attracted some stock market celebrities. The book by Nicolas Darvas (1960) with a captivating title *How I Made $2,000,000 in the Stock Market?* is an ideal example. Darvas, a dancer traveling around the globe, was hardly the type of a professional equity investor. On his tours, he only occasionally contacted his stockbroker through cable. As he describes in his book, his strategy was astonishingly simple: systematically reviewing newspapers, he would buy stocks at their new heights and systematically replace them with new market leaders. Following this straightforward technique, he asserted to make $2,000,000.

Another famous trader who strengthened the story of momentum investing was Richard Donchian. As a commodity advisor and trader, he used to publish a weekly newsletter describing his trend-following system based on 5-day and 20-day moving averages. His work, in turn, inspired other legendary traders Richard Dennis and Ed Seykota to train their group of investors which was later branded Turtle Traders. Interestingly, most of them become later exceptionally successful commodity trading advisors (CTAs) with Seykota famously mentoring Michael Marcus and David Druz, among many others.[2]

This anecdotal evidence, compelling as it is, still lacks the rigidity of proper scientific evidence. Admittedly, any comprehensive studies of momentum are hard to imagine in the pre-computer era. The first computer-based analysis was finally conducted by Levy in 1967, who first coined the phrase "relative strength", the early term for momentum, later renamed by academics. While Levy's precursory study falls short of the contemporary academic standards, covering only 625 stocks and ignoring both transaction costs and risk factors, its conclusion was clear: the top stock market performers yielded markedly higher returns over the subsequent six months than the market laggards.[3] The difference in returns between the past winners and losers amounted to 6.7 percentage points. Importantly, a bunch of later studies, which eventually accounted for trading costs and tested different equity and industry samples, essentially confirmed Levy's results (Akermann and Keller 1977; Bohan 1981; Brush and Bowles 1983). Levy was not wrong: stock market winners outperform losers.

Despite this early evidence, the momentum phenomenon failed to attract much attention from the academic community until in the 1990s the behavioral finance emerged offering logical and coherent explanation for the momentum effect. The groundbreaking article on momentum, "Returns to buying winners and selling losers: Implications for stock market efficiency", was published by Narasimhan Jegadeesh and Sheridan Titman in 1993. To this day, it remains the most frequently cited work on

[2] Other popular books depicting famous momentum traders include Chestnutt (1961), Haller (1965), Soros (2003), Covel (2007, 2009), O'Neil (2009), and the "Market wizards" series (Schwager 1994, 2003, 2012a, b).

[3] Later, in 1968, Levy expanded his thoughts to a full book on investing.

momentum ever written. Jegadeesh and Titman (1993) employed a practical rule-based approach: buying and holding a quantile of stocks that displayed the highest returns in the past while shorting the securities that delivered the lowest payoffs in the past. Having analyzed the price and return data on stocks listed on the NYSE and AMEX for years 1965–1989, the authors discovered that the stocks winning over past 6–12 months continued to outperform the losing stocks on a risk-adjusted basis by about 1% monthly over the subsequent 6–12 months. More importantly, this pattern seemed to be persistent over time. A decade later, Jegadeesh and Titman (2001) replicated their study to see whether the momentum would still hold. The results remained intact: in the 1990–1998 period, the past winners still continued to outperform the past losers by a substantial amount.

Jegadeesh and Titman's discovery (1993) was a scientific breakthrough. From the realm of stock market astrology, the momentum phenomenon was once for all elevated to the respectful halls of universities. Having sparked interest among academicians, the seminal paper triggered an extraordinary proliferation of momentum studies. Now momentum can be still called the most intensively researched topic in finance even with Eugene Fama, Nobel Prize laureate and a famous apostle of the stock market efficiency, finally calling momentum "the center stage anomaly of recent years". At the moment, a search for "momentum" in the Social Science Research Network eLibrary produces 3605 manuscripts, with over a thousand written in the past three years. While momentum's effectiveness in equities is regarded a well-established fact, the current scientific investigations have formed four major pursuits: (1) examining momentum across different markets and asset classes, (2) searching to explain its origins, (3) enhancing momentum-based strategies, and (4) researching the statistical properties of momentum-generated returns.

The final conclusion looming from this wealth of research is straightforward: the momentum phenomenon is one of the most robust, pervasive, and ubiquitous financial market anomalies ever discovered. It is truly beyond count now how many times the effect was proven in the US stock market, and the studies of Fama and French (2008) or Chan et al. (2012) may just serve as the most well-known example. Outside the USA, the momentum effect has been documented in developed (Rouwenhorst 1998; Chan et al. 2000; Griffin et al. 2005), emerging (Rouwenhorst 1999), and frontier markets (de Groot et al. 2012b). Recent years have brought a number of research investigating momentum across a wide spectrum of countries and timeframes as we can see in Table 2.1 including, for instance, Jacobs and Müller (2017a, b) who tested momentum within 39 countries for years 1980–2015.

Interestingly, the momentum effect seems to be effective not only anywhere but apparently any time, forming one of the most reliable and long-standing anomalies ever known. According to recent studies, the momentum strategy has worked well for over two centuries, as evidenced by Chabot et al. who found that momentum delivered satisfactory profits even in the Victorian age and Geczy and Samonov (2016) who in an incredible research effort demonstrated the effectiveness of momentum in the US equity market since 1800. Bearing that in mind, it is hard to regard momentum as a simple data-mining accident.

With all the overwhelming evidence, one of the most amazing characteristics of momentum is that it works virtually everywhere: being observable not only in individual stocks but also across entire portfolios. There is plenty of evidence that the momentum effect emerges in industry portfolios and country equity indices.[4] In other words, when deciding in which

Table 2.1 Studies of momentum in international stock markets

Paper	*Research period*	*Number of examined countries*
Griffin et al. (2003)	1926–2000	39
Chui et al. (2010)	1980–2003	55
Park and Kim (2013)	1990–2010	14
Fan et al. (2015)	1989–2009	43
Li and Wei (2015)	1988–2013	36
Schmidt et al. (2015)	1986–2012	21
Jacobs (2016)	1994–2013	45
Jacobs and Müller (2017a, b)	1980–2015	39

Note: Own elaboration

[4] See, for industry portfolio, Pan et al. (2004), Moskowitz and Grinblatt (1999), Faber (2010), Chen et al. (2012), Andreu et al. (2013), Szakmary and Zhou (2015), Plessis and Hallerbach (2016); for equity indices, Balvers and Wu (2006), Bhojraj and Swaminathan (2006), Muller and Ward (2010), Asness et al. (1997), Chan et al. (2000), Vu (2012), Andreu et al. (2013), Evans and Schmitz (2015), Grobys (2015), Zaremba (2016d), Zaremba and Andreu Sánchez (2017), Zaremba and Umutlu (2018a, b), Guilmin (2015), or Zaremba and Shemer (2017).

country you should invest, do look at the past performance, as here again top-performing stock market indices continue to overperform.

This pervasive pattern is found not only in equities but also across virtually all possible asset classes. The examples include treasury bonds, corporate bonds, commodities, currencies, real estate investment trusts (REITs), and interest rates, including even specific asset classes like Islamic bonds.[5]

Apart from equities and other asset classes, momentum sometimes appears in places that at first sight seem astonishing, like equity anomalies. Having analyzed returns on the 15 well-known equity anomalies in the US equity market, Avramov et al. (2016b) discovered that the anomalies that performed well in the most recent month continued to do well in the future, which was later confirmed in emerging markets (Zaremba and Szyszka 2016) and also—in a broader understanding—in international style or factor portfolios.[6] How should we interpret this? When choosing an equity strategy—whether based on value, low risk, or quality—it's worth keeping an eye on its past performance, regardless, in effect, of the observation period. Whether focusing on the last month, last year, or five years, the winner strategies tend to continue winning. This phenomenon is hardly limited to equities; it could be applied to, for instance, country asset allocation techniques or government bond strategies (Zaremba 2015a, 2017a) as successful approaches are more likely to succeed in the future.

[5] See, for government bonds, Luu and Yu (2012), Asness et al. (2013), Duyvesteyn and Martens (2014), Hambusch et al. (2015), Zaremba and Czapkiewicz (2017a, b), and Zaremba and Schabek (2017); for corporate bonds: Gebhardt et al. (2005), Pospisil and Zhang (2010), Kim et al. (2012), Jostova et al. (2013), de Carvalho et al. (2014), Israel et al. (2016), Barth et al. (2017), van Zundert (2017), Lin et al. (2017), and Houweling and van Zundert (2017); for interest rates, Durham (2013); for currencies, Okunev and White (2000), Bianchi et al. (2005), Menkoff et al. (2011), Burnside et al. (2011), Pojarliev and Levich (2013), Kroencke et al. (2013), Amen (2013), Accominotti and Chambers (2014), Olszewski and Zhou (2014), Orlov (2015), Bae and Elkamhi (2015), Filippou et al. (2015), and Grobys et al. (2016); for commodities, Pirrong (2005), Miffre and Rallis (2007), Fuertes et al. (2010), Gorton et al. (2013), de Groot et al. (2014), Szymanowska et al. (2014), Fuertes et al. (2015), and Zaremba (2016); and for real estate and REITs, Hung and Glascock (2010), Beracha and Skiba (2011), Goebel et al. (2012), Ro and Gallimore (2013), Feng et al. (2014)., and Moss et al. (2015).

[6] See, for factor portfolios, Zaremba and Shemer (2016a, c, e, and Ehsani (2017); for style indices, Chen and De Bondt (2004), Tibbs et al. (2008), Clare et al. (2010), and Chen et al. (2012).

So far we have talked only about the strategies within individual asset classes. Can we then benefit from the momentum phenomenon when choosing an asset class at the highest level of asset allocation? Absolutely! Blitz and van Vliet (2008) showed that past winners among asset classes are likely to remain winners while past laggards continue to stay behind which has been subsequently confirmed by many other researchers.[7]

While this wealth of evidence can be called direct, the validity of the momentum strategy can also be supported indirectly—by technical analysis. In reality, most of the quantitative technical trading systems, employed, for example, by professional Commodity Trading Advisors (Fung and Hsieh 1997; Lhabitant 2008), rely on trend following, a concept closely related to a type of price momentum sometimes called "time-series momentum" (discussed later in this chapter). Over the last decades, the profitability of the technical signals has been scrutinized in numerous research papers, with some studies relatively simple, but the recent ones, in particular, growing in sophistication. In a simpler research paper—a study from 1988 by Lukac et al.—the authors tested an array of trading strategies, including the so-called price channels, moving averages, oscillators, stop-loss orders, and the combinations of all these techniques stemming from the trend-following philosophy. The authors ensured robustness of their results and considered plenty of issues, including various portfolio optimization methods, alternative levels of trading costs, applying their system to a number of different commodity markets, also, adjusting the strategy returns for risk. As a result, 7 out of the 12 systems they tested provided both significant and positive abnormal returns. In other words, some of them—though not all—appeared effective, confirming, at least partly, the validity of the trend-following approach.

As indicated, the early examinations, of which the study by Lukac et al. (1988) may serve as a classical example, may seem relatively simple compared to the following studies visibly gaining in sophistication. For example, in 2005 in his research, Roberts utilized a complicated genetic algorithm to investigate the performance of as many as 20,000 random investment rules. He employed state-of-the-art simulation techniques and made his results robust to many considerations. Furthermore, in a recent "survey" paper, two researchers, Park and Irwin (2007), took a Herculean effort and reviewed almost a hundred various studies devoted to technical

[7] See, for example, Wang and Kochard (2011), Kim (2012), Asness et al. (2013), Bhansali et al. (2015), Baz et al. (2015), and Cooper et al. (2017).

analyses classifying them as "early" or "modern" according to the sophistication and quality of the testing procedures. In general, the "early" studies showed that the technical trading signals are able to deliver decent profits in futures markets and currency markets, yet tending to perform poorly in equity markets, whereas the "modern" studies were on average even more optimistic, showing that technical trading generated consistent economic profits in a variety of speculative markets. Among all of the studies reviewed by Park and Irwin (2007), the majority—59%—displayed positive results of technical trend-following strategies; the further 20% proved negative, while 19% of the studies produced mixed results. Summing up, the technical analysis appears to work well, with some studies however casting doubt on this proposition.

Why Momentum Works?

Once momentum was proved effective, it was time to question its origins. Although technical trading strategies always appealed to investors, the academic community was rather reserved. This caution stemmed most likely from two essential issues (Irwin and Park 2008). First, the initial formal academic attempts to verify the efficiency of technical analysis were unable to deliver convincing proofs.[8] Second, the idea that technical analysis could be profitable, stood in stark opposition to the main paradigm of the time—the efficient market hypothesis (EMH)—which largely dominated the thinking of the 1960s and 1970s. The term "efficient market hypothesis" was originally coined in 1967 by Harry Roberts who was also the first person to distinguish between the weak and strong forms of efficiency that later became the canonical taxonomy in the research of Eugene Fama (1970), the Nobel prize laureate. In essence, the EMH assumes that in the informationally efficient market, the prices should always perfectly reflect all the available information. The classification of the EMH differentiates its three forms: weak, semi-strong, and strong, dependent on what categories of information we refer to. In particular, the weak form has the strongest link to the technical analysis, because it considers the past prices. In other words, when the market is informationally efficient in its weak form, all of the information on past prices should be included, or "priced", in the current prices. Why? Because if thousands of stock market investors

[8] See, for example, Fama and Blume (1966), van Horne and Parker (1967, 1968), or Jensen and Benington (1970).

make their best efforts to exploit the technical trading opportunities in the equity market, then it is quite likely that any possible profits will rapidly dry up. To put it in different words, there is no place for any abnormal returns to be gained by technical analysis. As the famous economist Paul Samuelson (1965, p. 44) concluded, "There is no way of making an expected profit by extrapolating past changes in the future price, by chart or any other esoteric devices of magic or mathematics. The market quotation in t already contains in itself all that can be known about the future and in that sense has discounted future contingencies as much as it is humanly possible." How strong was the belief of the academic community in the EMH is also well expressed by another quote by Michael Jensen (1978), who famously wrote, "I believe there is no other proposition in economics which has more solid empirical evidence supporting it than the efficient market hypothesis."

Despite this rigid and categorical approach implied by the EMH, some later views were slightly more generous toward the profitability of technical trading. In particular, Grossman and Stiglitz (1976, 1980) indicated an interesting paradox in the reasoning pointing out that if financial markets are truly efficient, then its participants might have no incentive to either conduct any analysis or implement any strategies, especially if these processes require devotion of their time and money. In a nutshell, some investors may intentionally choose not to follow any technical analysis to avoid putting their efforts in something that is finally ineffective. These so-called *noise traders*, may, in turn, create opportunities for someone who does decide to follow the technical strategies. In other words, by voluntarily withdrawing from implementing some strategies, they produce profit opportunities for others. Moreover, the higher the costs of examining and implementing some investment techniques, the more investors might be prone to shy away from technical tools, thus, making these strategies even more effective. Summing up, Grossman and Stiglitz seem to say: do not worry that much, there is still some hope for trend following.[9]

To a great extent, the ideas of Grossman and Stiglitz changed the broadly held view on technical analysis and led to consider trend following

[9] The noisy rational expectations model in its most original form does not fully allow for technical analysis, because Grossman and Stiglitz (1976, 1980) assume that uninformed investors have rational expectations about future prices. Nonetheless, this gap has been filled by subsequent variations of this model, for example, Hellwig (1982), Brown and Jennings (1989), and Blume et al. (1994).

a more legitimate approach to market analysis. Hence, further explanations of momentum were quick to follow. While two or three years ago momentum appeared puzzling to the academic community, calling it now "an anomaly" could sound a little insolent. Although the jury on the sources of momentum is still out, now the finance literature offers a number of plausible explanations with opposite camps: supporters of neoclassical (rational) and behavioral finance still entangled in dispute.

The explanations of risk-based momentum go back to the ideas of Conrad and Kaul (1993) who saw its origin in the cross-sectional variation of expected stock returns. According to the researchers, the momentum effect might emerge simply because of the higher long-run returns. In other words, some firms systematically deliver higher returns. If we place the best performing companies in one portfolio, the investment, comprising outperforming stocks, is likely to continue to outperform in the future. Plain and simple. To gain a better perspective, let's assume that the market consists of only two firms. The first operates a safe and stable business, and its shares yield a stable 5% return per year. The other, rather inexperienced and risky, sees its share highly volatile for which the more careful, risk-averse investors would expect a return of at least 10% leading the shares to appreciate approximately 10% per year. Now let's think about momentum portfolios. In finance "laboratories", momentum strategies are usually implemented by sorting: you rank the equities by their past returns and go long in the stocks with the best performance, simultaneously shortening the worst performers. If an investor employed this strategy in our market of two stocks, they would most likely go long in the risk stock yielding 10% per year, and go short in the safe stocks delivering 5% per year. And, indeed, this portfolio will probably display positive returns, as it is long in the company that is characterized by a higher rate of return. The trouble lies only in the source of this outperformance. The better performing stocks display no sophisticated momentum-specific characteristics that add an extra return premium—being only more risky. In consequence, the momentum investor in this example loads his portfolio with excessive risk—giving the only reason for momentum to work. No magic involved. The momentum is not driven by any short-run conditional payoffs; it is rather a result of cross-sectional variation in long-run unconditional returns.

The theory seemed straightforward and coherent until a number of further studies refuted it, showing it is not the same risky stocks that comprise momentum portfolios. On the contrary, momentum is driven by rotating companies and stocks, systematically updating the winners and losers portfolios (Jegadeesh and Titman 2001; Grundy and Martin 2001).

Most equity anomalies are usually explained in one of the two ways: either as a consequence of the underlying risk factors or as a manifestation of investor irrationality that cannot be easily arbitraged away. Here, the momentum case is not that different. A number of studies suggest that the momentum profitability might be associated with countrywide (or even international) risk factors related to liquidity fluctuations or macroeconomy, for example, cycle (Chordia and Shivakumar 2002), economic growth shocks (Ahn et al. 2003), aggregate liquidity (Pastor and Stambaugh 2003), consumption (Bansal et al. 2005), and industrial production (Liu and Zhang 2008). Moreover, one study by Sagi and Seasholes (2007) linked momentum profits with firm-specific characteristics, like revenue, volatility, or costs of goods sold, whereas another influential research by Cooper et al. (2017) linked momentum to global macroeconomic risks across multiple asset groups. The authors proved that momentum might serve as a proxy for a set of global macroeconomic risks which, when efficiently combined, can explain the momentum abnormal profits. The risk factors included the growth rate of industrial production, unexpected inflation, change in expected inflation, and both term and default spread. Recreating momentum strategies using the stocks with the required exposure to these risk factors displays considerable powers to explain momentum.

Nevertheless, risk-based explanations of momentum have these shortcomings. On the one hand, they are challenged by the contradictory evidence (e.g., Griffin et al. 2003, Avramov et al. 2006a, b); on the other hand, when examining a large number of factors, the pitfalls of overfitting bias and data mining pose a significant threat. In effect, behavioral advocates, proposing markedly different explanations, seem to be winning the argument.

Behavioral explanations point to a series of psychological biases and frictions that affect the market price and lead a market trend to substitute an immediate price correction in reaction to the new information. To better explain this concept, let's take a look at the example depicted in Fig. 2.1.[10]

Let us imagine the unexpected positive news: a company has just acquired its competitor at an advantageous price or a quarterly report exceeding the analysts' revenue and earnings estimates. How would the

[10] This example is inspired by Hurst et al. (2013).

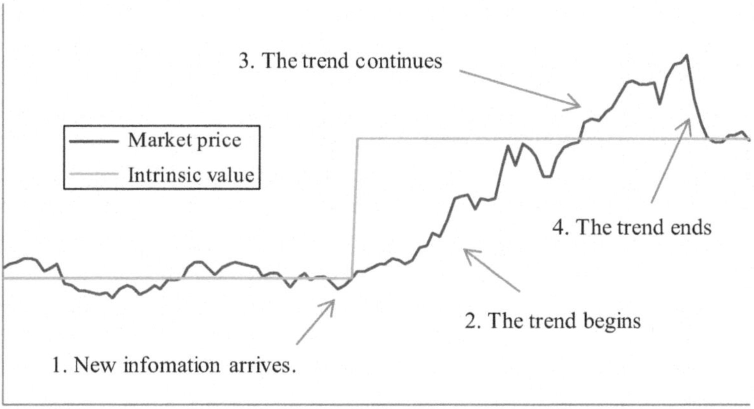

Fig. 2.1 Life-cycle of a trend (Source: Own elaboration)

market react in the ideally "efficient" world? Stock market investors should immediately recalculate the value of the company and start trading at a new level. The news would affect both buyers and sellers. No one would be willing to sell the stocks at the previous price, as the firm's value has increased—the sellers would fix their offer prices at a new higher level, with no intention to sell cheaper. For the same reason, the buyers will also accept the higher price knowing that the company is now more valuable, and not wanting to be outbid. In other words, the price of a stock would immediately adjust to the new information, subsequently remaining relatively stable, waiting patiently for the arrival of the next new piece of information, whether positive or negative.

In the real world, however, the picture is likely to be different. Human investors, who are affected by a number of behavioral biases, may assess the situation differently. First, investors have a tendency to underreact to newly arrived information. Thus, instead of the instant price increase, we are more likely to see a trend-like price movement. The underreaction phenomenon in the equity, and in general financial markets, stems from the following two crucial tendencies.

Anchoring The term "anchoring" describes a psychological bias in which stock market investors (as well all individuals) persistently stick to one initial value or arbitrary point of reference. A great example of this phenomenon was demonstrated by Kahneman and Tversky in their research article published in 1974. In their experiment, both authors spun a wheel containing numbers from 1 to 100, and, subsequently, asked the experiment participants to estimate the percentage of African countries in the United Nations. Unsurprisingly, few participants knew the correct answer. Interestingly, however, their guesses strangely correlated with the random numbers prompted by the wheel. For instance, if the wheel indicated 10, the average estimate given by the participants amounted to 25%. However, if the number on the wheel was 60, the mean estimate astonishingly rose to 45%. The subjects of this experiment unconsciously "anchored" their answer to a random number, even if it in no way related to the question.

Importantly, the anchoring bias is not only an experimental curiosity. It exerts a real impact on various investment decisions in financial markets. An excellent example was provided by Northcraft and Neale (1987) who asked real estate agents to estimate the value a certain property. All the participants were given exactly the same information with only a single exception: the listing price was different ranging from $119,900 to $149,900. While the estate agents denied their valuations would be influenced by the listing price, the outcomes evidently were. In the cases where the listing price was $119,900, the mean appraisal value equaled $116,833; while with the higher listing price of $149,900, the average appraisal value surged to $144,454.

Importantly for the equity investors, the anchoring effect reaches beyond the real estate. If stock market investors adhere to a past price without any reasonable justification, in consequence, the price is likely to underreact to any new information.[11]

Disposition Effect The disposition effect is another phenomenon which is very likely to facilitate the momentum pattern. While the fundamental advice for every stock market trader applying trend-following techniques is to "cut your losses and let your profits run", the majority of investors find it hard to follow. In reality, they tend to sell appreciating stocks too early and stick on to the losers for too long, as they prefer cashing in gains rather than owning up to losses.

[11] For further discussion on the anchoring effect and its implications for underreaction, see also Slovic and Lichtenstein (1971), Watson and Buede (1987), Reidpath and Diamond (1995), and Barberis et al. (1998).

This so-called disposition effect is one the most extensively examined and described phenomenon in behavioral finance. Let's examine a few examples. In 1998, a famous study by Odean investigated trades from 10,000 accounts of US discount brokers in the 1987–1993 period. In particular, the research analyzed the investors' behavior patterns following appreciations and depreciations of stocks in their portfolios. As observed, the investors were roughly 50% more likely to sell the stocks after their prices increased in comparison to price decreases. Importantly, the disposition effect is not only the problem of individual investors; it impacts all types of stock market participants households (Barber and Odean 2000, 2004) and professional futures traders (Locke and Mann 2005) as it does for many types of securities, including treasury futures (Heisler 1994) and mutual funds (Calvet et al. 1992; Ivkovic and Weisbenner 2009). In fact, the differences in the magnitude of the disposition effect between individual and professional investors are surprisingly small.

The disposition effect may add in two ways to the initial underpricing and, in consequence, to the emergence of the trend in the market. First, the investors who sell too early after the gains may create a downward price pressure, slowing down the price adjusting to the new information. Second, the late-sellers following losses may keep prices from falling as rapidly as they should have in order to reflect the new information instantly in the prices (Hurst et al. 2013).[12]

These two behavioral effects—the disposition effect and anchoring—are the most likely contributors to the initial underreaction in the development of the trend. However, once the trend is in motion, some other behavioral biases step in to contribute to its continuation and the subsequent overreaction. These phenomena are herding, feedback trading, confirmation bias, and representativeness (Hurst et al. 2013).

Herding The herding behavior could be described as a tendency of individuals to mimic the actions of a larger group even if individually the person would take a different decision (Bikhchandani et al. 1992). Academicians indicate two basic reasons for herding. On the one hand, it is driven by the social pressure of conformity. On the other hand, it is the

[12] For further essential references for the disposition effect, see Shefrin and Statman (1985), Weber and Camerer (1998), Frazzini (2006), and Barberis and Xiong (2009). Moreover, an interesting survey of theory and evidence is provided by Kaustia (2010).

belief upheld by most people that a large group cannot be wrong. How often do we evaluate our actions by checking what other people are doing? In financial markets, the herd behavior may manifest in a special way: by pushing investors to buy the same assets and thus reinforcing the trend. Interestingly, herding was found not only among individual investors but also among professionals preparing investment newsletters (Graham 1999) or stock recommendations (Welch 2000).

Feedback Trading The psychological phenomenon of feedback trading is in a way closely related to herding. The concept of feedback trading refers to a tendency in investors' behavior when a positive result, as for instance a successful trade, boosts the investor's confidence to pursue the same behavior in the future. If we have bought stocks and earned a decent profit, then we should continue buying the same shares, right? A consequence of this way of thinking may be simple: investors are prone to purchasing the stocks that are rising and selling the stocks that are falling. Such a cycle of positive feedback may considerably strengthen the trend in the market.[13]

Confirmation Bias and Representativeness These two effects, especially when taken together, might form another important contributor to the trend development. Frequently, when a stock investor investigates a company, they frequently have a preconceived opinion which they then use to filter the incoming new information: paying particular attention to the news supporting their opinion and simultaneously rationalizing, or simply ignoring, the contradictory information. In consequence, investors usually tend to focus on information that confirms their initial opinion about a business, rather any evidence to the contrary. The result? The perception of the company in the investor's eyes might be markedly leaning toward their initial preconception.[14]

[13] There are many theoretical models of feedback trading, developed by, for example, Shiller (1984), de Long et al. (1990a, b), Cutler et al. (1990), Hong and Stein (1999), and Shleifer (2000). Empirical evidence on this phenomenon could be found in Shiller (1988), de Long et al. (1990b), De Bondt (1993), Nosfinger and Sias (1999), and Bange (2000).

[14] Key studies regarding the confirmation bias include Lord et al. (1979), Forsythe et al. (1992), Pouget and Villeneuve (2012), and Bowden (2015). Moreover, further references regarding this phenomenon are in Rabin and Schrag (1999) and Pouget and Villeneuve (2008).

There is plenty of scientific evidence that stock market investors are influenced by the confirmation bias (Wason 1960; Tversky and Kahneman 1974) and that this phenomenon is further amplified by the effect of representativeness, a heuristic generating a broad array of biases. One of them—"*base rate neglect*"—has been skillfully encapsulated by Tversky and Kahneman (1974) in the following description of Linda:

> Linda is 31 years old, single, outspoken, and very bright. She majored in philosophy. As a student, she was deeply concerned with issues of discrimination and social justice, and also participated in anti-nuclear demonstrations. (Tversky and Kahneman 1974)

So how did the majority of participants responded to the question about the probability of "Linda being a bank teller" versus "Linda being a bank teller and active in the feminist movement"? Naturally, most people opted for the latter statement. In fact, the latter statement is clearly less probable since the population of bank tellers who simultaneously are feminist activist is clearly smaller than the broader population of bank tellers, in general.

Another manifestation of the representativeness heuristic is called "size neglect" stemming from the observation that people often fail to account properly for a size of the sample when attempting to assess the probability of a future event. The so-called hot hand phenomenon may serve as an excellent example. Sports fans sometimes believe that a basketball player who has made three shots in a row is on a hot streak and, therefore, is likely to score again. Despite the popular belief, there is literally no academic evidence to support the hot hand effect (Gilovich et al. 1985). The size neglect may equally affect the equity market. The stock market investors may be led to see a trend where it does not exists. Three or four consecutive price increases in a row may be sufficient to create an impression of a trend in the minds of trend-seeking investors while, in fact, these could be only three consecutive random price increases.[15]

To sum up, the market participants tend to look for information that confirms their current beliefs, and the past price appreciation may be

[15] The representativeness heuristic was initially discussed in a series of papers authored by Kahneman and Tversky (Kahneman and Tversky 1972; Tversky and Kahneman 1971, 1974, 1982). The impact on stock market investors, which eventually leads to overreaction, was documented in the papers of Kaestner (2006), Frieder (2008), Alwathainani (2012), and Boussaidi (2013).

perceived as the representative of the future price movements. In consequence, investors may be eager to pour more funds into financial assets, for example, stocks, that had risen in prices, while at the same time withdrawing cash from firms whose stock price has just fallen. Both actions are likely to reinforce the trend in prices, leading eventually to overvaluation (Daniel et al. 1998; Barberis et al. 1998).

Finally, in the case of an upward trend, all the above biases may lead to overvaluation, strengthening the trend for a limited time. The overvalued stock will most likely eventually revert to its intrinsic value in a pattern called "long-run reversal", which leads to systematical poor returns of the firms that performed very well in the past few years.[16]

The biases and heuristics presented above encapsulate the behavioral explanation of the momentum effect, which, along the risk-based explanation, is perhaps the most broadly acknowledged. While the tensions between the risk-based and behavioral explanations dominate the current academic discussion, we do also have completely new approaches to explain momentum often referring to completely unrelated phenomena. A separate array of models concentrates on the market microstructure, for example, the order flow (Osler 2000). The take-profit and stop-loss orders placed by investors tend to concentrate in very specific market areas: around the market tops and bottoms or round price numbers. Hence, their simultaneous activation may lead to either a sharp rise or significant decline in prices, becoming a self-fulfilling prophecy of the momentum effect in the market. This type of price fluctuations may justify the profitability of, for instance, short-term break-out systems.

Further, some researchers indicate that various financial or non-financial institutions may contribute to the trend formation. Silber (1994) partly blames central banks—important FX market players—whose pursuit of their individual goals may sometimes hinder an immediate and full discounting of the fundamental information on the currency markets, leading to the formation of trend. A central bank may strive to weaken the currency to boost the economy, while the fundamental intrinsic value would suggest the currency to be much stronger. If the central bank does engage in excessive money printing, the currency will most likely strengthen in the end, but the upward move will be alleviated by the central bank

[16] Evidence of the long-run underperformance is documented by, among others, De Bondt and Thaler (1985), Moskowitz et al. (2012), and Asness et al. (2013). We will also discuss this effect more in detail in further sections of this book.

actions, turning it into an appreciation trend. Furthermore, Garleanu and Pedersen (2007) see a source of the trend formation in risk management practices of some financial institutions, including banks, insurance companies, or investment funds which usually employ backward-looking risk measures, calculated based on historical data from a trailing period. In consequence, if there is a sharp decline in stock prices, the rising levels of risk indicators may force the financial institutions to sell some of its securities in the portfolios. This massive fire-sale may subsequently lead to further price decreases.

While there are other hypothesis theories, for example, the chaos theory (Clyde and Osler 1997), they seem much less discussed.

Although the discussion on the explanation of the momentum phenomenon still continues, the scientific community is now light years away from the time when the EMH dominated the minds of academicians and market practitioners. Today, momentum is not only empirically well documented, but it is being attempted to be fully explained. It appears to be a healthy and reliable return pattern grounded on solid foundations, in both theoretical and empirical terms.

Improving the Momentum

So far our discussion has concentrated on the basic relative momentum strategies where the investor sorts the stocks on their trailing past returns. As usual, however, the devil is in the details, and even the basic momentum strategy could be approached in a multiple ways impacting the final performance. Especially as the recent research on momentum has significantly gained in sophistication with the researchers constantly seeking for better, improved, and more precise momentum measures that would lead to better risk-return profiles. Let us then review some of the popular momentum-based techniques.

Classical Momentum The standard momentum strategy could be traced back to the seminal paper of Jegadeesh and Titman (1993) who employed specific "contingency" tables together with a range of sorting and holding periods for their portfolios. The researchers observed that the stocks that performed well over the past 6–12 months continued to outperform in the next 3–12 months. In other words, the optimal ranking period ranged between 6 and 12 months. Still, which exact ranking period is the best? The last two decades of further research has built a consensus among the momentum researchers agreeing on the most common approach of sorting stocks on their 12-month performance skipping the most recent month (cumulative or mean return in months $t-12$ to $t-2$). What are the reasons for that peculiar sorting period? There are at least three separate ones. First, stock prices tend to exhibit a short-term reversal effect, that is, when the price changes in the most recent period (e.g., a month) tend to revert partly in the following month (Lehmann 1990; Jegadeesh 1990; Da et al. 2014). Skipping this last month in the momentum measurement allows disentangling the momentum effect. Second, the momentum profitability depends to some extent on the sorting period which for some periods is stronger than for others. Historically, the 12-month ranking period has proven particularly efficient. The third reason concerns the seasonal anomalies in the stock market, which may affect equity prices. Specifically, it is related to one particular anomaly: the January effect. The January effect is a calendar month anomaly implying that small-capitalization companies tend to deliver particularly high returns in the first year of the month (Keim 1983a, b). The January effect is one the most intensively discussed and examined phenomena in asset pricing. Usually, it is explained by the behavior of individual investors, who—on the one hand—are tax sensitive and—on the other hand—hold a lot of small stocks in their portfolios, at least compared to the institutional investors. Such investors are prone to selling stocks for tax reasons at the year-end, reinvesting the proceeds in January.[17] So why might the January effect be important for the momentum measurement? If the sorting period is shorter than the full calendar year, the resulting selection of stocks will be a consequence of the specific calendar months included in the ranking period. If this period includes January, then small firms are very likely to be overweighted as performing particularly well in this period. Analogously, in the other months the stock selection would lean toward large companies. In fact, this cross-sectional seasonality could be extended also to other groups of stocks, for example, value or quality stocks. A simple way to overcome this problem is to base the ranking on a period close approximating a full calendar year.

Improving the Momentum Measurement Methods As momentum is now a broadly recognized and well-documented phenomenon, no longer do academicians seem to discuss *whether* the momentum exists, but rather

[17] The link between the size premium and the January effect was discussed by, for example, Easterday et al. (2009), Haug and Hirschey (2006), or Zhang and Jacobsen (2012).

why it exists and *how to improve* the momentum strategies. Let us now focus on the latter aspect. The recent decade has brought a cornucopia of ideas how to improve the momentum performance, in respect of both risk and return. Albeit some resemble only optimization exercises, some may serve as valuable tools for momentum investors.

Echo, or the intermediate momentum, is one of the ideas to enhance the momentum profitability by optimizing the measurement period and stepping away from the broadly acknowledged "12-month trailing with the most recent month skipped". An interesting initiative was undertaken by Robert Novy-Marx who in 2012 wrote his paper provocatively entitled "Is Momentum Really Momentum?" According to his research, the classical momentum effect is driven primarily by firm's performance 7 to 12 months prior the portfolio formation and not by a tendency of rising and falling stocks to keep rising and falling. Novy-Marx showed that the strategies based on the most recent performance would still generate positive returns, yet less profitable than those based on the intermediate past sorting periods. Thus, the phenomenon is not really momentum, but rather an echo in return reoccurring after six months! Interestingly, Novy-Marx (2012) found this phenomenon very robust, holding true in international equity indices, currencies, and commodities, and his research was published in the *Journal of Financial Economics*, one of the most reputable academic journals in finance.

This, however, is hardly the end of the story. Some further controversy was added by Amit Goyal and Sunil Wahal (2015) in their paper entitled "Is Momentum an Echo?", aimed at reexamining the Novy-Marx's approach. Casting doubt on the "echo effect", the authors pointed to its poor theoretical motivation stating that "it is hard to imagine a story that could generate such an effect on prices; even the age-old "relative strength" trading strategies of Wall-Street lore have nothing to say about such an effect. For financial economists, the challenge to theory is enormous. No existing theory, whether behavioral or rational, predicts an echo in returns."

Even more importantly, Goyal and Wahal identified another hole in the "intermediate momentum". Having conducted an extensive out-of-sample test in search for the same echo effect across 37 countries, including both developed and emerging markets, in the period 1980–2010, the researchers found almost nothing. With the sole exception of Japan and the USA, nowhere else did they find any convincing evidence of the echo effect concluding that the profitability of the classical and intermediate momentum effects is indistinguishable anywhere else outside the US market. Furthermore, a closer investigation of the full term structure of returns within the American market shows that the superior performance of strategies based on the "echo" effect is driven by the presence of reversal (or at least no continuation) from the month prior the most recent month (month −2 of the month of the returns). "The true puzzle is not why intermediate horizon returns forecast future returns better than recent horizon returns, but why return reversals from month −1 also extend (somewhat) to month −2," they concluded.

Summing up, the evidence for the superior performance of the intermediate momentum over the classical momentum still remains doubtful. It seems that the classical momentum based on the lagged 11 months will remain the dominant concept, at least for some time into the future.

Adjustment of Momentum Signals for Volatility Another drawback of the momentum effect is that it tends to gravitate strongly toward volatile stocks. Simply put, these assets are more likely to exhibit extreme positive or negative returns and, in consequence, to be picked up in the momentum selection. Let's consider two groups of stocks of large and small businesses. Small companies are usually much more volatile, more often yielding either very high or very low returns. There are a number of different reasons for that: first, a less stable financial situation more vulnerable to the swings in economy, and second, usually less liquid stocks whose price may rapidly rise or fall in reaction to the demand or supply pressure. Momentum portfolios are usually formed by sorting stocks on their historical returns and then forming the long and short portfolios of equities with the highest and lowest payoffs. Such portfolios are then quite likely to be overpopulated by volatile stocks. Importantly, this is also the case for other asset classes. In bonds, for instance, the classical long-momentum portfolio might be dominated by high-duration bonds during bull markets (under falling interest rates) and low-duration bonds during bear markets (when interest rates are rising).

This effect of the volatility on the momentum strategy might be detrimental in two ways. First, the portfolios overpopulated with volatile stock might simply become exceedingly volatile. In other ways, if we find a way to alleviate this problem, it would most likely reduce the risk of the momentum strategies. Second, the long-run volatility of stocks in the momentum portfolios might impact their profitability. As there is plenty of evidence that volatile stocks tend to underperform safe stocks (Blitz and van Vliet 2007), this phenomenon may also impede the momentum profits. Although we discuss this phenomenon in a separate chapter showing how to profit from it, in this case, it is clearly a burden.

One way to overcome it would be to scale the momentum signal by their volatility. In other words, not to sort the stocks on their past returns, but rather to divide the past cumulative returns by their standard deviation. This simple tweak allows to deal with the volatility issues improving on the performance of the momentum strategy (Ilmanen 2011; Shaik 2011; Dudler et al. 2015; Clare et al. 2016). Here, the sorting period also approximates 12 months, analogously to the classical momentum, so the return predictive signal for sorting stocks ($ADJ - MOM_{RAW}$), for stock i, in month t, may look as follows:

$$ADJ - MOM_{RAW,i,t} = \frac{\sum_{t-12}^{t-1} R_{i,t} / 12}{\sqrt{\sum_{t-12}^{t-1} \left(R_{i,t} - \overline{R_i}\right)^2 / 12}}, \tag{2.2}$$

where $\overline{R_i}$ is the mean monthly log-return from $t-12$ to $t-1$. Importantly, this way of improving the momentum efficiency, with some slight modifications, has been also successfully applied to corporate and government bonds, as a way of alleviating the influence of duration.[18]

Reducing Factor Exposure: Residual Momentum Another problem concerning momentum lies in the time-varying exposure of stocks to various risk factors. Let's illustrate it with a simple example using the famous capital asset pricing model (abbreviated CAPM, Sharpe 1964) and the influence of stock market beta. The CAPM assumes that each stock can be characterized by its "market beta", a special parameter indicating the asset's risk in comparison to the broad market portfolio. Putting it simple,

[18] Some bond strategies also use simpler measures to cope with the impact of influence, like sorting the bonds on change in yields-to-maturity or on return difference with a duration-matched benchmark bonds. A discussion and examination of bond momentum strategies could be found in following studies: for government bonds, Luu and Yu (2012), Asness et al. (2013), Duyvesteyn and Martens (2014), Hambusch et al. (2015), Zaremba and Czapkiewicz (2017a, b), and Zaremba and Schabek (2017); and for corporate bonds, Gebhardt et al. (2005), Pospisil and Zhang (2010), Kim et al. (2012), Jostova et al. (2013), de Carvalho et al. (2014), Israel et al. (2016), Barth et al. (2017), van Zundert (2017), Lin et al. (2017), and Houweling and van Zundert (2017).

the market beta shows the ratio by which the stock should rise in a bull market relative to the broad market portfolio, or it should fall in a downturn. If the stock beta is 1.5 under a positive excess return of 10%, we may expect the stock to earn a return of approximately 15%. Conversely, when the market falls with an excess return of −10%, the stock beta of 1.5 indicates a likely fall of over 15% in the same period. We usually call the stocks with beta above one aggressive, or cyclical, because they rise and fall more excessively than the market portfolio over the same time. These stocks might include, for instance, high-tech companies, luxury goods manufacturers, construction companies, or other businesses where demand varies significantly over the business cycle.

On the other hand, when the beta remains below one, amounting, for example, to 0.5, the stock will "underreact" the market swings. If the market rises 10%, it will rise around 5%; if the market decreases 10%, it will also drop by approximately 5%. These equities are often described as defensive and typically include companies with a very stable demand over the business cycle, such as the utilities, pharmaceuticals, or food manufacturers.

So what is beta's role in momentum? Let's imagine a powerful bull market. Which equities are more likely to be included in the top-momentum portfolios: high-beta or low-beta? Naturally, high-beta: as bearing bigger market exposure, they would be more likely to earn higher returns. Yet again, they end up in the top-momentum portfolio not because of some special "momentum characteristics"—but due to being simply riskier and exhibiting larger betas.

What are the consequences of this bias? On the one hand, the momentum portfolios might gravitate toward riskier (high-beta) stocks, thus, increasing the overall systematic risk of the momentum portfolio. Second, and more importantly, the high-beta stocks have been found to underperform the low-beta stocks (Frazzini and Pedersen 2014). In consequence, the bias toward the high-beta stocks may not only increase the risk but also impede the portfolio's profitability.

Importantly, the inclination of high-momentum portfolios to gravitate toward high-beta stocks is not limited to the stock market beta and could be extended to other types of factor exposure, for instance, to value, small-cap, or high-quality stocks. To illustrate this, let's imagine a huge credit crunch hitting the stock market. In panic, all the investors would rush to transfer their capital from the risky stocks to the high-quality securities. Hence, afterwards the long-momentum portfolio would likely include many high-quality firms. But again, the reason does not lie in any special momentum-related characteristics of these stocks—as they were just lucky enough to display a solid exposure to the well-performing factor.

Luckily, there is a standard solution to this problem: instead of calculating the momentum signals based on raw returns, replace them by the residuals from the factor model, which are parts of returns that cannot be explained by the factor models. The strategy follows a two-step procedure: first, we control for some common risk factors and in the second step compute the momentum signals on the residuals which are left unexplained by these risk factors.

Technically, the first step is to estimate the factor model for each of the securities in the portfolio with the usual estimation period revolving around five years. The most popular models include the CAPM (e.g., Chaves 2012) or the three-factor model of Fama and French (1993), applied, for example, by Blitz et al. (2011).

As the two-step procedure is usually based on the 60-month estimation period for each stock-month return observation, the investor should simply follow the following CAPM regression:

$$R_{i,t} - R_{f,t} = \alpha_{CAPM,i} + \beta_{MKT,i} MKT_t + \varepsilon_{CAPM,i,t}, \tag{2.3}$$

where MKT_t is the excess return on the market portfolio in month t, $R_{f,t}$ is the risk-free return in month t, $\alpha_{CAPM,i}$ and $\beta_{MKT,i}$ are regression parameters, and $\varepsilon_{CAPM,i,t}$ is the residual (error term). The intercept $\alpha_{CAPM,i}$ (Jensen's alpha) measures the average abnormal return, and $\beta_{MKT,i}$ is the exposure to stock market risk.

Alternatively, one can also use the Fama-French three-factor model:

$$R_{i,t} - R_{f,t} = \alpha_{FF,i} + \beta_{MKT,i} MKT_t + \beta_{SMB,i} SMB_t + \beta_{HML,i} HML_t + \varepsilon_{FF,i,t} \tag{2.4}$$

where SMB_t and HML_t are factor returns corresponding with size and value effects in month t, respectively; $\alpha_{FF,i}$, $\beta_{MKT,i}$, $\beta_{SMB,i}$, and $\beta_{HML,i}$ are the model's parameters; and $\varepsilon_{FF,i,t}$ is the residual from the model. The SMB_t is the return on a diversified long-short portfolio which is long (short) in the small (large) countries, industries, or companies, and the HML_t return is based on long-short portfolios which are long (short) in the high (low) book-to-market (abbreviated as BM) portfolios.

In the second step, an investor should compute the residual momentum signal based on CAPM (MOM_{CAPM}) as the mean residual during, usually, a trailing 12-month period:

$$MOM_{CAPM,i,t} = \sum_{t-12}^{t-1} \varepsilon_{CAPM,i,t} / 12. \tag{2.5}$$

The procedure to calculate the signal based on the three-factor model MOM_{FF} is very similar to MOM_{CAPM}, but the investor should use the residuals from the three-factor model instead of the CAPM:

$$MOM_{FF,i,t} = \sum_{t-12}^{t-1} \varepsilon_{FF,i,t} / 12. \tag{2.6}$$

The residual momentum strategy has been extensively tested within both the US and international markets (Blitz et al. 2011, 2017), successfully reducing the risk of the momentum strategies by decreasing their factor exposure.

The strategy has further evolved into two interesting propositions. First, Grundy and Martin (2001) and Hühn and Scholz (2017) have offered a strategy called "alpha momentum", which although very similar to the residual momentum requires the equity rankings to be based on alphas from the factor models instead of the averaged residuals. Mathematically, both approaches are very similar.

The second strategy proposed by Zaremba and Umutlu (2018a, b) aims to enhance the performance of the residual momentum by addressing the bias of residual momentum, and the raw return momentum effect, to gravitate toward stocks of high idiosyncratic volatility which leads to overweighting high idiosyncratic volatility stocks in momentum portfolios. This, in turn, can result not only in more volatile payoffs but also in lower profitability, as the companies characterized by high idiosyncratic volatility tend to underperform, on a risk-adjusted basis, the companies with low idiosyncratic volatility (Ang et al. 2006b), even though to this day the country-level relationship between the idiosyncratic risk and expected returns remains blurred (Umutlu 2015). In 2017, Zaremba and Umutlu offered a solution to this problem. In an attempt to take the best of the two worlds, volatility-adjusted momentum and residual momentum, they scaled the past residuals by their volatility to obtain the volatility-adjusted residual momentum (VARMOM).

Subsequently, the researchers tested the efficiency of their international asset allocation strategy across 51 country indices and 936 industry portfolios both from developed and emerging markets. The VARMOM trading strategy significantly outperformed and subsumed the standard momentum strategy, increasing the Sharpe ratios two to three times. Importantly, at least at the country-level, the volatility-adjusted residual momentum subsumed and explained the standard momentum. To conclude, most of the evidence confirms that the strategy of adjusting momentum signals by volatility scaling, or controlling for the factor exposure, may markedly improve the risk-return profile of the momentum strategies.

Capturing Behavioral Biases There are a number of enhancements targeting the behavioral aspect of momentum explanations. To illustrate this point let us examine the effect of overreaction, which according to some psychologists becomes amplified when there is a continuous flow of positive or negative information which come in small pieces. Thus, the more consistent the information flow, the stronger the overreaction, and, hence, the stronger trend in the market. Trying to capture this phenomenon, Grinblatt and Moskowitz (2004) double-sorted stocks on their prior returns and the number of months with either positive or negative returns in the ranking period and proved that selecting stocks that displayed a certain level of consistency in payoffs, at least five positive (or negative) returns in the formation period, would markedly improve the momentum performance.

Seeking for Inefficiencies According to the behavioral explanations of momentum, momentum is a result of psychological biases that cannot be easily arbitraged away. Hence, the momentum effect should appear the strongest in the market segments which are relatively less informationally efficient or, in other words, where the new information is slowly and incorrectly reflected in the prices.

While this supposition has been indeed confirmed in a number of studies adopting different perspectives and approaches, the unanswered question regards the method how to identify these "less efficient" market segments. It is usually done by implementing some types of double-sorts:

the first, based on a proxy for efficiency, and then by running a momentum strategy among the less efficient stocks. So what could constitute an "efficiency measure"? The usual candidates include:

1. **Size**. Momentum is usually stronger among smaller companies with lower institutional ownership and analysts' coverage. As a rule, the smaller the company, the stronger the momentum.
2. **Book-to-market ratio.** A high book-to-market ratio may be a proxy for credit risk, and in consequence, it may disallow, or at least discouraged, such stocks for trading to many sophisticated investors as momentum is stronger among "value" companies than among "growth" companies.
3. **Mutual fund ownership.** This is another proxy for the engagement and interest of sophisticated investors as the momentum effect appears stronger among firms experiencing large changes in mutual fund ownership.
4. **Analyst coverage.** As another measure related to the institutional investors and their activities, higher analyst coverage indicates quick dissemination and proper communication of new information to investors, making stock market anomalies more likely to occur in the market segments with lower analyst coverage. As a rule, the momentum effect emerges usually stronger among companies with low analyst coverage.
5. **Age**. The younger the company, the less known it is. The companies operating in the equity market longer offer investors a longer track record of financial statements with its corporate failures and successes. Without the access to historical information, the markets are more likely to be less efficient and, thus, create more opportunities for all momentum, or any anomaly, traders.
6. **Credit rating**. Low credit rating effectively deters many institutional investors from entering certain market segments. In consequence, the equities are analyzed and investigated less carefully and mostly by individual investors which can significantly decrease the level of efficiency. In 2007, Avramov et al. identified a strong and robust link between momentum and credit rating, clearly documenting that the momentum effect is driven almost exclusively by low-credit-rating securities. Interestingly, this effect prevails for both equities and corporate bonds.

7. **Idiosyncratic risk.** Companies displaying high idiosyncratic risk usually present a problem for institutional investors as their performance may differ markedly from the benchmark. Additionally, stocks with high idiosyncratic risk are more difficult to hedge against as most liquid future contracts track major stock market indices. As high idiosyncratic volatility is usually a trait of small and illiquid companies, the higher the idiosyncratic volatility (or lower the R-squared coefficient), the more pronounced the momentum profits.

All the above characteristics can help us identify the less efficient market segments and, hence, improve the momentum profits.[19] As a rule, the more neglected the company is, the higher momentum profits may arise.[20] Nonetheless, investors should be very cautious when implementing such optimized strategies as momentum's behavior may sometimes prove counterintuitive: for instance, Lee and Swaminathan (2000) found stronger momentum among liquid companies, that is, firms with a high turnover ratio.

Timing the Momentum

Although the momentum profits vary over time, with intertwining periods of success and disappointment, they tend to generate profits. For instance, between the end of World War II and the year 2008, the simple momentum strategy of going long in the 10% of previous year's winners and shorting the 10% of the previous year's looser delivered an annualized return of 16.5% with a notably low volatility. Nonetheless, there have been periods of utter failure, as observed by Victor Niederhoffer, a famous quantitative trader, it resembled "collecting nickels and dimes in front of a steamroller", which pointed to earning profit on most days only to suffer disastrous losses in a collapse of the market.[21]

[19] Key references include, for size, Jegadeesh and Titman (1993), Hong et al. (2000), Zhang (2006); for age, Zhang (2006); for book-to-market ratio, Asness (1997), Daniel and Titman (1999), Sagi and Seasholes (2007); for credit rating, Avramov et al. (2007); for analysts coverage, Hong et al. (2000); for idiosyncratic risk, Zhang (2006), Jiang et al. (2005), analyst forecast dispersion (Zhang 2006), R2 (Hou et al. 2006); for mutual fund ownership, Chen et al. (2002).

[20] Da et al. (2014) argue that it is not only important how the information is processed by the market but also how it is feed thereto, as momentum tends to be stronger among the companies with information arriving in small amounts.

[21] See Stockopedia (2012).

This has been thoroughly researched by Kent Daniel who in his study "Momentum Crashes" identified several such momentum calamities over the last 100 years.[22] A perfect example could be the period between March and May 2009. In three months, the winner portfolio rose by a modest 6.5% while the loser portfolio increased by 156%, delivering a huge blow for the entire long-short portfolio. This "momentum crash" wiped out all of the momentum profits generated for over a decade.

As a rule of thumb, the momentum strategy works best when the trend is stable and consistent and delivers low returns or even losses when the trend abruptly changes. Yet we can still delve into more sophisticated strategies to time the momentum strategies.

Calendar Effects Momentum seasonality patterns, as already identified by some previous studies, Haug and Hirschey (2006) and Ji et al. (2017), in particular, indicate that the momentum strategy tends to deliver disappointing returns in January. The results seem convincing, especially given the extent of the data. For instance, Haug and Hirschey (2006) investigated over two centuries of stock returns, spanning from 1802 to 2014, proving the momentum strategy to underperform in January. Having extended the examination to country equity indices, Zaremba (2015c) identified a similar pattern, while Sias (2007) furthered the investigations to show that the seasonal regularities in momentum payoffs do not limit to January. In fact, the momentum profits tend to concentrate in the last months of the year, particularly in December, and turn out the most disastrous in January.

What could be the source of the January effect in the momentum returns? There are at least two potential explanations. The first hypothesis points to the tax-motivated trading. At the end of a year, investors are more likely to contemplate saving money by avoiding paying taxes. The last thing on their mind at the year-end is to record a big capital gain. Realized losses, on the other hand, can be used to offset gains on other trades. These two mechanisms are likely to facilitate momentum profits as sticking to the winners and selling the losers is the essence of momentum trading.

The second explanation refers to "window dressing". This term is usually used to describe a behavior of some institutional investors or professional money managers to cater for less sophisticated clients. Having

[22] See also Grobys (2016).

originated from the retail industry, the term described a practice of arranging window stores to make them more appealing to potential customers. In the investment industry, however, the practice rather than windows involves financial statements.

In most countries, money managers are obliged to report their portfolio holdings on a quarterly or annual basis. As a client, what type of stocks would you prefer to see there? The well-performing equities that excelled over the last years? Or maybe the market laggards, perhaps even teetering on the verge of bankruptcy? As everyone likes owning the shiny, well-performing securities, some money managers simply cater for these needs, buying the well-performing stocks at the year (or quarter) end, and selling the bad performers. They will most likely unwind these trades; this, however, will never surface in the statement. This can additionally amplify the momentum profits at the year-end, significantly influencing the profitability of the trend-following strategies.

Bull and Bear Markets Some researchers, including Daniel et al. (1998) and Hong and Stein (1999), point to cognitive biases as prominent momentum drivers. They assume that investors' overconfidence, jointly with the self-attribution bias, lead to overreaction which in turn drives momentum returns. Following these arguments, Cooper et al. (2004) have concluded that momentum should increase following bull markets and weaken following bear markets as the overconfidence should surge in response to market increases strengthening the overreactions and thus generating greater momentum in the short run. The researchers have examined the theory testing directly the momentum profitability following bull and bear markets. Having studied the US stocks from 1929 to 1995, they found the six-month momentum strategy would generate a significant mean monthly profit of 0.93% in the periods following bull markets, and an insignificant loss of −0.37% following the bear markets. In other words, all the payoffs from the momentum strategy appear to be only generated in the post-bull market period, while in the post-bear market period it is best to adopt another strategy.

Liquidity and Volatility Another predictors of momentum profits are volatility and liquidity. While Avramov et al. (2016b) have proved momentum profits to be significantly lower following periods of illiquid market states, Wang and Xu (2015) documented that elevated market volatility impedes momentum. Combining these observations, Jacobs (2015) investigated the effect of an aggregate measure of market-wide limits on arbitrage on expected momentum profits to conclude that periods of high limits on arbitrage might be harmful to the momentum strategy. Thus, when following the momentum approach any volatility peaks or abrupt liquidity drops may signal the high time to switch to alternative investment techniques.

Investor Sentiment As according to the behavioral finance, market anomalies are driven by investor irrationality that cannot be quickly arbitraged away, besides the limits on arbitrage, the biggest factor is investor sentiment. Thus the momentum strategy should overperform in periods of high investor sentiment and record lower profits in the times of low investor sentiment. This expectation has been both tested and confirmed by Stambaugh et al. (2012) on the US market, which proves investors' sentiment to be a valuable predictor.

Combining Momentum with Other Signals To outperform the classic momentum strategy, we will need a momentum strategy enhanced by equally effective strategies which would well synergies with momentum. Fortunately, finance literature gives us hints on how to combine momentum with other profitable ranking technique.

Long-Run Reversal The behavioral explanation of momentum draws upon the underreaction and overreaction cycle. Following this idea, to find the top-performing assets we would apply the momentum strategy to the assets already undervalued as a result of a prolonged overreaction to bad news. In this case, the standard momentum signal may be regarded a catalyst signaling the end of the bad times and the stock to revert to its intrinsic value. Analogously, to find stocks to short, we would focus on the overvalued assets and use the abrupt downward move as a signal of the trend change. Thus, long-run reversal and momentum can be effectively combined, which was proved by Balvers and Wu (2006) who developed an integrated model of reversal and momentum documenting both theoretically and empirically the huge potential in combining the two strategies.

Value Investing The value investing effect is closely related to the long-run reversal strategy, and its payoffs display strong correlations with long-run reversal. Once Asness et al. (2013) found that value and momentum were, in fact, negatively correlated with each other, it became possible to combine them with signals to perform well in virtually any possible asset class, including stocks, corporate and government bonds, commodities, currencies, and equity indices.[23]

Skewness Motivated by the earlier research suggesting that the time-series of momentum returns is negatively skewed (Daniel and Moskowitz 2013; Barroso and Santa-Clara 2015), Jacobs et al. (2016) examined the link between the expected skewness of individual stock returns and their momentum. The researchers hypothesized that the outperformance of winners is partly driven by negative skewness whereas the poor performance of losers in part derives from their positive skewness. If losers are on average more positively skewed than winners, then the resulting winners-losers momentum portfolio will be negatively skewed. Following that reasoning, Jacobs et al. (2016) assumed that in the cross-section of stocks the average profitability of long-short momentum returns would increase in line with the difference in the level of skewness of the long and short leg of the portfolio. In consequence, the momentum technique could be greatly enhanced by skewness. Having investigated data from the US stock market for almost 80 years, the researchers provided convincing evidence to prove this conjecture: skewness-enhanced momentum delivers approximately two times higher returns than standard momentum. So to make your momentum strategy more profitable, when building portfolio, overweight stocks with the left-skewed return distributions, and underweight the right-skewed ones.

Alternative Trend-Following Signals

While so far we have discussed only the classical momentum strategy, which relies on ranking stocks on their past performance, either raw or modified, the finance literature offers us a wealth of other momentum-related strategies which differ, in particular, in the calculation and implementation methods, keeping, however, the same underlying philosophy: the trend is you friend, so stick to the winners.

Break-Out Strategies Break-out strategies belong to the oldest type of trend-following techniques based on a simple observation of the market. Whenever

[23] For momentum in equity indices, see also Zaremba (2016, 2017c).

the prices exceeded a long-term peak, it would signal the likelihood of the upward trend to continue. On the other hand, when the prices dropped below the long-run minimum, it would suggest that the price decline will go on. Although the fundamental challenge embedded in this type of strategies is their largely subjective character, academic researchers have ventured to translate these "opinions" into numbers and subject them to a rigid quantitative trading system. In 2004 George and Hwang sorted stocks on their distance to the 52-week high or the maximum price over trailing 52 weeks and found that the stocks approaching their 52-week high would vividly outperform. The effect was later confirmed by Liu et al. (2011), who replicated this approach in international markets to find this strategy producing profits in 18 of the 20 markets studied, with significant profits in 10 markets. However, as a high turnover strategy, there is a threat that the abnormal returns will no longer remain significant after accounting for transaction costs.

Interestingly, the profits in the 52-week high momentum technique are independent of the classical momentum effect. In other words, these two strategies, although seemingly fairly similar, may actually stem from a different underlying economic mechanism. In practice, therefore, both strategies can be efficiently combined to improve the momentum performance. As found by George and Hwang, when double-sorting on momentum and the distance to 52-week high, the momentum performance markedly improved, which was later examined and confirmed in many other international markets.[24]

Finally, the 52-week high strategy has been improved on in an analogous way as the standard momentum. For instance, Chen and Yang (2016) showed that the 52-week high displayed an echo effect, just like the momentum phenomenon. In other words, increasing the skip period between the date of portfolio formation and the date of portfolio purchase by 3–6 months markedly improved performance in nearly all the cases. Summing up, the 52-week high seems to be an intriguing variation of the momentum strategy which still deserves further investigation.

[24] Some alternative return-based improvements of the momentum strategy may include focusing on firms showing more extreme returns in the formation period (Bandarchuk and Hilscher 2013) or more consistent returns in the formation period (Grinblatt and Moskowitz 2004). Further investigations of the interactions of the 52-week high effect and momentum could be found in, for example, Bhootra and Hur (2013), Hao et al. (2016), and Lee and Piqueira (2017).

Time-Series Momentum Time-series momentum, also called absolute momentum, is another category of momentum strategies which has been attracting particular interest in recent years, sparked mostly by the groundbreaking study of Moskowitz et al. (2012) entitled "Time Series Momentum". Contrary to relative momentum, time-series momentum measures directly the price change relative to its past values, largely ignoring the performance of other assets. In practice, the indicators used for relative momentum may vary. For example, Moskowitz et al. (2012) examined rules that generated a buy signal when the price outperformed its historical record of, for instance, 200 days. On the other hand, Antonacci (2013, 2015) verified whether the excess return in the past period was either positive or negative, hinging all trading rules upon this one observation. In their construction, all time-series momentum strategies closely correspond to various technical analysis tools based on a similar underlying intuition. For example, the strategies formed upon moving averages can be considered a strain of time-series momentum techniques, as these two approaches are both empirically and theoretically closely intertwined. In fact, as argued by Levine and Pedersen (2016), they are their equivalent representations in their most general forms capturing also many other types of technical indicators.

Although both types of momentum strategies follow similar underlying economic intuition, their behavior is far from identical. In practice, to improve the risk-return profile they could be applied simultaneously (Antonacci 2015).[25]

Regardless how we measure the time-series momentum, it is a powerful return pattern that has been documented across a broad array of equity markets and asset classes, including indices, currencies, commodities, and bond futures.[26]

Moving Averages The technical trading strategies based on moving averages are one of the oldest tools in technical analysis. The underlying concept is fairly similar to the idea of time-series momentum: the current price is compared to its historical values to derive the return predictive signal. The only difference lies in the definition of the "historical price".

[25] The time-series momentum could be also improved by applying some ideas similar to the traditional momentum, like volatility scaling (Dudler et al. 2014; Kim et al. 2016).

[26] For evidence, see, for example, Baltas and Kosowski (2012a, b), Cheema et al. (2017). Georgopoulou and Wang (2016), Goyal and Jegadeesh (2017), Hurst et al. (2017), Maymin et al. (2014), and Zhou and Zhu (2013).

In standard momentum, we compare the current price with some value from a specific point in time in the past, for instance, a year ago. In the moving-average approach, we compare the price with the average price value over a period of time, for instance, the previous year. In the simplest terms, moving (or trailing) average price is calculated as a simple arithmetic average following this formula (2.7) (Lhabitant 2008):

$$MA_{i,t} = \frac{1}{N} \sum_{t-k-N+1}^{k} P_{i,t}, \tag{2.7}$$

whereby N represents the number of periods used for the calculation of a moving average; k is the relative position of the current period in the total number of the analyzed periods; and $P_{i,t}$ is the price of the security i at the time t. The average is unweighted, so any historical price occurring in recent periods will have equal importance in the calculation. Historically, equity investors used to draw a line in a chart representing an average smoothed price of historical time series. The example is presented in Fig. 2.2.

These types of strategies have gained significant popularity among technical traders, as the averages are well defined in statistics, generally understandable and easily implementable for testing transactional systems. As the moving average may be based on periods of different lengths, such

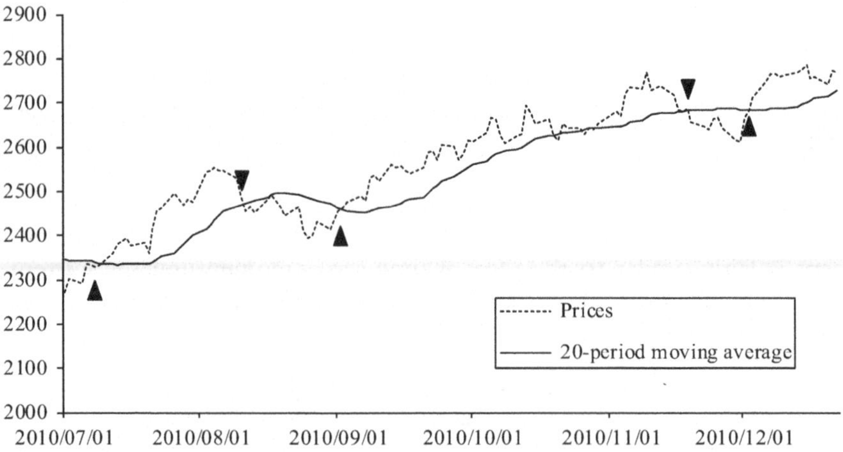

Fig. 2.2 Moving average—an example

as days, minutes, or individual ticks, we may have, for example, a 20-day moving average. In calculation of the average value the "eldest" price, elder than 21 sessions, will be dropped each day and a newer price, from the last session, will be added. The moving average has the advantage of smoothing the market time series. When the market is characterized by a general upward trend but occasionally distorted by lower prices, the moving average would "silence" the noise and allow the technical analyst to recognize the current trend.

As mentioned earlier, the moving average does not anticipate changes in the market but, as a result of analyzing historical quotations, becomes a lagging indicator, systematically following the market price. This effect becomes visible when overlaying the prices graphs of a given security with the moving average.

Moving average effectively "catches" the trend smoothing at the same time the quotations. In the growing market, the moving average stays below the current quotations due to a lagging mechanism embedded into the average, making the average show the "old" trend. Conversely, in a declining market, the average will stay above the market prices. This relationship creates one of the most common signals to buy or sell in technical analysis. If the intersection of the average represents the trend change, the rule reads as follows: buy when the market price crosses the moving average from below, and sell when the market price crosses the moving average from above. Figure 2.3 presents the buy-and-sell signals on a sample chart.

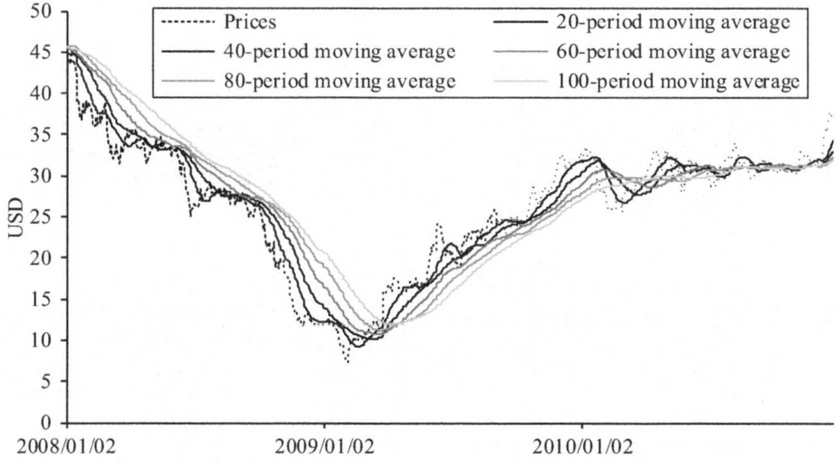

Fig. 2.3 Sample buy-and-sell signals based on moving average

Moving averages can be calculated based on periods of various lengths which considerably impact both the behavior and generation method of trading signals. When based on short periods, moving averages follow the market more closely and although allowing a faster trend identification, they also generate more buy-and-sell signals, largely false, which would also entail higher transaction costs. This can be particularly troublesome during side trends when there is no upward or downward trend in the market. On the other hand, long-term moving averages synthesize more historical prices, which makes them less responsive to current prices fluctuations (Fig. 2.4). As a result, these averages generate fewer false signals, but they can lead to missed investment opportunities. Figure 2.4 shows averages of sample quotations following 20, 40, 60, 80, and 100 sessions.

Unfortunately, there is no definitive answer resolving which moving average we should use. However, market practice shows that main long-term trends are well illustrated by a 40-week (200-session) average, medium-term trends by a 40-session average and short-term movements by a 20-session or a shorter average (Lhabitant 2008). The length of the moving average does also depend on the nature of the market, its variability, existing cycles, and so on. Other considerations include, for example, which prices (closing, average, maximum, minimum, opening, etc.) the system should be based on or what threshold must be exceeded above (below) the average to generate a buy (sell) signal. Although the most basic

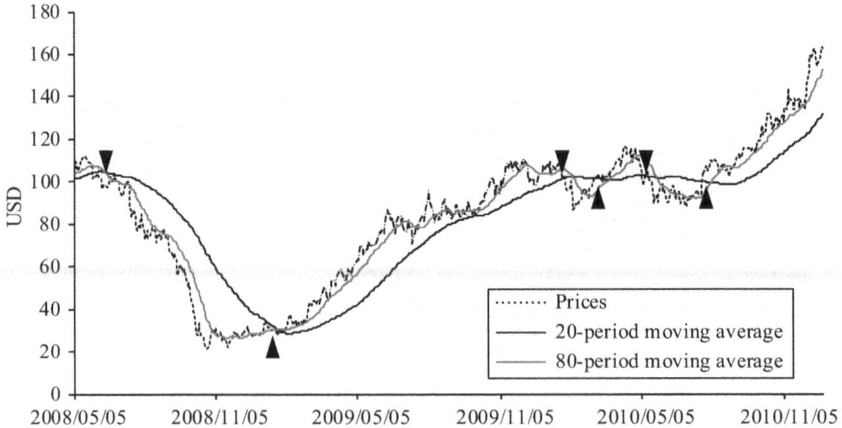

Fig. 2.4 Comparison of moving averages

principles for the transactional systems are relatively simple, one should be aware of the details and the long calibration time needed to adjust the rules to the specifics of individual markets, so that, at a later time, the system could operate seamlessly, without any interference of the author.

Classical arithmetic average, one variant of moving averages, can be computed in various ways. Most recently, for instance, the exponential moving average has grown in popularity as it depends more on the recent price movements compared to the arithmetic average.

So how are the moving-average signals generated? The most common approach, as already mentioned, is taking a long position when the stock exceeds the moving average, and a short position when the price stays under. In other words, we go long when the current price divided by the value obtained from Eq. 2.7 is above a unity and short when it stays below. Alternatively, we can also introduce minimum bands or rank the markets on the distance to the historical average as all the approaches seem to perform well, having been documented in many studies. While the moving average appears to be one of the simplest and most powerful trend-following signals, the underlying principle remains similar for all momentum strategies: stick to the winners and get rid of the losers.

As we have seen, moving averages prove successful in predicting future returns and finance literature brims with studies showcasing how these technical trading signals can be translated into profitable strategies. Perhaps the most comprehensive empirical study has been done by Glabadanidis who in his study entitled "Market Timing with Moving Averages" reported striking evidence of the extraordinary performance of the moving-average trading strategy. Further comparative studies examined a number of technical trading systems documenting the moving averages perform well regardless of the geographical coverage (Jacobs 2015; Zaremba and Szyszka 2016; Zaremba 2017b).

The title of king of moving-average strategies should be awarded to Valeriy Zakamulin, a professor at Adger University in Norway, who in his series of research papers thoroughly investigated the profitability of the moving average-based cross-sectional return patterns. Unfortunately, this strain of research casts also some doubt on the usefulness of the trailing averages. In his study of 2016 (Zakamulin 2016a) "Revisiting the Profitability of Market Timing with Moving Averages", the professor declared that at best the performance of the moving average strategy only marginally outperformed the corresponding buy-and-hold strategy. Moreover, in his later paper titled "A Comprehensive Look at the Empirical Performance of Moving Average Trading Strategies", Zakamulin (2015a) extended his examination to a 155-long study period again to conclude no statistically significant evidence that "market timing strategies outperformed the market in the second half of our sample", with little to be done to improve this performance.[27]

Trend Factor The trend factor is an interesting extension to the trend-following strategies introduced by Han et al. One fundamental problem in implementing the trend-following strategies based on moving averages is selecting the horizons for calculating the moving averages. Interestingly, oscillating between the short- and long-term horizons may impact the performance. The short-term moving averages, driven by momentum effect, may lead to positive correlation of signals with future returns whereas the very-long-run averages may gravitate toward mean reversion, displaying negative correlation with future returns. Furthermore, as the market behavior may change over time, the moving average, once most reliable, may turn obsolete. Which horizon of the moving average should we then use? According to Han, Zhou, and Zhu:… all of them!

Han et al. (2016) proposed a novel approach to the moving-range strategy, incorporating the entire range of moving-average strategies. Their approach to ranking stocks followed a two-step procedure. In the first step, they conducted a cross-sectional regression on moving averages with various lags: 3-, 5-, 10-, 20-, 50-, 100-, 200-, 400-, 600-, 800-, and 1000-days. The signals indicated the daily, weekly, monthly, quarterly, one-year, two-year, three-year, and four-year price trends of the underlying stock. Subsequently, they used the predictions from the regression to select the best assets for their portfolios. Having recorded astonishingly good results, the researchers concluded that the trend factor strategy "outperforms substantially the well-known short-term reversal, momentum, and long-term reversal factors, which are based on the three price trends separately, by more than doubling their Sharpe ratios. During the recent financial crisis, the trend factor earns 0.75% per month, while the market loses −2.03% per month, the short-term reversal factor loses −0.82%, the momentum factor loses −3.88%, and the long-term reversal factor barely gains 0.03%. The performance of the trend factor is robust to alternative formations and to a variety of control variables."

Acceleration While the momentum strategy captures how quickly the prices appreciate in the preceding months, it misses to account for the

[27] See, also, Zakamulin (2015b, 2016b).

pace the prices change: accelerating or decelerating. Pursuing this issue, Ardila et al. (2015) examined the price-acceleration-based strategy relying their sorts in the portfolio formation process not only on the raw returns in the preceding 12 months, but rather on a difference in the returns between the most recent 6 months (*t*–6 to *t*–1), and the preceding 6 months (*t*–12 to *t*–7). As they persuasively documented, the changes in momentum, or the acceleration, defined as the first difference in the successive returns, displayed better performance and higher explanatory power than momentum, which the researchers considered an imperfect proxy for acceleration.

This effect was further researched by Chen et al. (2017a), who examined the US equity market from 1962 to 2014, to find the acceleration and deceleration patterns in historical prices predictive of future expected returns in momentum investing. The authors proved that the winners with accelerated historical price increases deliver higher future expected returns while losers with accelerated historical price decreases underperform in the future. Thus, the profitability of holding past accelerated winners and shorting past accelerated losers turned out markedly higher than the momentum profits. Looking for explanations, Chen et al. (2017) attributed the outperformance to behavioral phenomena: the extrapolative bias and overreaction.[28]

Empirical Test of Momentum Strategies

Among momentum strategies, we tested three different techniques within the broad concept of momentum: the *classical relative momentum*, *moving-average*, and *time-series momentum*.

Following the *classical momentum strategy*, we sorted all the stocks on the cumulative return within the months *t*–12 to *t*–2 or, in other words, on the trailing 12 months with the most recent month discarded from the calculations. We followed the same approach in all the countries and ranked the stocks monthly to identify the top and bottom quintiles, that is, the 20% of stocks with the highest and the lowest historical return. Subsequently, we equal-weighted the returns in order to form portfolios and finally calculated the return on a long-short portfolio, which was long in the top-momentum portfolio and short in the bottom-momentum. The results are reported in Table 2.2.

[28] The concepts of acceleration and so-called gamma factor had been discussed also earlier in Andersen et al. (2000).

Table 2.2 The performance of international momentum portfolios

Country	*Top portfolio mean return*	*Bottom portfolio mean return*	*Average number of firms*	*T-B portfolio*		*Standard deviation*	*Sharpe ratio*	*Beta*	*Alpha*	
				Mean return	*t-stat*				*Value*	*t-stat*
Australia	1.94	−0.43	44	2.37***	*(7.97)*	4.89	1.68	−0.10	2.45***	*(8.21)*
Austria	1.14	0.70	7	0.44	*(0.97)*	7.54	0.20	−0.02	0.46	*(0.99)*
Belgium	1.91	0.13	11	1.77***	*(4.32)*	6.75	0.91	−0.17	1.89***	*(4.61)*
Canada	1.60	−0.13	90	1.73***	*(3.97)*	7.14	0.84	0.02	1.71***	*(3.90)*
Denmark	1.80	0.35	11	1.45***	*(3.95)*	6.05	0.83	−0.12	1.57***	*(4.22)*
Finland	1.63	0.57	11	1.06**	*(2.54)*	6.89	0.53	−0.02	1.09**	*(2.57)*
France	1.65	0.33	45	1.32***	*(3.20)*	6.79	0.67	−0.07	1.36***	*(3.28)*
Germany	1.56	−0.28	40	1.84***	*(4.33)*	6.98	0.91	0.04	1.82***	*(4.25)*
Greece	1.49	−0.58	13	2.07***	*(2.64)*	12.86	0.56	0.05	2.06***	*(2.63)*
Hong Kong	0.07	−0.47	22	0.53	*(1.00)*	8.78	0.21	0.00	0.53	*(0.99)*
Ireland	1.43	0.27	4	1.15	*(1.25)*	15.14	0.26	0.05	1.12	*(1.21)*
Israel	1.60	0.47	15	1.13**	*(2.30)*	8.06	0.48	−0.01	1.13**	*(2.30)*
Italy	1.49	−0.04	26	1.53***	*(3.90)*	6.44	0.82	0.05	1.50***	*(3.82)*
Japan	0.50	0.17	314	0.33	*(0.96)*	5.67	0.20	−0.07	0.33	*(0.97)*
The Netherlands	1.39	0.35	18	1.03**	*(2.52)*	6.73	0.53	−0.06	1.07***	*(2.61)*
New Zealand	1.42	0.37	4	1.05**	*(2.36)*	7.30	0.50	−0.04	1.08**	*(2.40)*

Norway	2.07	−0.32	14	2.38***	*(4.69)*	8.35	0.99	0.06	2.33***	*(4.56)*
Portugal	1.50	−0.70	4	2.20***	*(4.49)*	8.04	0.95	0.00	2.20***	*(4.47)*
Singapore	0.28	−0.30	11	0.57	*(1.22)*	7.72	0.26	−0.10	0.63	*(1.34)*
Spain	1.36	0.05	17	1.31***	*(3.68)*	5.85	0.78	−0.04	1.34***	*(3.74)*
Sweden	1.86	0.65	25	1.21***	*(2.83)*	7.03	0.60	0.03	1.18***	*(2.73)*
Switzerland	1.78	0.36	28	1.42***	*(4.10)*	5.70	0.86	−0.11	1.50***	*(4.28)*
UK	1.49	−0.08	112	1.57***	*(4.34)*	5.95	0.92	−0.09	1.61***	*(4.44)*
USA	1.21	0.56	672	0.65	*(1.55)*	6.88	0.33	−0.22	0.80*	*(1.91)*
World (EW)	1.42	0.08	1557	1.34***	*(4.94)*	4.45	1.04	−0.08	1.38***	*(5.06)*
World (VW)	1.13	0.20	1557	0.93***	*(2.82)*	5.39	0.60	−0.14	1.00***	*(3.04)*

Note: The table reports the monthly returns on the portfolios from sorts on the average return in months t–12 to t–2. "Average number of firms" is the mean monthly number of companies in the quintile portfolios. ***Top portfolio*** and ***bottom portfolio*** are quintile portfolios including the stocks with the highest and lowest historical returns, respectively. *T-B* ***portfolio*** is long in the top portfolio and short in the bottom portfolio. The Sharpe ratio is expressed on an annualized basis. The alpha and beta are derived from the CAPM. Mean returns, standard deviations and alphas are expressed in percentage. Asterisks *, **, and *** indicate values significantly different from zero at the 10%, 5%, and 1% levels, respectively

The results in Table 2.2 undoubtedly confirm momentum to be a powerful and robust investment strategy. The top-momentum portfolios significantly outperformed the bottom-momentum portfolios in 18 out of 24 countries examined. Furthermore, in all the countries, the momentum strategy delivered alphas also significant from the CAPM. Naturally, the mean returns and alphas on long-short portfolios varied: for instance, in Japan—which is well known for poor momentum performance—the long-short portfolio yielded only 0.33% per month. In Australia, on the other hand, the same strategy delivered 2.37% per month. Evidently, the volatility of the strategies was country-specific: the standard deviation of monthly returns ranged from 5.70% (Switzerland) to 15.14% (Ireland) monthly.

Figures 2.5 and 2.6 present the long-run returns on the global portfolios which equal-weight or value-weight all the single-country momentum strategies.

Both figures clearly confirm the momentum strategy as extremely impactful over the last two decades. The top-momentum stocks vividly outperformed both the market portfolio and the bottom portfolio stocks. The outperformance became more pronounced in the equally weighted

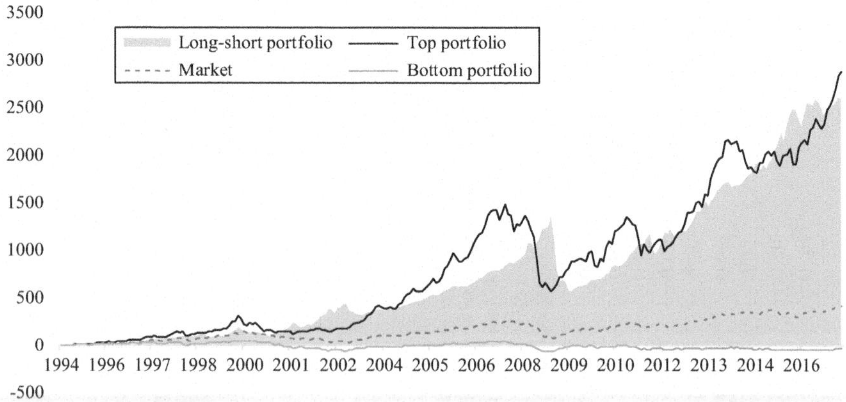

Fig. 2.5 Cumulative return on equal-weighted relative momentum portfolios. (Note: The figure displays the cumulative return on the equal-weighted quantile of the portfolios from sorts on the average return in months $t-12$ to $t-2$. *Top portfolio* and *bottom portfolio* are quintile portfolios including the stocks with the highest and lowest historical returns, respectively. Market is the value-weighted portfolio of all the country equity markets considered. All the returns are expressed in percentage)

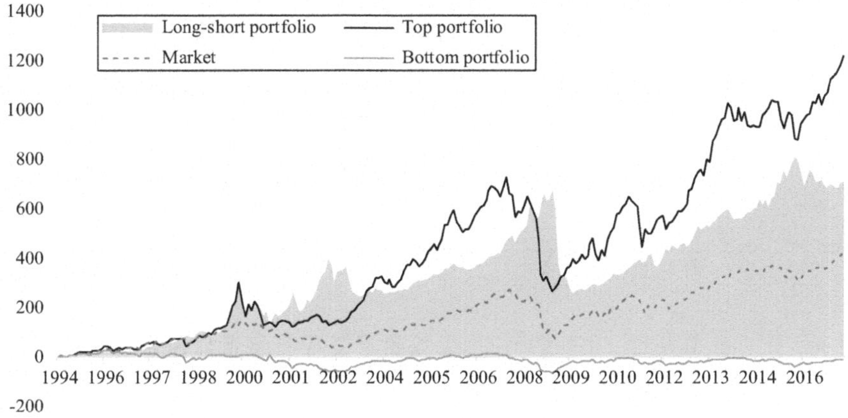

Fig. 2.6 Cumulative return on value-weighted relative momentum portfolios. (Note: The figure displays the cumulative return on the value-weighted quantile of the portfolios from sorts on the average return in months $t-12$ to $t-2$. *Top portfolio* and *bottom portfolio* are quintile portfolios including the stocks with the highest and lowest historical returns, respectively. Market is the value-weighted portfolio of all the country equity markets considered. All the returns are expressed in percentage)

portfolio than in the value-weighted portfolios, consistent with the well-known phenomena of stronger momentum among small companies.

Distinctively in Figs. 2.5 and 2.6, the momentum performance was neither smooth nor simple as the year 2009 brought a remarkable momentum crash. Still, its overall outperformance remains clear and undeniable.

Testing the second strategy, ***the moving-average approach***, we sorted stocks on the most recent price divided by the average price over the previous 12 months. The larger the ratio was, or in other words, the higher was the price above the moving average, the stronger the signal for the future returns. Conversely, the low price relative to the 12-month average would paint a rather gloomy future. Table 2.3 reports the performance of the moving-average strategies with stocks sorted into quintiles based on the distance to the 12-month trailing moving average.

Interestingly, the moving-average strategy outperformed even the simple relative momentum approach. In 21 of 24 countries, the strategy delivered both significant and positive CAPM alphas. These included even Japan, where momentum usually disappoints. The mean return on the

Table 2.3 The performance of international moving-average portfolios

Country	*Top portfolio mean return*	*Bottom portfolio mean return*	*Average number of firms*	*T-B portfolio*		*Standard deviation*	*Sharpe ratio*	*Beta*	*Alpha*	
				Mean return	*t-stat*				*Value*	*t-stat*
Australia	1.00	0.10	46	0.90***	*(4.40)*	3.37	0.93	−0.05	0.94***	*(4.57)*
Austria	1.41	0.70	7	0.72**	*(2.16)*	5.45	0.45	−0.08	0.76**	*(2.28)*
Belgium	1.71	0.93	12	0.78***	*(2.80)*	4.56	0.59	−0.01	0.79***	*(2.81)*
Canada	1.57	0.09	95	1.48***	*(4.73)*	5.13	1.00	−0.01	1.49***	*(4.72)*
Denmark	2.02	0.88	12	1.14***	*(3.91)*	4.78	0.82	−0.07	1.20***	*(4.07)*
Finland	1.99	0.94	11	1.04***	*(3.27)*	5.24	0.69	−0.02	1.06***	*(3.29)*
France	1.64	0.84	47	0.80***	*(3.31)*	3.95	0.70	−0.01	0.80***	*(3.30)*
Germany	1.46	0.15	43	1.31***	*(4.75)*	4.55	1.00	0.03	1.30***	*(4.65)*
Greece	1.25	−0.54	14	1.79***	*(2.65)*	11.09	0.56	−0.06	1.80***	*(2.66)*
Hong Kong	1.12	−1.68	23	2.80***	*(6.04)*	7.63	1.27	−0.05	2.84***	*(6.08)*
Ireland	1.46	1.10	4	0.35	*(0.42)*	13.94	0.09	0.00	0.36	*(0.42)*
Israel	1.32	1.41	15	−0.09	*(−0.28)*	5.38	−0.06	0.03	−0.10	*(−0.30)*
Italy	1.02	0.28	28	0.74***	*(3.46)*	3.54	0.73	0.02	0.73***	*(3.39)*
Japan	0.85	0.13	325	0.72***	*(2.69)*	4.42	0.57	0.18	0.71***	*(2.71)*
The Netherlands	1.59	0.60	19	0.99***	*(3.62)*	4.49	0.76	0.03	0.97***	*(3.53)*
New Zealand	0.93	0.79	5	0.15	*(0.36)*	6.64	0.08	−0.06	0.19	*(0.47)*

Norway	1.50	−0.12	15	1.62***	*(4.33)*	6.16	0.91	−0.04	1.65***	*(4.38)*
Portugal	0.91	−0.31	4	1.22***	*(3.13)*	6.39	0.66	−0.10	1.25***	*(3.22)*
Singapore	0.42	−1.10	12	1.53***	*(4.03)*	6.22	0.85	0.04	1.50***	*(3.96)*
Spain	1.44	0.29	18	1.15***	*(4.59)*	4.12	0.97	−0.02	1.17***	*(4.62)*
Sweden	2.22	0.82	26	1.40***	*(5.07)*	4.53	1.07	−0.07	1.47***	*(5.30)*
Switzerland	1.44	0.99	29	0.44***	*(2.60)*	2.81	0.55	0.05	0.41**	*(2.38)*
UK	1.09	0.40	118	0.69***	*(4.52)*	2.49	0.95	−0.08	0.72***	*(4.76)*
USA	1.82	0.73	716	1.09***	*(3.35)*	5.37	0.71	−0.03	1.12***	*(3.37)*
World (EW)	1.38	0.35	1644	1.03***	*(7.41)*	2.29	1.56	−0.05	1.06***	*(7.59)*
World (VW)	1.44	0.40	1644	1.04***	*(5.15)*	3.32	1.09	−0.03	1.06***	*(5.18)*

Note: The table reports the monthly returns on the portfolios from sorts on the distance of current price to the 12-month moving average. The calculations were made based on monthly observations. "Average number of firms" is the mean monthly number of companies in the quintile portfolios. ***Top portfolio*** and ***bottom portfolio*** are quintile portfolios including the stocks with the highest and lowest distance to the moving average, respectively. ***T-B portfolio*** is long in the top portfolio and short in the bottom portfolio. The Sharpe ratio is expressed on an annualized basis. Both alpha and beta are derived from the CAPM. Mean returns, standard deviations, and alphas are expressed in percentage. Asterisks *, **, and *** indicate values significantly different from zero at the 10%, 5%, and 1% levels, respectively global long-short momentum portfolios exceeded 1% per month, irrespective of the weighting scheme. Importantly, the moving-average strategies proved slightly less volatile than the classic momentum strategies. The standard deviations on the global portfolios reached only 2.29% and 3.32% for the equal-weighted and value-weighted portfolios. In consequence, the Sharpe ratios markedly exceeded their counterparts in the classic momentum approach, rising about 50%, to 1.56 and 1.09 annually, for the equal-weighted and capitalization-weighted strategies, respectively.

Figures 2.7 and 2.8 display cumulative returns on the moving-average portfolios confirming again the impressive profitability of this strategy: for example, the top equal-weighted portfolio delivered as much as 2700% over the years 1994–2017.

Finally, testing the third strategy, *time-series momentum*, we followed a straightforward procedure for portfolio formation. Having sorted all the stocks on their cumulative return in the trailing 12 months with the most recent month skipped—which was identical for the classic momentum approach—we assumed long position in all the stocks with positive returns and short in the securities with negative returns. Analogously as before,

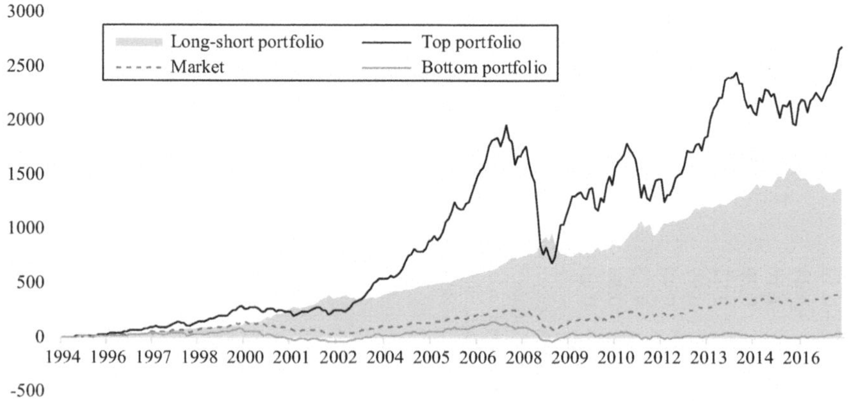

Fig. 2.7 Cumulative return on the equal-weighted moving-average portfolios. (Note: The figure displays the cumulative return on the equal-weighted quantile of the portfolios from sorts on the distance of current price to the 12-month moving average. The calculations were made based on monthly observations. *Top portfolio* and *bottom portfolio* are quintile portfolios including the stocks with the highest and lowest historical returns, respectively. Market is the value-weighted portfolio including all the country equity markets considered. All the returns are expressed in percentage)

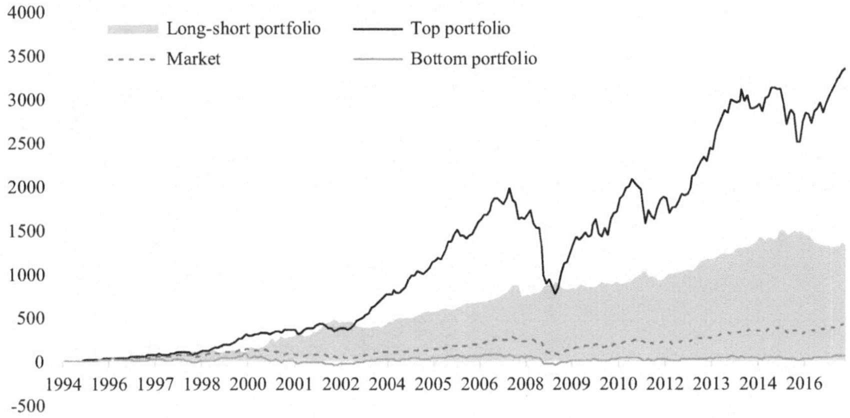

Fig. 2.8 Cumulative return on the value-weighted relative momentum portfolios. (Note: The figure displays the cumulative return on the equal-weighted quantile of the portfolios from sorts on the distance of current price to the 12-month moving average. The calculations were made based on monthly observations. Top portfolio and bottom portfolio are quintile portfolios including the stocks with the highest and lowest historical returns, respectively. Market is the value-weighted portfolio including all the country equity markets considered. All the returns are expressed in percentage)

we formed the equal-weighted long, short, and long-short portfolios. In other words, the mere sign—positive or negative—of the trailing 12-month return determined the position we should take in a given asset: long or short. Table 2.4 synthesizes the performance of the time-series strategies across the international equity markets.

The profits from the time-series momentum strategy seem exceptionally robust. Within the years 1995–2017, only one country in our sample did not deliver significant alpha: Singapore. In all of the other equity markets both the mean monthly returns and the alphas were positive and significant. The abnormal returns ranged from as much as 1.54% in Australia to only 0.21% (insignificant) in Japan, which is, actually, quite well known for the poor momentum performance.[29]

Taking a broader look at the global time-series momentum the equal-weighted portfolio including all the countries delivered the mean monthly

[29] For details, see Hanauer (2014), Teplova and Mikova (2015), and Chang et al. (2018).

Table 2.4 The performance of time-series momentum portfolios

Country	*Top portfolio mean return*	*Bottom portfolio mean return*	*Average number of firms*	*T-B portfolio*		*Standard deviation*	*Sharpe ratio*	*Beta*	*Alpha*	
				Mean return	*t-stat*				*Value*	*t-stat*
Australia	1.28	−0.22	155	1.50***	*(7.23)*	3.41	1.53	−0.05	1.54***	*(7.36)*
Austria	1.02	0.20	23	0.82**	*(2.16)*	6.21	0.46	−0.05	0.84**	*(2.22)*
Belgium	1.21	−0.08	39	1.29***	*(4.67)*	4.54	0.98	−0.11	1.37***	*(4.94)*
Canada	1.17	−0.11	297	1.28***	*(5.15)*	4.08	1.09	0.00	1.28***	*(5.09)*
Denmark	1.33	0.45	38	0.88***	*(3.19)*	4.51	0.67	−0.03	0.91***	*(3.26)*
Finland	1.26	0.49	37	0.77***	*(2.78)*	4.56	0.59	−0.07	0.84***	*(3.02)*
France	1.17	0.26	148	0.90***	*(3.84)*	3.87	0.81	−0.10	0.97***	*(4.11)*
Germany	1.11	−0.16	126	1.27***	*(5.02)*	4.14	1.06	−0.01	1.27***	*(5.02)*
Greece	0.99	−0.32	38	1.31**	*(2.46)*	8.72	0.52	0.03	1.30**	*(2.45)*
Hong Kong	0.27	−0.62	75	0.89**	*(2.18)*	6.73	0.46	0.03	0.87**	*(2.11)*
Ireland	1.19	0.17	16	1.03*	*(1.95)*	8.66	0.41	0.00	1.03*	*(1.94)*
Israel	1.23	0.34	50	0.90***	*(2.74)*	5.39	0.58	−0.06	0.91***	*(2.80)*
Italy	1.09	0.05	80	1.05***	*(4.56)*	3.78	0.96	0.00	1.05***	*(4.55)*
Japan	0.42	0.09	876	0.34*	*(1.77)*	3.11	0.37	−0.05	0.34*	*(1.79)*
The Netherlands	1.04	0.32	59	0.72***	*(2.65)*	4.46	0.56	0.00	0.72***	*(2.64)*
New Zealand	1.21	0.17	17	1.04***	*(3.22)*	5.29	0.68	0.01	1.03***	*(3.16)*

Norway	1.34	−0.16	48	1.50***	*(4.75)*	5.21	1.00	0.02	1.49***	*(4.65)*
Portugal	0.90	−0.60	13	1.49***	*(4.42)*	5.55	0.93	0.01	1.49***	*(4.39)*
Singapore	0.35	0.23	38	0.12	*(0.31)*	6.25	0.07	−0.16	0.21	*(0.55)*
Spain	1.09	0.02	57	1.07***	*(4.09)*	4.28	0.86	−0.04	1.10***	*(4.18)*
Sweden	1.44	0.46	87	0.97***	*(3.38)*	4.73	0.71	0.01	0.96***	*(3.31)*
Switzerland	1.38	0.21	92	1.17***	*(5.55)*	3.45	1.17	−0.07	1.22***	*(5.76)*
UK	1.04	−0.04	367	1.09***	*(5.36)*	3.33	1.13	−0.06	1.11***	*(5.46)*
USA	1.11	0.50	2122	0.61***	*(2.59)*	3.83	0.55	−0.12	0.69***	*(2.93)*
World (EW)	1.07	0.07	4900	1.00***	*(6.36)*	2.58	1.34	−0.07	1.03***	*(6.56)*
World (VW)	0.93	0.18	4900	0.76***	*(4.14)*	3.00	0.87	−0.09	0.80***	*(4.38)*

Note: The table reports the monthly returns on the time-series momentum portfolios. The calculations were made based on monthly observations. “Average number of firms” is the mean monthly number of companies in the quintile portfolios. ***Top portfolio*** and ***bottom portfolio*** are portfolios including the stocks with the positive and negative cumulative return over previous 12 months, respectively. ***T-B portfolio*** is long in the top portfolio and short in the bottom portfolio. The Sharpe ratio is expressed on an annualized basis. Both alpha and beta are derived from the CAPM. Mean returns, standard deviations, and alphas are expressed in percentage. Asterisks *, **, and *** indicate values significantly different from zero at the 10%, 5%, and 1% levels, respectively return of 1.00% and the monthly alpha amounting to 1.03%, with the impressive t-statistics exceeding 6. The volatility remained reasonably low—only 2.58% per month—so the Sharpe ratio proved very high reaching 1.34 and 0.87 in the equal-weighting and value-weighting approaches.

Our test indicates the time-series momentum as one of the most robust strategies delivering both high and stable returns around the world, as detailed in Figs. 2.9 and 2.10 presenting cumulative returns on the global time-series momentum portfolios, weighted equally and based on the country equity markets capitalizations.

Within the years 1995–2017 both the long-short equal-weighted and value-weighted time-series momentum portfolios, long (short) in the stocks that delivered positive (negative) returns over the previous 12 months, earned over 1200% and 600% respectively. Most notably, this wealth creation occurred without any major drawback, with the only exception of the famous momentum crash in 2009. Albeit simple, the time-series strategy appears most effective and reliable.

Discussing momentum-related strategies, we have shown various theoretical and empirical strategies assuming the continuation of the best per-

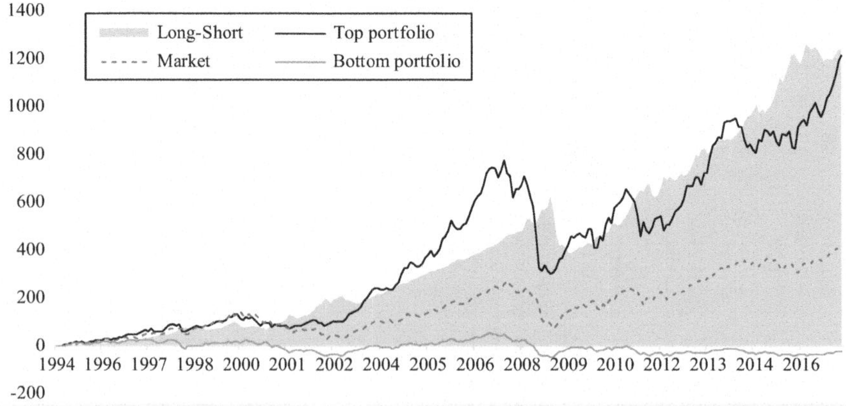

Fig. 2.9 Cumulative return on equal-weighted moving-average portfolios. (Note. The figure displays the cumulative return on the equal-weighted time-series momentum portfolios. The calculations were made based on monthly observations. *Top portfolio* and *bottom portfolio* are quintile portfolios including the stocks with the highest and lowest historical returns, respectively. Market is the value-weighted portfolio including all the country equity markets considered. All the returns are expressed in percentage)

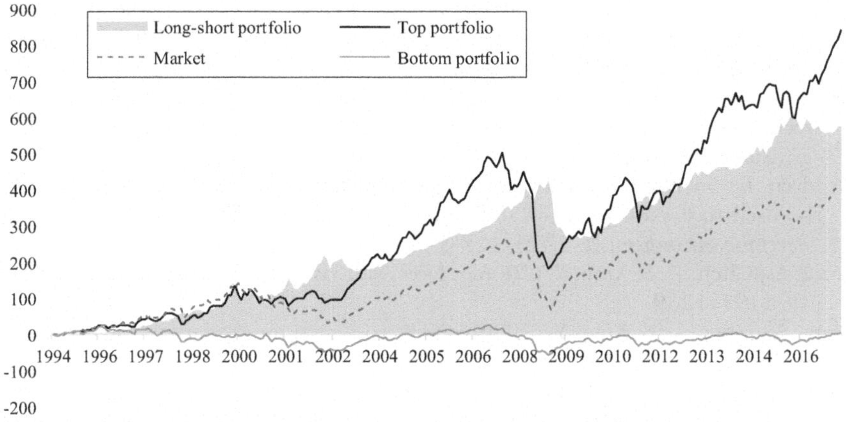

Fig. 2.10 Cumulative return on value-weighted relative momentum portfolios. (Note: The figure displays the cumulative return on the equal-weighted time-series momentum portfolios. The calculations were made based on monthly observations. *Top portfolio* and *bottom portfolio* are quintile portfolios including the stocks with the highest and lowest historical returns, respectively. *Market* is the value-weighted portfolio including all the country equity markets considered. All the returns are expressed in percentage)

forming assets to outperform and the poor performers to disappoint. While investors can benefit from this effect in numerous ways, the three simple strategies—relative momentum, time-series momentum, and moving averages—have proved profitable all around the world. Next, it's worth considering their complete opposite—return reversal.

References

Accominotti, O., & Chambers, D. (2014). *Out-of-sample evidence on the returns to currency trading*. Available at SSRN: https://ssrn.com/abstract=2293684 or https://doi.org/10.2139/ssrn.2293684. Accessed 21 Oct 2015.

Ahn, D.-H., Conrad, J., & Dittmar, R. (2003). Risk adjustment and trading strategies. *Review of Financial Studies, 16*(2), 459–485.

Akermann, C. A., & Keller, W. E. (1977). Relative strength does persist! *Journal of Portfolio Management, 4*(1), 38–45.

Alwathainani, A. M. (2012). Consistent winners and losers. *International Review of Economics and Finance, 21*, 210–220.

Amen, S. (2013). *Beta'em up: What is market beta in FX?* Available at SSRN: http://ssrn.com/abstract=2439854 or https://doi.org/10.2139/ssrn.2439854. Accessed 21 Oct 2015.

Andersen, J. V., Gluzman, S., & Sornette, D. (2000). Fundamental framework for technical analysis. *European Physical Journal B, 14*, 579–601. http://xxx.lanl.gov/abs/cond-mat/9910047

Andreu, L., Swinkels, L., & Tjong-A-Tjoe, L. (2013). Can exchange traded funds be used to exploit industry and country momentum? *Financial Markets and Portfolio Management, 27*(2), 127–148.

Ang, A., Chen, J., & Xing, Y. (2006a). Downside risk. *Review of Financial Studies, 19*, 1191–1239.

Ang, A., Chen, J., & Xing, Y. (2006b). The cross-section of volatility and expected returns. *Journal of Finance, 61*, 259–299.

Antonacci, G. (2013). *Absolute momentum: A simple rule-based strategy and universal trend-following overlay* (Research paper). Available at SSRN: http://ssrn.com/abstract=2244633 or https://doi.org/10.2139/ssrn.2244633. Accessed 18 Oct 2015.

Antonacci, G. (2015). *Dual momentum investing: An innovative strategy for higher returns with lower risk.* New York: McGraw Hill Education.

Ardila, D., Forrò, Z., & Sornette, D. (2015). *The acceleration effect and gamma factor in asset pricing* (Swiss Finance Institute research paper No. 15-30). Available at SSRN: https://ssrn.com/abstract=2645882 or https://doi.org/10.2139/ssrn.2645882. Accessed 21 Oct 2017.

Asness, C. S. (1997). The interaction of value and momentum strategies. *Financial Analysts Journal, 61*, 29–36.

Asness, C. S., Liew, J. M., & Stevens, R. L. (1997). Parallels between the cross-sectional predictability of stock and country returns. *Journal of Portfolio Management, 6*, 79–86.

Asness, C. S., Moskowitz, T. J., & Pedersen, L. H. (2013). Value and momentum everywhere. *Journal of Finance, 68*(3), 929–985.

Avramov, D., Chordia, T., & Goyal, A. (2006a). Liquidity and autocorrelations in individual stock returns. *Journal of Finance, 61*, 2365–2394.

Avramov, D., Chordia, T., & Goyal, A. (2006b). The impact of trades on daily volatility. *Review of Financial Studies, 19*(4), 1241–1277.

Avramov, D., Chordia, T., Jostova, G., & Philipov, A. (2007). Momentum and credit rating. *Journal of Finance, 62*, 2503–2520.

Avramov, D., Cheng, S., Schreiber, A., & Shemer, K. (2016b, in press). Scaling up market anomalies. *Journal of Investing*. Available at SSRN: https://ssrn.com/abstract=2709178 or https://doi.org/10.2139/ssrn.2709178. Accessed 23 Oct 2017.

Bae, J. W., & Elkamhi, R. (2015). *Global equity correlation in FX carry and momentum trades.* Available at SSRN: http://ssrn.com/abstract=2521608 or https://doi.org/10.2139/ssrn.2521608. Accessed 21 Oct 2015.

Baltas, A.-N., & Kosowski, R. (2012a). Momentum strategies in futures markets and trend-following funds. *SSRN Electronic Journal*. https://doi.org/10.2139/ssrn.1968996. Accessed 23 Oct 2017.

Baltas, A.-N., & Kosowski, R. (2012b). Improving time-series momentum strategies: The role of trading signals and volatility estimators. *SSRN Electronic Journal*. https://doi.org/10.2139/ssrn.2140091. Accessed 23 Oct 2017.

Balvers, R. J., & Wu, Y. (2006). Momentum and mean reversion across national equity markets. *Journal of Empirical Finance, 13*, 24–48.

Bandarchuk, P., & Hilscher, J. (2013). Sources of momentum profits: Evidence on the irrelevance of characteristics. *Review of Finance, 17*, 809–845.

Bange, M. M. (2000). Do the portfolios of small investors reflect positive feedback trading? *Journal of Financial and Quantitative Analysis, 35*, 239–255.

Bansal, R., Dittmar, R. F., & Lundblad, C. T. (2005). Consumption, dividends, and cross section of equity returns. *Journal of Finance, 60*(4), 1639–1672.

Barber, B. M., & Odean, T. (2000). Trading is hazardous to your wealth: The common stock investment performance of individual investors. *Journal of Finance, 55*(2), 773–806.

Barber, B. M., & Odean, T. (2004). Are individual investors tax savvy? Evidence from retail and discount brokerage accounts. *Journal of Public Economics, 88*(1–2), 419–442.

Barberis, N., & Xiong, W. (2009). What drives the disposition effect? An analysis of a long-standing preference-based explanation. *Journal of Finance, 64*(2), 751–784.

Barberis, N., Shleifer, A., & Vishny, R. (1998). A model of investor sentiment. *Journal of Financial Economics, 49*, 307–343.

Barroso, P., & Santa-Clara, P. (2015). Momentum has its moments. *Journal of Financial Economics, 116*(1), 111–120. https://doi.org/10.1016/j.jfineco.2014.11.010.

Barth, F., Scholz, H., & Stegmeier, M. (2017). *Momentum in the European corporate bond market: The role of characteristics-adjusted returns*. Available at SSRN: https://ssrn.com/abstract=2664491 or https://doi.org/10.2139/ssrn.2664491. Accessed 23 Oct 2017.

Baz, J., Granger, N. M., Harvey, C. R., Le Roux, N., & Rattray, S. (2015). *Dissecting investment strategies in the cross section and time series*. Available at SSRN: https://ssrn.com/abstract=2695101 or https://doi.org/10.2139/ssrn.2695101. Accessed 23 Oct 2017.

Beracha, E., & Skiba, H. (2011). Momentum in residential real estate. *Journal of Real Estate Finance and Economics, 43*(3), 299–320.

Bhansali, V., Davis, J., Dorsten, M. P., & Rennison, G. (2015). *Carry and trend in lots of places*. Available at SSRN: https://ssrn.com/abstract=2579089 or https://doi.org/10.2139/ssrn.2579089. Accessed 23 Oct 2017.

Bhojraj, S., & Swaminathan, B. (2006). Macromomentum: Returns predictability in international equity indices. *Journal of Business, 79*(1), 429–451.

Bhootra, A., & Hur, J. (2013). The timing of 52-week high price and momentum. *Journal of Banking & Finance, 37*(10), 3773–3782. https://doi.org/10.1016/j.jbankfin.2013.05.025.

Bianchi, R. J., Drew, M. E., & Polichronis, J. (2005). A test of momentum trading strategies in foreign exchange markets: Evidence from the G7. *Global Business and Economic Review, 7*(2/3), 155–179.

Bikhchandani, S., Hirshleifer, D., & Welch, I. (1992). A theory of fads, fashion, custom, and cultural change as informational cascades. *Journal of Political Economy, 100*(5), 992–1026.

Blitz, D. C., & van Vliet, P. (2007). The volatility effect: Lower risk without lower return. *Journal of Portfolio Management, 34*(1), 102–113. https://doi.org/10.3905/jpm.2007.698039.

Blitz, D. C., & van Vliet, P. (2008). Global tactical cross-asset allocation: Applying value and momentum across asset classes. *Journal of Portfolio Management, 35*(1), 23–38. https://doi.org/10.3905/JPM.2008.35.1.23.

Blitz, D., Huij, J., & Martens, M. (2011). Residual momentum. *Journal of Empirical Finance, 18*(3), 506–521. https://doi.org/10.1016/j.jempfin.2011.01.003.

Blitz, D., Hanauer, M. X., & Vidojevic, M. (2017). *The idiosyncratic momentum anomaly.* Available at SSRN: https://ssrn.com/abstract=2947044. Accessed 23 Oct 2017.

Blume, L., Easley, D., & O'Hara, M. (1994). Market statistics and technical analysis: The role of volume. *Journal of Finance, 49*, 153–181.

Bohan, J. (1981). Relative strength: Further positive evidence. *Journal of Portfolio Management, 8*(1), 36–39.

Boussaidi, R. (2013). Representativeness heuristic, investor sentiment and overreaction to accounting earnings: The case of the Tunisian stock market. *Procedia – Social and Behavioral Sciences, 81*, 9–21.

Bowden, M. P. (2015). A model of information flows and confirmatory bias in financial markets. *Decisions in Economics and Finance, 38*(2), 197–215.

Brown, D. P., & Jennings, R. H. (1989). On technical analysis. *Review of Financial Studies, 2*, 527–551.

Brush, J. S., & Bowles, K. E. (1983). The predictive power in relative strength and CAPM. *Journal of Portfolio Management, 9*(4), 20–23.

Burnside, A. C., Eichenbaum, M., & Rebelo, S. T. (2011). Carry trade and momentum in currency markets. *Annual Review of Financial Economics, 3*, 511–535.

Calvet, L. E., Lakonishok, J., & LeBaron, B. (1992). Simple technical trading rules and the stochastic properties of stock returns. *Journal of Finance, 47*(5), 1731–1764.

Chan, K., Hameed, A., & Tong, W. (2000). Profitability of momentum strategies in the international equity markets. *Journal of Financial and Quantitative Analysis, 35*(2), 153–172.

Chan, L. K. C., Jegadeesh, N., & Lakonishok, J. (2012). Momentum strategies. *Journal of Finance, 51*(5), 1681–1713.

Chang, R. P., Ko, K.-C., Nakano, S., & Rhee, S. G. (2018). Residual momentum in Japan. *Journal of Empirical Finance, 45*, 283–299. https://doi.org/10.1016/j.jempfin.2017.11.005.

Chaves, D. B. (2012). *Eureka! A momentum strategy that also works in Japan.* Available at SSRN: https://ssrn.com/abstract=1982100 or https://doi.org/10.2139/ssrn.1982100. Accessed 23 Oct 2017.

Cheema, M. A., Nartea, G. V., & Man, Y. (2017, in press). Cross-sectional and time series momentum returns and market states. *International Review of Finance.* https://doi.org/10.1111/irfi.12148.

Chen, H. S., & De Bondt, W. (2004). Style momentum within the S&P-500 index. *Journal of Empirical Finance, 11*, 483–507.

Chen, A.-S., & Yang, W. (2016). Echo effects and the returns from 52-week high strategies. *Finance Research Letters, 16*, 38–46. https://doi.org/10.1016/j.frl.2015.10.015.

Chen, J., Hong, H., & Stein, J. C. (2002). Breadth of ownership and stock returns. *Journal of Financial Economics, 66*, 171–205.

Chen, L. H., Jiang, G. J., & Zhu, X. (2012). Do style and sector indexes carry momentum? *Journal of Investment Strategies, 1*(3), 67–89.

Chen, L.-W., Yu, H.-Y., & Wang, W.-K. (2017). Evolution of historical prices in momentum investing. *Journal of Financial Markets*, in press. Available at SSRN: https://ssrn.com/abstract=3009059. Accessed 21 Oct 2017.

Chen, L.-W., Yu, H.-Y., & Wang, W.-K. (2017a, in press). Evolution of historical prices in momentum investing. *Journal of Financial Markets.* Available at SSRN: https://ssrn.com/abstract=3009059. Accessed 21 Oct 2017.

Chestnutt, G. A. (1961). *Stock market analysis: Facts and principles.* Larchmont: American Investors Service.

Chordia, T., & Shivakumar, L. (2002). Momentum, business cycle, and time varying expected returns. *Journal of Finance, 57*(2), 985–1019.

Chui, A. C. W., Titman, S., & Wei, J. K. C. (2010). Individualism and momentum around the world. *Journal of Finance, 65*(1), 361–392.

Clare, A., Sapuric, S., & Todorovic, N. (2010). Quantitative or momentum-based multi-style rotation? UK experience. *Journal of Asset Management, 10*, 370–381.

Clare, A., Seaton, J., Smith, P. N., & Thomas, S. (2016). The trend is our friend: Risk parity, momentum and trend following in global asset allocation. *Journal of Behavioral and Experimental Finance, 9*, 63–80. https://doi.org/10.1016/j.jbef.2016.01.002.

Clyde, W. C., & Osler, C. L. (1997). Charting: Chaos theory in disguise? *Journal of Futures Markets, 17*, 489–514.

Conrad, J., & Kaul, G. (1993). Long-term market overreaction or biases in computer returns? *Journal of Finance, 48*(1), 39–63.

Cooper, M. J., Gutierrez, R. C., Jr., & Hameed, A. (2004). Market states and momentum. *Journal of Finance, 59*(3), 1345–1365. https://doi.org/10.1111/j.1540-6261.2004.00665.x.

Cooper, H., Mitrache, A., & Priestley, R. (2017). *A global macroeconomic risk model for value, momentum, and other asset classes.* Available at SSRN: https://ssrn.com/abstract=2768040. Accessed 23 Oct 2017.

Covel, M. W. (2007). *The complete turtle trader: How 23 novice investors became overnight millionaires.* New York: HarperCollins Publishers.

Covel, M. W. (2009). *Trend following: Learn to make millions in up or down markets.* London: FT Press.

Cowles, A., III, & Jones, H. E. (1937). Some a posteriori probabilities in stock market criteria. *Econometrica, 5*(3), 280–294.

Cutler, D. M., Poterba, J. M., & Summers, L. H. (1990). Speculative dynamics and the role of feedback traders. *American Economic Review, 80*, 63–68.

Da, Z., Liu, Q., & Schaumburg, E. (2014). A closer look at the short-term return reversal. *Management Science, 60*, 658–674.

Da, Z., Gurun, U., & Warachka, M. (2014). Frog in the pan: Continuous information and momentum. *Review of Financial Studies, 27*, 2171–2218.

Daniel, K. D., & Moskowitz, T. J. (2013). *Momentum crashes* (Swiss Finance Institute research paper No. 13-61; Columbia Business School research paper No. 14-6; Fama-Miller working paper). Available at SSRN: http://ssrn.com/abstract=2371227 or https://doi.org/10.2139/ssrn.2371227. Accessed 17 Nov 2015.

Daniel, K., & Titman, S. (1999). Market efficiency in an irrational world. *Financial Analysts Journal, 55*, 28–40.

Daniel, K., Hirshleifer, D., & Subrahmanyam, A. (1998). A theory of overconfidence, selfattribution, and security market under- and over-reactions. *Journal of Finance, 53*, 1839–1885.

Darvas, N. (1960). *How I made $2,000,000 in the stock market.* Larchmont: American Research Council.

de Bondt, W. E. M. (1993). Betting on trends: Intuitive forecasts of financial risk and return. *International Journal of Forecasting, 9*, 355–371.

de Carvalho, R. L., Dugnolle, P., Lu, X., & Moulin, P. (2014). Low-risk anomalies in global fixed income: Evidence from major broad markets. *Journal of Fixed Income, 23*(4), 51–70. https://doi.org/10.3905/jfi.2014.23.4.051.

de Groot, W., Pang, J., & Swinkels, L. A. P. (2012b). The cross-section of stock returns in frontier emerging markets. *Journal of Empirical Finance, 19*(5), 796–818.

de Groot, W., Karstansje, D., & Zhou, W. (2014). Exploiting commodity momentum along the futures curves. *Journal of Banking & Finance, 48*, 79–93.

de Long, B. J., Shleifer, A., Summers, L. H., & Waldmann, R. J. (1990a). Noise trader risk in financial markets. *Journal of Political Economy, 98*, 703–738.

de Long, J. B., Shleifer, A., Summers, L. H., & Waldmann, R. J. (1990b). Positive feedback investment strategies and destabilizing rational speculation. *Journal of Finance, 45*(2), 379–395.

De Bondt, W. F. M., & Thaler, R. (1985). Does the stock market overreact? *Journal of Finance, 40*(3), 793–805.

Dudler, M., Gmuer, B., & Malamud, S. (2014). *Risk adjusted time series momentum* (Swiss Finance Institute research paper No. 14-71). Available at

SSRN: https://ssrn.com/abstract=2457647 or https://doi.org/10.2139/ssrn.2457647. Accessed 23 Oct 2017.

Dudler, M., Gmur, B., & Malamud, S. (2015). Momentum and risk adjustment. *Journal of Alternative Investment, 18*(2), 91–103. https://doi.org/10.3905/jai.2015.18.2.091.

Durham, J. B. (2013). *Momentum and the term structure of interest rates* (FRB of New York staff report No. 657). Available at SSRN: http://ssrn.com/abstract=2377379 or https://doi.org/10.2139/ssrn.2377379. Accessed 20 Oct 2015.

Duyvesteyn, J., & Martens, M. (2014). Emerging government bond market timing. *Journal of Fixed Income, 23*(3), 36–49.

Easterday, K. E., Sen, P. K., & Stephan, J. (2009). The persistence of the small firm/January effect: Is it consistent with investors' learning and arbitrage efforts? *Quarterly Review of Economics and Finance, 49*(3), 1172–1193.

Ehsani, S. (2017). *Factor momentum and the momentum factor.* Available at SSRN: https://ssrn.com/abstract=3014521. Accessed 23 Oct 2017.

Evans, A., & Schmitz, C. (2015). *Value, size and momentum on equity indices – A likely example of selection bias* (WINTON Global Investment Management working paper). Available at https://www.wintoncapital.com/assets/documents/research-papers/ValueSizeMomentumonEquityIndices2015-09-07.pdf. Accessed 11 Nov 2015.

Faber, M. T. (2010). *Relative strength strategies for investing.* Available at SSRN: http://ssrn.com/abstract=1585517 or https://doi.org/10.2139/ssrn.1585517. Accessed 21 Oct 2015.

Fama, E. F. (1970). Efficient capital markets: A review of theory and empirical work. *Journal of Finance, 25*(2), 383–417.

Fama, E. F., & Blume, M. E. (1966). Filter rules and stock market trading. *Journal of Business, 39*(1), 226–241.

Fama, E. F., & French, K. R. (1993). Common risk factors in the returns on stocks and bonds. *Journal of Financial Economics, 33*, 3–56. https://doi.org/10.1016/0304-405X(93)90023-5.

Fama, E. F., & French, K. R. (2008). Dissecting anomalies. *Journal of Finance, 63*(4), 1653–1678.

Fan, S., Opsal, S., & Yu, L. (2015). Equity anomalies and idiosyncratic risk around the world. *Multinational Finance Journal, 19*(1), 33–75.

Feng, Z., Price, S. M., & Sirmans, C. F. (2014). The relation between momentum and drift: Industry-level evidence from equity Real Estate Investment Trusts (REITs). *Journal of Real Estate Research, 36*(3), 407.

Filippou, I., Gozluklu, A. E., & Taylor, M. P. (2015). *Global political risk and currency momentum.* Available at SSRN: http://ssrn.com/abstract=2517400 or https://doi.org/10.2139/ssrn.2517400. Accessed 21 Oct 2015.

Forsythe, R., Nelson, F., Neumann, G., & Wright, J. (1992). Anatomy of an experimental stock market. *American Economic Review, 82*, 1142–1161.

Frazzini, A. (2006). The disposition effect and underreaction to news. *Journal of Finance, 61*(4), 2017–2046.

Frazzini, A., & Pedersen, L. H. (2014). Betting against beta. *Journal of Financial Economics, 111*, 1–25. https://doi.org/10.1016/j.jfineco.2013.10.005.

Frieder, L. (2008). Investor and price response to patterns in earnings surprises. *Journal of Financial Markets, 11*, 259–283.

Fuertes, A. M., Miffre, J., & Rallis, G. (2010). Tactical allocation in commodity futures markets: Combining momentum and term structure signals. *Journal of Banking and Finance, 34*, 2530–2548.

Fuertes, A. M., Miffre, J., & Fernández-Pérez, A. (2015). Commodity strategies based on momentum, term structure and idiosyncratic volatility. *Journal of Futures Markets, 35*(3), 274–297.

Fung, W., & Hsieh, D. A. (1997). Survivorship bias and investment style in the returns of CTAs. *Journal of Portfolio Management, 24*(1), 30–41.

Garleanu, N., & Pedersen, L. H. (2007). Liquidity and risk management. *American Economic Review, 97*, 193–197.

Gartley, H. M. (1935). *Profits in the stock market*. Pomeroy: Lambert Gann Publishing.

Gartley, H. M. (1945). Relative velocity statistics: Their application in portfolio analysis. *Financial Analyst Journal, 51*(1), 18–20.

Gebhardt, W. R., Hvidkjaer, S., & Swaminathan, B. (2005). Stock and bond market interaction: Does momentum spill over? *Journal of Financial Economics, 75*(3), 651–690.

Geczy, C., & Samonov, M. (2016). Two centuries of price-return momentum. *Financial Analysts Journal, 72*(5), 32–56. https://doi.org/10.2469/faj.v72.n5.1.

Georgopoulou, A., & Wang, G. J. (2016, in press). The trend is your friend: Time-series momentum strategies across equity and commodity markets. *Review of Finance*. Available at SSRN: http://ssrn.com/abstract=2618243. Accessed 11 Sept 2017.

Gilovich, T., Vallone, R., & Tversky, A. (1985). The hot hand in basketball: On the misperception of random sequences. *Cognitive Psychology, 17*, 295–314.

Goebel, P. R., Harrison, D. M., Mercer, J. M., & Whitby, R. J. (2012). REIT momentum and characteristic-related REIT Returns. *Journal of Real Estate Finance and Economics, 47*(3), 564–581.

Gorton, G. B., Hayashi, F., & Rouwenhorst, K. G. (2013). The fundamentals of commodity futures returns. *Review of Finance, 17*, 35–105.

Goyal, A., & Jegadeesh, N. (2017). *Cross-sectional and time-series tests of return predictability: What is the difference?* (Swiss Finance Institute research paper No. 15-13). Available at SSRN: https://ssrn.com/abstract=2610288 or https://doi.org/10.2139/ssrn.2610288. Accessed 23 Oct 2017.

Goyal, A., & Wahal, S. (2015). Is momentum and echo? *Journal of Financial and Quantitative Analysis, 50*(6), 1237–1267. https://doi.org/10.1017/S0022109015000575.

Graham, J. R. (1999). Herding among investment newsletters: Theory and evidence. *Journal of Finance, 54*(1), 237–268.

Griffin, J. M., Ji, X., & Martin, S. J. (2003). Momentum investing and business cycle risk: Evidence from pole to pole. *Journal of Finance, 58*(6), 2515–2547.

Griffin, J., Ji, X., & Martin, S. J. (2005). Global momentum strategies: A portfolio perspective. *Journal of Portfolio Management, 31*(2), 23–39.

Grinblatt, M., & Moskowitz, T. M. (2004). Predicting stock price movements from past returns: The role of consistency and tax-loss selling. *Journal of Financial Economics, 71*, 541–579.

Grobys, K. (2015, forthcoming). Another look at momentum crashes: Momentum in the European monetary union. *Applied Economics*. Available at SSRN: http://ssrn.com/abstract=2564488 or https://doi.org/10.2139/ssrn.2564488. Accessed 11 Nov 2015.

Grobys, K. (2016). Another look at momentum crashes: Momentum in the European monetary union. *Applied Economics, 48*(19), 1759–1766.

Grobys, K., Heinonen, J.-P., & Kolari, J. W. (2016). *Is currency momentum driven by global economic risk?* Available at SSRN: http://ssrn.com/abstract=2619146 or https://doi.org/10.2139/ssrn.2619146. Accessed 28 Aug 2015.

Grossman, S. J., & Stiglitz, J. E. (1976). Information and competitive price systems. *American Economic Review, 66*, 246–253.

Grossman, S. J., & Stiglitz, J. E. (1980). On the impossibility of informationally efficient markets. *American Economic Review, 70*, 393–408.

Grundy, B. D., & Martin, J. S. (2001). Understanding the nature of the risks and the sources of the rewards to momentum investing. *Review of Financial Studies, 14*(1), 29–78.

Guilmin, G. (2015). *The effective combination of risk-based strategies with momentum and trend following*. Available at SSRN: http://ssrn.com/abstract=2556747 or https://doi.org/10.2139/ssrn.2556747. Accessed 11 Oct 2015.

Han, Y., Zhou, G., & Zhu, Y. (2016, June). *A trend factor: Any economic gains from using information over investment Horizons?* Available at SSRN: https://ssrn.com/abstract=2182667 or https://doi.org/10.2139/ssrn.2182667.

Haller, G. (1965). *The Haller theory of stock market trends*. West Palm Beach: Gilber Haller.

Hanauer, M. (2014). Is Japan different? Evidence on momentum and market dynamics. *International Review of Finance, 14*(1), 141–160.

Hao, Y., Chu, H.-H., Ho, K.-Y., & Ko, K.-C. (2016). The 52-week high and momentum in the Taiwan stock market: Anchoring or recency biases? *International Review of Economics & Finance, 43*, 121–138. https://doi.org/10.1016/j.iref.2015.10.035.

Haug, M., & Hirschey, M. (2006). The January effect. *Financial Analyst Journal, 62*(5), 78–88.

Heisler, J. (1994). Loss aversion in a futures market: An empirical test. *Review of Futures Markets, 13*(3), 793–822.

Hellwig, M. (1982). Rational expectations equilibrium with conditioning on past prices: A mean-variance example. *Journal of Economic Theory, 26*, 279–312.

Hong, H., & Stein, J. (1999). A unified theory of underreaction, momentum trading, and overreaction in asset markets. *Journal of Finance, 54*(6), 2143–2184.

Hong, H., Lim, T., & Stein, J. C. (2000). Bad news travels slowly: Size, analyst coverage, and the profitability of momentum strategies. *Journal of Finance, 55*(1), 265–295.

Hou, K., Peng, L., & Xiong, W. (2006). *$R^2$and price inefficiency* (Research in Financial Economics in its series working paper series with number 2006-23). Available at http://www.cob.ohio-state.edu/fin/dice/papers/2006/2006-23.pdf. Accessed 9 Sept 2017.

Houweling, P., & van Zundert, J. (2017). Factor investing in the corporate bond market. *Financial Analysts Journal, 73*(2), 100–115. https://doi.org/10.2469/faj.v73.n2.1.

Hühn, H. L., & Scholz, H. (2017). *Alpha momentum and price momentum*. Available at SSRN: https://ssrn.com/abstract=2287848 or https://doi.org/10.2139/ssrn.2287848. Accessed 23 Oct 2017.

Hambusch, G., Hong, K. J., & Webster, E. (2015). Enhancing risk-adjusted return using time series momentum in sovereign bonds. *Journal of Fixed Income, 25*(1), 96–111. https://doi.org/10.3905/jfi.2015.25.1.096.

Hung, K., & Glascock, J. L. (2010). Volatilities and momentum returns in real estate investment trusts. *Journal of Real Estate Finance and Economics, 41*(2), 126–149. https://doi.org/10.1007/s11146-008-9165-8.

Hurst, B. K., Ooi, Y. H., & Pedersen, L. H. (2013). Demystifying managed futures. *Journal of Investment Management, 11*(3), 42–58.

Hurst, B., Ooi, Y. H., & Pedersen, L. H. (2017). *A century of evidence on trend-following investing*. Available at SSRN: https://ssrn.com/abstract=2993026. Accessed 23 Oct 2017.

Ilmanen, A. (2011). *Expected returns: An investor's guide to harvesting market rewards*. Hoboken: Wiley.

Irwin, S. H., & Park, C. H. (2008). The profitability of technical analysis in commodity markets. In F. J. Fabozzi, R. Fus, & D. G. Kaiser (Eds.), *The handbook of commodity investing*. Hoboken: John Wiley & Sons.

Israel, R., Palhares, D., & Richardson, S. A. (2016). *Common factors in corporate bond and bond fund returns*. Available at SSRN: https://ssrn.com/abstract=2576784 or https://doi.org/10.2139/ssrn.2576784. Accessed 23 Oct 2017.

Ivkovic, Z., & Weisbenner, S. (2009). Individual investor mutual fund flows. *Journal of Financial Economics, 92*(2), 223–237.

Jacobs, H. (2015). What explains the dynamics of 100 anomalies? *Journal of Banking & Finance, 57*, 65–85. https://doi.org/10.1016/j.jbankfin.2015.03.006.

Jacobs, H. (2016). Market maturity and mispricing. *Journal of Financial Economics, 122*(2), 270–287. https://doi.org/10.1016/j.jfineco.2016.01.030.

Jacobs, H., & Müller, S. (2017a). *Anomalies across the globe: Once public, no longer existent?* Available at SSRN: https://ssrn.com/abstract=2816490 or https://doi.org/10.2139/ssrn.2816490. Accessed 23 Oct 2017.

Jacobs, H., & Müller, S. (2017b). *...and nothing else matters? On the dimensionality and predictability of international stock returns.* Available at SSRN: https://ssrn.com/abstract=2845306 or https://doi.org/10.2139/ssrn.2845306. Accessed 23 Oct 2017.

Jacobs, H., Regele, T., & Weber, M. (2016). *Expected skewness and momentum.* Available at SSRN: https://ssrn.com/abstract=2600014 or https://doi.org/10.2139/ssrn.2600014. Accessed 11 Sept 2017.

Jaffarian, E. (2009). Managed futures. In K. Wilkens-Christopher (Ed.), *CAIA level II. Advanced core topics in alternative investments.* Hoboken: John Wiley & Sons.

Jegadeesh, N. (1990). Evidence of predictable behavior of security returns. *Journal of Finance, 45,* 881–898.

Jegadeesh, N., & Titman, S. (1993). Returns to buying winners and selling losers: Implications for stock market efficiency. *Journal of Finance, 48,* 65–91.

Jegadeesh, N., & Titman, S. (2001). Profitability of momentum strategies: An evaluation of alternative explanations. *Journal of Finance, 56*(2), 599–720.

Jensen, M. C. (1978). Some anomalous evidence regarding market efficiency. *Journal of Financial Economics, 6*(2–3), 95–101.

Jensen, M. C., & Benington, G. A. (1970). Random walks and technical theories: Some additional evidence. *Journal of Finance, 25*(2), 469–482.

Ji, X., Martin, S., & Yao, Y. (2017, in press). Macroeconomic risk and seasonality in momentum profits. *Journal of Financial Markets.* https://doi.org/10.1016/j.finmar.2017.04.002.

Jiang, G., Lee, C. M., & Zhang, Y. (2005). Information uncertainty and expected returns. *Review of Accounting Studies, 10,* 185–221.

Jostova, G., Nikolova, S., Philipov, A., & Stahel, C. W. (2013). Momentum in corporate bond returns. *Review of Financial Studies, 26*(7), 1649–1693.

Kaestner, M. (2006). Anomalous price behaviour following earnings surprises: Does representativeness cause overreaction? *Revue de l'Association Francaise de Finance, 27,* 5–31.

Kahneman, D., & Tversky, A. (1972). Subjective probability: A judgment of representativeness. *Cognitive Psychology, 3,* 430–454.

Kaustia, M. (2010). Disposition effect. In H. K. Baker & J. R. Nofsinger (Eds.), *Behavioral finance.* Hoboken: John Wiley & Sons, chapter 10.

Keim, D. (1983a). Size-related anomalies and stock return seasonality: Further empirical evidence. *Journal of Financial Economics, 12,* 13–32.

Keim, D. (1983b). Stock return seasonality and the size effect. *Journal of Financial Economics, 12,* 13–32.

Kim, D. (2012). Cross-asset style momentum. *Asia-Pacific Journal of Financial Studies, 41*(5), 610–636. https://doi.org/10.1111/j.2041-6156.2012.01084.x.

Kim, H., Arvind, M., & Petkevich, A. (2012). *Sources of momentum in bonds* (Mays Business School research paper No. 2012-40). Available at SSRN: http://ssrn.

com/abstract=2054711 or https://doi.org/10.2139/ssrn.2054711. Accessed 20 Oct 2015.

Kim, A. Y., Tse, Y., & Wald, J. K. (2016). Time series momentum and volatility scaling. *Journal of Financial Markets, 30*, 103–124. https://doi.org/10.1016/j.finmar.2016.05.003.

Kroencke, T. A., Schindler, F., & Schrimpf, A. (2013). International diversification benefits with foreign exchange investment styles. *Review of Finance, 18*(5), 1847–1883.

Lee, E., & Piqueira, N. (2017). Short selling around the 52-week and historical highs. *Journal of Financial Markets, 33*, 75–101. https://doi.org/10.1016/j.finmar.2016.03.001.

Lee, C. M., & Swaminathan, B. (2000). Price momentum and trading volume. *Journal of Finance, 55*, 2017–2069.

Lefevre, E. (2010). *Reminiscences of a stock operator: With new commentary and insights on the life and times of Jesse Livermore*. Hoboken: John Wiley & Sons.

Lehmann, B. N. (1990). Fads, martingales, and market efficiency. *Quarterly Journal of Economics, 105*(1), 1–28.

Levine, A., & Pedersen, L. H. (2016). Which trend is your friend? *Financial Analysts Journal, 72*(3), 51–66. https://doi.org/10.2469/faj.v72.n3.3.

Levy, R. A. (1967). Relative strength as a criterion for investment selection. *Journal of Finance, 22*(4), 595–610.

Levy, R. A. (1968). *The relative strength concept of common stock price forecasting*. Larchmont: Investors Intelligence.

Lhabitant, F. S. (2008). Commodity trading strategies: Examples of trading rules and signals from the CTA sector. In F. J. Fabozzi, R. Fuss, & D. G. Kaiser (Eds.), *The handbook of commodity investing*. Hoboken: John Wiley & Sons.

Li, F. W., & Wei, J. K. C. (2015). Momentum life cycle around the world: The roles of individualism and limits to arbitrage. In *Asian Finance Association (AsianFA) 2015 Conference Paper*. Available at SSRN: http://ssrn.com/abstract=2565305 or https://doi.org/10.2139/ssrn.2565305. Accessed 20 Oct 2015.

Lin, H., Wu, C., & Zhou, G. (2017). *Does momentum exist in bonds of different ratings?* Available at SSRN: https://ssrn.com/abstract=2872382 or https://doi.org/10.2139/ssrn.2872382. Accessed 23 Oct 2017.

Liu, L. X., & Zhang, L. (2008). Momentum profits, factor pricing, and macroeconomic risk. *Review of Financial Studies, 21*(6), 2417–2448.

Liu, M., Liu, Q., & Ma, T. (2011). The 52-week high momentum strategy in international stock markets. *Journal of International Money and Finance, 30*, 180–204.

Locke, P. R., & Mann, S. C. (2005). Professional trader discipline and trade disposition. *Journal of Financial Economics, 76*(2), 401–444.

Lord, C., Ross, L., & Lepper, M. (1979). Biased assimilation and attitude polarization: The effects of prior theories on subsequently considered evidence. *Journal of Personality and Social Psychology, 37*, 2098–2109.

Lukac, L. P., Brorsen, B. W., & Irwin, S. H. (1988). A test of futures market disequilibrium using twelve different technical trading systems. *Applied Economics, 20*(5), 523–639.

Luu, B. V., & Yu, P. (2012). Momentum in government-bond markets. *Journal of Fixed Income., 22*(2), 72–79.

Maymin, P. Z., Maymin, Z. G., & Fisher, G. S. (2014). Momentum's hidden sensitivity to the starting day. *Journal of Investing, 23*(2), 114–123. https://doi.org/10.3905/joi.2014.23.2.114.

Menkoff, L., Sarno, L., Schmeling, M., & Schrimpf, A.(2011). *Currency momentum strategies.* Available at SSRN: http://ssrn.com/abstract=1809776 or https://doi.org/10.2139/ssrn.1809776. Accessed 21 Oct 2015.

Miffre, J., & Rallis, G. (2007). Momentum strategies in commodity futures markets. *Journal of Banking & Finance, 31*(6), 1863–1886. https://doi.org/10.1016/j.jbankfin.2006.12.005.

Moskowitz, T. J., & Grinblatt, M. (1999). Do industries explain momentum? *Journal of Finance, 54*(4), 1249–1290.

Moskowitz, T. J., Ooi, Y. H., & Pedersen, L. H. (2012). Time series momentum. *Journal of Financial Economics, 104*(2), 228–250.

Moss, A., Clare, A., Thomas, S. H., & Seaton, J. (2015). Trend following and momentum strategies for global REITs. *Journal of Real Estate Portfolio Management, 21*(1), 21–31.

Muller, C., & Ward, M. (2010). Momentum effects in country equity indices. *Journal for Studies in Economics and Econometrics, 34*(1), 111–127.

Northcraft, G. B., & Neale, M. (1987). Experts, amateurs, and real estate: An anchoring-and-adjustment perspective on property pricing decisions. *Organizational Behavior and Human Decision Processes, 39*, 84–97.

Nosfinger, J. R., & Sias, R. W. (1999). Herding and feedback trading by institutional and individual investors. *Journal of Finance, 54*(6), 2263–2295.

Novy-Marx, R. (2012). Is momentum really momentum? *Journal of Financial Economics, 103*, 429–453.

O'Neil, W. (2009). *How to make money in stocks: A winning system in good times and bad* (4th ed.). New York: McGraw Hill Education.

Okunev, J., & White, D. (2000). Do momentum based strategies still work in foreign currency markets. *Journal of Financial and Quantitative Markets, 38*(2), 422–457.

Olszewski, F., & Zhou, G. (2014). Strategy diversification: Combining momentum and carry strategies within a foreign exchange portfolio. *Journal of Derivatives & Hedge Funds, 19*(4), 311–320.

Orlov, V. (2015). *Currency momentum, carry trade and market illiquidity.* 27th Australasian Finance and Banking Conference 2014 Paper.

Osler, C. L. (2000). Support for resistance: Technical analysis and intraday exchange rates. *Economic Policy Review, 6*, 53–65.

Pan, M. S., Liano, K., & Huang, G.-C. (2004). Industry momentum strategies and autocorrelations in stock returns. *Journal of Empirical Finance, 11*(2), 185–202.

Park, C.-H., & Irwin, S. H. (2007). What do we know about the profitability of technical analysis? *Journal of Economic Surveys, 21*(4), 786–826.

Park, K.-I., & Kim, D. (2013). Sources of momentum profits in international stock markets. *Accounting and Finance, 54*(2), 567–589.

Pastor, L., & Stambaugh, R. F. (2003). Liquidity risk and expected stock returns. *Journal of Political Economy, 111*(3), 642–685.

Pirrong, C. (2005). *Momentum in futures markets* (EFA 2005 Moscow meetings paper). Available at SSRN: http://ssrn.com/abstract=671841 or https://doi.org/10.2139/ssrn.671841. Accessed 21 Oct 2015.

Plessis, J., & Hallerbach, W. G. (2016). Volatility-weighting applied to momentum strategies. *Journal of Alternative Investments*. https://doi.org/10.3905/jai.2016.2016.1.050.

Pojarliev, M., & Levich, R. M. (2013). *A new look at currency investing*. CFA Institute Research Foundation Monograph. Available at SSRN: http://ssrn.com/abstract=2571391. Accessed 20 Oct 2015.

Pospisil, L., & Zhang, J. (2010). Momentum and reversal effects in corporate bond prices and credit cycles. *Journal of Fixed Income, 20*(2), 101–115.

Pouget, S., & Villeneuve, S. (2008). *Price formation with confirmation bias*. Available at http://www.creedexperiment.nl/enable2008/pouget.pdf. Accessed 24 Oct 2015.

Pouget, S., & Villeneuve, S. (2012). *A mind is a terrible thing to change: Confirmation bias in financial markets* (IDEI working papers 720). Toulouse: Institut d'Économie Industrielle (IDEI). Available at http://idei.fr/sites/default/files/medias/doc/wp/2012/wp_idei_720.pdf. Accessed 24 Oct 2015.

Rabin, M., & Schrag, J. (1999). First impressions matter: A model of confirmatory bias. *Quarterly Journal of Economics, 114*, 37–82.

Reidpath, D. D., & Diamond, M. R. (1995). A nonexperimental demonstration of anchoring bias. *Psychological Reports, 76*, 800–802.

Rhea, R. (1932). *The Dow theory*. New York: Barrons.

Ro, S. H., & Gallimore, P. (2013). Real estate mutual funds: Herding, momentum trading and performance. *Real Estate Economics, 42*(1), 190–222.

Rouwenhorst, G. K. (1998). International momentum strategies. *Journal of Finance, 53*(1), 267–284.

Rouwenhorst, G. K. (1999). Local return factors and turnover in emerging stock markets. *Journal of Finance, 54*, 1439–1464.

Sagi, J., & Seasholes, M. (2007). Firm-specific attributes and the cross section of momentum. *Journal of Financial Economics, 84*(2), 389–434.

Samuelson, P. A. (1965). Proof that properly anticipated prices fluctuate randomly. *Industrial Management Review, 6*, 41–49.

Schmidt, P. S., von Arx, U., Schrimpf, A., Wagner, A. F., & Ziegler, A. (2015). *Size and momentum profitability in international stock markets* (Swiss Finance Institute Research paper No. 15-29). Available at SSRN: http://ssrn.com/

abstract=2642185 or https://doi.org/10.2139/ssrn.2642185. Accessed 20 Oct 2015.

Schwager, J. D. (1994). *The new market wizards: Conversations with America's top traders*. New York: HarperCollins.

Schwager, J. D. (2003). *Stock market wizards: Interviews with America's top stock traders*. New York: HarperBusiness.

Schwager, J. D. (2012a). *Hedge fund market wizards: How winning traders win?* Hoboken: John Wiley & Sons.

Schwager, J. D. (2012b). *Market wizards, updated: Interviews with top traders*. Hoboken: John Wiley & Sons.

Seamans, G. (1939). *The seven pillars of stock market success*. Brightwaters: Windsor Books.

Shaik, R. (2011). *Risk-adjusted momentum: A superior approach to momentum investing* (White paper). Bridgeway Capital Management. Available at http://www.dorseywright.com/downloads/hrs_research/Momentum%20White%20Paper%202011%20Fall.pdf

Sharpe, W. F. (1964). Capital asset prices: A theory of market equilibrium under conditions of risk. *Journal of Finance, 19*(3), 425–442.

Shefrin, H., & Statman, M. (1985). The disposition to sell winners too early and ride losers too long: Theory and evidence. *Journal of Finance, 40*(3). Papers and Proceedings of the Forty-Third Annual Meeting American Finance Association, Dallas, Texas, December 28–30, pp. 777–790.

Shiller, R. J. (1984). *Stock prices and social dynamics* (Cowles Foundation Paper #616, pp. 457–510). Available at http://www.econ.yale.edu/~shiller/pubs/p0616.pdf. Accessed 9 Oct 2017.

Shiller, R. J. (1988). Portfolio insurance and other investor fashions as factors in the 1987 stock market crash. *NBER Macroeconomic Annual, 3*, 287–296.

Shleifer, A. (2000). *Inefficient markets: An introduction to behavioral finance*. Oxford: Oxford University Press.

Sias, R. (2007). Causes and seasonality of momentum profits. *Financial Analysts Journal, 63*(2), 48–54.

Silber, W. L. (1994). Technical trading: When it works and when it doesn't. *Journal of Derivatives, 1*, 39–44.

Slovic, P., & Lichtenstein, S. (1971). Comparison of Bayesian and regression approaches to the study of information processing in judgement. *Organizational Behavior and Human Performance, 6*, 649–744.

Soros, G. (2003). *The alchemy of finance*. Hoboken: John Wiley & Sons.

Stambaugh, R. F., Yu, J., & Yuan, Y. (2012). The short of it: Investor sentiment and anomalies. *Journal of Financial Economics, 104*(2), 288–302. https://doi.org/10.1016/j.jfineco.2011.12.001.

Stockopedia. (2012). *What is a momentum crash and why does it happen?* Available at http://www.businessinsider.com/what-is-a-momentum-crash-and-why-does-it-happen--2012-11. Accessed 10 Sept 2017.

Szakmary, A. C., & Zhou, X. (2015). Industry momentum in an earlier time: Evidence from the Cowles data. *Journal of Financial Research, 38*(3), 319–347.

Szymanowska, M., de Roon, F., Nijman, T., & van den Goorbergh, R. (2014). An anatomy of commodity futures risk premia. *Journal of Finance, 69*(1), 453–482.

Teplova, T., & Mikova, E. (2015). New evidence on determinants of price momentum in the Japanese stock market. *Research in International Business and Finance, 34*, 84–109.

Tibbs, S. L., Eakins, S. G., & DeShurko, W. (2008). Using style momentum to generate alpha. *Journal of Technical Analysis, 65*, 50–56.

Tversky, A., & Kahneman, D. (1971). Belief in the law of small numbers. *Psychological Bulletin, 2*, 105–110.

Tversky, A., & Kahneman, D. (1974). Judgement under uncertainty: Heuristics and biases. *Science, 185*, 1124–1131.

Tversky, A., & Kahneman, D. (1982). Judgments of and by representativeness. In D. Kahneman, P. Slovic, & A. Tversky (Eds.), *Judgment under uncertainty: Heuristics and biases* (pp. 84–98). Cambridge: Cambridge University Press.

Umutlu, M. (2015). Idiosyncratic volatility and expected returns at the global level. *Financial Analysts Journal, 71*(6), 58–71.

van Horne, J. C., & Parker, G. G. C. (1967). The random-walk theory: An empirical test. *Financial Analyst Journal, 23*(6), 87–92.

van Horne, J. C., & Parker, G. G. C. (1968). Technical trading rules: A comment. *Financial Analyst Journal, 24*(4), 128–132.

van Zundert, J. (2017). *A new test for cross-sectional momentum*. Available at SSRN: https://ssrn.com/abstract=2880097. Accessed 23 Oct 2017.

Vinod, H. D., & Morey, M. R. (1999). *A double Sharpe ratio* (Working paper). Available at SSRN: http://papers.ssrn.com/sol3/papers.cfm?abstract_id=168748. Accessed 16 Oct 2017.

Vu, J. D. (2012). Do momentum strategies generate profits in emerging stock markets? *Problems and Perspectives in Management, 10*(3), 2012.

Wang, P., & Kochard, L. (2011). *Using a Z-score approach to combine value and momentum in tactical asset allocation*. Available at SSRN: https://ssrn.com/abstract=1726443 or https://doi.org/10.2139/ssrn.1726443. Accessed 23 Oct 2017.

Wang, K. Q., & Xu, J. (2015). Market volatility and momentum. *Journal of Empirical Finance, 30*, 79–91. https://doi.org/10.1016/j.jempfin.2014.11.009.

Wason, P. C. (1960). On the failure to eliminate hypotheses in a conceptual task. *Quarterly Journal of Experimental Psychology, 12*, 129–140.

Watson, S. R., & Buede, D. M. (1987). *Decision synthesis: The principles and practice of decision analysis*. Cambridge: Cambridge University Press.

Weber, M., & Camerer, C. F. (1998). The disposition effect in securities trading: An experimental analysis. *Journal of Economic Behavior and Organization, 33*(2), 167–184.

Welch, I. (2000). Herding among security analysts. *Journal of Financial Economics, 58*, 69–396.

Wyckoff, R. F. (1924). *How I trade in stocks and bonds: Being some methods evolved and adapted during my thirty-three years' experience in Wall Street.* New York: Magazine of Wall Street.

Zakamulin, V. (2015a). *A comprehensive look at the empirical performance of moving average trading strategies.* Available at SSRN: https://ssrn.com/abstract=2677212 or https://doi.org/10.2139/ssrn.2677212. Accessed 19 Oct 2017.

Zakamulin, V. (2015b). Market timing with a robust moving average. Available at SSRN: https://ssrn.com/abstract=2612307 or https://doi.org/10.2139/ssrn.2612307. Accessed 19 Oct 2017.

Zakamulin, V. (2016a). *Revisiting the profitability of market timing with moving averages.* Available at SSRN: https://ssrn.com/abstract=2743119 or https://doi.org/10.2139/ssrn.2743119. Accessed 19 Oct 2017.

Zakamulin, V. (2016b). *Market timing with moving averages: Anatomy and performance of trading rules.* Available at SSRN: https://ssrn.com/abstract=2585056 or https://doi.org/10.2139/ssrn.2585056. Accessed 19 Oct 2017.

Zaremba, A. (2015a). *The momentum effect in country-level stock market anomalies.* Available at SSRN: https://ssrn.com/abstract=2621236 or https://doi.org/10.2139/ssrn.2621236. Accessed 23 Oct 2017.

Zaremba, A. (2016). Investor sentiment, limits on arbitrage, and the performance of cross-country stock market anomalies. *Journal of Behavioral and Experimental Finance, 9*, 136–163. https://doi.org/10.1016/j.jbef.2015.11.007.

Zaremba, A. (2015c). The January seasonality and the performance of country-level value and momentum strategies. *Copernican Journal of Finance & Accounting, 2*, 195–209. http://apcz.pl/czasopisma/index.php/CJFA/article/view/CJFA.2015.024

Zaremba, A. (2015d). Country selection strategies based on value, size and momentum. *Investment Analyst Journal, 44*(3), 171–198.

Zaremba, A. (2016). Strategies based on momentum and term structure in financialized -commodity markets. *Business and Economics Research Journal, 7*(1), 31–46.

Zaremba, A. (2017a). Performance persistence of government bond factor premia. *Finance Research Letters, 22*, 182–189. https://doi.org/10.1016/j.frl.2016.12.022.

Zaremba, A. (2017b). *Performance persistence in anomaly returns: Evidence from frontier markets.* Available at SSRN: https://ssrn.com/abstract=3060876. Accessed 31 Oct 2017.

Zaremba, A. (2017c). Combining country equity selection strategies. *Contemporary Economics, 11*(1), 107–126. https://doi.org/10.5709/ce.1897-9254.231.

Zaremba, A., & Andreu Sánchez, L. (2017). *Paper profits or real money? Trading costs and stock market anomalies in country equity indices.* Available at https://doi.org/10.2139/ssrn.3038514

Zaremba, A., & Czapkiewicz, A. (2017a). Digesting anomalies in emerging European markets: A comparison of factor pricing models. *Emerging Markets Review, 31*, 1–15. https://doi.org/10.1016/j.ememar.2016.12.002.

Zaremba, A., & Czapkiewicz, A. (2017b, in press). The cross section of international government bond returns. *Economic Modelling*. https://doi.org/10.1016/j.econmod.2017.06.011.

Zaremba, A., & Schabek, T. (2017). Seasonality in government bond returns and factor premia. *Research in International Business and Finance, 41*, 292–302. https://doi.org/10.1016/j.ribaf.2017.04.036.

Zaremba, A., & Shemer, J. (2016a). *Country asset allocation*. New York: Palgrave Macmillan.

Zaremba, A., & Shemer, J. (2016b). Is small beautiful? Size effect in stock markets. *Country Asset Allocation*, 67–79. https://doi.org/10.1057/978-1-137-59191-3_4.

Zaremba, A., & Shemer, J. (2016c). Momentum effect across countries. *Country Asset Allocation*, 161–181. New York: Palgrave Macmillan. https://doi.org/10.1057/978-1-137-59191-3_10.

Zaremba, A., & Shemer, J. (2016d). Value versus growth: Is buying cheap always a bargain? *Country Asset Allocation*, 9–38. New York: Palgrave Macmillan. https://doi.org/10.1057/978-1-137-59191-3_2.

Zaremba, A., & Shemer, K. (2016e). *What drives the momentum in factor premia? Evidence from international equity markets*. Paper presented at the 20th EBES Conferences, September 28–30, 2016, Vienna, Austria.

Zaremba, A., & Shemer, J. (2016f). Testing the country allocation strategies. *Country Asset Allocation*, 123–136. New York: Palgrave Macmillan. https://doi.org/10.1057/978-1-137-59191-3_7

Zaremba, A., & Shemer, K. (2017, in press). Is there momentum in factor premia? Evidence from international equity markets. *Research in International Business and Finance*. https://doi.org/10.1016/j.ribaf.2017.12.002

Zaremba, A., & Szyszka, A. (2016). Is there momentum in equity anomalies? Evidence from the Polish emerging market. *Research in International Business and Finance, 38*, 546–564. https://doi.org/10.1016/j.ribaf.2016.07.004.

Zaremba, A., & Umutlu, M. (2018a, in press). Strategies can be expensive too! The value spread and asset allocation in global equity markets. *Applied Economics*.

Zaremba, A., & Umutlu, M. (2018b, in press). Less pain, more gain: Volatility-adjusted residual momentum in international equity markets. *Investment Analysts Journal*. https://doi.org/10.1080/10293523.2018.1469290.

Zhang, X. F. (2006). Information uncertainty and stock returns. *Journal of Finance, 61*(1), 105–101.

Zhang, C. Y., & Jacobsen, B. (2012). Are monthly seasonals real? A three century perspective. *Review of Finance, 17*(5), 1743–1785.

Zhou, G., & Zhu, Y. (2013). *An equilibrium model of moving-average predictability and time-series momentum*. Available at SSRN. doi: https://doi.org/10.2139/ssrn.2326650. Accessed 23 Oct 2017.

CHAPTER 3

Trees Do Not Grow to the Sky: Reversals in a Stock Market

"Trees do not grow to the sky"—this stock exchange maxim captures the essence of reversal strategies which belong to the oldest tools ever employed in technical trading. Their underlying principles remain surprisingly simple: if stock prices have significantly dropped, buy them, as they are likely to transform into winners. On the other hand, when the equities recorded a solid bull market, sell them short, as they are likely to lose.

What Is the Reversal Effect?

Interestingly, at first glance the mean reversion seems to contradict the momentum strategy, which interprets growing prices as a good sign and recommends keeping the stocks. The reversion strategy, on the other hand, advocates the opposite: you should stay away from a stock price that has risen, sticking more to the losers than the winners. How is it possible that both these strategies, so clearly contradicting, could be profitable? The answer lies in different time horizons.

To illustrate the mean reversion in prices, Vitali Kalesnik (2013) from Research Affiliates, an academically oriented money management company, drew an analogy with a pendulum which in a typical classroom experiment consists of a weight, called the bob, suspended from a pivot. Let us take a look at the Fig. 3.1.

What will happen once the bob has been moved from point A to B and then released? Swinging back it will pass from point A to C and continue

A. Zaremba, J. "Koby" Shemer, *Price-Based Investment Strategies*,
https://doi.org/10.1007/978-3-319-91530-2_3

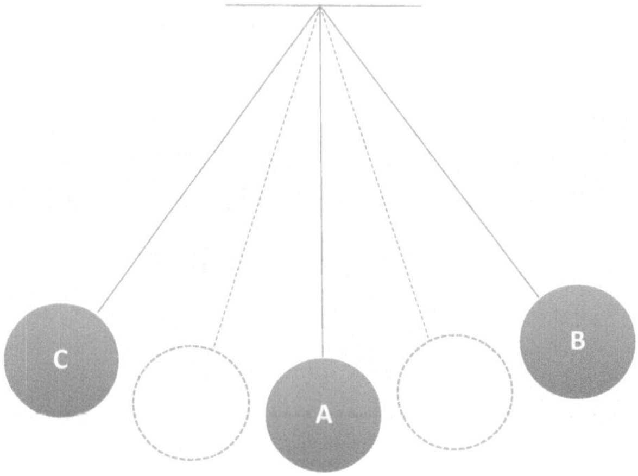

Fig. 3.1 Pendulum illustrating reversion to the mean. (Source: Own elaboration inspired by Kalesnik (2013))

swinging to and fro until it finally loses its energy and rests in the equilibrium point A. However, before the bob finds its balance in point A, it will be moving quite quickly, and its momentum will be the best indicator of both the speed and direction the bob will be moving in the immediate future. Nevertheless, in the long run, point A, which is the bob's average position, is the place where it is most likely to be found. Summing up, while in the short run the bob is likely to continue to move in the same direction, in the longer run, it will revert as the shorter and shorter swings are the process of reverting to the mean.

The physical example of a pendulum, ruled by the orderly Newtonian mechanics, is a clear and simple way of demonstrating a few irregularities. While the stock exchange reality is quite different, with the mean-reversion process being neither smooth nor deterministic, the crucial characteristics of this analogy remain very similar.

In the short run, recent price movements are indicative of the future. This phenomenon, as described in the previous chapter, suggests the trend of the securities that performed well in the past to continue to overperform, while the assets that displayed low performance are more likely to underperform. The long-run reversion implies this continuation tendency to be only temporary, as over time the prices are likely to revert to the average rather than to grow to the sky. Taking the long-term perspective, the equities that moved in one direction in the past will rather move to the opposite in the future.

Evidence of the Reversal Phenomenon

The investigations of mean reversion in equities have a very long history of academic research. In 1985 De Bondt and Thaler wrote their seminal paper "Does the Stock Market Overreact?" where they observed that "research in experimental psychology suggests that [...] most people tend to "overreact" to unexpected and dramatic news events." Following this observation, De Bondt and Thaler designed an investment strategy that could capture eventual profits resulting from the overreaction to its unquestionable success. The researchers found that stocks experiencing extreme returns in the past would exhibit subsequent long-run price reversals, which could persist even up to three to five years. Just as in the case of pendulum, the more extreme returns experienced in the past, the bigger subsequent reversals.

De Bondt and Thaler (1985) offered a "contrarian strategy" aimed at buying past losers, or undervalued stocks, and selling past winners, or overvalued stocks, to be tested it in the US stock market for the period ranging from 1930 to 1977.

The researchers computed each security's cumulative return for the 36 months starting December 1932, repeated this step 16 times to obtain 16 non-overlapping periods between 1930 and 1977. Next, for the each of the 16 portfolio formation dates, De Bondt and Thaler sorted the securities on the past 36-month trailing returns from the lowest to the highest. The bottom 35 equities, with the poorest performance, were then called loser portfolio, while the top 35 stocks, with the highest returns, became winners, to be finally compared.

Based on the 16 non-overlapping subperiods the researchers found that the losers outperformed winners by 24.6% over the following three years. Compared to the market-wide returns, the winner underperformed the market by 5% on average, while the losers earned 19.6% more than the market in the three-year portfolio formation.

The study also provided a few additional insights into the details of this strategy. First, they identified the performance of the reversal strategy especially strong in the first month following the portfolio formation, in January in particular. Second, they discovered the winner portfolio also displaying a higher beta which means that the long-term losers are not only more profitable but also safer than the winners. In their final observation, De Bondt and Thaler declared no reversal in the ranking periods of one year.

Interestingly, this last observation influenced the way the reversal strategy has been since implemented. If the latest 12 months do not contribute to the long-run reversal, why they should be used? In fact, utilizing this period could even prove counterproductive, as it is driving momentum, that is, a positive autocorrelation of returns. Therefore, many recent studies of the long-run reversal effect usually include sorting on the last 36–60 months and disregard the last 12 months.[1]

Summing up, the seminal study of De Bondt and Thaler (1985) brought convincing evidence for the long-run reversal in equity markets. While in the short term the relative strength, or momentum, may be the dominant force driving the prices, in the long run it is better to stick to the loser, as more likely to become winners in the future.

Since then, long-run reversal has been studied across various international stock markets, showcasing its significantly affecting price behavior in, for example, the UK, Spain, Germany, New Zealand, France, Australia, Canada, India, Malaysia, China, or even Sri Lanka, and Jordan.[2] The phenomenon was further researched in various asset classes, including corporate bonds, futures, country and industry indices, treasuries, commodities, and currencies.[3]

[1] The examples include Jacobs (2015, 2016), Zaremba and Szyszka (2016), Zaremba (2016, 2016d, 2017), Hou et al. (2017), and Jacobs and Müller (2017a).

[2] See, for USA, Campbell and Limmack (1997), Dissanaike (1997); for UK, Clare and Thomas (1995); for Spain, Alonso and Rubio (1990), Forner and Marhuenda (2003); for Germany: Stock (1990); for New Zealand, Swallow and Fox (1998); for France, Bacmann and Dubois (1998); for Poland, Sekuła (2015); for Australia, Brailsford (1992); for Canada, Kryzanowski and Zhang (1992); for Brazil, Da Costa (1994); for Malaysia, Ahmad and Hussain (2001) and Ali et al. (2011); for China, Wu (2011); for Sri Lanka: Tripathi and Aggarwal (2009); for Tunisia, Dhouib and Abaoub (2007); for South Africa, Page and Way (1992) and Hsieh and Hodnett (2011); for Turkey, Bildik and Gulay (2007); for Jordan, Saleh (2007); and for Egypt, Ismail (2012).

[3] See, for stocks, Alonso and Rubio (1990), Da Costa (1994), Baytas and Cakici (1999), George and Hwang (2007), Saleh and Sabbagh (2010), and Maheshwari and Dhankar (2015); for equity country indices, Richards (1997), Balvers et al. (2000), Balvers and Wu (2006), Spierdijk et al. (2012), Smith and Pantilei (2013), Malin and Bornholt (2013), Gharaibeh (2015), and Zaremba (2016d); for currencies, Chen and Jeon (1998), Sweeney (2006), Serban (2010), Chan (2013), and Kumar (2014); for futures markets, Monoyios and Sarno (2002), Chan (2013), and Lubnau and Todorova (2015); for government bonds, Park and Switzer (1996) and Khang and King (2004); for commodities, Irwin, Zulauf, and Jackson (1996), Andersson (2007), Miffre and Rallis (2007), and Chaves and Viswanathan (2016); for corporate bonds, Bhanot (2005) and Bali et al. (2017); and for industries, Bornholt et al. (2015).

In 2016, Arnott et al. even argued that the mean-reversion phenomenon affected entire strategies by reducing the future profitability of factor returns. In other words, the strategies that performed very well over years might, in turn, become expensive and underperform in the future.

Perhaps one of the most comprehensive studies of long-run reversal in the stock markets was conducted by Blackburn and Cakici. In their research published in the *Journal of Empirical Finance*, they investigated a huge sample covering 23 equity markets for years 1993–2014 to find evidence in support of the global presence of long-run reversals. As indicated, over the period of three years the positive return differential between loser stocks and winner stocks remained significant regardless of various considerations: controlling for size, valuation, or momentum although not equally strong in all global regions.

In the North America subsample, composed mainly of the US markets, the equal-weighted portfolio of stocks with the poorest returns over trailing 36 months outperformed the top performers by 0.80% on average. The situation was similar in Japan and in other Asian markets, with the return differential amounting to 1.03% and 0.54%, respectively. Interestingly, in the European sample, including the largest economies at the Old Continent, the contrarian strategy displayed rather disappointing results: the past losers earned on average 0.96% per month, while the past winners 1.23%. In other words, what was observed was more of a return continuation rather than reversal (Fig. 3.2).

Furthermore, the overperformance of the contrarian strategies was also significantly diminished when the portfolios were weighted on capitalization. In this case, in all the regions evaluated by Blackburn and Cakici (2017) the abnormal and raw returns diminished so markedly that they insignificantly differed from zero.

What was the reason for this poor performance? Perhaps the market became more efficient over the years, as the mean-reversion anomaly had been known for decades. In fact, a number of recent research have indicated that many anomalies are ruled by a sort of Murphy's law: once discovered, they tend to disappear (McLean and Pontiff 2016; Jacobs and Müller 2017a). Second, the recent period could prove extraordinary leading to reduced profits from long-run reversal strategies. Indeed, the falling payoffs to mean reversion have been observed in many places, and it is still unclear whether these are permanent or temporary changes in the market (Zaremba 2016d). Third, the reversal effect drivers may be particularly embedded in some market segments, for instance, in small stocks, which we will consider later.

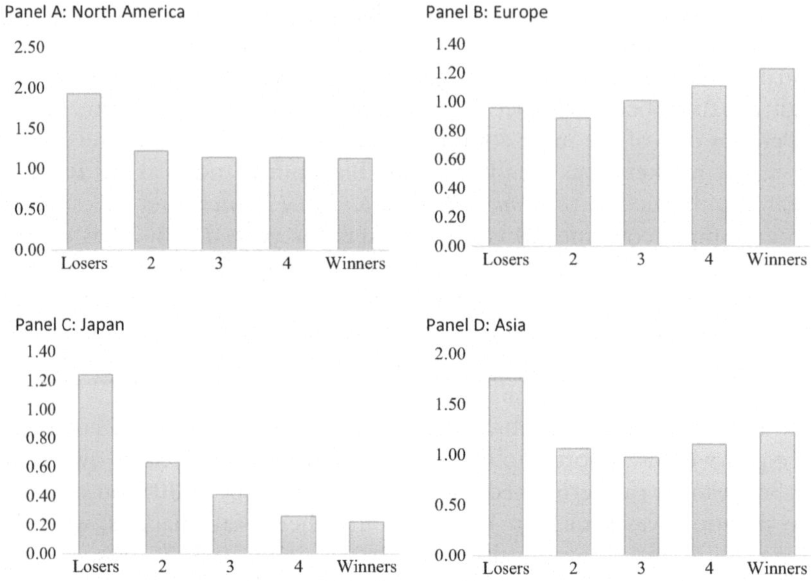

Fig. 3.2 Monthly returns on portfolios of stocks from sorts on long-run returns. (Note: The figure displays mean-monthly returns on equities in four global regions—North America, Europe, Japan, and Asia. The portfolios were formed from sorts into quintiles according to their three-year cumulative return measured over the months $t-36$ to $t-1$ with quintile 1 being the portfolio of losers and quintile 5 the portfolio of winners. The breakpoints were determined using the 20, 40, 60, and 80 percentiles of the stocks in the top 90% of the aggregate market capitalization. Time t returns from the equal-weighted and value-weighted portfolios comprising the stocks in each quintile were averaged across all months from 1993 to 2014. The data for the figures and the description was sourced from Table 2 in Blackburn and Cakici (2017))

As their last insight, Blackburn and Cakici (2017) stated that profits from the contrarian strategy are unevenly distributed. The charts for North America or Asia resemble the letter L, rather than any monotonically increasing profits. The conclusion? To benefit from the contrarian strategy, it is not enough to buy losers: we need "super-losers", that is, the companies with truly detrimental past performance that can turn out to be in the 20% of the worst performing stocks in the market.

Explaining the Reversal Effect

While most academics confirm the existence of long-run reversal in equities, the reasons behind it remain still controversial and hotly debatable. As for most stock market anomalies, we have two dominating theories: the behavioral and the risk approach, with only some slightly helpful marginal explanations concentrating on the measurement error or methodological issues.

The explanation of the long-run reversal effect may be interestingly related to the size and value effect. The first phenomenon relates to the tendency of small companies to outperform large businesses on a risk-adjusted basis. Analogously, the value effect refers to the tendency of stocks with low value-to-fundamental ratios to yield higher returns than the securities where this ratio is higher. Both effects have been long known to both the researchers and market practitioners, being intensively documented and thoroughly researched.[4] Clearly, if a small-business security has low valuation ratios, its price is likely to have recently decreased.[5] Other studies confirm the value and reversal strategy profits to be visibly correlated (Asness et al. 2013), and the long-run reversal payoffs to be an important component of the small-cap strategy. Therefore, the hypotheses explaining the reversal, value, and size effects appear interrelated (Zaremba and Umutlu 2018a).

Let's explore the potential explanations starting with the behavioral approach to the long-run reversal.[6]

Behavioral Mispricing The behavioral justification for the long-run reversal came forward directly after its discovery (Lakonishok et al. 1994). In essence, the theory indicated that the abnormal stock returns of the losers relative to the winners resulted from behavioral mispricing and investor irrationality. The mispricing results from a series of behavioral biases held by market participants, the most important of which is probably the so-called judgmental bias. This stems from the overreaction of investors who

[4] The two anomalies have been initially described in seminal papers of Basu (1983), Banz (1981), and Rosenberg et al. (1985). A comprehensive discussion and review of literature could be found in Zaremba and Shemer (2017).

[5] For further discussion of the relationship between size and long-run reversal, see Zarowin (1989, 1990).

[6] These issues have been also discussed and are partially sourced from Zaremba and Shemer (2017).

in their predictions too optimistically (or pessimistically) extrapolate either the past trends in prices or the fundamentals, like sales or earnings growth. According to this theory, winner companies with the good past record become overpriced, as investors expect the nice return to continue in the future. The overpricing should be reflected in the inflated valuation ratios making the long-run reversal closely related to the value vs. growth effect. In consequence, the firms with the lowest past record should become undervalued, also displaying low valuation ratios.

Having concentrated on value investing, Lakonishok et al. (1994) identified data patterns supporting the behavioral hypothesis: growth stocks displaying higher growth rates, yet tending to revert to the mean within years; analogously, while value stock grows slower, the growth stocks quickly accelerate. Summing up, there are real differences in growth rates between growth and values stocks, being, however, insufficient to justify the spread in the valuation ratios. The behavioral bias affects particularly less professional individual investors who are more prone to such psychological traps. Consistently, the profitability of value strategies is higher across stocks with low institutional ownership (Phalippou 2004).

The mispricing phenomenon resulting from the extrapolation biases could be subsequently amplified by agency problems. Stock market analysts, in their pursuit of commissions, try to persuade customers into buying stocks using good past performance and growth rates as a winning argument (Chan et al. 1995). Moreover, most winner and growth stocks come from the "shiny" and exciting industries, like new technologies, which attract a lot of media attention and analyst's coverage (Bhushan 1989; Jegadeesh et al. 2004) Thus, professional money managers gravitating toward glamorous growth stocks may fall for such investments lured by the potential benefits to their future careers.

Although such fad-induced mispricing may last for years (Shleifer and Vishny 1997), the valuation gap eventually closes: the earnings announcements awake the investors to the truth about the company's potential and its growth prospects, helping thus the prices move toward their "intrinsic value" (La Porta et al. 1997).

Another explanation of the value premium within the behavioral strain has been offered by Barberis and Huang (2001), who identified two psychological biases: mental accounting and loss aversion. The concept of loss aversion implies that investors suffer more from losses than they rejoice from equivalent gains making a series of losses a particularly painfully distressing experience for all stock market investors.[7] Additionally, biased by mental accounting, investors consider the performance of stocks in their portfolios individually, rather than considering the overall gains and losses across the entire portfolio. According to Barberis and Huang, the undervaluation of the loser stocks, or value stocks, may result from a very poor prior performance. The investors, regarding the stocks with dismal prior returns riskier, demand higher returns on their investments. In other words, what triggers the premium for the long-run losers is not the objective risk, but the risk perceived by investors influenced by the behavioral biases. This explanation is consistent with the observations of De Bondt and Thaler (1985) who have found the performance of value stocks correlated with the returns on companies that suffered long-term losses over past four to six years.

The behavioral explanation of stock market anomalies brings another implication: the mispricing resulting from reversals premium should be particularly high in the periods of levered investor irrationality, that is, following the times of high investor sentiment. This was proven by Baker and Wurgler in 2006 and subsequently an analogous pattern was identified by me at the country level (Zaremba 2016), having examined it with regard to the equity valuations: there too returns on the markets with low valuation multiples scored particularly high in comparison to the "growth countries" in months when the investor sentiment was high.

Finally, an interesting experiment was also performed by Du (2011) although indirectly linked to the long-term reversal, and more oriented toward the value effects. Having jointly tested the two competing explanations of the value premium, the risk compensation hypothesis and the investor sentiment story, Du found that while the value premium did correlate with the investor sentiment, it only loosely related to the state of economy. The researcher finally, concluded the notion of value premium resulting from risk difficult to disapprove.[8]

The Risk Story Another set of explanations refer to risk, notably with some authors arguing that the fluctuations in expected returns may stem from

[7] For further explanation of the concepts of loss aversion and mental accounting, see Szyszka (2013).

[8] This observation was later confirmed for the international markets by Chaves et al. (2012). On the contrary, Chui et al. (2013) found the behavior of the value premium consistent with the risk-based explanation but failed to support the mispricing hypothesis.

either the uncertainty of future economic conditions and the probability of survival in the event of economic depressions or military conflicts. Even more importantly, the long-run reversal appears also closely related to the value premium. In consequence, a review the risk-based hypothesis behind the value premium may provide some interesting insights in the search for the origins of the long-run reversal.

The risk-based explanation for the value effect was first laid out by Fama and French in their famous paper of 1992. The authors argued the reason behind the low price of value stocks to be bankruptcy risk; in other words, value companies were to be more prone to encounter financial distress.[9]

To some extent, the risk story has been since supported by the data: value portfolios, and frequently also the closely correlated long-run losers, do tend to lean heavily on the financially distressed stocks whereas the value stocks are more exposed to credit risk, making the value premium substantially influenced by the financial leverage (Ozdagli 2012; Cao 2015a).[10] Nonetheless, this explanation faces one problem: in practice, distressed stocks underperform the market. With ample evidence of high distress risk being in fact associated with lower returns (Dichev 1998; Griffin and Lemmon 2002; Piotroski 2000; Campbell et al. 2008), a research by de Groot and Huij (2011) indicated that contrary to popular beliefs value portfolios sometimes overweighted the least distressed stocks—and not only the most distressed ones.

Digging deeper into the value premium, which is closely linked with the long-run reversal, we will see that the non-market risk borne by companies may also be related to investments and production technologies used in business. This concept was further explored by Cochrane (1991, 1996), Zhang (2006), and Garlappi and Song (2013) who researched asset pricing framework in production companies. According to their findings, value firms are heavily burdened with hard assets and unproductive capital, which may turn against them in harsh economic periods during which they cannot easily and quickly divest by closing factories or selling unproductive assets. This lack of flexibility may translate into serious losses or even default. Growth firms, on the other hand, rely more on human

[9] For further discussion, see also Fama and French (1996).

[10] See Kang and Kang (2009), Avramov et al. (2013), Elgammal and McMillan (2014), Janssen (2014), Choi (2013), or Blitz et al. (2014b).

capital and intangible assets,[11] and as it is easier to dismiss a high-salary employee than to sell a factory, the underlying structure of production companies poses a fundamental risk which should be compensated with additional risk premium.[12]

Another interpretation of the non-market risk was offered by Doukas et al. (2004), who suggested that the risk could arise from the divergence of opinions on the company's future among market participants. When the investors substantially disagree about the company's prospects, the investment may seem riskier than in the case of a universal market consensus. Subsequently, however, the idea was challenged by Shon and Zhou (2010), who used the dispersion among analysts' forecasts as the proxy for testing the divergence of opinions. Surprisingly, they found firms with greater exposure to divergent opinions earning no higher excess and, historically, earning even slightly lower returns. These findings questioned the initial claim that divergence of opinions might really help explain the value premium.

The risk story causes ripples also at the country level. Undoubtedly, international investors face numerous risks of expropriation, currency devaluation, coups, or regulatory changes (Bekaert et al. 1996; Dahlquist and Bansal 2002a) which—due to their nature—are not fully reflected in the volatility of returns. A solid block of academic evidence suggests that these risks are, in fact, priced in. The markets considered riskier in terms of political, country, or economic risk are indeed associated with higher returns.[13] Exploring it further, Erb et al. (1996a, b) confirmed that riskier countries display lower price-to-book and price-to-earnings ratios, and higher dividend yields.

Besides the risk explanations more or less directly related to the "value vs. growth" phenomenon, a few are linked explicitly to the behavior of prices. Although many old models of the financial market, including those used by De Bondt and Thaler, assumed the risk level to remain unchanged between the period of portfolio ranking and formation, and the test (evaluation) period, it may not be true. Chan (1988) and Ball and Kothari (1989) challenged this view indicating that if a stock experienced a series

[11] The importance of human capital in explaining the value premium was also the subject of investigations by Hansson (2004), Santos and Veronesi (2006), Jank (2014), and Sylvain (2014).

[12] For further discussion, see also Carlson et al. (2004) and Cooper (2006).

[13] For further discussion on this issue, see Ferson and Harvey (1994), Erb et al. (1995, 1996a, b), Bekaert et al. (1996), Dahlquist and Bansal (2002a), Harvey (2004), Andrade (2009), and Zaremba (2016b, c).

of serious negative returns, it was likely to become riskier. The betas increasing from the rank period to the test period could imply higher future expected returns. Consistent with this hypothesis, these authors observed changes in betas over the study period which once accounted for significantly impeded the performance of the long-run reversal strategy, casting doubt on its economic significance.

In addition, Ball and Kothari (1989) have concentrated on the changes in leverage and argued that the negative serial correlation in returns is entirely driven by the time-series variation in risk. Their argument? A stock beta is closely related to leverage: the higher the leverage, the higher the beta. Moreover, a company's market value is a function of its stock price: if the stock price has been decreasing for a long time with no new stocks issued, the company's market value is certain to fall. If at the same time the debt remains constant, the leverage has to increase, increasing in turn both the beta and the expected return. In short, the longer and more severe the streak of past negative returns, the higher the future returns.

The arguments of Chan (1988), Ball and Kothari (1989) were hardly in line with the overreaction story of De Bondt and Thaler (1985, 1987). The two conflicting sides were reconciled by the work of Jones (1993), who indicated that the simple leverage cannot fully account for the changes in expected returns. His research showed that the risk exposures of stocks are asymmetric in bull and bear markets: tending to be higher in the up markets and lower in down markets. According to Jones, this pattern may also contribute to the mean-reversion phenomenon, being consistent with the rational time-varying expected returns.

Microstructure Effects Mean reversion, among many stock market anomalies, has been attempted to be explained with the microstructure issues. The overreaction hypothesis was applied for this purpose by Kaul and Nimalendrum (1990) and Conrad and Kaul (1993) who claimed the overreaction was caused by measurement errors in prices stemming from the bid-ask spreads. The authors indicated that the loser companies were smaller and had lower nominal prices than the large ones, so the changes of non-trading were higher. This may turn to totally spurious autocorrelation. Another caveat was added by Ball et al. (1995a), who observed that the loser stocks picked by De Bondt and Thaler were usually low priced, making them exceptionally sensitive to liquidity and microstructure effects. They also noticed the outcomes of De Bondt and Thaler (1985) to be sensitive to the selection of the formation month, in this case, December, while the selection of a different month, for instance, June or August, could make the results inconsistent with the overreaction hypothesis.

January Effect As already indicated it in the momentum section, the January effect is a tendency of stocks to perform in January, when small companies, in particular, tend to outperform the large ones. Interestingly, there is a lot of research implying that the January effect arises not only in stocks, but also across some strategies, of which the long-term reversal might be one.[14] In fact, Zarowin (1990) observed the return differential to exist only in January, whereas Conrad and Kaul (1998) having implemented a buy-and-hold strategy argued any abnormal returns in January arose due to the January effect. To conclude, the overreaction may be somehow driven, or at least biased, by some seasonal anomalies.

Survivorship Bias Survivorship bias is the distortion in results occurring when only the surviving companies are investigated. It is, in fact, a common problem in testing investment strategies as investors look only at those strategies that exist and ignore the ones that are no longer present in the market (due to delisting or bankruptcy). This may significantly contribute to the alleged overperformance of the loser stocks. How? Let us imagine a company undergoing serious financial problems: its standing deteriorates, the stock price plunges, and the bankruptcy seems looming ahead. As the company stock price is plummeting, it reaches ridiculously low valuation ratios, as no one wants to overpay for a company doomed to disappear from the market. If the situation improves, the prices may bounce back earning its investors substantial returns. On the other hand, if the company does go bankrupt, it drops out of the existing sample. We have a win-win situation: the worst market losers either recover or we disregard their performance, theoretically making money either way; in real life, however, we do lose when the company eventually goes under. The survivorship bias can significantly contribute to the long-run reversal (Loughran and Ritter 1996; Pepelas 2008) and, in more general terms, to the value premium (Banz and Breen 1986; Kothari et al. 1995).[15] In the most extreme cases, the value effect may even be completely eradicated by the survivorship bias.

[14] See, for example, Zarowin (1990), Pettengill and Jordan (1990), Jegadeesh (1991), Chopra et al. (1992), and Conrad and Kaul (1993).

[15] Importantly, it may influence not only stock returns but also, for example, funds. See, for example, Carpenter and Lynch (1999) for discussion.

One way of tackling the survivorship bias is to exclude a reasonable amount of time before the bankruptcy. For instance, Lakonishok et al. (1994) adhered to five years of prior data to classify their returns, additionally focusing on the 50% of the largest NYSE and AMEX companies, which were less affected by the bias (La Porta 1996). The authors found that the survivorship bias distorted the results, but it was far from being the main factor driving the performance. This is true for both long-run reversal (Loughran and Ritter 1996) and the value strategies. In fact, even in the emerging or frontier markets, the survivorship bias does not completely wipe out profitability of the value strategy. For example, Anghel et al. (2015) carefully examined the returns from the Romanian market having accounted for the survivorship bias, to conclude that the value portfolios consistently outperformed the growth socks. However, slightly less optimistic conclusions were reached by Andrikopoulos et al. (2006), who examined the UK equity market for the period 1987–2002. Having employed a different approach to Lakonishok's and utilized a survivorship-bias-free database including both listed and delisted stocks, they accounted for losses whenever a company went bankrupt. Once accounted for various statistical biases, including the survivorship bias, the researchers found the performance of value strategies deteriorating so much that the strategies proved no longer significant whether statistically or economically. Even if their results may be period specific, and the survivorship bias does not fully explain the value premium, it most certainly contributes to it and its potential influence should not be ignored. In essence, the results informative of the value premium are also promising for the closely linked long-run reversal effect.

Data Mining The last valid explanation of the long-run reversal effect says that there simply is no effect. The recent years have brought an array of studies on cross-sectional patterns in returns and alleged predictive signals of future payoffs. The research was at least partially driven by the investing industry as the results could be easily used as a springboard for higher salaries and bonuses. In 2016, Harvey et al. reviewed over 300 asset pricing factors from the equity universe documented in the top-tier academic journal. A year later, Hou, Xue, and Zhang extended the number of return regularities to over 400, giving only two examples of the large-scale review studies![16] Thus, this should hardly be surprising that

[16] For other studies reviewing a large number of anomalies, see Hou et al. (2011, 2015, 2016), Green et al. (2016), Jacobs and Müller (2017a, b), Zaremba (2016, 2017), Zaremba and Nikorowski (2017), and Zaremba and Andreu Sánchez (2017).

some of these return patterns are simply random phenomena emerging from data mining, as suggested by the infinite monkey theorem: if a bunch of monkeys pound on a typewriter, one will eventually compose Hamlet. The researchers Dimson and Marsh (1999) call it a Murphy's law of equity anomalies: once discovered, their profitability tends to evaporate.[17]

The phenomenon, whether down to the exploitation of the anomaly by professional investors, or due to false conclusions, presents a real challenge to the value anomaly. Acknowledging this, the researchers Lo and MacKinlay (1990) argued that data mining may lie behind some stock market anomalies, including the long-run reversal.

While this seems improbable, it is possible. The reversal strategy also has its weaknesses. The seminal studies of De Bondt and Thaler (1985) were carried out over a limited period: 1930–1977. The study of Blackburn and Cakici (2017) never delivered extremely optimistic results. Regarded as out-of-sample in both geographical and time-series terms, as it included both the countries and time periods that have never been researched before, it proved the reversal anomaly almost non-existent in Europe in the post-1990 period, and invisible in the value-weighted portfolios. Importantly, this phenomenon was not limited to individual equities. While early studies, for example, Balvers and Wu (2006), clearly identified the long-run reversal, in 2016, Zaremba demonstrated that over the last two decades the effect remained entirely unprofitable!

Notably, the disappointing performance of the long-run reversal could also be extended to the value effect. The seminal studies of Fama and French (1992, 1993) covered only a period of 28 years (1963–1991) for a single equity, opening up the possibility of a unique period of value stocks' abnormal returns. Indeed, a study by Israel and Moskowitz (2013) comprehensively examined value premium over a much longer period (1927–2011) only to identify the premium within the small-cap and mid-cap companies, proving the abnormal returns on value stocks insignificant among the largest 40% of the NYSE companies. Furthermore, having examined the subperiods, they found that the two largest quantiles exhibiting no reliable value premium in three out of four investigated subperiods. In fact, the value strategy performed well in large caps only within the 1970–1989 period, which coincides with the findings of Fama and French (1992, 1993).

Another Achilles' heel of the Fama and French (1992, 1993) studies was pointed out by Kothari et al. (1995), who examined a similar sample

[17] See also McLean and Pontiff (2016) and Jacobs and Müller (2017a).

using a different data source, interestingly, finding no evidence of any significant positive relation between the book-to-market ratio and the expected returns, leading him to conclude that the value premium could have simply emerged from the selection bias.

One of the deadliest blows to the value premium was finally delivered by Fama and French (2015). In a five-factor asset pricing model, the researchers successfully replaced the value factor with a combination of profitability and investment intensity, which suggested the value premium to be no anomaly per se, but rather a manifestation of other phenomena in the market.

To be fair, given the current state of research, we should admit that considering all the anomalies and asset pricing factors, the value premium is hardly the effect of data mining. The strongest proof is its pervasiveness. Having been identified across numerous stock markets and asset classes (Asness et al. 2013), the criticism raising the outperformance of the value stocks as a merely random event must be considered at least audacious, if not outright implausible.

Summing up, the existing academic evidence offers a few reasonable explanations of the long-run reversal anomaly. While the debate to what extent each contributes to the effect is still ongoing, the existence of this phenomenon is certainly theoretically justifiable.

Improving the Reversal Strategies

Having now investigated both the theoretical and empirical evidence for the long-run reversal, we can focus on the ways it can be further improved.

Optimize the Sorting Period The long-run reversal could be approached with various sorting periods. Most studies use ranking periods ranging from 36 to 60 months, with the 12 most recent months skipped. Although the exact results might differ in various studies, as a rule, the reversal effect emerges until the 60th month as proved also by Zaremba and Umutlu (2018b, c) who found a stronger outperformance of loser indices over winner indices in the 60-month sorting period (with the usual last 12 months dropped).

Focus on the Less-Efficient Markets Similarly to the momentum strategy, as an anomaly, the long-run reversal should appear stronger in the less informationally efficient market segments, that is, covered by few analysts, less investigated by sophisticated institutional investors, or simply less interesting to the general public. How to select the less efficient segments? At least two approaches seem justifiable based on the research of McLean (2010) who double-sorted the equities following the long-term return and idiosyncratic volatility. The stocks with high-idiosyncratic volatility having varied significantly from the market benchmark could not be used for efficient hedge against the market risk, while according to McLean (2010) the reversal effect worked almost solely in these stocks characterized by high-idiosyncratic risk. Having researched a sample of US equities for years 1965–2004, he discovered that the long-run losers outperformed the long-term winners by 1.241 percentage points in the quintile of the riskiest stocks. However, within the safest stocks, the return differential turned even slightly negative. Clearly, the long-term reversal works almost only for the stocks of high-idiosyncratic volatility.

Another proxy for efficiency is size. Paraphrasing Hong et al. (2000), in small stocks, news travel slowly (Fig. 3.3). It was also proved true for the long-reversal by Blackburn and Cakici (2017), summarized in Fig. 3.4.

Clearly, the long-run reversion effect originates from the smallest stock. Apart from Europe, where the anomaly was non-existent, the long-term reversal was driven almost solely by the smallest stocks in the market, having an important implication for, for example, portfolio construction. When implementing the long-term return strategy, using equal-weighted portfolios appears more reasonable, as they tend to overweight small companies which has been is also confirmed by Blackburn and Cakici (2017).

Empirical Test of Long-Run Reversal

Within the long-run reversal universe we tested the most fundamental *long-run reversal* strategy by sorting equities on the mean-monthly return in the trailing 60 months skipping the most recent 12 months. In other words, for each month we calculated the mean return in months t–60 to t–13 and sorted them accordingly. Subsequently, as in the case of momentum strategies, we formed quintile portfolios and assumed long position in the portfolio of stocks with the lowest historical return and the short position in the portfolio with the highest historical return. The results of this simple exercise across all the examined countries are reported in Table 3.1.

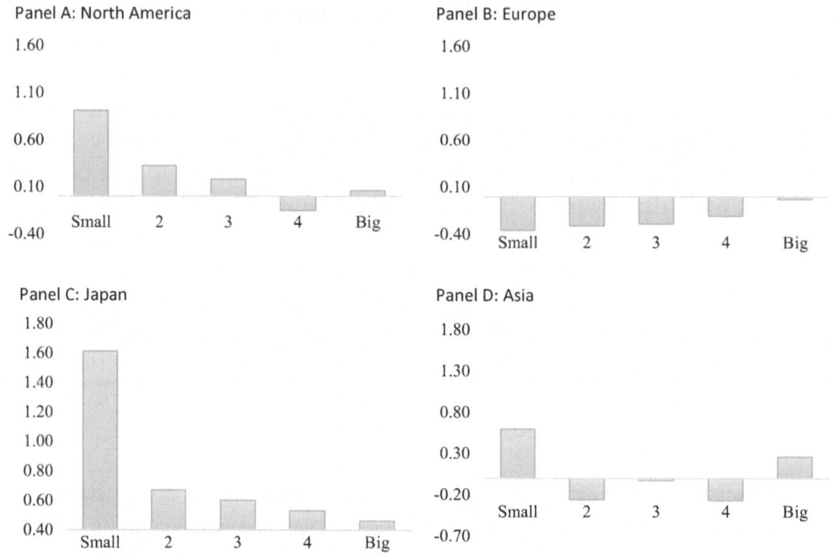

Fig. 3.3 Monthly returns on long-short portfolios of stocks from sorts on long-run returns within various size quantiles. (Note: The figure displays mean-monthly returns on equities in four global regions: North America, Europe, Japan, and Asia. This table reports the equal-weighted returns of portfolios formed by the independent double sort by market capitalization long-term return, that is, the three-year cumulative return measured over $t-36$ to $t-1$. REV breakpoints are determined using the 20%, 40%, 60%, and 80% percentiles of the 90% of stocks in the top 90% of aggregate market cap within the region. Size breakpoints are determined using the 3%, 7%, 13%, and 25% breakpoints of all the firms within the region. The sorts are conducted independently. The long-short portfolios are long (short) in the stocks with the lowest (highest) long-run returns. The data for the figures and the description is sourced from Table 6 in Blackburn and Cakici (2017))

The results proved faintly optimistic: the long-run reversal strategy yielded some profits, yet only in a few countries. In the USA, the long-short portfolio produced a mean-monthly return of 0.42% and a modestly significant alpha of 0.38%. Also, the Japanese mean payoffs and alphas were both significant and positive, equaling 0.51% in both cases while the third exception was Denmark with the long-short portfolios yielding 0.8% per month, but the long-horizon reversal strategy failed in all of the other covered countries.

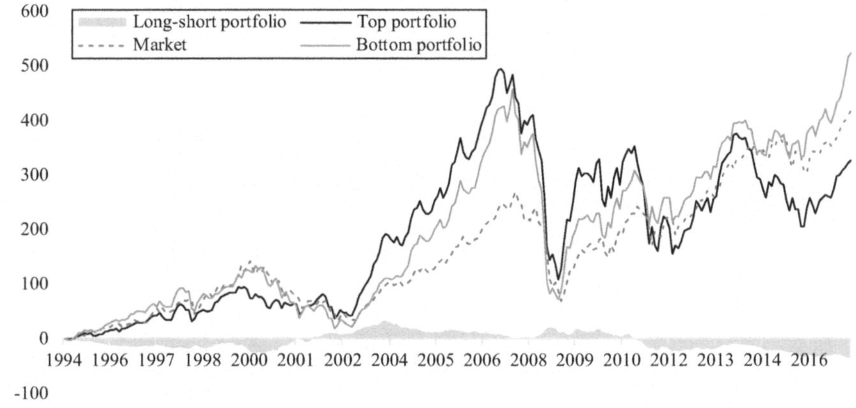

Fig. 3.4 Cumulative return on equal-weighted portfolios formed on long-run returns. (Note: The figure displays the cumulative return on equal-weighted quantile portfolios from sorts on the 60-month average return with the 12 most recent months skipped. The calculations were made on the basis of monthly observations. *Top portfolio* and *bottom portfolio* are quintile portfolios including the stocks with the worst and the best long-run performance, respectively. *T-B portfolio* is the portfolio long in the *top* portfolio and short in the *bottom* portfolio. Market is the value-weighted portfolio of all the country equity markets considered. All the returns are expressed in percentage)

Interestingly, however, disappointing, our results only slightly departed from the earlier evidence. For example, Blackburn and Cakici (2017) also found the reversal strategy particularly strong in the USA and Japan, with little evidence in other countries.

As the strategy proved profitable in two distinct markets, the USA and Japan, only the value-weighted global long-short portfolio displayed significant and positive mean-monthly returns, albeit very modest, amounting to only 0.25% per month, yet still positive. On the other hand, the equal-weighted returns displayed profits indistinguishable from zero.

Figures 3.4 and 3.5 present cumulative return on the equal-weighted and value-weighted global portfolios, respectively. Again, the cumulative returns on the value-weighted long-short strategies were positive, though modest, amounting to over 80%. On the other, the long-short equal-weighted strategies proved to deliver small losses.

In summary, while the performance of the long-run strategy yielded initially promising results, the recent performance proved somewhat

Table 3.1 The performance of international portfolios formed on long-run returns

Country	*Top portfolio mean return*	*Bottom portfolio mean return*	*Average number of firms*	*T-B portfolio*		*Standard deviation*	*Sharpe ratio*	*Beta*	*Alpha*	
				Mean return	*t-stat*				*Value*	*t-stat*
Australia	0.98	0.60	35	0.38	*(1.43)*	4.41	0.30	−0.04	0.41	*(1.52)*
Austria	0.66	1.01	5	−0.35	*(−0.55)*	10.44	−0.12	0.11	−0.41	*(−0.64)*
Belgium	1.10	0.92	9	0.18	*(0.57)*	5.11	0.12	−0.05	0.21	*(0.68)*
Canada	0.95	0.59	71	0.35	*(1.19)*	4.88	0.25	−0.08	0.41	*(1.36)*
Denmark	1.50	0.70	10	0.80**	*(2.49)*	5.28	0.53	0.00	0.80**	*(2.46)*
Finland	1.08	1.60	9	−0.52	*(−1.42)*	5.96	−0.30	−0.05	−0.47	*(−1.28)*
France	0.90	1.09	38	−0.19	*(−0.75)*	4.15	−0.16	0.06	−0.23	*(−0.89)*
Germany	0.77	0.90	32	−0.13	*(−0.53)*	4.10	−0.11	−0.02	−0.12	*(−0.49)*
Greece	0.26	0.49	10	−0.22	*(−0.28)*	13.34	−0.06	0.08	−0.23	*(−0.28)*
Hong Kong	−0.21	0.71	18	−0.92**	*(−1.98)*	7.62	−0.42	0.06	−0.97**	*(−2.07)*
Ireland	−0.40	1.39	3	−1.80**	*(−2.46)*	12.00	−0.52	−0.13	−1.71**	*(−2.33)*
Israel	1.03	0.74	11	0.28	*(0.56)*	8.33	0.12	−0.03	0.29	*(0.58)*
Italy	0.42	0.91	21	−0.49*	*(−1.66)*	4.88	−0.35	0.05	−0.52*	*(−1.75)*
Japan	0.63	0.12	282	0.51**	*(2.26)*	3.71	0.48	−0.03	0.51**	*(2.26)*
The Netherlands	0.84	1.02	15	−0.18	*(−0.63)*	4.63	−0.13	−0.03	−0.16	*(−0.57)*
New Zealand	0.23	1.14	3	−0.91*	*(−1.92)*	7.78	−0.41	−0.05	−0.87*	*(−1.82)*

Norway	0.44	0.88	10	−0.44	*(−1.11)*	6.57	−0.23	0.08	−0.50	*(−1.25)*
Portugal	0.50	0.76	3	−0.26	*(−0.56)*	7.59	−0.12	−0.06	−0.24	*(−0.52)*
Singapore	0.34	0.28	9	0.06	*(0.15)*	6.49	0.03	−0.03	0.08	*(0.20)*
Spain	0.63	0.94	15	−0.31	*(−0.98)*	5.15	−0.21	0.04	−0.34	*(−1.07)*
Sweden	1.21	1.13	19	0.08	*(0.27)*	4.80	0.06	0.03	0.05	*(0.17)*
Switzerland	1.23	0.89	24	0.34	*(1.48)*	3.72	0.31	0.07	0.28	*(1.24)*
UK	0.80	0.61	90	0.19	*(0.92)*	3.39	0.19	0.02	0.18	*(0.87)*
USA	1.26	0.84	526	0.42**	*(2.03)*	3.39	0.43	0.06	0.38*	*(1.81)*
World (EW)	0.71	0.84	1269	−0.13	*(−0.92)*	2.32	−0.19	−0.03	−0.12	*(−0.81)*
World (VW)	0.90	0.65	1269	0.25*	*(1.69)*	2.47	0.36	0.03	0.24	*(1.56)*

Note: The table reports the monthly returns on the portfolios from sorts on the 60-month average return with 12 most recent months skipped. The calculations were made on the basis of monthly observations. ***Top portfolio*** and ***bottom portfolio*** are quintile portfolios including the stocks with the worst and the best long-run performance, respectively. ***T-B portfolio*** is the portfolio long in the ***top*** portfolio and short in the ***bottom*** portfolio. The Sharpe ratio is expressed on an annualized basis. The alpha and beta are derived from the CAPM. Mean returns, standard deviations, and alphas are expressed in percentage. Asterisks *, **, and *** indicate values significantly different from zero at the 10%, 5%, and 1% levels, respectively

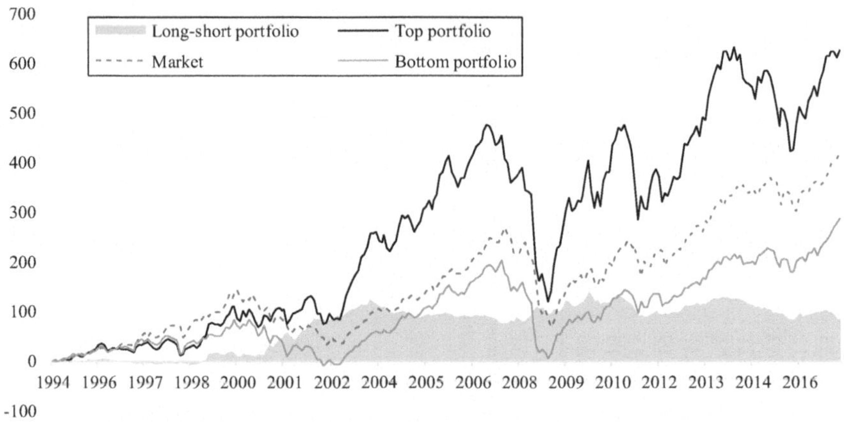

Fig. 3.5 Cumulative return on the value-weighted portfolios formed on the long-run return. (Note: The figure displays the cumulative return on the value-weighted quantile portfolios from sorts on the 60-month average return with the 12 most recent months skipped. The calculations were made on the basis of monthly observations. *Top portfolio* and *bottom portfolio* are quintile portfolios including the stocks with the worst and the best long-run performance, respectively. *T-B portfolio* is the portfolio long in the *top* portfolio and short in the *bottom* portfolio. Market is the value-weighted portfolio of all the country equity markets considered. All the returns are expressed in percentage)

mixed. Our own analysis, in line with the latest research papers, confirmed the long-term reversal to emerge only in some markets over last two decades, luckily, also the largest ones: the USA and Japan.

Having explored the long-run reversal strategy, it is now time to examine its short-term relative: namely, short-run reversal.

Short-Term Reversal: A Younger Cousin?

When adopting a really long-term approach of multiple years, we can see stocks reverse: with long-run losers turning into winners and initial winners degrading to losers. In the medium term of 12 months, however, continuation, or as we call it here, momentum, rules the roost. The top performing stocks continue to dominate, and the laggards generally lag behind. So which trend do we see in an even shorter term: continuation or reversal? In the shortest run, the stock returns appear to … reverse again.

The short-term reversal anomaly belongs to the oldest patterns discovered in equity markets. While the evidence could be traced back to Fama (1965), the seminal study was conducted by Lehmann in 1990. In his paper titled "Fads, Martingales, and Market Efficiency", he examined returns in the US equity market for years 1934 to 1987. Lehmann simply ranked the securities on their returns in the most recent week. Subsequently, he formed an artificial portfolio that was held over next seven days and repeated the operation every week. What Lehmann (1990) found was that the losers and winners displayed a sizable return reversal the following week. The stocks with positive returns (winners) in the most recent week typically recorded negative returns in the following week (ranging on average from −0.35% to −0.55% per week). Conversely, those with negative returns (losers) in the prior week typically displayed positive returns in the subsequent week (ranging from 0.86% to 1.24% per week on average). Summing up, a contrarian strategy based on a zero-investment portfolio which is long on both past losers and past winners generated abnormal returns of over 2% per month. A very similar research to Lehmann's (1990) was later conducted by Jegadeesh (1990), who proved the short-term reversal effective also within a monthly horizon, that is, applying both a monthly ranking period and a monthly holding period.

The short-term reversal effect was later verified in the US equity market in alternative samples and time periods. The evidence was very supportive, confirming the tendency of recent losers to outperform recent winners.[18] Furthermore, Jacobs and Müller (2017b) later reexamined the anomaly in an extensive sample of 44 country stock markets for the years 1989–2015. The research confirmed the effectiveness of the strategy both in developed and emerging markets. Subsequent research indicates that the short-run reversal exists not only on the level of individual stocks, but it could also be implemented across industries. In other words, the industries that performed particularly well (poor) over the last month are likely to turn into the next month losers (winners) (Hameed and Mian 2015).[19]

[18] Campbell et al. (1993), Ball et al. (1995a), Conrad et al. (1997), Da and Schaumburg (2007), Avramov et al. (2006a, b), Huang et al. (2010), de Groot et al. (2012), Nagel (2012), Da et al. (2011, 2014a), and Cakici and Topyan (2014).

[19] We should admit here the existence of some evidence casting doubt on the presence of the short-term reversal effect. In particular, in less developed and frontier markets the short-term reversal effect tends to transform into short-term continuation (Zaremba and Szyszka 2016; Zaremba and Czapkiewicz 2017; Zaremba 2017).

Why would this strategy work? Why would the most recent winners underperform the losers and so clearly contradict the momentum framework? As usual, one reason is rooted in behavioral finance, while the other in the underlying risk factors which initially might not appear obvious. The behavioral explanation, supported by Shiller (1984), Black (1986), Stiglitz (1989), Summers and Summers (1989), and Subrahmanyam (2005), indicates that the payoffs to the short-run reversal stem from investor overreactions, fads, and other cognitive biases. For example, if the news of an attractive merger or exceptional contract stirs the market, investors flock to buy the stocks, elevating the price. In the following month, the arbitrageurs step in selling the stocks and restoring the equilibrium. Analogously, when in one month investors sell a stock too rapidly, it becomes undervalued in the eyes of more rational investors who, in turn, buy it, causing a price increase the following month. This explanation focuses on behavior, or sentiment, driven factors.

The Other Perspective Concentrates on Risk In essence, it refers to the price pressure that can occur when the short-term demand curve of a stock is downward sloping and/or the supply curve is upward sloping (see, e.g., Grossman and Miller 1988 or Jegadeesh and Titman 1995). For example, according to Campbell et al. (1993), uninformed trades lead to a temporary price concession that, when absorbed by liquidity providers, leads to a reversal in price that serves as compensation for those who provide liquidity. To put it simply, there is a group of investors who in bad times will lend the stockholders a hand and purchase the stocks they would like to get rid of as quickly as possible. This help, however, comes at a price. The helping buyers never want to overpay, and charge for providing the liquidity. In the subsequent month, when the market stress is over, the prices are likely to re-emerge, allowing the liquidity providers to capitalize their profits.

Consistent with this mechanism, Avramov et al. (2006a, b) argued that the short-run reversal strategy profits result mainly from positions in illiquid and small stocks. Furthermore, Pastor and Stambaugh (2003) suggested even directly measuring illiquidity by the occurrence of the initial price change and subsequent reversal.

Interestingly, the two explanations are not necessarily mutually exclusive which entails further questioning. For example, if the overreaction to new information drives the reversal, then it would be interesting to identify the type of information. Analogously, if the reversal results from liquidity shocks, one would like to know the absolute and relative natures of such shocks. In this context, an interesting exercise was conducted by Da et al. (2011), who decomposed the profits from the short-term reversal strategy into four components related to (a) inter-industry return momentum, (b) within-industry variation in expected returns, (c) underreaction to within-industry cash flow shocks, and (d) a residual component. By focusing on the residual return, these authors were able to isolate the true driver of return reversal, substantially improving the performance of the strategy. Within their sample of US stocks for the period from 1982 to 2009, the residual-based short-term reversal strategy—assuming sorting stocks based on the prior-month residual return—delivered a monthly alpha of 1.34% with a highly significant *t*-statistic of 9.28. This abnormal return was particularly impressive given that their sample included predominantly large and liquid stocks covered by an equity analyst. For comparison, the classical reversal strategy generated a monthly alpha of mere 0.33% insignificantly differing from zero. Da et al. (2011) having conducted a few further tests concluded that not only was the reversal effect much stronger than previously reported, but it also stemmed from a dual source: driven by liquidity shocks on the long side and by investor overreaction on the short side.

The short-run reversal strategy seems sufficiently documented and supported by at least two credible explanations. The natural extending question should be, then, can we improve it even further? Indeed, the finance literature offers us a few tricks to enhance the short-run reversal performance.

Trick 1. Beware of the trading costs. As it was found by Avramov et al. (2006a, b), the reversal profits tend to concentrate in small and illiquid stocks, when bid-ask spreads are likely to be broad and transaction costs elevated. Thus, de Groot et al. (2012) showed that once the trading costs are taken into account, the reversal payoffs are likely to fall markedly. However, limiting the stock universe to only large caps significantly reduces the trading costs. What is more, when you apply some more sophisticated portfolio formation algorithms, the decreased turnover might reduce the trading costs even further, improving the reversal strategy post-cost performance.

Trick 2. Combine reversal with the momentum. Similarly, to the long-run reversal, the short-term reversal could be also efficiently combined with momentum. In particular, Zhu and Yung (2016) documented the magnitude of price reversals of short-term winners and losers as markedly related to the past medium-term performance. In consequence, short-term reversal strategies work best in the momentum-loser quintile whereas momentum strategies excel in the short-term-winner quintile. What Zhu and Yung (2016) have shown is that equity investors could yield higher momentum profits by considering short-term performance.

Trick 3. Consider the volatilities. Wei and Yang (2012) showed the importance of not only size or liquidity, but also stock volatility. For small companies, no reversals are observed when volatilities are higher, and for large stocks, reversals prevail only in low-volatility stocks.[20]

Trick 4. Focus on the residuals. Similarly, to momentum, the short-run reversal may partly result from the returns on the underlying return factors, for example, value or size effects. In other words, the conventional strategy displays dynamic exposures to the classical asset pricing factors. As these factor bets are implicitly and inversely related to the actual factor returns over the formation month, the short-run reversal strategy might be negatively exposed to the short-term momentum effect in factor returns documented by, for example, Moskowitz and Grinblatt (1999), Chen and De Bondt (2004), or Avramov et al. (2017). In consequence, the dynamic factor exposures of a reversal strategy might negatively influence its profitability. To overcome this problem, Blitz et al. (2013a) have introduced a short-term reversal strategy based on residual stock returns which does not only exhibit such dynamic factor exposures but its returns are higher and substantially less volatile than those of a conventional short-term reversal strategy, also maintaining a very stable profitability over time.

The reversal strategies are interesting potential components of an investment portfolio, although their recent results are somewhat mixed. Definitely, although these approaches are based on mean historical returns: the only varying variable is, in this case, sorting horizon. In the next chapter, we will leave the mean aside and focus on the second moment of the return distribution: variance. We will now explore the relation between the risk measures derived from prices and future performance.

[20] See, also, Wei (2011).

References

Ahmad, Z., & Hussain, S. (2001). KLSE long run overreaction and the Chinese New Year effect. *Journal of Business, Finance, and Accounting, 28*(1–2), 63–112.

Ali, N., Nassair, A. M., Hassan, T., & Abidin, S. Z. (2011). Stock overreaction behaviour in Bursa Malaysia: Does the length of formation period matter? *British Journal of Economics Finance and Management Sciences, 2*(2), 42–56.

Alonso, A., & Rubio, G. (1990). Overreaction in the Spanish equity market. *Journal of Banking and Finance, 14*, 469–481.

Andersson, H. (2007). Are commodity prices mean reverting? *Applied Financial Economics, 17*(10), 769–783. https://doi.org/10.1080/09603100600749204.

Andrade, S. C. (2009). A model of asset pricing under country risk. *Journal of International Money and Finance, 28*(4), 671–695.

Andrikopoulos, P., Daynes, A., Latimer, D., & Pagas, P. (2006). The value premium and methodological biases: Evidence from the UK equity market. *Investment Management and Financial Innovation, 3*(1), 40–59.

Anghel, A., Dumitrescu, D., & Tudor, C. (2015). Modeling portfolio returns on Bucharest Stock exchange using the Fama-French multifactor model. *Romanian Journal of Economic Forecasting, 17*(1), 22–46.

Asness, C. S., Moskowitz, T. J., & Pedersen, L. H. (2013). Value and momentum everywhere. *Journal of Finance, 68*(3), 929–985.

Avramov, D., Chordia, T., & Goyal, A. (2006a). Liquidity and autocorrelations in individual stock returns. *Journal of Finance, 61*, 2365–2394.

Avramov, D., Chordia, T., & Goyal, A. (2006b). The impact of trades on daily volatility. *Review of Financial Studies, 19*(4), 1241–1277.

Avramov, D., Chordia, T., Jostova, G., & Philipov, A. (2013). Anomalies and financial distress. *Journal of Financial Economics, 108*(1), 139–159.

Avramov, D., Kaplanski, G., & Levy, H. (2017). *Talking numbers: Technical versus fundamental investment recommendations.* Available at SSRN: https://ssrn.com/abstract=2648292 or https://doi.org/10.2139/ssrn.2648292. Accessed 21 Oct 2017.

Bacmann, J. F., & Dubois, M. (1998). *Contrarian strategies and cross-autocorrelations in stock returns: Evidence from France.* Available at SSRN: https://ssrn.com/abstract=138176 or https://doi.org/10.2139/ssrn.138176. Accessed 23 Oct 2017.

Baker, M., & Wurgler, J. (2006). Investor sentiment and the cross-section of stock returns. *Journal of Finance, 61*(4), 1645–1680.

Bali, T. G., Subrahmanyam, A., & Wen, Q. (2017). *Return-based factors for corporate bonds.* Available at SSRN: https://ssrn.com/abstract=2978861 or https://doi.org/10.2139/ssrn.2978861. Accessed 23 Oct 2017.

Ball, R., & Kothari, S. (1989). Non stationary expected returns: Implications for test of market efficiency and serial correlation in returns. *Journal of Financial Economics, 25*, 51–74.

Ball, R., Kothari, S., & Shanken, J. (1995a). Problems in measuring portfolio performance: An application to contrarian investment strategies. *Journal of Financial Economics, 38*, 79–107.

Balvers, R. J., & Wu, Y. (2006). Momentum and mean reversion across national equity markets. *Journal of Empirical Finance, 13*, 24–48.

Balvers, R., Wu, Y., & Gililand, E. (2000). Mean reversion across national stock markets and parametric contrarian investment strategies. *Journal of Finance, 55*(2), 745–772. https://doi.org/10.1111/0022-1082.00225.

Banz, R. W. (1981). The relationship between return and market value of common stocks. *Journal of Financial Economics, 9*, 3–18.

Banz, R., & Breen, W. (1986). Sample dependent results using accounting and market data: Some evidence. *Journal of Finance, 41*(4), 779–793.

Barberis, N., & Huang, M. (2001). Mental accounting, loss aversion, and individual stock returns. *Journal of Finance, 56*(4), 1247–1292.

Basu, S. (1983). The relationship between earnings yield, market value and return for NYSE common stocks: Further evidence. *Journal of Financial Economics, 12*, 129–156.

Baytas, A., & Cakici, N. (1999). Do markets overreact: International evidence. *Journal of Banking and Finance, 23*, 1121–1144.

Bekaert, G., Erb, C. B., Harvey, C. R., & Viskanta, T. E. (1996). *The cross-sectional determinants of emerging equity market returns.* Retrieved from https://www0.gsb.columbia.edu/faculty/gbekaert/PDF_Papers/The_cross-sectional_determinants.pdf. Accessed 21 Sept 2015.

Bhanot, K. (2005). What causes mean reversion in corporate bond index spreads? The impact of survival. *Journal of Banking and Finance, 29*(6), 1385–1403. https://doi.org/10.1016/j.jbankfin.2004.04.003.

Bhushan, R. (1989). Firm characteristics and analyst following. *Journal of Accounting and Economics, 11*(2–3), 255–274.

Bildik, R., & Gulay, G. (2007). Profitability of contrarian strategy: Evidence from the Istanbul stock exchange. *International Review of Finance, 7*(1–2), 61–87.

Black, F. (1986). Noise. *Journal of Finance, 41*, 529–543.

Blackburn, D. W., & Cakici, N. (2017). Overreaction and the cross-section of returns: International evidence. *Journal of Empirical Finance, 42*, 1–14. https://doi.org/10.1016/j.jempfin.2017.02.001.

Blitz, D., Huij, J., Lansdorp, S., & Verbeek, M. (2013a). Short-term residual reversal. *Journal of Financial Markets, 16*, 477–504.

Blitz, D., Pang, J., & van Vliet, P. (2013b). The volatility effect in emerging markets. *Emerging Markets Review, 16*, 31–45.

Blitz, D., van der Grient, B., & Hanauer, M. (2014b). *What drives the value premium?* (White paper). Robeco. Available at https://www.robeco.com/images/20141016-what-drives-the-value-premium-june-2014.pdf. Accessed 13 Oct 2015.

Bornholt, G., Gharaibeh, O., & Malin, M. (2015). Industry long-term return reversal. *Journal of International Financial Markets, Institutions and Money, 38*, 65–78. https://doi.org/10.1016/j.intfin.2015.05.013.

Brailsford, T. (1992). A test for the winner-loser anomaly in the Australian equity market: 1958–87. *Journal of Business Finance and Accounting, 19*(2), 225–241.

Cakici, N., & Topyan, K. (2014). *Risk and return in Asian emerging markets.* New York: Springer.

Campbell, K., & Limmack, R. J. (1997). Long term overreaction in the UK stock market and size adjustments. *Applied Financial Economics, 7*, 537–548.

Campbell, J., Grossman, S. J., & Wang, J. (1993). Trading volume and serial correlation in stock returns. *Quarterly Journal of Economics, 108*(4), 905–939.

Campbell, C. J., Rhee, S. G., Du, Y., & Tang, N. (2008). *Market sentiment, IPO underpricing, and valuation* (Working paper). Available at SSRN: http://ssrn.com/abstract=1108540 or https://doi.org/10.2139/ssrn.1108540. Accessed 22 Nov 2015.

Cao, V. N. (2015a). What explains the value premium? The case of adjustment costs, operating leverage and financial leverage. *Journal of Banking & Finance, 59*, 350–366.

Cao, X. (2015b). *Are idiosyncratic skewness and idiosyncratic kurtosis priced?* (Brock University working paper). Available at https://dr.library.brocku.ca/handle/10464/6426. Accessed 14 Oct 2017.

Carlson, M., Fisher, A., & Giammarino, R. (2004). Corporate investment and asset price dynamics: Implications for the cross section of returns. *Journal of Finance, 59*(6), 2577–2603.

Carpenter, J. N., & Lynch, A. W. (1999). Survivorship bias and attrition effects in measures of performance persistence. *Journal of Financial Economics, 54*, 337–374.

Chan, K. (1988). On the contrarian investment strategy. *Journal of Business, 61*, 147–163.

Chan, E. P. (2013). Mean reversion of currencies and futures. In *Algorithmic trading: Winning strategies and their rationale.* Hoboken: John Wiley & Sons, Inc. https://doi.org/10.1002/9781118676998.ch5.

Chan, L. K. C., Jegadeesh, N., & Lakonishok, J. (1995). Evaluating the performance of value versus glamour stocks: The impact of selection bias. *Journal of Financial Economics, 38*(3), 269–296.

Chaves, D. B., & Viswanathan, V. (2016). Momentum and mean-reversion in commodity spot and futures markets. *Journal of Commodity Markets, 3*(1), 39–53.

Chaves, D. B., Hsu, J. C., Kalesnik, V., & Shim, Y. (2012). *What drives the value effect? Risk versus mispricing: Evidence from international markets* (Working paper). Available at SSRN: http://ssrn.com/abstract=1940504 or https://doi.org/10.2139/ssrn.1940504. Accessed 23 Oct 2017.

Chen, H. S., & De Bondt, W. (2004). Style momentum within the S&P-500 index. *Journal of Empirical Finance, 11*, 483–507.

Chen, S.-N., & Jeon, K. (1998). Mean reversion behavior of the returns on currency assets. *International Review of Economics & Finance, 7*(2), 185–200. https://doi.org/10.1016/S1059-0560(98)90039-9.

Choi, J. (2013). What drives the value premium? The role of asset risk and leverage. *Review of Financial Studies, 26*(11), 2845–2875.

Chopra, N., Lakonishok, J., & Ritter, J. (1992). Measuring abnormal performance. *Journal of Financial Economics, 31*, 235–268.

Chui, A. C. W., Wei, J. K. C., & Xie, F. (2013). *Explaining the value premium around the world: Risk or mispricing?* (Working paper). Available at http://repository.ust.hk/ir/Record/1783.1-66583

Clare, A., & Thomas, S. (1995, October). The overreaction hypothesis and the UK stock market. *Journal of Business & Accounting, 22*(7), 961–973.

Cochrane, J. H. (1991). Production-based asset pricing and the link between stock returns and economic fluctuations. *Journal of Finance, 46*, 209–237.

Cochrane, J. H. (1996). A cross-sectional test of an investment-based asset pricing model. *Journal of Political Economy, 104*, 572–621.

Conrad, J., & Kaul, G. (1993). Long-term market overreaction or biases in computer returns? *Journal of Finance, 48*(1), 39–63.

Conrad, J., Gultekin, M. N., & Kaul, G. (1997). Profitability of short-term contrarian strategies: Implications for market efficiency. *Journal of Business & Economic Statistics, 15*(3), 379–386. https://doi.org/10.2307/1392341.

Conrad, J., & Kaul, G. (1998). An anatomy of trading strategies. *Review of Financial Studies, 11*(3), 489–519.

Cooper, I. (2006). Asset pricing implications of non-convex adjustment costs and irreversibility of investment. *Journal of Finance, 61*(1), 139–170.

Da Costa, N. C. (1994). Overreaction in the Brazilian stock market. *Journal of Banking and Finance, 18*, 633–642.

Da, Z., & Schaumburg, E. (2007). *Target prices, relative valuations and the premium for liquidity provision* (AFA 2007 Chicago meetings paper). University of Notre Dame.

Da, Z., Liu, Q., & Schaumburg, E. (2011). *Decomposing short-term return reversal* (Federal Reserve Bank of New York staff report No. 513). Available at https://www.newyorkfed.org/medialibrary/media/research/staff_reports/sr513.pdf. Accessed 9 Oct 2017.

Da, Z., Liu, Q., & Schaumburg, E. (2014a). A closer look at the short-term return reversal. *Management Science, 60*, 658–674.

Dahlquist, M., & Bansal, R. (2002a). *Expropriation risk and return in global equity markets* (EFA 2002 Berlin meetings presented paper). Available at

SSRN: http://ssrn.com/abstract=298180 or https://doi.org/10.2139/ssrn.298180. Accessed 21 Sept 2015.

de Groot, W., & Huij, J. (2011). *Are the Fama-French factors really compensations for distress risk?* (Working paper). Available at SSRN: http://ssrn.com/abstract=1840551 or https://doi.org/10.2139/ssrn.1840551. Accessed 12 Oct 2015.

de Groot, W., Huij, J., & Zhou, W. (2012). Another look at trading costs and short-term reversal profits. *Journal of Banking and Finance, 36*(2), 371–382. https://doi.org/10.1016/j.jbankfin.2011.07.015.

DeBondt, W. F. M., & Thaler, R. (1985). Does the stock market overreact? *Journal of Finance, 40*(3), 793–805.

DeBondt, F., & Thaler.R. (1987). Further evidence on the investor overreaction and stock market seasonality. *Journal of Finance, 42*, 557–581.

Dhouib, F. H., & Abaoub, E. (2007). Does the Tunisian stock market overreact? *Asian Academy of Management Journal of Accounting and Finance, 3*(2), 83–107.

Dichev, I. D. (1998). Is the risk of bankruptcy a systematic risk? *Journal of Finance, 53*(3), 1131–1147.

Dimson, E., & Marsh, P. (1999). Murphy's law and market anomalies. *Journal of Portfolio Management, 25*(2), 53–69.

Dissanaike, G. (1997). Do stock market investors overreact? *Journal of Business and Accounting, 24*, 27–49.

Doukas, J. A., Kim, C., & Pantzalis, C. (2004). Divergent opinions and the performance of value stocks. *Financial Analyst Journal, 60*(6), 55–64.

Du, D. (2011). Value premium and investor sentiment. *Advances in Behavioral Finance & Economics: The Journal of the Academy of Behavioral Finance, 1*(2), 87–101.

Elgammal, M. M., & McMillan, D. G. (2014). Value premium and default risk. *Journal of Asset Management, 15*, 48–61.

Erb, C. B., Harvey, C. R., & Viskanta, T. E. (1995). Country risk and global equity selection. *Journal of Portfolio Management, 21*(2), 74–83.

Erb, C. B., Harvey, C. R., & Viskanta, T. E. (1996a). Expected returns and volatility in 135 countries. *Journal of Portfolio Management, 22*(3), 46–58.

Erb, C. B., Harvey, C. R., & Viskanta, T. E. (1996b). Political risk, economic risk, and financial risk. *Financial Analyst Journal, 52*(6), 29–46.

Fama, E. F. (1965). The behavior of stock-market prices. *Journal of Business, 38*(1), 34–105.

Fama, E. F., & French, K. R. (1992). The cross-section of expected returns. *Journal of Finance, 47*, 427–466.

Fama, E. F., & French, K. R. (1993). Common risk factors in the returns on stocks and bonds. *Journal of Financial Economics, 33*, 3–56. https://doi.org/10.1016/0304-405X(93)90023-5.

Fama, E. F., & French, K. R. (1996). Multifactor explanations of asset pricing anomalies. *Journal of Finance, 51*(1), 55–84.

Fama, E. F., & French, K. R. (2015). A five-factor asset pricing model. *Journal of Financial Economics, 116*(1), 1–22. https://doi.org/10.1016/j.jfineco.2014.10.010.

Ferson, W. E., & Harvey, C. R. (1994). Sources of risk and expected returns in global equity markets. *Journal of Banking and Finance, 18*, 775–803.

Forner, C., & Marhuenda, J. (2003). Contrarian and momentum strategies in the Spanish stock market. *European Financial Management, 9*(1), 67–88.

Garlappi, L., & Song, Z. (2013). *Can investment shocks explain value premium and momentum profits?* (Working paper). Available at http://finance.sauder.ubc.ca/~garlappi/Papers/IShockReturn_Dec_10.pdf. Accessed 13 Oct 2015.

George, T. J., & Hwang, C.-Y. (2007). Long-term return reversals: Overreaction or taxes? *Journal of Finance, 62*(6), 2865–2896.

Gharaibeh, O. K. (2015). Long-term contrarian profits in the Middle East market indices. *Research Journal of Finance and Accounting, 6*(16). Available at SSRN: https://ssrn.com/abstract=2684807. Accessed 23 Oct 2017.

Green, J., Hand, J. R. M., & Zhang, F. (2016). *The characteristics that provide independent information about average U.S. monthly stock returns.* Available at SSRN: https://ssrn.com/abstract=2262374 or https://doi.org/10.2139/ssrn.2262374. Accessed 23 Oct 2017.

Griffin, J. M., & Lemmon, M. L. (2002). Book-to-market equity, distress risk, and stock returns. *Journal of Finance, 57*, 2317–2336.

Grossman, S., & Miller, M. H. (1988). Liquidity and market structure. *Journal of Finance, 43*, 617–633.

Hameed, A., & Mian, G. M. (2015). Industries and stock return reversals. *Journal of Financial and Quantitative Analysis, 50*(1–2), 89–117.

Hansson, B. (2004). Human capital and stock returns: Is the value premium an approximation for return on human capital? *Journal of Business Finance & Accounting, 31*(3–4), 333–358.

Hao, Y., Chu, H.-H., Ho, K.-Y., & Ko, K.-C. (2016). The 52-week high and momentum in the Taiwan stock market: Anchoring or recency biases? *International Review of Economics & Finance, 43*, 121–138. https://doi.org/10.1016/j.iref.2015.10.035.

Harvey, C. R. (2004). Country risk components, the cost of capital, and returns in emerging markets. In S. Wilkin (ed.), *Country and political risk: Practical insights for global finance* (pp. 71–102). London: Risk Books. Available at SSRN: http://ssrn.com/abstract=620710 or https://doi.org/10.2139/ssrn.620710. Accessed 21 Sept 2015.

Hong, H., Lim, T., & Stein, J. C. (2000). Bad news travels slowly: Size, analyst coverage, and the profitability of momentum strategies. *Journal of Finance, 55*(1), 265–295.

Hou, K., Karolyi, G. A., & Kho, B. C. (2011). What factors drive global stock returns? *Review of Financial Studies, 24*(8), 2527–2574. https://doi.org/10.1093/rfs/hhr013.

Hou, K., Xue, C., & Zhang, L. (2015). Digesting anomalies: An investment approach. *Review of Financial Studies, 28*(3), 650–705. https://doi.org/10.1093/rfs/hhu068.

Hou, K., Xue, C., & Zhang, L. (2017). *Replicating Aanomalies.* Fisher College of Business Working Paper No. 2017-03-010; Charles A. Dice Center Working Paper No. 2017-10. Available at SSRN: https://ssrn.com/abstract=2961979 or https://doi.org/10.2139/ssrn.2961979. Accessed 30 Sept 2017.

Hsieh, H.-H., & Hodnett, K. (2011). Tests of overreaction hypothesis and the timing of mean reversals on the JSE Securities Exchange (JSE): The case of South Africa. *Journal of Applied Finance and Banking, 1*(1), 107–130.

Huang, W., Liu, Q., Rhee, S. G., & Zhang, L. (2010). Return reversals, idiosyncratic risk, and expected returns. *Review of Financial Studies, 23*, 147–168.

Irwin, S. H., Zulauf, C. R., & Jackson, T. E. (1996). Monte Carlo analysis of mean reversion in commodity futures prices. *American Journal of Agricultural Economics, 78*(2), 387–399.

Ismail, E. (2012). Do momentum and contrarian profits exist in the Egyptian stock market? *International Research Journal of Finance and Economics, 87*, 48–72.

Israel, R., & Moskowitz, T. J. (2013). The role of shorting, firm size, and time on market anomalies. *Journal of Financial Economics, 108*(2), 275–301.

Jacobs, H. (2015). What explains the dynamics of 100 anomalies? *Journal of Banking & Finance, 57*, 65–85. https://doi.org/10.1016/j.jbankfin.2015.03.006.

Jacobs, H. (2016). Market maturity and mispricing. *Journal of Financial Economics, 122*(2), 270–287. https://doi.org/10.1016/j.jfineco.2016.01.030.

Jacobs, H., & Müller, S. (2017a). *Anomalies across the globe: Once public, no longer existent?* Available at SSRN: https://ssrn.com/abstract=2816490 or https://doi.org/10.2139/ssrn.2816490. Accessed 23 Oct 2017.

Jacobs, H., & Müller, S. (2017b). *...and nothing else matters? On the dimensionality and predictability of international stock returns.* Available at SSRN: https://ssrn.com/abstract=2845306 or https://doi.org/10.2139/ssrn.2845306. Accessed 23 Oct 2017.

Jank, S. (2014). *Specialized human capital, unemployment risk, and the value premium* (Working paper). Available at SSRN: http://ssrn.com/abstract=2526119 or https://doi.org/10.2139/ssrn.2526119. Accessed 15 Sept 2017.

Janssen, L. (2014). *The effect of credit risk on stock returns.* Available at http://arno.uvt.nl/show.cgi?fid=135567. Accessed 15 Sept 2015.

Jegadeesh, N. (1990). Evidence of predictable behavior of security returns. *Journal of Finance, 45*, 881–898.

Jegadeesh, N. (1991). Seasonality in stock price mean reversion: Evidence from U.S. and the U.K. *Journal of Finance, 46*(4), 1427–1444. https://doi.org/10.1111/j.1540-6261.1991.tb04624.x.

Jegadeesh, N., & Titman, S. (1995). Short-horizon return reversals and the bid-ask spread. *Journal of Financial Intermediation, 4*, 116–132.

Jegadeesh, N., Kim, J., Krische, S., & Lee, C. M. C. (2004). Analyzing the analysts: When do recommendations add value? *Journal of Finance, 59*(3), 1083–1124.

Jones, S. (1993). Another look at time varying risk and return in a long horizon contrarian trading strategy. *Journal of Financial Economics, 33*, 67–93.

Kalesnik, V. (2013). *Smart beta and the pendulum of mispricing* (Research affiliates white paper). Available at https://www.researchaffiliates.com/en_us/publications/articles/s_2013_09_smart-beta-and-the-pendulum-of-mispricing.html

Kang, C. O., & Kang, H. G. (2009). The effect of credit risk on stock returns. *Journal of Economic Research, 14*, 49–67.

Kaul, G., & Nimalendrum, M. (1990). Price reversals: Bid-ask errors or market overreaction. *Journal of Financial Economics, 28*, 67–93.

Khang, K., & King, T. D. (2004). Return reversals in the bond market: Evidence and causes. *Journal of Banking and Finance, 28*(3), 569–593.

Kothari, S. P., Shanken, J., & Sloan, R. (1995). Another look at the cross-section of expected stock returns. *Journal of Finance, 50*(1), 185–224.

Kryzanowski, L., & Zhang, H. (1992). The contrarian investment strategy does not work in Canadian markets. *Journal of Financial and Quantitative Analysis, 27*(3), 383–395.

Kumar, P. (2014). *Need for mean reversion in forecasting emerging market exchange rates.* Available at SSRN: https://ssrn.com/abstract=2547451 or https://doi.org/10.2139/ssrn.2547451. Accessed 23 Oct 2017.

La Porta, R. (1996). Expectations and the cross-section of stock returns. *Journal of Finance, 51*(5), 1715–1742.

La Porta, R., Lakonishok, J., Shleifer, A., & Vishny, R. (1997). Good news for value stocks: Further evidence on market efficiency. *Journal of Finance, 52*(2), 859–874.

Lakonishok, J., Schleifer, A., & Vishny, R. W. (1994). Contrarian investment, extrapolation, and risk. *Journal of Finance, 49*(5), 1541–1578.

Lehmann, B. N. (1990). Fads, martingales, and market efficiency. *Quarterly Journal of Economics, 105*(1), 1–28.

Lo, A., & MacKinlay, C. (1990). Data-snooping biases in tests of financial asset pricing models. *Review of Financial Studies, 3*(3), 431–467.

Loughran, T., & Ritter, J. R. (1996). Long-term market overreaction: The effect of low-priced stocks. *Journal of Finance, 51*(5), 1959–1970. https://doi.org/10.1111/j.1540-6261.1996.tb05234.x.

Lubnau, T., & Todorova, N. (2015). Trading on mean-reversion in energy futures markets. *Energy Economics, 51*, 312–319. https://doi.org/10.1016/j.eneco.2015.06.018.

Maheshwari, S., & Dhankar, R. S. (2015). The long-run return reversal effect: A re-examination in the Indian stock market. *Journal of Business Inquiry, 14*(2). Available at https://uvu.edu/woodbury/docs/jbi-09-15-208.pdf

Malin, M., & Bornholt, G. (2013). Long-term return reversal: Evidence from international market indices. *Journal of International Financial Markets, Institutions and Money, 25*, 1–17. https://doi.org/10.1016/j.intfin.2013.01.002.

McLean, R. D. (2010). Idiosyncratic risk, long-term reversal, and momentum. *Journal of Financial and Quantitative Analysis, 45*, 883–906.

McLean, D., & Pontiff, J. (2016). Does academic research destroy stock return predictability? *Journal of Finance, 71*(1), 5–32. https://doi.org/10.1111/jofi.12365.

Miffre, J., & Rallis, G. (2007). Momentum strategies in commodity futures markets. *Journal of Banking & Finance, 31*(6), 1863–1886. https://doi.org/10.1016/j.jbankfin.2006.12.005.

Monoyios, M., & Sarno, L. (2002). Mean reversion in stock index futures markets: A nonlinear analysis. *Journal of Futures Markets, 22*(4), 285–314. https://doi.org/10.1002/fut.10008.

Moskowitz, T. J., & Grinblatt, M. (1999). Do industries explain momentum? *Journal of Finance, 54*(4), 1249–1290.

Nagel, S. (2012). Evaporating liquidity. *Review of Financial Studies, 25*(7), 2005–2039. https://doi.org/10.1093/rfs/hhs066.

Ozdagli, A. K. (2012). Financial leverage, corporate investment, and stock returns. *Review of Financial Studies, 25*, 1033–1069.

Page, M., & Way, C. (1992). Stock market overreaction: The South African evidence. *Investment Analysts Journal, 21*, 35–49.

Park, T. H., & Switzer, L. N. (1996). Mean reversion of interest-rate term premiums and profits from trading strategies with treasury futures spreads. *Journal of Futures Markets, 16*(3), 331–352. https://doi.org/10.1002/(SICI)1096-9934(199605)16:3<331::AID-FUT5>3.0.CO;2-K.

Pastor, L., & Stambaugh, R. F. (2003). Liquidity risk and expected stock returns. *Journal of Political Economy, 111*(3), 642–685.

Pepelas, A. (2008). *Testing the overreaction hypothesis in the UK Stock market by using inter & intra industry contrarian strategies*. Available at SSRN: https://ssrn.com/abstract=1282776 or https://doi.org/10.2139/ssrn.1282776. Accessed 23 Oct 2017.

Pettengill, G., & Jordan, B. (1990). The overreaction hypothesis, firm size and stock market seasonality. *Journal of Portfolio Management, 16*(3), 60–64.

Phalippou, L. (2004). *What drives the value premium* (INSEAD working paper). Available at http://www3.nd.edu/~pschultz/Phalippou.pdf. Accessed 13 Oct 2015.

Piotroski, J. D. (2000). Value investing: The use of historical financial statement information to separate winners from losers. *Journal of Accounting Research, 38*, 1–52.

Richards, A. J. (1997). Winner-loser reversals in national stock market indices: Can they be explained? *Journal of Finance, 52*(5), 2129–2144. https://doi.org/10.1111/j.1540-6261.1997.tb02755.x.

Rosenberg, B., Reid, K., & Lanstein, R. (1985). Persuasive evidence of market inefficiency. *Journal of Portfolio Management, 11*, 9–17.

Saleh, W. (2007). Overreaction: The sensitivity of defining the duration of formation period. *Applied Financial Economics, 17*, 45–61.

Saleh, W., & Al Sabbagh, O. (2010). Short-term stock price momentum, long-term stock price reversal and the effect of information uncertainty. *International Journal of Accounting and Finance, 2*(1), 1–48.

Santos, T., & Veronesi, P. (2006). Labor income and predictable stock returns. *Review of Financial Studies, 19*(1), 1–44.

Sekuła, P. (2015). Nadreaktywność GPW w Warszawie – analiza empiryczna. *Zeszyty Naukowe Uniwersytetu Szczecińskiego nr 855, "Finanse, Rynki Finansowe, Ubezpieczenia", 74*(1), 171–180.

Serban, A. F. (2010). Combining mean reversion and momentum trading strategies in foreign exchange markets. *Journal of Banking & Finance, 34*(11), 2720–2727. https://doi.org/10.1016/j.jbankfin.2010.05.011.

Shiller, R. J. (1984). *Stock prices and social dynamics* (Cowles Foundation Paper #616, pp. 457–510). Available at http://www.econ.yale.edu/~shiller/pubs/p0616.pdf. Accessed 9 Oct 2017.

Shleifer, A., & Vishny, R. W. (1997). The limits of arbitrage. *Journal of Finance, 52*(1), 35–55.

Shon, J., & Zhou, P. (2010). Do divergent opinions explain the value premium? *Journal of Investing, 19*(2), 53–62.

Smith, D. M., & Pantilei, V. S. (2013, forthcoming). Do 'dogs of the world' bark or bite? Evidence from single-country ETFs. *Journal of Investing*. Available at SSRN: https://ssrn.com/abstract=2279246 or https://doi.org/10.2139/ssrn.2279246. Accessed 23 Oct 2017.

Spierdijk, L., Bikker, J. A., & van den Hoek, P. (2012). Mean reversion in international stock markets: An empirical analysis of the 20th century. *Journal of International Money and Finance, 31*(2), 228–249. https://doi.org/10.1016/j.jimonfin.2011.11.008.

Stiglitz, J. E. (1989). Using tax policy to curb speculative trading. *Journal of Financial Services, 3*, 101–115.

Stock, D. (1990). Winner and loser anomalies in the German stock market. *Journal of Institutional and theoretical Economics, 146*(3), 518–529.

Subrahmanyam, A. (2005). Distinguishing between rationales for short-horizon predictability of stock returns. *Financial Review, 40*, 11–35.

Summers, L. H., & Summers, V. P. (1989). When financial markets work too well: A cautious case for a securities transactions tax. *Journal of Financial Services, 3*, 261–286.

Swallow, S., & Fox, M. A. (1998). *Long run overreaction on the New Zealand Stock Exchange* (Commerce Division discussion paper, 48). Available at http://citeseerx.ist.psu.edu/viewdoc/download?doi=10.1.1.568.515&rep=rep1&type=pdf

Sweeney, R. J. (2006). Mean reversion in G-10 nominal exchange rates. *Journal of Financial and Quantitative Analysis, 41*(3), 685–708 http://www.jstor.org/stable/27647266.

Sylvain, S. (2014). *Does human capital risk explain the value premium puzzle?* (Working paper). Available at SSRN: http://ssrn.com/abstract=2400593 or https://doi.org/10.2139/ssrn.2400593. Accessed 30 Sept 2017.

Szyszka, A. (2013). *Behavioral finance and capital markets: How psychology influences investors and corporation.* New York: Palgrave Macmillan.

Tripathi, V., & Aggarwal, S. (2009). The overreaction effect in Indian stock market. *Asian Journal of Business and Accounting, 2*(1–2), 93–114.

Wei, J. Z. (2011). *Do momentum and reversals coexist?* Available at SSRN: https://ssrn.com/abstract=1679464 or https://doi.org/10.2139/ssrn.1679464. Accessed 10 Oct 2017.

Wei, J. Z., & Yang, L. (2012). *Short-term momentum and reversals in large stocks.* Available at SSRN: https://ssrn.com/abstract=2029984 or https://doi.org/10.2139/ssrn.20299849. Accessed 10 Oct 2017.

Wu, Y. (2011). Momentum trading, mean reversion and overreaction in Chinese stock market. *Review of Quantitative Finance and Accounting, 37*(3), 301–323.

Zakamulin, V. (2015). Market timing with a robust moving average. Available at SSRN: https://ssrn.com/abstract=2612307 or https://doi.org/10.2139/ssrn.2612307. Accessed 19 Oct 2017.

Zaremba, A. (2016). Has the long-term reversal reversed? Evidence from country equity indices. *Romanian Journal of Economic Forecasting, 19*(1), 88–103. http://www.ipe.ro/rjef/rjefl_16/rjefl_2016p88-103.pdf.

Zaremba, A. (2016a). Investor sentiment, limits on arbitrage, and the performance of cross-country stock market anomalies. *Journal of Behavioral and Experimental Finance, 9*, 136–163. http://dx.doi.org/10.1016/j.jbef.2015.11.007

Zaremba, A. (2016b). Strategies based on momentum and term structure in financialized -commodity markets. *Business and Economics Research Journal, 7*(1), 31–46.

Zaremba, A. (2016c). Risk-based explanation for the country-level size and value effects. *Finance Research Letters, 18*, 226–233. https://doi.org/10.1016/j.frl.2016.04.020.

Zaremba, A. (2016d). Has the long-term reversal reversed? Evidence from country equity indices. *Romanian Journal of Economic Forecasting, 19*(1), 88–103. http://www.ipe.ro/rjef/rjefl_16/rjefl_2016p88-103.pdf

Zaremba, A. (2017). *Performance persistence in anomaly returns: Evidence from frontier markets.* Available at SSRN: https://ssrn.com/abstract=3060876. Accessed 31 Oct 2017.

Zaremba, A., & Szyszka, A. (2016). Is there momentum in equity anomalies? Evidence from the Polish emerging market. *Research in International Business and Finance, 38*, 546–564. https://doi.org/10.1016/j.ribaf.2016.07.004.

Zaremba, A., & Andreu Sánchez, L. (2017). *Paper profits or real money? Trading costs and stock market anomalies in country equity indices.* Available at https://doi.org/10.2139/ssrn.3038514

Zaremba, A., & Czapkiewicz, A. (2017). Digesting anomalies in emerging European markets: A comparison of factor pricing models. *Emerging Markets Review, 31*, 1–15. https://doi.org/10.1016/j.ememar.2016.12.002.

Zaremba, A., & Nikorowski, J. (2017). *Trading costs, short sale constraints, and the performance of stock market anomalies in Emerging Europe.* Available at SSRN: https://ssrn.com/abstract=2778063. Accessed 23 Oct 2017.

Zaremba, A., & Shemer, K. (2017, in press). Is there momentum in factor premia? Evidence from international equity markets. *Research in International Business and Finance.* https://doi.org/10.1016/j.ribaf.2017.12.002

Zaremba, A., & Umutlu, M. (2018a, in press). Strategies can be expensive too! The value spread and asset allocation in global equity markets. *Applied Economics.*

Zaremba, A., & Umutlu, M. (2018b). Size matters everywhere: Decomposing the small country and small industry premia. *The North American Journal of Economics and Finance, 43*, 1–18. https://doi.org/10.1016/j.najef.2017.09.002.

Zaremba, A., & Umutlu, M. (2018c). *Opposites attract: Alpha momentum and alpha reversal in country and industry equity indexes* (Unpublished working paper).

Zarowin, P. (1989). Does the stock market overreact to corporate earnings information? *Journal of Finance, 44*, 1385–1399.

Zarowin, P. (1990). Size, seasonality, stock market and overreaction. *Journal of Financial and quantitative Analysis, 25*, 113–125.

Zhang, X. F. (2006). Information uncertainty and stock returns. *Journal of Finance, 61*(1), 105–101.

Zhu, Z., & Yung, K. (2016). The interaction of short-term reversal and momentum strategies. *Journal of Portfolio Management, 42*(4), 96–107. https://doi.org/10.3905/jpm.2016.42.4.096.

CHAPTER 4

No Pain, No Gain? The Puzzle of Risk-Return Relationship

The relationship between price risk and future returns has become one of the most fascinating and controversial issues in finance revolving around one of the most profound questions in finance: are safe investment better than risky ones? Although for over 70 years, researchers have strived to understand the relationship, it still remains full of puzzles.

The Low-Risk Anomaly

Although the common view is that risky investments should offer higher expected returns, why is it so? Let us consider two companies with exactly the same market value and financial situation, including expected profits, dividends, and expected returns. Albeit nearly identical, the companies have a single minor difference: one is a small, risky, and volatile, while the other is big, sage, and stable. Which company would the investors prefer? Unsurprisingly, the latter. This demand will clearly impact both the prices and the expected returns as the investors will likely sell the volatile, risky stock and buy the safe securities. Who wouldn't when both deliver the same payoffs? As a result, the risky stock's price will go down while the safe stock will strengthen. If the financial prospects of the companies remain the same, and both companies continue to offer identical dividends, the cheaper, risky company will eventually deliver higher returns than the more expensive safer business. What will be the difference in returns? This value, showing the additional return the investors expect on holding riskier assets, is called a "risk premium".

A. Zaremba, J. "Koby" Shemer, *Price-Based Investment Strategies*,
https://doi.org/10.1007/978-3-319-91530-2_4

The investigation of the risk-return relationship gave birth to a number of illustrious models of which perhaps the best known is the capital asset-pricing model (abbreviated CAPM, Sharpe 1964).[1] As a simple model, the CAPM was invented by William Sharpe for three main purposes: to explain the reasons for portfolio diversification, to create a framework for the valuation of assets in conditions of risk, and to explain differences in the long-term returns on various assets.[2] The CAPM laid the foundation for many performance evaluation methods in investment portfolio management, owing to its core assumption that volatility of any financial instrument can be broken down into two parts: a systematic and specific risk. The systematic risk stems from general changes in market conditions and relates to the volatility of the market portfolio, whereas the specific risk also relating to volatility, however, driven not by the market but by the internal situation in the company. In other words, losses ensuing a market crash are more of a systematic nature while the losses from an employee strike belong to the specific risk category.

The CAPM model has vital implications for both portfolio construction and diversification. When building a portfolio, systematic risks of individual stock simply add up; however, specific risks, not being correlated, set each other off. Therefore, in a well-diversified portfolio, the influence of the specific risk is generally negligible, and in a well-functioning market, a rational investor may ignore the specific risk and concentrate solely on the systematic part. Why would the investor even consider the specific risk if it could be easily diversified away at no cost?

This important implication of the CAPM model—stating that the investors should be only compensated for the systematic risk because the specific risk can be easily and almost entirely eliminated—is reflected in its elementary equation:

$$R_{i,t} = \alpha_i + R_{f,t} + \beta_{rm,i} \cdot \left(R_{mt} - R_{f,t} \right) + \varepsilon_{i,t}, \tag{4.1}$$

where $R_{i,t}$, $R_{m,t}$, and $R_{f,t}$ are returns on the analyzed security or portfolio i, the market portfolio, and risk-free returns at time t, and α_i and $\beta_{rm,i}$ are

[1] The detailed characteristics of the Sharpe model was extensively presented in a number of financial textbooks, for example, Francis (1990), Elton and Gruber (1995), Campbell et al. (1997), Cochrane (2005), or Wilmott (2008).

[2] Treynor (1961, 1962), Lintner (1965a, b), and Mossin (1966) developed a similar model at the same time, so all four of them, including Sharpe (1964), are now considered to be the fathers of the CAPM model.

regression parameters. $\beta_{rm,i}$ is the measure of the systematic risk. It informs us how aggressively the stock reacts to the changes in prices in the broad market. Basically, the CAPM formula implies that the excess returns on the investigated security or portfolio should increase linearly with the systematic risk measured with beta: the higher the risk, the higher the expected return.

In summary, the fundamental assumption of the CAPM is the existence of a positive relationship between the systematic stock market risk measured with betas and the expected returns, which was initially identified by a series of tests in the US stock market.[3] Although the CAPM is built upon the modern portfolio theory, under which investors should diversify risk by holding a portfolio of various stocks, the portfolios, for various reasons, often end up poorly diversified (Goetzman and Kumar 2008). In such portfolios, the idiosyncratic volatility, that is, the volatility not stemming from broad market fluctuations, should positively correlate with the expected returns in the cross-section analysis. This was originally proven by both theoretical analysis and empirical evidence confirming that securities with higher idiosyncratic risk yield higher average returns.[4] As both the systematic and idiosyncratic risks make up total volatility, this total parameter should also positively correlate with returns. Several studies have confirmed this assumption showing the risk measures related to the total variability as positively correlated with the expected returns. For instance, Bali and Cakici (2004) found a strong positive link between the average returns and value at risk (VaR), which proved robust against different investment horizons and various levels of loss probability. In addition, Ang et al. (2006a) focusing on the downside risk showed that a cross-section analysis of stock returns reflected a significant downside risk premium.[5]

However, many other research studies directly contradict these theories, pointing to the phenomenon called a "low-risk anomaly" (Ang 2014, p. 332), indicating this relationship to be frequently reversed: in other words, safer investments generate higher returns whether risk-adjusted or even raw.

The evidence for this anomaly has been pouring in from numerous studies conducted since its first discovery. In 1970 Friend and Blume examined the stock returns for the period 1960–1968 with the use of both

[3] Examples include Black et al. (1972), Fama and MacBeth (1973), Blume (1970), Miller and Scholes (1972), and Blume and Friend (1973).

[4] See Levy (1978), Tinic and West (1986), Merton (1987), and Malkiel and Xu (1997, 2004).

[5] The issues discussed in this section have been also described in Zaremba (2016a).

the CAPM beta and volatility. In the summary the researchers concluded that "risk-adjusted performance is dependent on risk. The relationship is inverse and highly significant" (Friend and Blume 1970). Shortly afterward, this observation was confirmed by Haugen and Heins (1975), who analyzed the US stock market in the period between 1926 and 1971, concluding that "over the long run, stock portfolios with lesser variance in monthly returns have experienced greater average returns than their 'riskier' counterparts" (Haugen and Heins 1975). Also, as a predictor of stock returns, market beta appeared far from ideal. Probably the first challenge was posed by Jensen et al. (1972) who wrote that despite the positive correlation between beta and returns, it was probably "too flat" compared to the CAPM predictions, which results in abnormal returns on low-beta stocks. The relevance of the CAPM was finally questioned by a seminal research of Fama and French (1992) who proved that when considering the size and value effects, "beta shows no power to explain average returns" (Fama and French 1992). These studies gave birth to further studies supplying plenty of evidence on the relationships between risk and future returns in the US and other international equity markets.[6]

Measuring the Risk

Risk in investing is usually defined as the unpredictability of future returns and measured in various ways. Most recent studies conclude that the risk-return relationship is rather negatively correlated. At the same time, studies considering downside risk or VaR lead to contradictory conclusions. Let's shortly review the most popular measures employed in low-risk investing.

Standard Deviation

As one of the most popular measures of risk in finance, standard deviation reflects the situation when we buy a bottle of Coke of precisely 1 liter, yet as it happens one bottle contains slightly less, say 0.98 liter, while the other

[6]For the US equity markets, see Black (1993), Haugen and Baker (1991, 1996), Falkenstein (1994), Chan et al. (1999), Jagannathan and Ma (2003), Clarke et al. (2006), Ang et al. (2006b), and Clarke et al. (2010); for global equity markets, see Blitz and van Vliet (2007), Ang et al. (2009), Baker et al. (2011), Dimitriou and Simos (2011), Baker and Haugen (2012), Blitz et al. (2013b), and Walkshausl (2014a, b).

slightly more, for example, 1.01 liter. The measure of the actual amount of Coke above and below the 1-liter requirement is the standard deviation.

Whenever investors evaluate the past returns, the standard deviation tells them how the returns on average disperse around the mean. Most frequently market practitioners calculate the measure on an annual basis, investigating how much the yearly returns on average deviated from the annual mean.

A commonsense intuition would dictate that the higher the standard deviation, the higher the expected returns, simply because investors favor stable stocks over volatile stocks, thus making them cheaper, which leads to higher expected returns. This could not be further from the truth. Based on the existing evidence, the relationship between the standard deviation and future returns gravitates toward the negative correlation, irrespective of the calculation method. To this conclusion, Blitz and van Vliet sorted stocks on the past three-year volatility, derived from monthly returns, and researched the performance of the international stocks in the FTSE World Index throughout the 1985–2006 period. The researchers found the decile portfolio of low-volatility companies outperforming the same portfolio of high-volatility companies on average by 5.9% per annum.

In 2011, Baker et al. examined quantile portfolios formed on the standard deviation of monthly returns using the date from the past five years. Having tested the US companies within the 1968–2008 period, they arrived at a similar conclusion: the high-volatility stocks underperformed the low-volatility stocks by 11.2% annually.

Finally, van Vliet et al. (2011) compared the performance of volatile and safe stocks under various methodological choices, considering various capitalizations, sorting period, and risk measures, which also confirmed the profitability of the low-volatility approach as robust compared to numerous methodological variations.

This anomaly is not only a stock market phenomenon, but it has been confirmed to expand over corporate bond markets, treasuries, and commodities.[7] However, in some universes, the low-volatility anomaly is

[7]The evidence is provided in the following studies: for commodities, Blitz and de Groot (2014) and Szymanowska et al. (2014); for treasury bonds, de Carvalho et al. (2014), Zaremba and Schabek (2017), and Zaremba and Czapkiewicz (2017a, b); for corporate bonds, Houweling et al. (2012), de Carvalho et al. (2014), Houweling and Zundert (2014), and Ng and Phelps (2015). Some papers also find evidence for the low-volatility effect appearing in country equity indices, but this evidence is not very convincing. It rather seems

hardly a reliable phenomenon. Analyzing the risk-return relationship across country equity indices, in 2010 Bali and Cakici examined returns from 37 countries within the period from 1973 to 2006. The authors formed tertile portfolios composed of country equity indices from sorts on total volatility on a monthly basis to discover risky countries markedly outperforming safe markets. For instance, when computing daily returns volatility over the six-month period, the portfolio of the safest countries earned on average 0.81% a month, while the portfolios of most volatile countries delivered the mean return of 1.45%. In all the variants, the volatile portfolios would always outperform the stable portfolios by at least a half of the percentage point. In other words, the low-volatility anomaly seems nonexistent at the country level because the higher the risk grows, the higher the returns follow.[8]

Systematic Risk Market Risk

The total volatility of a given security may be split into two basic parts, derived from the underlying source. Systematic risk—the first category—results from market-wide price swings and correlates with changes in interest rates, pricing of credit risk, fluctuations of the business cycle, and so on. The other category, idiosyncratic (or specific) risk, contrary to the systematic risk, relates to a single security and reflects its products, people, operations, and other firm-specific activities, as well as the company-specific share related demand and supply patterns.

Using appropriate econometric tools, we can split the two types of risk and easily attribute the extent to which the two categories of risk contribute to the firm's overall risk. The systematic part is usually calculated with beta, which econometrically is the regression coefficient of the portfolio excess returns on the excess returns on the market portfolio. As mentioned in the momentum section, simply speaking, beta expresses how aggressively the stock prices change in response to the market-wide fluctuation. Risky, high-beta stocks fluctuate more than the market tending to rise higher in the bull market and fall more rapidly in the bear market. A stock with a beta of two would be expected to rise twice as much as the

in line with the theoretical expectations of the classical models; these are the risky markets, which yield higher returns. In early 1996, Erb et al. compared the returns and volatilities across a panel of 28 equity market indices within the years 1979–1995. They discovered the relation between these two metrics rather weak, albeit generally positive, particularly among the emerging equity markets.

[8] See Liang and Wei (2016) and Zaremba (2016b) for further evidence.

market during upward moves, but then to decline also twice as much during price market-wide price decreases.

Under the CAPM, beta is the core determinator of securities' expected returns where higher beta means higher future returns which intuitively seems very understandable. The reality, however, proves to be rather surprising. Since Frazzini and Pedersens' comprehensive research (2014), we know that this simplistic risk-return relation is very far from true.

In their seminal paper of 2014 titled "Betting Against Beta", Frazzini and Pedersen questioned the relation between systematic risk and future returns. Having formed portfolios of different securities based on their past beta measures, they discovered that the low-beta assets delivered, actually, markedly higher risk-adjusted returns, or so-called alphas, than the risky high-beta assets, which visibly underperformed. The phenomenon turned out to be not only astonishing but also *strikingly pervasive.* Frazzini and Pedersen identified this phenomenon not only in 19 out of 20 country equity markets but also across plenty of other asset classes, just to mention treasuries, equity indices, credit indices, sovereign bonds, commodities, and currencies. Throughout all these markets, the lower risk turned out to be associated with higher risk-adjusted returns! Furthermore, in another study Asness et al. (2014) revealed that the profitability of low-beta investing is not a simple consequence of industry bets which favor stable industries.

How convincing is the evidence delivered by Frazzini and Pedersen can be also seen in Fig. 4.1. For modeling and asset-pricing purposes the authors also designed a factor portfolio, essentially a long-short portfolio of stocks ranked by their beta. The long side of this trade comprised low-beta stocks while the short side the high-beta stocks. While the short side was additionally deleveraged, the long side was leveraged so that they both had the same systematic risk level: the portfolio's beta equal to one. In consequence, the beta of the entire long-short portfolio should amount to zero, implying the lack of any abnormal returns. Figure 4.1 details the performance of the long-short betting-against-beta (BAB) portfolio plotted against the market portfolio. Finally, the cumulative profit on the BAB portfolio composed of global stocks in years 1987–2017 reached over 1300% exceeding more than five times the total excess return on the value-weighted market portfolio of global stocks. Furthermore, the outperformance was consistent and stable in time.

At the country level, however, the picture loses its clarity. In respect of country equity indices, the relationship between beta and the returns seems rather weak, if not downright nonexistent. Although Frazzini and

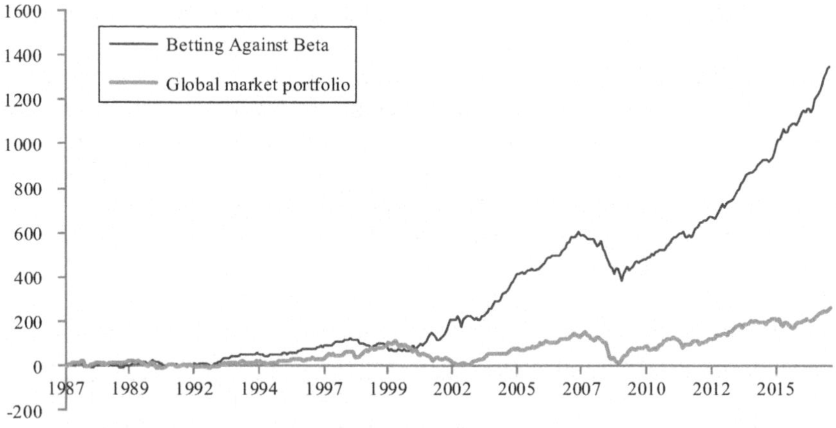

Fig. 4.1 The profitability of the betting-against-beta portfolio (%). (Note: The figure depicts the cumulative excess returns on the betting-against-beta portfolio and on the capitalization-weighted global portfolio of global stocks from 24 international markets in the period from February 1987 to August 2017. The underlying data is sourced as of 17 September 2017 from the website of QR Capital Management, LLC: https://www.aqr.com/library/data-sets/. Copyright ©2014 Andrea Frazzini and Lasse Heje Pedersen)

Pedersen (2014) argued the low-beta markets outperformed the high-beta markets, their study covered merely 13 indices from the developed markets. Also, other studies have struggled to confirm any relations between past beta and index returns. Bali and Cakici (2010), who examined 37 countries in the 1973–2006 period, identified no reliable relation between past beta and future returns. The authors showed the tertile portfolio of high-beta markets with raw returns per month 0.13%–0.29% higher than in the low-beta portfolio. The outperformance, however, was still too small to be statistically significant. Similar results were also reached in other studies which relied on even broader and fresher samples.[9]

Idiosyncratic Risk

While the systematic risk is what equally affects all the companies in the market, the idiosyncratic risk is company specific and could be also viewed as the difference between the market volatility and the systematic risk.

[9] See Liang and Wei (2006) or Zaremba (2016b).

Although the idiosyncratic risk could be calculated using various models, let us begin with the simple CAPM. In the CAPM framework, the idiosyncratic risk should never be priced; in other words, it should not be the determinant of expected future returns. Why? The company-specific risks are by definition uncorrelated, so substantial diversification benefits could be achieved by holding even a relatively small number of various securities.[10] After all, why the investor should be rewarded for the risk that could be so easily eliminated?

Alas, the existing evidence on how the idiosyncratic risk is actually priced in the market is not that straightforward. Indeed, some studies document a positive relationship between the future returns and idiosyncratic risk[11] with the more recent evidence showing the relationship as rather negative: the higher the idiosyncratic risk, the lower the return.

A seminal study on the impact of the idiosyncratic risk on future profits was carried out by Ang et al. in 2006. The authors examined the performance of quantile portfolio formed by ranking stocks on their idiosyncratic volatility in the US equity market within the years 1963–2000 to discover the securities with the top idiosyncratic volatility measured over the past month underperforming by as much as 12.7% per year compared to the low-risk stocks. In their later study conducted in 2009 (Ang et al. 2009), the authors extended their research sample to other international markets only to find that this surprising pattern works not only in the USA but also in many other countries. For instance, in Europe the risky stocks underperformed the safe by 4.9%, and in Asia by 3.2%. Thus, investors should avoid all high-idiosyncratic risk stocks[12] bearing in mind that a similar pattern has been also found in other asset classes, for example, commodities.[13]

Interestingly, the idiosyncratic volatility tends to perform differently at the portfolio level than in s individual stocks. The majority of research points to the risky (volatile) countries as yielding higher returns compared to the safe national markets. For instance, in 2015 Umutlu examined the payoffs on 23 local country indices sourced from Thomson Reuters and found the tertile portfolio of the stock market indices with high country-specific risk producing higher returns than the safe countries in the years 1973 to 2011, with the difference ranging from 0.21% to 0.37% dependent on the

[10] A review of relevant studies is provided by Alexeev and Tapon (2012).

[11] See Merton (1987) and Malkiel and Xu (2004).

[12] For further evidence, see Bali and Cakici (2008), Fu (2009), Clarke et al. (2010), van Vliet et al. (2011), and Fink et al. (2010).

[13] See Bernard et al. (2013), Fernandez-Perez et al. (2014), or Fuertes et al. (2015).

methodological choices. Still, the outperformance was regarded too small to be statistically significant. However, according to a prior study by Bali and Cakici, who examined 37 countries from 1973 to 2006, the low-risk countries outperformed high-risk countries by around 0.50% per month.

What is the source of this difference? The reason may lie in the sample: the idiosyncratic volatility determines future returns better in illiquid and small markets rather than in large and liquid environments. While Umutlu focused predominantly on the developed markets, Bali and Cakici (2010) extended their reach to emerging markets. Given that the cross-country capital mobility constraints make diversifying across emerging markets much more difficult for an average country-level investor, it should come as no surprise that taking up the idiosyncratic risk is primarily rewarded in the undeveloped markets.

Following this reasoning, in his recent study Zaremba (2016b) designed a portfolio from two-way independent sorts on both idiosyncratic volatility and stock market capitalization. The broad sample covered 78 national stock markets, including developed, emerging, and frontier markets, for the period 1999–2014. Zaremba documented the spread in returns between the risky and safe countries growing much wider within the small markets. In the class of small countries, the markets with high-idiosyncratic risk outperformed the markets of low risk by 1.20% per month whereas in the medium and large markets the differences amounted to only 0.39% and 0.50%, respectively. The detailed returns on the nine size-risk portfolios are reported in Fig. 4.2.

However compelling it may look, in a real world profiting from the performance of the portfolios formed on idiosyncratic volatility within the small markets may pose a significant challenge. First, the markets are truly small, with far less developed investment infrastructure than in the USA, Japan, or the eurozone; thus, quickly shifting capital between countries might cause problems. Second, the volatility of the strategies adopted in small markets also rises markedly.[14]

In idiosyncratic volatility crucial is the method of measurement. Among various approaches and nuances in methodology, the following three questions remain crucial:

1) What is the data frequency? In most research papers, the idiosyncratic volatility is measured either based on daily or monthly returns.

[14] Further evidence on the relationship between idiosyncratic volatility and future returns in the cross-country section can also be found in Hueng and Yau (2013).

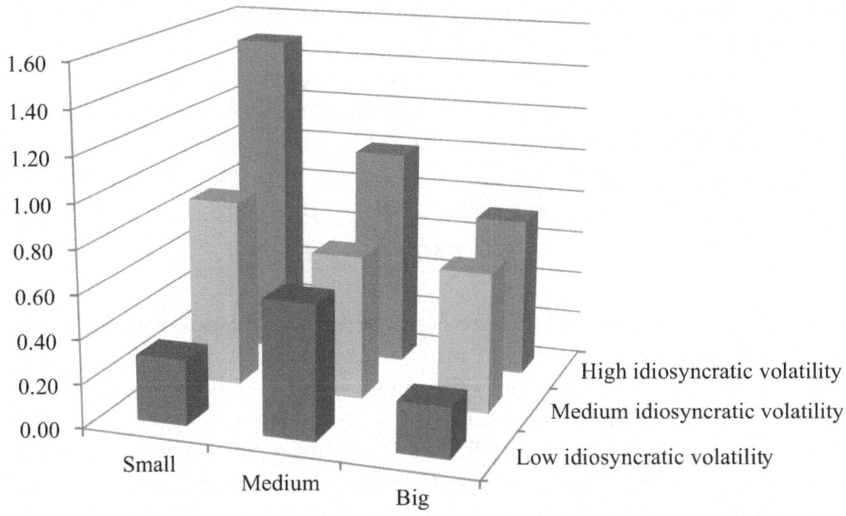

Fig. 4.2 Performance country portfolios from sorts on idiosyncratic volatility and size. (Note: The figure reports mean monthly excess returns (expressed in percentage) on portfolios from double sorts on idiosyncratic volatility and total stock market capitalization within the sample of 78 countries for years 1999–2014, self-developed based on the data from Table 3 in Zaremba's research (2016b))

2) How long is the lookback period? The ranking period is generally linked to the data frequency: for high-frequency data (e.g., daily), the sorting periods tend to be short (e.g., a month); for monthly data, the ranking periods usually approach two or three years.
3) Which model is used to estimate the idiosyncratic volatility? Among many approaches, we present the most practical below.

The most common method in the literature for estimating the idiosyncratic volatility is employing a broadly acknowledged asset-pricing model with the CAPM model as the simplest but not the only option. As presented in the momentum section, the Fama-French three-factor model also captures the value and size effects within the stock market. The model is based on three major factors driving equity returns: market excess return, representing the market risk factor; the return small-minus-big portfolio return, related to the small-firm effect in the equity market; and the return on the high-minus-low portfolio, representing the relative performance of the value stocks vs. the growth stocks. The three-factor model implies that these three effects account for a large portion of the cross-sectional differences in stock market returns with the idiosyncratic risk showing us the measure after controlling for these risk factors.

To control for even more risk factors, we should follow the example of Carhart (1997), who also included the momentum factor:

$$R_{i,t} - R_{f,t} = \alpha_{FF,i} + \beta_{MKT,i} MKT_t + \beta_{SMB,i} SMB_t + \beta_{HML,i} HML_t + \beta_{UMD,i} UMD_t + \varepsilon_{i,t} \quad (4.2)$$

where SMB_t, HML_t, and UMD_t are factor returns corresponding with size, value, and momentum effects in month t, respectively; $\alpha_{FF,i}$, $\beta_{MKT,i}$, $\beta_{SMB,i}$, $\beta_{HML,i}$, and $\beta_{UMDL,i}$ are the model's parameters; and $\varepsilon_{FF,i,t}$ is the residual from the model. The SMB_t is the return on a diversified long-short portfolio which is long (short) in the small (large) countries, industries, or companies, and the HML_t return is based on long-short portfolios which are long (short) in the high (low) book-to-market (abbreviated as BM) portfolios, identically as in the Fama-French three-factor model. The fourth factor, UMD_t, is the return on the long-short portfolio which goes long (short) the securities with the highest (lowest) past return.

Finally, we can also adopt the recent five-factor model of Fama and French (2015). Compared to the Carhart's model, the five-factor model disregards the UMD_t and the momentum factor but adds another two factors representing investment and profitability:

$$R_{i,t} - R_{f,t} = \alpha_{FF,i} + \beta_{MKT,i} MKT_t + \beta_{SMB,i} SMB_t + \beta_{HML,i} HML_t + \beta_{RMW,i} RMW_t + \beta_{CMA,i} CMA_t + \varepsilon_{i,t} \quad (4.3)$$

while the SMB_t and HML_t factors are identical as in the four-or three-factor model, whereas the RMW_t and CMA_t factors are innovations. The RMW_t refers to the robust-minus-weak portfolio, which is a diversified long-short portfolio, going long (short) the profitable (unprofitable stocks). The gross profitability, interpreted as a ratio of gross profits to assets, is in this case most frequently used as a proxy for profitability. The model relies on numerous studies indicating that profitable companies tend to outperform non-profitable ones.[15] Another factor relates to the

[15] For references on various measures of profitability, see, for example, for the gross-profitability, Novy-Marx (2013); Fama and French (2006), Balakrishnan et al. (2010), and Kogan

conservative-minus-aggressive (abbreviated CMA) portfolio, which is long (short) the stocks conducting few (a lot of) investment. It stems from the observation that firms with conservative investment policy tend to underperform companies with an aggressive investment policy.[16] As the five-factor model very well describes the cross-section of returns, it can be also successfully used to estimate the idiosyncratic risk.

However, in the case of the multifactor models used to estimate the idiosyncratic volatility, it is crucial to mind the source of the data for the models. Anyone trying to calculate the idiosyncratic risk based on the models will need two inputs: (1) returns on the given securities and (2) returns on the asset-pricing factors for the model—SMB, HML, UMD, and so on. While the first item seems relatively easy to obtain—based on the stock prices and dividends paid—the second may first appear more sophisticated. While computing the factor returns is both time consuming and data demanding, luckily, the factor returns for the majority of developed countries are readily available from at least two credible sources: from the personal website of Kenneth R. French, a long-time research partner of the Nobel laureate Eugene Fama,[17] and from the AQR website[18] operated by AQR Capital Management, an investment management company strongly tied to academia and founded by Clifford Asness. As very reliable, stable, and regularly updated both sources can be of great use for individual research.

Having discussed the alternative model used to estimate the idiosyncratic volatility, we must acknowledge here another option: of using no model. As proposed in a few studies, the "model-less" approach to computing the idiosyncratic risk defines it as a volatility of excess returns over the average of all of the assets in the sample.[19] This measure, however simple, works properly.

and Papanikolaou (2013); for ROE, Haugen and Baker (1996), Chen et al. (2011a), and Wang and Yu (2013).

[16] For evidence, see Lakonishok et al. (1994), Chan et al. (2001), Fairfield (2003), Titman et al. (2004), Eberhardt et al. (2004), Gu (2005), Anderson and Garcia-Feijoo (2006), Cooper et al. (2008), Hirshleifer et al. (2013), and Lou (2014).

[17] http://mba.tuck.dartmouth.edu/pages/faculty/ken.french/data_library.html.

[18] https://www.aqr.com/library/data-sets.

[19] For further readings on these types of measures, see Goyal and Santa-Clara (2003), Bali et al. (2005), Bekaert et al. (2012), Garcia et al. (2014), Verousis and Voukelatos (2015), and Kim and Lee (2017).

Although the methods vary greatly in approach and sophistication, the final results point to the same conclusion: the more idiosyncratic risk, the poorer the return.

VaR

VaR is another straightforward risk measure to have gained in popularity in recent decades as a useful statistical tool to quantify financial risk in investment portfolios. Its strength lies in its simplicity: it could be expressed in a single intuitive number. Also, it could be defined either in absolute terms (value, e.g., in US dollars) or in relative terms (percentage). Formally, VaR is defined as "an estimate of a loss over a fixed time horizon that would be equaled or exceeded with a specified probability" (Alexander and Sheedy 2004, p. 76). A portfolio manager may determine to have 1%-month VaR of 20%, accepting a 5% chance of the portfolio losing more than 20% of its value in any given month. In other words, the loss of 20% or more is expected to occur every 100 months.

In practice, VaR usually comes in three possible variants (Jorion 2007, pp. 241–264):

- Historical VaR, based on the past track record
- Monte Carlo VaR, using simulation methods
- Analytical VaR, assuming normal, or log-normal, distribution of rates of return, using standard deviations and correlations

From the investor's point of view, the VaR can report on risk characteristics that escape many classical measures, including the standard deviation as the VaR concentrates on the tail risk, that is, the risk of extreme negative events, which is hardly captured by simpler volatility measures. Consequently, it would be possible to verify whether this risk is priced in by investors or, in other words, whether investors demand higher returns for the stocks with high VaR.

This very question was posed in 2004 by Bali and Cakici. The pair tried to find any relationship in the US market between VaR and future returns in years 1965–2001 and finally succeeded. Having simplified VaR to a percentile of past returns, Bali and Cakici then sorted the stocks into decile portfolios based on their metric. As a result, the decile of stocks with the highest 5% VaR outperformed the decile of stocks with the lowest 5% VaR by 0.96% per month. These abnormal returns resulted from the specific methodological choices of the VaR calculations. Subsequent studies confirmed this cross-sectional pattern also in Taiwan or Pakistan, and among other asset classes, like hedge funds.[20]

Importantly, the stock-level return pattern related to VaR seems analogous at the level of country equity indices, particularly among small countries which resembles the role of the idiosyncratic risk at the individual stock level. According to a study by Zaremba (2016b), to test returns on 78 markets in the 1999–2014 period, the high VaR markets indeed yielded higher returns than the low VaR markets. The results, however, were driven by a modest number of extremely small countries, so in effect the anomaly might prove difficult to turn profitable. Furthermore, the anomaly appeared so weak that it finally disappeared completely in different portfolio weighting schemes (Zaremba 2015).

Exposure to Non-market Risk Factors

While we focused entirely on the systematic exposure to the market risk when describing the low-beta anomaly, finance literature also offers other definitions of systematic risk. Ang et al. (2006a, b) first recognized the importance of the exposure to total volatility risk pointing out that when sorting stocks on the beta of all of the stocks in the market, the high-beta stocks underperformed the low-beta stocks. In other words, the low-volatility anomaly emerged not only for the classic volatility but also in the exposure to aggregate volatility.[21] Notably, an interesting concept is also the "bear beta" proposed by Lu and Murray (2017), measuring the exposure to the bear market risk. Also this variable displays significant correlation with future returns.

Other risk factors applicable here may seem even more exotic. For instance, Huang and Miao (2016) sorted the markets on the exposure to the oil risk, that is, a regression coefficient of stock returns on light sweet crude oil future returns to find the stocks with the low oil risk outperforming the equities with high oil risk. The final difference may also lie in the very process of calculating beta. Here again Ang et al. (2006b) proved the importance of not generic beta but a "downside beta", that is, the beta coefficient calculated based on only negative returns as a variable strongly indicative of the future returns.

[20] For Taiwan, Chen et al. (2014); for Pakistan, Iqbal et al. 2013, Iqbal and Azher (2014); and for hedge funds, Bali et al. (2007).

[21] For various measures, see Goyal and Santa-Clara (2003), Bali et al. (2005), Bekaert et al. (2012), Garcia et al. (2014), Verousis and Voukelatos (2015), Kim and Lee (2017), and Zaremba and Andreu Sanchez (2017).

Non-price Risks

Concentrating on price-based investing, we have now discussed predominantly the risk measures that could be obtained based on prices and returns. Some investors, however, may also want to take a broader look including the non-price risks, at least for robustness purposes, to investigate the extent the risk-return relationships hold under different measures. Can the low-risk anomaly—heretofore emerging as one of the dominant forces shaping the future returns—be proxied with non-price indicators? It can be done.

Looking at the discussion of "quality investing" within the framework of fundamental investing, we can see the highlighted relation between the fundamental quality of a company and its future stock market performance. At first, it seems only rational to assume that investors should be willing to pay more for companies displaying higher quality characteristics. Consequently, higher prices should imply lower expected returns. To put it simply: the higher the quality, the lower the returns.

Still, a substantial part of recent publications seems to indicate that quality is not fully priced in, proving that historically quality stocks outperformed low-quality securities. This counterintuitive phenomenon has been confirmed by many studies and led to many ways of understanding quality through, for example, credit standing, leverage, growth, accruals, or profitability.[22] Furthermore, the synthesized measures of quality, which integrate a range of various metrics, appear to be positively correlated with future returns.

Interestingly, at the level of countries, the relationship between returns and "fundamental risks" appear more "traditional"—when allocating asset across countries, investors are exposed to various risks and "shocks" related to currency devaluation, coups, expropriation, or regulatory changes (Bekaert et al. 1996; Dahlquist and Bansal 2002a, b), which seem particularly timely nowadays when the global financial turmoil has forced many governments to seize the assets of its citizens, and military conflicts and political instability spread chaos across numerous countries in Africa, Europe, and the Middle East.

[22] For evidence, see, for leverage and credit standing, Penman et al. (2007), Campbell et al. (2008), Hahn and Lee (2009), and George and Hwang (2010); for growth, Mohanram (2005); for accruals, Sloan (1996), and Richardson et al. (2005); for balance sheet liquidity, Palazzo (2012); for profitability, Griffin and Lemmon (2002), Fama and French (2006), and Novy-Marx (2013); and for aggregated measures, Asness et al. (2017).

What is then the role of these alternative risks in the international portfolio? If posing real threats to the investor's wealth should also be rewarded with additional payoffs. Indeed, according to many researchers, these political, financial, and economic risks are priced in at the country level, making investments in riskier countries associated with higher expected returns. This phenomenon was investigated in an article by Erb et al. published in 1995. Having examined the impact of country credit risk, the authors proved it a powerful predictor of future returns, especially within emerging markets. After forming quartile portfolios based on the *Institutional Investor*'s semiannual surveys, the researchers calculated mean returns in the 1980–1993 period, having based their analysis on 40 markets, both developed and emerging. As a result, the quartile portfolio of the riskiest countries delivered returns on average 11.6 percentage points higher per annum than the safe markets. Still, across the developed markets the differences in returns were relatively small being driven predominantly by the emerging markets. While the lowest credit-risk emerging-market portfolio earned on average only 7.9% per year, the riskiest markets delivered the mean annual return of 34.3%, with a very similar level of volatility for both portfolios. In other words, Erb et al. (1995) strongly reinforced the concept of the high sovereign credit risk providing additional premium for global equity investors. Nonetheless, their relatively short study period and the lack of reliable robustness tests may still be considered as its weakness.

One interesting contribution was also made by Zaremba (2016c) by employing the risk measures calculated by the Economist Intelligence Unit and future returns on country equity indices. The study focused on both composite risk assessments and component risks related to sovereign credit, currency, banking sector, economic structure, and political situation. Zaremba found the equal-weighted portfolio of risky countries outperformed the safe countries by approximately 0.50 percentage points per month. Although the general conclusion was clear—the higher the risk, the higher the return—the application of this cross-sectional pattern still posed a significant challenge for general investment practice. The abnormal performance proved insignificant for capitalization-weighted and liquidity-weighted portfolios as well as within many other subgroups across the sample with the profitability completely disappearing in the years following the global financial crisis. Summing up, the fundamental evidence seems to support the observations from the price-based universe. For individual equities, the low fundamental quality is associated with higher returns, as it is the case with the low-risk anomaly in the price-based world. At the index level, the high-risk assets tend to deliver higher long-run returns—with the risk measured either with price-based or fundamental indicators.

In the case of individual stock returns, the low-risk anomaly stands out a powerful cross-sectional pattern showing that both low-volatile and low-beta companies grossly outperform their risky counterparts. At the country level, however, a similar effect is hardly so evident, in fact, the link between beta and returns appears very weak against the predictions of the CAPM, even if the idiosyncratic risk is rewarded with higher profits.[23]

Why the Low-Risk Anomaly Exists?

To recognize the nature of these discrepancies, and to determine the applicability of the risk-based strategies at the country level, we should first better understand the root cause of the low-risk anomaly. The explanations fall into two main categories: (1) investors' behavior and psychology and (2) limits to arbitrage.

Within the behavioral finance framework, a few phenomena seem to explain the low-risk anomaly.

Preference for Lotteries Both lotteries and roulette wheels are great manifestations of this simple truth: people love gambling. Although casinos are widely recognized for negative expected returns, as players on average lose the bet, gaming houses have had their clientele for centuries.

In many respects, buying volatile individual stocks resemble a lottery, with securities used as betting instruments. Although to a large extent this phenomenon results from the skewness of return distribution, it is, at the same time, strongly linked to volatility (Mitton and Vorkink 2007; Boyer et al. 2010).[24] If a start-up high-tech company fails, we can lose all our investment, but if it becomes another Microsoft, the stock price can rise exponentially. As in general, individual investors show clear preference for such low-priced, volatile, lottery-like stocks (Kumar 2009); this has

[23] This section has been inspired and sourced from Zaremba and Shemer (2017).

[24] Interestingly, some studies argue low-volatility anomaly to be just a manifestation of various skewness related effects; see, for example, Schneider et al. (2016).

reflected in high demand and, thus, inflated prices of these lottery-like securities as indicated by an array of circumstantial evidence.[25]

Perhaps the most seminal paper attempting to explain the low-beta effect with the lottery demand was published by Bali, Brown, Murray, and Tang in 2017. In their study, these authors implemented the low-beta strategy after controlling for the lottery demand. They did it by various ways, for example, by neutralizing the lottery demand before sorting the stocks or including lottery factors in their regression specifications. Once the lottery demand was controlled, the low-beta strategy was no longer profitable. In other words, when we account for the preference for lotteries, the low-beta anomaly ceases to exist. This evidence provides a serious support for the lottery-based explanation of the low-risk effect.

Representativeness As we have already discussed representativeness in the momentum chapter, let's only refer to the experimental story of Linda who was assumed by most interviewees to be a female activist although it was certainly not the most probable proposition. Does the representativeness bias relate to the low-volatility anomaly? Clearly, Baker et al. (2011) did argue to that effect. Considering a substantial investment in potentially another Apple or Microsoft, that is, a risky high-tech company which may dominate and their stock price surge by thousands of percentage, a layman investor might feel inclined to buy such risky and volatile stocks, ignoring the fact that only a few such investments prove finally successful. This excessive irrational demand drives the overpricing.

Overconfidence As another mighty behavioral phenomenon, overconfidence leads us to believe we know more than we do.[26] According to the classic example, 93% of US car drivers place themselves above the median when assessing their own driving skills (Svenson 1981) which is naturally unlikely from the mathematical standpoint. Stock market investors can hardly be free from such widespread overconfidence which can only prove detrimental to their long-term performance as overconfident investors tend to trade more than others, and the additional trades generate no better performance but only higher transaction costs.

[25] See, for example, Tversky and Kahneman (1992), Barberis and Huang (2008), or Bali et al. (2011).

[26] Seminal papers on this issue include Fischhoff et al. (1977) and Alpert and Raiffa (1982).

Overconfidence may also impact investors' predictions of future returns or their judgment of companies' financial standing. When asked to estimate the population of Massachusetts and to provide a 90% confidence interval most responders tend to give too narrow responses, proving thus the prevalent tendency to make estimates markedly more accurate compared to the factual knowledge (Baker et al. 2011).

Why overconfidence produces undesired effects in the stock market? When valuing stocks, an overconfident investor may be unrealistically optimistic, risk blind and forming overly optimistic, precise predictions. This is particularly visible in more uncertain outcomes, for example, in returns on volatile equities (Baker et al. 2011). In consequence, the overconfidence effect may eventually lead to overpricing risky stocks and, thus, to their lower long-run return (Cornell 2009).

Greed and Envy One of the most profound assumptions of the traditional financial models, including the CAPM, state that equity investors aim to maximize their personal wealth, making no allowances for the wealth of others. To put it differently: it is not how much others have, but how much I have. At the first glance, the difference may seem subtle as the growth of absolute wealth usually goes hand in hand with the growth of the relative wealth. Nevertheless, there are some marginal discrepancies that, in the end, may lead to substantial differences in pricing of financial assets in stock markets.

In practice, however, real investors usually behave slightly different: contrary to the CAPM assumptions, many happiness studies have proven the relative gain as much more important than the absolute wealth[27] with perhaps the most well-known study, the Easterlin Paradox, first conducted by Richard Easterlin in 1974, according to which happiness within a society is largely unaffected by the level of absolute wealth growing over time. Another intriguing manifestation of the relative utility concept was discovered in 2011 by Frank who gave the participants two alternatives: to earn \$100,000 when others make \$90,000 or gain \$110,000 when others earn \$200,000. In the world of absolute wealth preference, the answer would be simple: the more the better. In reality, however, it is far from true: the overwhelming majority opted for the first proposition, being perfectly happy to earn less as long as gaining more than others.

[27] For example, Ferrer-i-Carbonell (2005), Luttmer (2005), Clark and Oswald (1996), and Knight et al. (2009).

Till now, the concept of relative utility has been broadly acknowledged and incorporated in many financial and economic models, importantly, also by the professional financial industry.[28] More and more often, portfolio managers are assessed based on their historical portfolio returns relative to the benchmark, rather than based on their absolute performance.[29] In other words, usually, it is not as important to produce high absolute returns as to outperform the peers. Currently over 90% of US mutual funds are benchmarked against one common index (Sensoy 2009). This has important implication for asset pricing, as asset managers may be more prone to minimizing benchmark-relative risk (the so-called tracking error) while ignoring the total risk. Assuming, therefore, that there is a positive relationship between the stock market beta, or systematic risk, and future returns, and that we have two assets with identical tracking error but different systematic risk, the portfolio manager will opt for the one with higher beta as it is associated with higher expected returns. This way, investors may generate excessive demand for the high-beta stocks, driving the overvaluation relative to the CAPM model.[30]

Attention Grabbing As the national equity markets are nowadays populated with thousands of stocks, for an individual investor knowing all the securities and then filtering out the losers might prove truly overwhelming. In consequence, equity investors usually concentrate on stocks that easily attract their attention (Barber and Odean 2008), that is, the equities which recently appeared in the news, delivered extreme returns, or experienced abnormally high volumes in the given period. Usually, these attention-grabbing stocks tend to display above average return volatility and belong to the "shiny" economy sectors, like the high-tech industry. As a result, this phenomenon may generate excessive demand, increasing prices and decreasing the expected returns for risky stocks. As more boring and stable companies are likely to be ignored, this contributes to lowering their stock prices and reduced future payoffs.

Interestingly, Falkenstein (1996) observed the preference for attention-grabbing stocks is not limited to individual investors as institutional investors, including mutual funds, also tend to hold shares of companies more frequently portrayed in the news, potentially adding to the excessive demand.

[28] See Abel (1990), Gali (1994), Campbell and Cochrane (1999), Heaton and Lucas (2000), Lettau and Ludwigson (2001), DeMarzo et al. (2004), or Roussanov (2010).

[29] See Sharpe (1981) or Roll (1992).

[30] For further models and references, see Falkenstein (2009, 2012), Blitz et al. (2013b), and Brennan et al. (2012).

This behavioral phenomenon may also well explain the grounds for the low-volatility anomaly, but it falls short to justify its existence. If the market is efficient, such anomalies should be rapidly arbitraged away by professional investors constantly seeking new profit opportunities. As this doesn't happen, something must stand in the way. We can name at least three constraints preventing investors from arbitraging away the low-risk anomaly, related to leverage, short selling, and regulation.

Leverage Constraints When planning to take on more risk in an equity portfolio, we face two choices: either to leverage the low-risk stocks or to buy more high-beta equities. While not always be available, the leverage option can be further restricted by, for example, margin rules, tax regulations, or bankruptcy laws. Thus, when leveraging becomes impossible, the only solution is buying high-beta stocks. As a result, the more restricted the leverage availability, the higher the demand for high-beta stocks, which is directly causing the overvaluation of high-beta stocks.

Numerous academic studies have delivered both theoretical and empirical evidence confirming that leverage constraints can reinforce the low-risk anomaly.[31] Yet they still fail to explain why the low-risk securities yield returns higher than the market portfolio.

Short-Selling Constraints This is closely related to the limits imposed on the leverage availability. If valuations of the high-beta stocks become too elevated, one way to return to the equilibrium prices is for the short sellers to borrow the overpriced stocks and sell them in the market. If the short selling becomes impossible, the pricing might remain distorted leading to other misrepresentations in the risk-return relationship in the market (de Giorgi et al. 2013; Ho and Sraer 2015). According to even the oldest financial models, for example, Miller's (1977), when even a little short-selling activity is available, the prices might be determined by a small minority with the most optimistic expectations. This mechanism may directly contribute to the volatility anomaly.

Regulatory Constraints Most investment regulations, either national or international, fail to recognize low-volatility stocks as a separate asset class, as opposed to equities or bonds. An investment policy may indicate that

[31] See, for example, Brennan (1971), Black (1972, 1993), and Frazzini and Pedersen (2014).

the portfolio manager is allowed to allocate at maximum 60% of his portfolio into stocks and 40% into bonds, while the same risk level could be also achieved by investing 80% of the portfolio into low-volatility stocks and 20% in bond; this, however, stretches beyond the tools available to the asset manager, who, to maximize his equity exposure is forced to go for high-beta stocks. Thus, such regulations may also contribute to boosting demand for risky companies (Blitz et al. 2014a).

Other supplemental theories only partially explain the phenomenon. While some studies raise the data-mining concerns pointing to the results proving sensitive to liquidity effects and portfolio weighting schemes,[32] the volatility effect seems too pervasive to be a mere data-mining anomaly. Further evidence provided Martellini (2008) indicating the possibility of the low-volatility anomaly to be related to delisting bankrupt public companies. As a result, the volatility-based strategies are implemented only to the survivors causing the high-risk companies substantially outperform the safe businesses.

A further study into various explanations was carried out by Hou and Loh in 2015, with the researchers declaring the lottery preference as the most promising explanation, ironically, having argued earlier that a set of explanations linked to the lottery preference could explain away a half of the puzzles in individual stocks leaving the other half unexplained. Thus, although the current academic knowledge offers an array of explanations of the low-risk anomaly, clearly some important phenomena still seem waiting to be discovered.

Empirical Tests of Risk-Based Strategies

Although controversial, the risk-return relationship can become a useful predictor of future returns. Let us then analyze—based on the real stock market data—how such strategies have performed over the last two decades.

In this section, we will showcase two risk-based strategies—each implying a different relationship with risk. The first strategy assuming lower risk to bring the higher returns is based on *idiosyncratic volatility*. The second, assuming the contrary, relies on *VaR* as the predictor of future payoffs. Importantly, none of these strategies requires any built-in deleveraging or leveraging mechanism for the long or short sides of the trades, being both simple and easy to implement.

[32] The evidence is provided by, for example, Bali and Cakici (2008) and Han and Lesmond (2011).

Simply implementing ***idiosyncratic volatility***, each month we calculated the idiosyncratic volatility derived from the trailing 60-month returns. To measure the idiosyncratic risk, we applied the simple CAPM model. As a proxy for the market portfolio, we referred to the most representative and popular index for each country, for instance, S&P500 for the USA and DAX for Germany. Having computed the idiosyncratic volatility, we subsequently ranked all the companies on this variable each month. We assumed a long position in the quintile of stocks with the lowest idiosyncratic risk and a short position in a quintile of securities with the highest idiosyncratic risk. The results are reported in Table 4.1.[33]

Clearly, as reliable return predictor of future stock returns, the idiosyncratic volatility failed to reach the level of, for instance, momentum, although its performance proved definitely interesting. The mean monthly returns on the long-short portfolios were historically positive in 23 out of 24 countries, although the mean was significant only in 10 national markets. The significant CAPM alpha was identified in 13 countries, namely Australia, Canada, France, Germany, Greece, Hong Kong, Israel, Japan, the Netherlands, Singapore, Spain, Sweden, and the UK. The equal-weighted return on all the country portfolios also displayed significant alpha amounting to 0.75% per month whereas the alpha of the portfolio of countries weighted on their capitalization was slightly lower and amounted to 0.55%.

Clearly, a drawback of the long-short low-idiosyncratic risk strategy was its volatility. The standard deviation of the equal-weighted global portfolio reached 3.68%, remarkably exceeding the instances of other tested strategies. Furthermore, the value-weighted portfolio proved even more volatile, with the standard deviation arriving at 5.85%. These high volatilities naturally translated into relatively disappointing Sharpe ratios of 0.61 and 0.26, respectively.

Additionally, Figs. 4.3 and 4.4 display the cumulative returns on the global portfolios. Indeed, the low-idiosyncratic risk strategies yielded attractive returns, but not free from risk. The long-short portfolios had experienced many crashes and drawdowns that definitely would be a bad experience for the investor's pocket.

Considering the ***VaR strategy***, advocating forming portfolios based on the historical VaR, we used a return predicting variable closely following the approach of Bali et al. (2011). In particular, we sorted all the

[33] Importantly, in this exercise we first averaged the time-series of log-returns and subsequently converted it into the standard returns.

Table 4.1 The performance of international portfolios formed on idiosyncratic risk

Country	*Top portfolio mean return*	*Bottom portfolio mean return*	*Average number of firms*	*T-B portfolio*		*Standard deviation*	*Sharpe ratio*	*Beta*	*Alpha*	
				Mean return	*t-stat*				*Value*	*t-stat*
Australia	1.08	−0.44	31	1.52***	*(3.48)*	7.14	0.73	−0.23	1.70***	*(3.90)*
Austria	0.11	0.59	5	−0.48	*(−1.24)*	6.37	−0.26	0.04	−0.50	*(−1.28)*
Belgium	0.82	0.59	9	0.24	*(0.62)*	6.26	0.13	−0.25	0.42	*(1.10)*
Canada	0.84	−0.07	65	0.91*	*(1.96)*	7.58	0.41	−0.17	1.03**	*(2.21)*
Denmark	1.12	0.79	9	0.33	*(0.83)*	6.57	0.17	−0.19	0.51	*(1.27)*
Finland	0.94	0.47	10	0.47	*(1.12)*	6.90	0.24	−0.10	0.57	*(1.36)*
France	0.95	0.24	37	0.71*	*(1.73)*	6.69	0.37	−0.14	0.80*	*(1.95)*
Germany	0.71	−0.11	32	0.82*	*(1.68)*	7.99	0.36	−0.14	0.91*	*(1.85)*
Greece	0.47	−1.42	9	1.92***	*(3.12)*	10.02	0.66	0.03	1.92***	*(3.11)*
Hong Kong	0.50	−1.97	21	2.52***	*(4.85)*	8.44	1.02	−0.12	2.61***	*(5.01)*
Ireland	0.90	0.51	3	0.39	*(0.48)*	13.18	0.10	0.08	0.33	*(0.41)*
Israel	0.92	0.16	13	0.75**	*(2.16)*	5.71	0.46	0.04	0.74**	*(2.13)*
Italy	0.20	−0.10	19	0.30	*(0.92)*	5.40	0.19	0.03	0.29	*(0.87)*
Japan	0.35	−0.20	280	0.55	*(1.59)*	5.71	0.33	−0.22	0.57*	*(1.65)*
The Netherlands	1.01	0.42	12	0.59	*(1.50)*	6.43	0.32	−0.21	0.73*	*(1.87)*
New Zealand	0.73	0.60	3	0.13	*(0.55)*	3.75	0.12	−0.03	0.15	*(0.66)*
Norway	0.19	−0.03	11	0.22	*(0.49)*	7.26	0.10	−0.06	0.27	*(0.61)*
Portugal	−0.02	−0.17	3	0.15	*(0.30)*	8.03	0.06	−0.04	0.16	*(0.34)*
Singapore	0.07	−1.03	9	1.11***	*(3.26)*	5.58	0.69	0.00	1.11***	*(3.23)*
Spain	0.86	0.05	14	0.81**	*(2.48)*	5.31	0.52	−0.10	0.88***	*(2.70)*
Sweden	1.28	0.15	21	1.13***	*(2.82)*	6.57	0.59	−0.20	1.32***	*(3.32)*
Switzerland	0.91	0.76	23	0.15	*(0.41)*	6.09	0.09	−0.21	0.30	*(0.81)*

(*continued*)

Table 4.1 (continued)

Country	*Top portfolio mean return*	*Bottom portfolio mean return*	*Average number of firms*	*T-B portfolio*		*Standard deviation*	*Sharpe ratio*	*Beta*	*Alpha*	
				Mean return	*t-stat*				*Value*	*t-stat*
UK	0.81	0.35	75	0.46	*(1.32)*	5.66	0.28	−0.25	0.57*	*(1.68)*
USA	0.98	0.96	453	0.02	*(0.05)*	7.78	0.01	−0.20	0.16	*(0.33)*
World (EW)	0.70	0.04	1166	0.65***	*(2.91)*	3.68	0.61	−0.16	0.74***	*(3.32)*
World (VW)	0.76	0.32	1166	0.44	*(1.23)*	5.85	0.26	−0.22	0.55	*(1.55)*

Note: The table reports the monthly returns on the portfolios from sorts on the trailing 60-month idiosyncratic risk from the CAPM. The calculations were made on the basis of monthly observations. ***Top portfolio*** and ***bottom portfolio*** are quintile portfolios including the stocks with the lowest and the highest idiosyncratic risk, respectively. ***T-B portfolio*** goes long in the top portfolio and short in the bottom portfolio. The Sharpe ratio is expressed on an annualized basis. The alpha and beta are derived from the CAPM. Mean returns, standard deviations, and alphas are expressed in percentage. Asterisks *, **, and *** indicate values significantly different from zero at the 10%, 5%, and 1% level, respectively

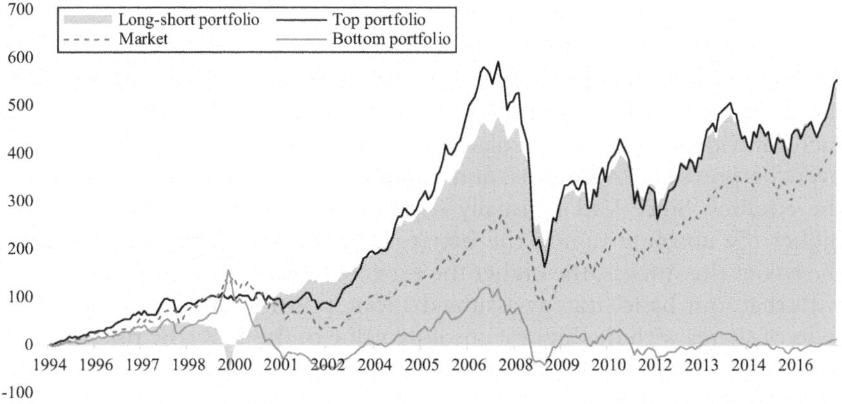

Fig. 4.3 Cumulative return on equal-weighted portfolios formed on idiosyncratic risk. (Note: The figure displays the cumulative return on the equal-weighted quantile of the portfolios from sorts on the trailing 60-month idiosyncratic risk from the CAPM. The calculations were made based on monthly observations. *Top portfolio* and *bottom portfolio* are quintile portfolios including the stocks with the lowest and the highest idiosyncratic risk, respectively. Market is the value-weighted portfolio of all the country equity markets considered. All the returns are expressed in percentage)

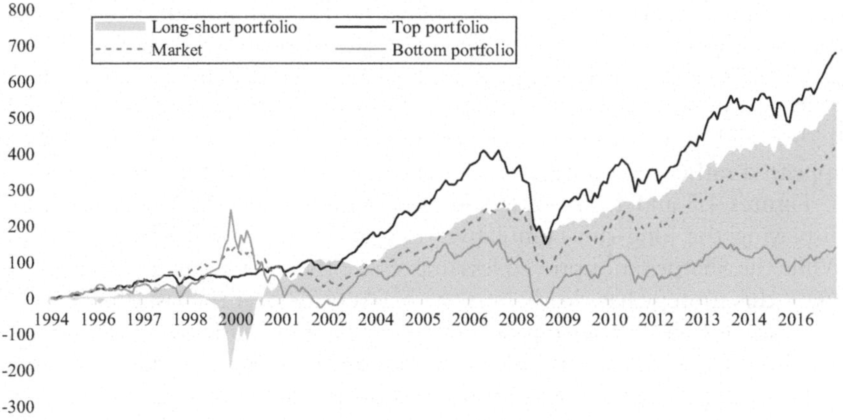

Fig. 4.4 Cumulative return on value-weighted portfolios formed on idiosyncratic risk. (Note: The figure displays the cumulative return on the value-weighted quantile of the portfolios from sorts on the trailing 60-month idiosyncratic risk from the CAPM. The calculations were made based on monthly observations. *Top portfolio* and *bottom portfolio* are quintile portfolios including the stocks with the lowest and the highest idiosyncratic risk, respectively. Market is the value-weighted portfolio of all the country equity markets considered. All the returns are expressed in percentage)

equities in the sample on their empirical VaR using the 5% cutoff based on the 24-month trailing monthly returns. In other words, each month for each individual stock we calculated the 5% percentile of monthly returns over the previous 24 months, and based on this variable, we then sorted the equities. Since VaR is usually negative, the lower the VaR value (or higher the absolute value), the better. In other words, in this approach, the riskier the stock is, the higher the expected future returns. Consistently with that, our basic strategy assumed a long position in the quintile portfolio of shares with the highest absolute value of the VaR (the riskiest) and the short position in the portfolio of shares with the lowest absolute value of the VaR (the safest).

The performance of the VaR portfolios in international equity markets is presented in Table 4.2.

Although the alphas on the long-short portfolio proved historically positive in all the 24 countries considered, only in a half of them these values significantly differed from zero. The precise alphas varied monthly from 0.26% in Ireland to 2.01% in Greece. In the largest of the considered markets, the USA, the alpha amounted to 0.90% with the corresponding *t*-statistic of 1.58. The VaR strategy displayed a slightly higher volatility than, for example, the very common momentum strategy. The standard deviation of returns ranged from 6.02% to 15.78%, and the volatility of the equal-weighted and value-weighted global portfolios equaled 5.50% and 7.03%, respectively. The profitability of the equally and value-weighted global portfolios remained similar: the long-short portfolios delivered 0.79% and 0.84% per month, respectively. Finally, the Sharpe ratios appeared rather moderate, at least compared with the earlier strategies.

Figures 4.5 and 4.6 provide additional insights into the VaR strategy by displaying the long-run cumulative returns on the global VaR portfolios. While the Sharpe ratios proved less impressive then in the case of other strategies, this strategy has clearly beat the markets for over the last 20 years.

So far, we have reviewed the strategies related to historical volatility or, in a broader sense, to the risk of investment securities. As we have seen, some strategies can serve as an interesting predictor of future returns in selecting securities even if the direction of the risk-return relationship still remains to some extent controversial. What about other moments of the return distribution? Does the shape matter? Could the skewness of the return distribution help? We will probe these questions in the next chapter.

Table 4.2 The performance of international portfolios formed on VaR

Country	*Top portfolio mean return*	*Bottom portfolio mean return*	*Average number of firms*	*T-B portfolio*		*Standard deviation*	*Sharpe ratio*	*Beta*	*Alpha*	
				Mean return	*t-stat*				*Value*	*t-stat*
Australia	0.94	0.03	46	0.91**	*(2.28)*	6.57	0.48	−0.13	1.01**	*(2.51)*
Austria	1.00	0.33	7	0.67	*(1.12)*	9.89	0.24	−0.17	0.76	*(1.27)*
Belgium	1.05	0.71	12	0.35	*(0.77)*	7.40	0.16	−0.25	0.53	*(1.17)*
Canada	1.28	−0.05	94	1.33**	*(2.47)*	8.81	0.52	−0.11	1.40***	*(2.60)*
Denmark	1.21	0.66	12	0.55	*(1.45)*	6.24	0.31	−0.09	0.64*	*(1.66)*
Finland	1.31	1.08	11	0.23	*(0.49)*	7.77	0.10	−0.18	0.41	*(0.87)*
France	1.17	0.58	47	0.60	*(1.23)*	8.00	0.26	−0.11	0.67	*(1.37)*
Germany	0.98	0.24	43	0.74	*(1.38)*	8.85	0.29	−0.13	0.82	*(1.51)*
Greece	1.15	−0.86	13	2.01**	*(2.40)*	13.76	0.51	−0.02	2.01**	*(2.39)*
Hong Kong	0.73	−0.96	23	1.68***	*(2.67)*	10.37	0.56	−0.21	1.84***	*(2.93)*
Ireland	1.16	0.88	4	0.28	*(0.30)*	15.78	0.06	0.03	0.26	*(0.27)*
Israel	1.39	0.82	15	0.57	*(1.03)*	9.13	0.22	0.00	0.57	*(1.03)*
Italy	0.99	0.26	28	0.73*	*(1.74)*	6.89	0.37	0.00	0.73*	*(1.73)*
Japan	0.51	−0.16	324	0.67	*(1.61)*	6.84	0.34	−0.23	0.68*	*(1.67)*
The Netherlands	1.19	0.57	19	0.61	*(1.25)*	8.06	0.26	−0.12	0.69	*(1.40)*
New Zealand	1.06	0.53	5	0.53	*(1.28)*	6.79	0.27	0.06	0.48	*(1.16)*
Norway	0.92	−0.02	15	0.94*	*(1.72)*	8.96	0.36	−0.07	1.00*	*(1.82)*
Portugal	0.55	−0.12	4	0.67	*(1.39)*	8.00	0.29	−0.20	0.75	*(1.55)*
Singapore	0.85	−0.59	12	1.44***	*(3.17)*	7.47	0.67	0.00	1.44***	*(3.14)*
Spain	0.99	0.00	18	0.99**	*(2.39)*	6.83	0.50	−0.10	1.07**	*(2.55)*
Sweden	1.51	0.75	26	0.75	*(1.57)*	7.91	0.33	−0.15	0.90*	*(1.86)*
Switzerland	1.10	0.86	29	0.24	*(0.60)*	6.51	0.13	−0.20	0.38	*(0.95)*

(*continued*)

Table 4.2 (continued)

Country	*Top portfolio mean return*	*Bottom portfolio mean return*	*Average number of firms*	*T-B portfolio*		*Standard deviation*	*Sharpe ratio*	*Beta*	*Alpha*	
				Mean return	*t-stat*				*Value*	*t-stat*
UK	0.95	0.15	117	0.79**	*(2.16)*	6.02	0.46	−0.12	0.85**	*(2.31)*
USA	1.26	0.51	712	0.74	*(1.32)*	9.25	0.28	−0.23	0.90	*(1.58)*
World (EW)	1.05	0.26	1637	0.79**	*(2.37)*	5.50	0.50	−0.20	0.90***	*(2.69)*
World (VW)	1.03	0.19	1637	0.84**	*(1.97)*	7.03	0.41	−0.21	0.95**	*(2.22)*

Note: The table reports the monthly returns on the portfolios from sorts on the 24-month VaR. The VaR was calculated as the fifth percentile of the 24-month trailing monthly returns. The calculations were made based on monthly observations. *Top portfolio* and *bottom portfolios* are quintile portfolio including the stocks with the lowest (usually highest absolute value) and the highest (usually lowest absolute value) VaR, respectively. *T-B portfolio* goes long in the top portfolio and short in the bottom portfolio. The Sharpe ratio is expressed on an annualized basis. The alpha and beta are derived from the CAPM. Mean returns, standard deviations, and alphas are expressed in percentage. Asterisks *, **, and *** indicate values significantly different from zero at the 10%, 5%, and 1% level, respectively

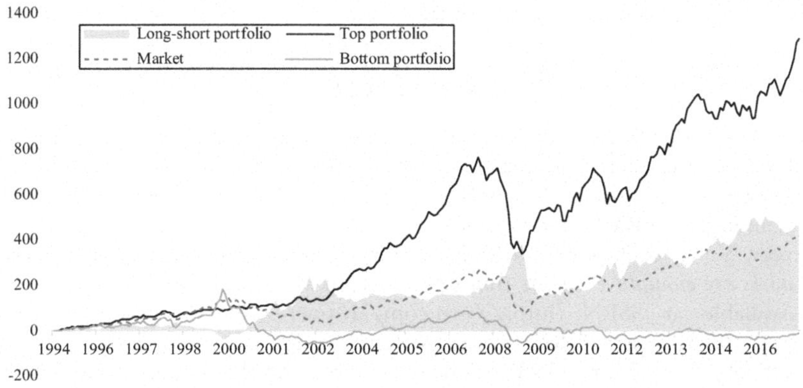

Fig. 4.5 Cumulative return on equal-weighted portfolios formed on VaR. (Note: The figure displays the cumulative return on the equal-weighted quantile of the portfolios from sorts on the 24-month VaR. The VaR was calculated as the fifth percentile of the 24-month trailing monthly returns. The calculations were made based on monthly observations. *Top portfolio* and *bottom portfolio* are quintile portfolios including the stocks with the lowest (usually highest absolute value) and the highest (usually lowest absolute value) VaR, respectively. Market is the value-weighted portfolio of all the country equity markets considered. All the returns are expressed in percentage)

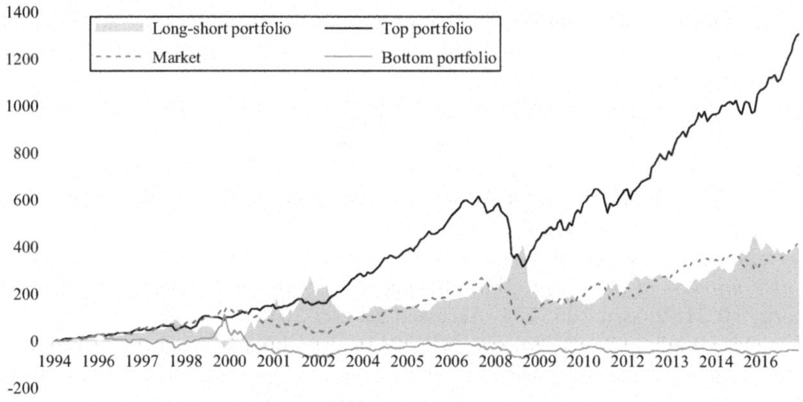

Fig. 4.6 Cumulative return on value-weighted portfolios formed on VaR. (Note: The figure displays the cumulative return on the value-weighted quantile of the portfolios from sorts on the 24-month VaR. The VaR was calculated as the fifth percentile of the 24-month trailing monthly returns. The calculations were made based on monthly observations. *Top portfolio* and *bottom portfolio* are quintile portfolios including the stocks with the lowest (usually highest absolute value) and the highest (usually lowest absolute value) VaR, respectively. Market is the value-weighted portfolio of all the country equity markets considered. All the returns are expressed in percentage)

References

Abel, A. B. (1990). Asset prices under habit formation and catching up with the Joneses. *American Economic Review, 80*(2), 38–42.

Alexander, C., & Sheedy, E. (2004). *A guide to risk management best practices.* Wilmington: PRMIA Publications.

Alexeev, V. V., & Tapon, F. (2012). *Equity portfolio diversification: How many stocks are enough? Evidence from five developed markets* (FIRN research paper). Available at SSRN: http://ssrn.com/abstract=2182295 or https://doi.org/10.2139/ssrn.2182295. Accessed 26 Oct 2015.

Alpert, M., & Raiffa, H. (1982). A progress report on the training of probability assessors. In D. Kahneman, P. Slovic, & A. Tversky (Eds.), *Judgment under uncertainty: Heuristics and biases* (pp. 294–305). New York/Cambridge: Cambridge University Press.

Anderson, C. W., & Garcia-Feijoo, L. (2006). Empirical evidence on capital investment, growth options, and security returns. *Journal of Finance, 61*, 171–194.

Ang, A. (2014). *Asset management: A systematic approach to factor investing.* New York: Oxford University Press.

Ang, A., Chen, J., & Xing, Y. (2006a). Downside risk. *Review of Financial Studies, 19*, 1191–1239.

Ang, A., Chen, J., & Xing, Y. (2006b). The cross-section of volatility and expected returns. *Journal of Finance, 61*, 259–299.

Ang, A., Hodrick, R., Xing, Y., & Zhang, X. (2009). High idiosyncratic volatility and low returns: International and further U.S. evidence. *Journal of Financial Economics, 91*, 1–23.

Asness, C. S., Frazzini, A., & Pedersen, L. H. (2014). Low-risk investing without industry bets. *Financial Analyst Journal, 70*(4), 24–41.

Asness, C. S., Frazzini, A., & Pedersen, L. H. (2017). *Quality minus junk.* Available at SSRN: https://ssrn.com/abstract=2312432 or https://doi.org/10.2139/ssrn.2312432. Accessed 23 Oct 2017.

Baker, N. L., & Haugen, R. A. (2012). *Low risk stocks outperform within all observable markets of the world* (Working paper). Available at SSRN: https://doi.org/10.2139/ssrn.2055431. Accessed 25 Oct 2015.

Baker, M., Bradley, B., & Wurgler, J. (2011). Benchmarks as limits to arbitrage: Understanding the low-volatility anomaly. *Financial Analyst Journal, 67*(1), 40–54.

Balakrishnan, K., Bartov, E., & Faurel, L. (2010). Post loss/profit announcement drift. *Journal of Accounting and Economics, 50*, 20–41.

Bali, T. G., & Cakici, N. (2004). Value at risk and expected stock returns. *Financial Analyst Journal, 60*(2), 57–73.

Bali, T. G., & Cakici, N. (2008). Idiosyncratic volatility and the cross section of expected returns. *Journal of Financial and Quantitative Analysis, 43*(1), 29–58.

Bali, C., & Cakici, N. (2010). World market risk, country-specific risk and expected returns in international stock markets. *Journal of Banking and Finance, 34*, 1152–1165.

Bali, T. G., Cakici, N., Yan, X., & Zhang, Z. (2005). Does idiosyncratic risk really matter? *Journal of Finance, 60*(2), 905–929.

Bali, T. G., Gokcan, S., & Liang, B. (2007). Value at risk and the cross-section of hedge fund returns. *Journal of Banking & Finance, 31*(4), 1135–1166.

Bali, T., Cakici, N., & Whitelaw, R. F. (2011). Maxing out: Stocks as lotteries and the cross-section of expected returns. *Journal of Financial Economics, 99*(2), 427–446.

Barber, B., & Odean, T. (2008). All that glitters: The effect of attention on the buying behavior of individual and institutional investors. *Review of Financial Studies, 21*(2), 785–818.

Barberis, N., & Huang, M. (2008). Stocks as lotteries: The implications of probability weighting for security prices. *American Economic Review, 98*(5), 2066–2100.

Bekaert, G., Erb, C. B., Harvey, C. R., & Viskanta, T. E. (1996). *The cross-sectional determinants of emerging equity market returns.* Retrieved from https://www0.gsb.columbia.edu/faculty/gbekaert/PDF_Papers/The_cross-sectional_determinants.pdf. Accessed 21 Sept 2015.

Bekaert, G., Hodrick, R. J., & Zhang, X. (2012). Aggregate idiosyncratic volatility. *Journal of Financial and Quantitative Analysis, 47*(6), 1155–1185.

Bernard, S., Leippold, M., & Lohre, H. (2013). *Risk-based commodity investing* (Working paper). Available at http://viessmanncentre.ca/wp-content/uploads/2014/05/Bernardi_Leiphold_Lohre1.pdf. Accessed 24 Oct 2015.

Black, F. (1972). Capital market equilibrium with restricted borrowing. *Journal of Business, 45*, 44–455.

Black, F. (1993). Beta and returns. *Journal of Portfolio Management, 20*(1), 8–18.

Black, F., Jensen, M. C., & Scholes, M. S. (1972). The capital asset pricing model: Some empirical tests. In M. C. Jensen (Ed.), *Studies in the theory of capital markets* (pp. 79–121). New York: Praeger Publishers.

Blitz, D., Pang, J., & van Vliet, P. (2013b). The volatility effect in emerging markets. *Emerging Markets Review, 16*, 31–45.

Blitz, D. C., & van Vliet, P. (2007). The volatility effect: Lower risk without lower return. *Journal of Portfolio Management, 34*(1), 102–113. https://doi.org/10.3905/jpm.2007.698039.

Blitz, D., & de Groot, W. (2014). Strategic allocation to commodity factor premiums. *Journal of Alternative Investments, 17*(2), 103–115.

Blitz, D., Falkenstein, E., & van Vliet, P. (2014a). Explanations for the volatility effect: An overview based on the CAPM assumptions. *Journal of Portfolio Management, 40*(3), 61–76.

Blume, M. E. (1970). Portfolio theory: A step towards its practical application. *Journal of Business, 43*(2), 152–174.

Blume, M. E., & Friend, I. (1973). A new look at the capital asset pricing model. *Journal of Finance, 28*(1), 19–34.

Boyer, B., Mitton, T., & Vorkink, K. (2010). Expected idiosyncratic skewness. *Review of Financial Studies, 23*(1), 169–202.

Brennan, M. (1971). Capital market equilibrium with divergent borrowing and lending rates. *Journal of Financial and Quantitative Analysis, 6*(5), 1197–1205.

Brennan, M. J., Cheng, X., & Li, F. (2012). Agency and institutional investment. *European Financial Management, 18*(1), 1–27.

Campbell, J. Y., & Cochrane, J. H. (1999). By fore of habit: A Consumption-based explanation of aggregate stock market behavior. *Journal of Political Economy, 107*(2), 205–251.

Campbell, J. Y., Lo, A. W., & MacKinlay, A. C. (1997). *The econometrics of financial markets*. Princeton: Princeton University Press.

Campbell, C. J., Rhee, S. G., Du, Y., & Tang, N. (2008). *Market sentiment, IPO underpricing, and valuation* (Working paper). Available at SSRN: http://ssrn.com/abstract=1108540 or https://doi.org/10.2139/ssrn.1108540. Accessed 22 Nov 2015.

Carhart, M. M. (1997). On persistence in mutual fund performance. *Journal of Finance, 52*(1), 57–82.

Chan, L., Karceski, J., & Lakonishok, J. (1999). On portfolio optimization: Forecasting covariances and choosing the risk model. *Review of Financial Studies, 12*, 937–974.

Chan, L. K., Lakonishok, J., & Sougiannis, T. (2001). The stock market valuation of research and development expenditures. *Journal of Finance, 56*, 2431–2456.

Chen, L., Li, S., & Wang, J. (2011a). Liquidity, skewness and stock returns: Evidence from Chinese stock market. *Asia-Pacific Financial Markets, 18*, 405–427.

Chen, D.-H., Chen, C. D., & Wu, S. C. (2014). VaR and the cross-section of expected stock returns: An emerging market evidence. *Journal of Business Economics and Management, 15*(3), 441–459.

Clark, A., & Oswald, A. (1996). Satisfaction and comparison income. *Journal of Public Economics, 61*(3), 359–381.

Clarke, R., de Silva, H., & Thorley, S. (2006). Minimum-variance portfolios in the US equity market. *Journal of Portfolio Management, 33*(1), 10–24.

Clarke, R., de Silva, H., & Thorley, S. (2010). Know your VMS exposure. *Journal of Portfolio Management, 36*(2), 52–59.

Cochrane, J. H. (2005). *Asset pricing*. Princeton: Princeton University Press.

Cooper, M. J., Gulen, H., & Schill, M. J. (2008). Asset growth and the cross-section of stock returns. *Journal of Finance, 63*, 1609–1651.

Cornell, B. (2009). The pricing of volatility and skewness: A new interpretation. *Journal of Investing, 18*(3), 27–30.

Dahlquist, M., & Bansal, R. (2002a). *Expropriation risk and return in global equity markets* (EFA 2002 Berlin meetings presented paper). Available at SSRN: http://ssrn.com/abstract=298180 or https://doi.org/10.2139/ssrn.298180. Accessed 21 Sept 2015.

Dahlquist, M., & Bansal, R. (2002b). *Expropriation risk and return in global equity markets* (EFA 2002 Berlin meetings presented paper). Available at SSRN: http://ssrn.com/abstract=298180 or https://doi.org/10.2139/ssrn.298180. Accessed 30 Sept 2017.

de Carvalho, R. L., Dugnolle, P., Lu, X., & Moulin, P. (2014). Low-risk anomalies in global fixed income: Evidence from major broad markets. *Journal of Fixed Income, 23*(4), 51–70. https://doi.org/10.3905/jfi.2014.23.4.051.

de Giorgi, E. G., Post, T., & Yalcin, A. (2013). *A concave security market line.* Available at SSRN: http://ssrn.com/abstract=1800229 or https://doi.org/10.2139/ssrn.1800229. Accessed 25 Sept 2017.

DeMarzo, P., Kaniel, R., & Kremer, I. (2004). Diversification as a public good: Community effects in portfolio choice. *Journal of Finance, 59*(4), 1677–1715.

Dimitriou, D., & Simos, T. (2011). The relationship between stock returns and volatility in the seventeen largest international stock markets: A semi-parametric approach. *Modern Economy, 2*, 1–8.

Easterlin, R. (1995). Will raising the incomes of all raise the happiness of all? *Journal of Economic Behavior and Organization, 27*, 35–47.

Eberhardt, A. C., Maxwell, W. F., & Siddique, A. R. (2004). An examination of long-term abnormal stock returns and operating performance following R&D increases. *Journal of Finance, 59*, 623–650.

Elton, E. J., & Gruber, M. J. (1995). *Modern portfolio theory and investment analysis.* Hoboken: John Wiley & Sons.

Erb, C. B., Harvey, C. R., & Viskanta, T. E. (1995). Country risk and global equity selection. *Journal of Portfolio Management, 21*(2), 74–83.

Fairfield, P. M. (2003). Accrued earnings and growth: Implications for future profitability and market mispricing. *Accounting Review, 58*, 353–371.

Falkenstein, E. G. (1994). *Mutual funds, idiosyncratic variance, and asset returns* (PhD thesis). Northwestern University. Available at http://www.researchgate.net/publication/269698051. Accessed 25 Oct 2015.

Falkenstein, E. (1996). Preferences for stock characteristics as revealed by mutual fund portfolio holdings. *Journal of Finance, 51*(1), 111–135.

Falkenstein, E. G. (2009). *Risk and return in general: Theory and evidence.* Available at SSRN: http://ssrn.com/abstract=1420356 or https://doi.org/10.2139/ssrn.1420356. Accessed 28 Oct 2015.

Falkenstein, E. G. (2012). *The missing risk premium: Why low volatility investing works.* CreateSpace Independent Publishing Platform.

Fama, E. F., & French, K. R. (1992). The cross-section of expected returns. *Journal of Finance, 47*, 427–466.

Fama, E. F., & French, K. R. (2006). Profitability, investment and average returns. *Journal of Financial Economics, 82*, 491–518.

Fama, E. F., & French, K. R. (2015). A five-factor asset pricing model. *Journal of Financial Economics, 116*(1), 1–22. https://doi.org/10.1016/j.jfineco.2014.10.010.

Fama, E. F., & MacBeth, J. D. (1973). Risk, return and equilibrium: Empirical tests. *Journal of Political Economy, 81*(3), 607–636.

Fernandez-Perez, A., Fuertes, A.-M., & Miffre, J. (2014). *Is idiosyncratic volatility priced in commodity futures markets?* Available at SSRN: http://ssrn.com/abstract=2120587 or https://doi.org/10.2139/ssrn.2120587. Accessed 24 Oct 2015.

Ferrer-i-Carbonell, A. (2005). Income and well-being: An empirical analysis of the comparison income effect. *Journal of Public Economics, 89*(5–6), 997–1019.

Fink, J., Fink, K., & He, H. (2010). Idiosyncratic volatility measures and expected return. *Financial Management, 41*(3), 519–553.

Fischhoff, B., Slovic, P., & Lichtenstein, S. (1977). Knowing with certainty: The appropriateness of extreme confidence. *Journal of Experimental Psychology: Human Perception and Performance, 3*(4), 552–564.

Francis, J. C. (1990). *Investments: Analysis and management*. New York: McGraw Hill Higher Education.

Frazzini, A., & Pedersen, L. H. (2014). Betting against beta. *Journal of Financial Economics, 111*, 1–25. https://doi.org/10.1016/j.jfineco.2013.10.005.

Friend, I., & Blume, M. (1970). Measurement of portfolio performance under uncertainty. *American Economic Review, 60*, 561–575.

Fu, F. (2009). Idiosyncratic risk and the cross-section of expected returns. *Journal of Financial Economics, 91*(1), 24–37.

Fuertes, A. M., Miffre, J., & Fernández-Pérez, A. (2015). Commodity strategies based on momentum, term structure and idiosyncratic volatility. *Journal of Futures Markets, 35*(3), 274–297.

Gali, J. (1994). Keeping up with the Joneses: Consumption externalities, portfolio choice, and asset prices. *Journal of Money, Credit and Banking, 26*(1), 1–8.

Garcia, R., Mantilla-Garcia, D., & Martellini, L. (2014). A model-free measure of aggregate idiosyncratic volatility and the prediction of market returns. *Quantitative Analysis, 49*(5–6), 1133–1165. https://doi.org/10.1017/S0022109014000489.

George, T. J., & Hwang, C. Y. (2010). A resolution of the distress risk and leverage puzzles in the cross section of stock returns. *Journal of Financial Economics, 96*, 56–79.

Goetzman, W., & Kumar, A. (2008). Equity portfolio diversification. *Review of Finance, 12*(3), 433–463. https://doi.org/10.1093/rof/rfn005.

Goyal, A., & Santa-Clara, P. (2003). Idiosyncratic risk matters! *Journal of Finance, 58*(3), 975–1008.

Griffin, J. M., & Lemmon, M. L. (2002). Book-to-market equity, distress risk, and stock returns. *Journal of Finance, 57*, 2317–2336.

Gu, F. (2005). Innovation, future earnings, and market efficiency. *Journal of Accounting, Auditing and Finance, 20*, 385–418.

Hahn, J., & Lee, H. (2009). Financial constraints, debt capacity, and the cross-section of stock returns. *Journal of Finance, 64*, 891–921.

Han, Y., & Lesmond, D. (2011). Liquidity biases and the pricing of cross-sectional idiosyncratic volatility. *Review of Financial Studies, 24*, 1590–1629.

Haugen, R. A., & Baker, N. (1991). The efficient market inefficiency of capitalization-weighted stock portfolios. *Journal of Portfolio Management, 17*(1), 35–40.

Haugen, R. A., & Baker, N. L. (1996). Commonality in the determinants of expected stock returns. *Journal of Financial Economics, 41*(3), 401–439.

Haugen, R. A., & Heins, A. J. (1975). Risk and the rate of return on financial assets: Some old wine in new bottles. *Journal of Financial and Quantitative Analysis, 10*(5), 775–784.

Heaton, J. C., & Lucas, D. J. (2000). Portfolio choice and asset prices: The importance of entrepreneurial risk. *Journal of Finance, 55*(3), 1163–1198.

Hirshleifer, D., Hsu, P.-H., & Li, D. (2013). Innovative efficiency and stock returns. *Journal of Financial Economics, 107*, 632–654.

Ho, H. G., & Sraer, D. A. (2015, forthcoming). Speculative betas. *Journal of Finance*. Available at SSRN: https://ssrn.com/abstract=1967462 or https://doi.org/10.2139/ssrn.1967462. Accessed 23 Oct 2017.

Hou, K., & Loh, R. (2016). Have we solved the idiosyncratic volatility puzzle? *Journal of Financial Economics, 121*(1), 167–194. https://doi.org/10.1016/j.jfineco.2016.02.013.

Houweling, P., & van Zundert, J. (2014). *Factor investing in the corporate bond market*. Available at SSRN: http://ssrn.com/abstract=2516322 or https://doi.org/10.2139/ssrn.2516322. Accessed 25 Oct 2015.

Houweling, P., Beekhuizen, P., Bus, S., Haesen, D., Kwaak, P., Verberk, V., & Wang, R. (2012). *The low risk anomaly in credits* (Robeco Research note). Available at https://www.robeco.com/images/the-low-risk-anomaly-in-credits.pdf. Accessed 24 Oct 2015.

Huang, D., & Miao, J. (2016). *Oil prices and the cross-section of stock returns*. Available at SSRN: https://ssrn.com/abstract=2847514. Accessed 23 Oct 2017.

Hueng, C. J., & Yau, R. (2013). Country-specific idiosyncratic risk and global equity index returns. *International Review of Economics & Finance, 25*, 325–337.

Iqbal, J., & Azher, S. (2014). Value-at-risk and expected stock returns: Evidence from Pakistan. *Lahore Journal of Economics, 19*(2), 71–100.

Iqbal, J., Azher, S., & Ijaz, A. (2013). Predictive ability of value-at-risk methods: Evidence from the Karachi Stock Exchange-100 Index. *IUP Journal of Financial Risk Management, 10*(1), 26–40.

Jagannathan, R., & Ma, T. (2003). Risk reduction in large portfolios: Why imposing the wrong constrains helps. *Journal of Finance, 58*(4), 1651–1684.

Jensen, M. C., Black, F., & Scholes, M. S. (1972). The capital asset pricing model: Some empirical tests. In M. C. Jensen (Ed.), *Studies in the theory of capital markets*. New York: Praeger Publishers.

Jorion, P. (2007). *Financial Risk Manager Handbook*. Wiley, Hoboken.

Kim, J., & Lee, C. (2017). *Idiosyncratic volatility and stock return predictability: Evidence from the Korean stock market*. Available at http://www.kafo.or.kr/board_common/file_download.asp?Board_Key=144&File_Key=226&flag=2. Accessed 6 Sept 2017.

Knight, J., Song, L., & Gunatilaka, R. (2009). Subjective well-being and its determinants in rural China. *China Economic Review, 20*(4), 635–649.

Kogan, L., & Papanikolaou, D. (2013). Firm characteristics and stock returns: The role of investment specific shocks. *Review of Financial Studies, 25*, 2718–2759.

Kumar, A. (2009). Who gambles in the stock market? *Journal of Finance, 64*(4), 1889–1933.

Lakonishok, J., Schleifer, A., & Vishny, R. W. (1994). Contrarian investment, extrapolation, and risk. *Journal of Finance, 49*(5), 1541–1578.

Lettau, M., & Ludvigson, S. (2001). Consumption, aggregate wealth, and expected stock returns. *Journal of Finance, 56*(3), 815–849.

Levy, H. (1978). Equilibrium in an imperfect market: A constraint on the number of securities in the portfolio. *American Economic Review, 68*, 643–658.

Liang, S. X., & Wei, K. C. J. (2006). *Volatility and stock market returns around the world* (Working paper). Available at: https://www.eurofidai.org/Xin_Liang.pdf. Accessed 26 Oct 2015.

Liang, S. X., & Wei, K. C. J (2016). Volatility risk factors and stock returns around the world: Implications for multinational corporations. In *Asian Finance Association (AsFA) 2013 Conference*. Available at SSRN: https://ssrn.com/abstract=2217622 or https://doi.org/10.2139/ssrn.2217622. Accessed 23 Oct 2017.

Lintner, J. (1965a). The valuation of risk assets and the selection of risky investments in stock portfolios and capital budgets. *Review of Economics and Statistics, 47*(1), 13–37.

Lintner, J. (1965b). Security prices, risk and maximal gains from diversification. Journal of Finance, *20*(4), 587–615.

Lou, D. (2014). Attracting investor attention through advertising. *Review of Financial Studies, 27*, 1797–1829.

Lu, Z., & Murray, S. (2017, in press). Bear beta. *Journal of Financial Economics*. Available at SSRN: https://ssrn.com/abstract=2871737 or https://doi.org/10.2139/ssrn.2871737. Accessed 25 Feb 2018.

Luttmer, E. (2005). Neighbors as negatives: Relative earnings and well-being. *Quarterly Journal of Economics, 120*(3), 963–1002.

Malkiel, B., & Xu, Y. (1997). Risk and return revisited. *Journal of Portfolio Management, 23*(3), 9–14. https://doi.org/10.3905/jpm.1997.409608.

Malkiel, B., & Xu, Y. (2004). *Idiosyncratic risk and security returns* (AFA 2001 New Orleans meetings). Available at SSRN: http://ssrn.com/abstract=255303 or https://doi.org/10.2139/ssrn.255303. Accessed 25 Oct 2015.

Martellini, L. (2008). Toward the design of better equity benchmarks: Rehabilitating the tangency portfolio from modern portfolio theory. *Journal of Portfolio Management, 34*(4), 34–41.

Merton, R. (1987). A simple model of capital market equilibrium with incomplete information. *Journal of Finance, 42*, 483–510.

Miller, E. M. (1977). Risk, uncertainty, and divergence of opinion. *Journal of Finance, 32*(4), 1151–1168.

Miller, M. H., & Scholes, M. (1972). Rates of return in relation to risk: A reexamination of some recent findings. In M. C. Jensen (Ed.), *Studies in the theory of capital markets*. New York: Praeger.

Mitton, T., & Vorkink, K. (2007). Equilibrium underdiversification and the preference for skewness. *Review of Financial Studies, 20*(4), 1255–1288.

Mohanram, P. (2005). Separating winners from losers among low book-to-market stocks using financial statement analysis. *Review of Accounting Studies, 10*, 133–170.

Mossin, J. (1966). Equilibrium in a capital asset market. *Econometrica, 35*(4), 768–783.

Ng, K. Y., & Phelps, B. D. (2015). The hunt for a low-risk anomaly in the USD corporate bond market. *Journal of Portfolio Management, 42*(1), 63–84.

Novy-Marx, R. (2013). The other side of value: The gross profitability premium. *Journal of Financial Economics, 108*, 1–28.

Palazzo, B. (2012). Cash holdings, risk, and expected returns. *Journal of Financial Economics, 104*, 162–185.

Penman, S., Richardson, S., & Tuna, I. (2007). The book-to-price effect in stock returns: Accounting for leverage. *Journal of Accounting Research, 45*, 427–467.

Richardson, S., Sloan, R. G., Soliman, M., & Tuna, I. (2005). Accrual reliability, earnings persistence and stock prices. *Journal of Accounting and Economics, 39*, 437–485.

Roll, R. (1992). A mean/variance analysis of tracking error. *Journal of Portfolio Management, 18*(4), 13–22.

Roussanov, N. (2010). Diversification and its discontents: Idiosyncratic and entrepreneurial risk in the quest for social status. *Journal of Finance, 65*(5), 1755–1788.

Schneider, P., Wagner, C., & Zechner, J. (2016). *Low risk anomalies?* (CFS WP No. 550). Available at SSRN: https://ssrn.com/abstract=2858933. Accessed 23 Oct 2017.

Sensoy, B. (2009). Performance evaluation and self designated benchmark indexes in the mutual fund management industry. *Journal of Financial Economics, 92*(1), 25–39.

Sharpe, W. F. (1964). Capital asset prices: A theory of market equilibrium under conditions of risk. *Journal of Finance, 19*(3), 425–442.

Sharpe, W. F. (1981). Decentralized investment management. *Journal of Finance, 36*(2), 217–234.

Sloan, R. G. (1996). Do stock prices reflect information in accruals and cash flows about future earnings? *Accounting Review, 71*, 289–315.

Svenson, O. (1981). Are we all less risky and more skillful than our fellow drivers? *Acta Psychologica, 47*(2), 143–148.

Szymanowska, M., de Roon, F., Nijman, T., & van den Goorbergh, R. (2014). An anatomy of commodity futures risk premia. *Journal of Finance, 69*(1), 453–482.

Tinic, S. M., & West, R. R. (1986). Risk, return and equilibrium: A revisit. *Journal of Political Economy, 94*, 126–147.

Titman, S., Wei, K. J., & Xie, F. (2004). Capital investments and stock returns. *Journal of Financial and Quantitative Analysis, 39*, 677–700.

Treynor, J. L. (1961). *Market value, time, and risk.* Available at SSRN: http://ssrn.com/abstract=2600356 or https://doi.org/10.2139/ssrn.2600356. Accessed 17 Oct 2015.

Treynor, J. L (1962). *Toward a theory of market value of risky assets* (Unpublished manuscript). Final version in *Asset Pricing and Portfolio Performance* (pp. 15–22), 1999, Robert A. Korajczyk (ed.). London: Risk Books. Available also at SSRN: http://ssrn.com/abstract=628187 or https://doi.org/10.2139/ssrn.628187. Accessed 17 Oct 2015.

Tversky, A., & Kahneman, D. (1992). Advances in prospect theory: Cumulative representation of uncertainty. *Journal of Risk and Uncertainty, 5*(4), 297–323.

van Vliet, P., Blitz, D., & van der Grient, B. (2011). *Is the relation between volatility and expected stock returns positive, flat or negative?* Available at SSRN: http://ssrn.com/abstract=1881503 or https://doi.org/10.2139/ssrn.1881503. Accessed 25 Oct 2015.

Verousis, T., & Voukelatos, N. (2015). *Cross-sectional dispersion and expected returns.* Available at SSRN: https://ssrn.com/abstract=2734192 or https://doi.org/10.2139/ssrn.2734192. Accessed 23 Oct 2017.

Walkshausl, C. (2014a). International low-risk investing. *Journal of Portfolio Management, 41*(4), 45–56.

Walkshausl, C. (2014b). The MAX effect: European evidence. *Journal of Banking and Finance, 42*(1), 1–10. https://doi.org/10.1016/j.jbankfin.2014.01.020.

Wang, H., & Yu, J. (2013). *Dissecting the profitability premium* (AFA 2013 San Diego meetings paper). Retrieved from SSRN: https://doi.org/10.2139/ssrn.1711856. Accessed 4 Nov 2015.

Wilmott, P. (2008). *Paul Wilmott on quantitative finance*. Hoboken: John Wiley & Sons.

Zaremba, A. (2015). The January seasonality and the performance of country-level value and momentum strategies. *Copernican Journal of Finance & Accounting, 2*, 195–209. http://apcz.pl/czasopisma/index.php/CJFA/article/view/CJFA.2015.024

Zaremba, A. (2016a). Investor sentiment, limits on arbitrage, and the performance of cross-country market anomalies. *Journal of Behavioral and Experimental Finance*, 9, 136–163. http://dx.doi.org/10.1016/j.jbef.2015.11.007.

Zaremba, A., & Shemer, J. (2016a). *Country asset allocation*. New York: Palgrave Macmillan.

Zaremba, A. (2016b). Is there low-risk anomaly across countries? *Eurasian Economic Review*, 69(1), 45–65.

Zaremba, A. (2016c). *Country risk and expected returns across global equity markets*. Available at SSRN: https://ssrn.com/abstract=2778061. Accessed 23 Jan 2018.

Zaremba, A., & Andreu Sánchez, L. (2017). *Paper profits or real money? Trading costs and stock market anomalies in country equity indices*. Available at https://doi.org/10.2139/ssrn.3038514

Zaremba, A., & Czapkiewicz, A. (2017a). Digesting anomalies in emerging European markets: A comparison of factor pricing models. *Emerging Markets Review, 31*, 1–15. https://doi.org/10.1016/j.ememar.2016.12.002.

Zaremba, A., & Czapkiewicz, A. (2017b, in press). The cross section of international government bond returns. *Economic Modelling*. https://doi.org/10.1016/j.econmod.2017.06.011.

Zaremba, A., & Schabek, T. (2017). Seasonality in government bond returns and factor premia. *Research in International Business and Finance, 41*, 292–302. https://doi.org/10.1016/j.ribaf.2017.04.036.

Zaremba, A., & Shemer, K. (2017, in press). Is there momentum in factor premia? Evidence from international equity markets. *Research in International Business and Finance*. https://doi.org/10.1016/j.ribaf.2017.12.002.

CHAPTER 5

Are Stocks Lotteries? The Shape of Distribution Matters

According to the classical asset pricing models, a successful investor needs to mind only two things: return and risk, and while risk as a potential consequence seems obvious, its measurement and understanding, however, have always presented a challenge. Ever since Markowitz introduced his mean-variance paradigm, it has become commonly understood that all the risk relevant to portfolio selection is captured by the second moment of the return distribution, or variance (squared standard deviation). Therefore, investors should build their portfolios by striking an optimal trade-off between the portfolio's expected returns and its future standard deviation. The most prominent financial model dominating for the last 60 years—the capital asset pricing model (CAPM) by Sharpe (1964), Lintner (1965a, b), and Mossin—is based precisely on this concept. In other words, the expected return on any security should equal the risk-free rate of return plus the risk premium, which equals stock market beta multiplied by the market risk premium.

The Role of the Shape of the Distribution

The idea behind interpreting risk as standard deviation of returns is elementary. The standard deviation, as the square root of variance, presents the potential dispersion of future returns. The less we know about the future outcome, the riskier the stock. This definition, simple as it seems, does have an important caveat which may escape the commonsense understanding of

A. Zaremba, J. "Koby" Shemer, *Price-Based Investment Strategies*,
https://doi.org/10.1007/978-3-319-91530-2_5

risk: the standard deviation is symmetrical. Irrespective of whether the return unexpectedly rises or sinks under the mean—it is all considered as risk. Does it comply with the way investors understand risk? If I expect to earn 10%, but there is a chance to win 20%, is that a risk? Not really. Thus the critical element is the left side of the distribution, namely the likelihood of losing.

Summing up, it is not merely the dispersion of the return distribution that matters to investors, but also its shape. This has been known under different names like "tail risk", or "skewness". So what precisely is skewness? It is a metric capturing the asymmetry of return distribution and, in essence, emerges in two forms: positive or negative. Positive skewness signals that data points are skewed to the right; thus, there are more extreme positive returns than in the case of a normal distribution (e.g., Panel A of Fig. 5.1). On the contrary, negative skewness indicates more extreme losses (e.g., Panel B of Fig. 5.1).

Investment assets can display various return distributions. Corporate bonds tend to the left-skewed distribution: the investor usually earns regular, steady, small returns, which only sometimes happen to be diminished by singular large losses resulting from a default. A private equity fund, on the other hand, displays positive skewness as nine out of ten start-up companies are likely to fail, and the only one stands the chance to become a new Microsoft.

So which distribution do investors prefer? At first sight, it may appear that investors prefer positive skewness, like lottery tickets, to large negative drops resulting from possible crashes. The lottery-type stocks might thus be more expensive, and, indeed, we find anecdotal evidence to support this prediction: many, both individual and institutional, investors

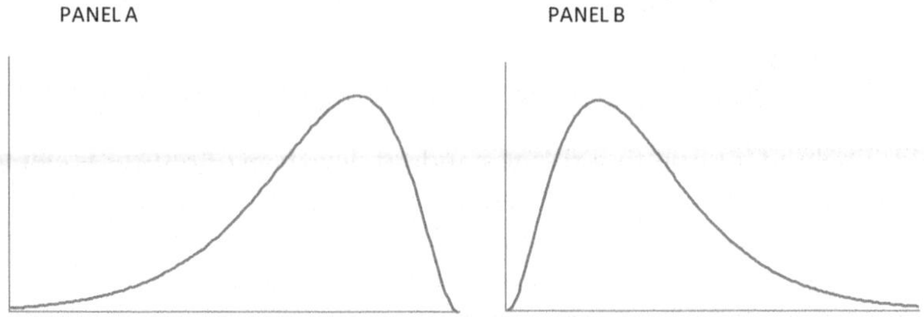

Fig. 5.1 Skewness of return distributions. Panel A: left-skewed distribution. Panel B: right-skewed distribution. (Note: Own elaboration)

used this argumentation to justify the high prices of internet stocks at the end of previous century. Even Alan Greenspan, the Chairman of Federal Reserve, argued a "lottery premium" in internet equities during his hearing before the Senate Budget Committee on 28 January 1999:

> The size of that potential market is so huge that you have these pie-in-the-sky type of potentials for a lot of different vehicles. And undoubtedly, some of these small companies, whose stock prices are going through the roof, will succeed. And they well may justify even higher prices. The vast majority are almost sure to fail. That's the way the markets work in this regard.... What lottery managers have known for centuries is that you could get somebody to pay for a one-in-a-million shot, more than the value of that chance. In other words, people pay more for a claim on a very big payoff, and that's where the profits from lotteries have always come from. (Stevenson 1999)

The theoretical considerations, however, are not all that obvious (Ilmanen 2011). A plausible counterargument has been risen by Nassim Taleb, the bestselling author of *The Black Swan* (2007) and *Fooled by Randomness* (2005). He pointed out that some money managers may actually prefer negative skewness, suggesting that professional asset managers may prefer frequent small gains and infrequent huge loses risking rather occasional "blowups" than continuous "bleeding". From the business perspective, underperforming peers in normal times is bad, while outperforming them consistently, even by small amounts, helps to attract clients and increase the value of asset under the company's management.

So what does the data say? The majority of the studies indicate that investors do prefer positive skewness to negative jumps. In other words, they both "like lottery tickets and fear crashes" (Ilmanen 2011). The precise results, however, heavily depend on how the skewness is measured. Therefore, before we move to the review of the actual evidence on skewness-based investing, let us first dig deeper into why the skewness actually matters to investors. As pointed out by Ilmanen (2011), the preference for positive skewness is driven rather by the desire for exceptional upside than the protection against the downside. Investors are prone to overpay for securities that have an asymmetrically large upside, resembling the lottery buyers overpaying more when the jackpot is outsized (compared to other rewards) or racetrack punters overpaying for long shots. Still, a viable contributor is the search for downside protection.

Why the Skewness Matters?

As usual in finance, we have a few explanations of the skewness phenomenon: some gravitating toward neoclassical, or "rational", finance and some focusing more on the behavioral aspect. The earliest models incorporating skewness in the portfolio construction appeared long before the dawn of behavioral finance. The idea of considering skewness in determining optimal investments was first introduced by Arditti (1967, 1971), who provided both theoretical and empirical evidence that investors demand a lower (higher) rate of return on investments whose return distributions are positively (negatively) skewed. This analysis was later extended by Scott and Horvath (1980), who analyzed not only skewness but also multiple higher moments of the distribution, including kurtosis, proving that positive values of odd (even) moments command negative (positive) risk premia and vice versa for negative values.[1] In other words, higher values of even moments, that is, variance and kurtosis, are associated with higher future returns, while higher values of odd moments, that is, skewness, are associated with lower expected returns. Analogously, lower values of even moments, that is, variance and kurtosis, are associated with lower future returns, while lower values of odd moments, that is, skewness, are associated with higher expected returns.

Once the basic relationships had been established, the time came for a revised asset pricing model that would take into account the higher moments. This was done by Kraus and Litzenberg (1976) who in essence, extended the CAPM by stating that the expected returns are not only determined by the amount of undiversifiable variance, but also by the security's skewness. Similarly, in the Kraus and Litzenberg model (1976), the unsystematic risk—relative to both skewness and variance—is diversifiable and, thus, does not impact expected return. In other words, if investors can easily eliminate some risk, then it is irrelevant to the valuation. This analysis was subsequently extended by Harvey and Siddique (2000), who incorporated systematic skewness in their asset pricing model by developing a special co-skewness measure that we will look into below.

Another set of explanations revolve around behavioral issues and, in particular, around preference for lotteries. These explanations refer to the stories behind the low-risk anomaly that we have discussed in the previous chapter. For example, in 2007 Mitton and Vorkink developed a model

[1] Similar evidence was provided by Dittmar (2002) and Kimball (1993).

assuming the existence of a group of investors with a direct preference for positive skewness: the "lotto investors". The group would care little about the expected profit, willing to sacrifice the Sharpe ratio, if only to achieve higher skewness. Why would they choose such securities? Although not excessively profitable on average, these stocks still offered a chance for huge payoffs. The researchers concluded that "lotto investors" would deliberately hold undiversified portfolios as the more diversified portfolio means lower skewness, and skewness is what they seek. Across the financial markets, the authors found large segments of individual investors exhibiting lotto preferences: on average not outperforming, but likely to make it as jackpot winners (Ilmanen 2011).

Interestingly, other studies specify who the lotto players are. Kumar (2009) and Kumar et al. (2011), researching data from a major US discount brokerage house, indicated that the strongest inclination for lottery stocks showed poor, uneducated men, mainly from Catholic, African American, or Hispanic minority, that is, people with the worst economic prospects within the American society, for whom both lotteries and lottery stocks may offer the only hope for gaining wealth. As a rule, retail investors are more likely to show lottery-type preferences than institutional investors with the inclination rising in economically challenging times.

Lottery preferences have been further explored by Barberis and Huang (2008) in their famous paper "Stocks as Lotteries". The authors argued that investors overvalued and in effect overweighted low-probability events which led them to overpay for assets with positive skewness. In general, investors prefer stocks with high-idiosyncratic volatility and large skewness, with an elevated chance of such low-probability payoffs. The overvalued stocks have higher prices and, hence, lower subsequent returns. By the way, the inclination to lotteries is also strongly supported by the findings in neuroscience with a number of studies confirming that large payoffs attract far more attention than the low payoffs. The "reflexive brain" focuses much more on the size of the reward rather than on its probability. Finally, another supportive evidence was delivered by Cornell (2009), who argued that equity investors overconfident in their stock-picking skills would "want the most bang for the buck in their investments and often prefer high-volatility, high-skewness stocks, making them overpriced" (Ilmanen 2011).

One particularly interesting insight related to the skewness phenomenon was made by Barberis et al. (2016). The authors directly tested the hypothesis assuming that when considering money allocation to a stock, "investors mentally represent the stock by the distribution of its past returns and then evaluate this distribution in the way described by prospect theory." Subsequently, the researchers built a model of asset prices in which some investors would follow this reasoning and assigned "scores" linked to the interpretation of the distribution to particular stocks. They found that a stock whose past return distribution had a high (low) prospect theory value earned on average a low (high) subsequent return. Their results were very robust, verifying the validity of the hypothesis not only in the US market but also across the majority of the 46 equity markets. To sum up, Barberis et al. (2016) found that the interpretation of payoffs via the prospect theory—just like in case of sorts on skewness—may be viably translated into economic profits.

Measuring Skewness

Thus, these theoretical considerations provide solid grounds to state that the prospect shape of the return distribution indeed plays a role in determining future returns. Let's look into the empirical evidence. Skewness has proved a powerful determinator of future returns across numerous markets and asset classes, not only for US equities but also across many national markets, including China, India, Russia, or Poland.[2] In 2016 Barberis et al. researched 46 international equity markets and confirmed their findings in most of the markets identifying fairly promising outcomes not only at the level of individual securities but also at the country level. More broadly, skewness preference has also been observed in individual equity options (Boyer and Vorkink 2014), commodities (Fernandez-Perez et al. 2017), bonds (Yang et al. 2010), and even equity indices (Harvey 2000; Zaremba and Novak 2015). The precise results, however, vary significantly—in particular under various return measurement methods. So, how can we best measure the skewness and do particular measures translate into profitable strategies? We have three most popular types—total skewness, co-skewness, and idiosyncratic skewness—and a range of other related measures, which can be calculated based on different data periods and frequencies.

[2] See, for the US market, Harvey and Siddique (2000), Dittmar (2002), Kapadia (2006), Barberis and Huang (2008); for China, Chen et al. (2011); for India, Narayan and Ahmed (2014); for Russia, Teplova and Mikova (2011); and for Poland, Zaremba and Nowak (2015).

Total Skewness Total skewness is perhaps the most straightforward measure; it is calculated as a sample historically realized skewness of stock returns:

$$Skew_i \frac{\frac{1}{n}\sum_{i=1}^{n}\left(R_{i,t}-\overline{R_i}\right)^3}{\left(\frac{1}{n}\sum_{i=1}^{n}\left(R_{i,t}-\overline{R_i}\right)^2\right)^{\frac{3}{2}}}, \tag{5.1}$$

where $R_{i,t}$ is the return on stock I during period t, n is the number of periods used in the calculation, and $\overline{R_i}$ is the average periodic return on stock i over all of the periods included in the calculations (Bali et al. 2016). The total realized skewness was considered, for example, by Amaya et al. (2015), and the comprehensive evidence was delivered by Bali et al. (2016). The authors thoroughly investigated the application of various skewness measures in the US market, finding the results highly dependent on both the return intervals and estimation period. Bali et al. (2016) formed ten portfolios from sorts on the realized skewness and, subsequently, evaluated their performance. In particular, they formed a long-short portfolio which was long in the stocks with the highest skewness and short in the securities with the lowest skewness. When the portfolio components were equally weighted, the portfolios delivered significant and negative returns only when the return interval was very short, for example, one day, with the estimation period kept also short, below the level of months. The lowest (negative) returns were recorded for the one-month sorting period. Interestingly, for all longer periods, ranging up to even five years, the returns were insignificantly different from zero. When the portfolios were value weighted, some of the abnormal returns on the long-short portfolios turned positive, meaning that the right-skewed stocks outperformed the left-skewed stocks. Importantly, also Zaremba and Andreu Sánchez (2017), who reviewed an array of strategies implemented in country equity indices, found the skewness-based portfolio not delivering the performance in line with the expectations. Summing up, the total skewness seems to be an indicator which is highly dependent on the measurement technique and should be employed only with cautions.

Co-skewness Just like with variance split into systematic and idiosyncratic risk, the total skewness might also be divided into two parts: systematic and idiosyncratic skewness. The later component should be, at least theoretically, diversifiable. If so, then investors should with no difficulty eliminate the idiosyncratic component making it in consequence, irrelevant to asset pricing as opposed to the systematic component which should definitely play a role. This exact concept was proposed and directly examined by Harvey and Siddique (2000).

The systematic skewness, or co-skewness, as it is frequently described, was calculated by Harvey and Siddique (2000) as the slope coefficient on the squared market return from a multiple regression of stock's excess returns on the excess returns of the market portfolio and squared excess returns on the market portfolio. In other words, it is the CoSkewi coefficient from the following equation:

$$r_{i,t} = \alpha + \beta_{MKT,i} MKT_t + CoSkew_i MKT_t^2 + \varepsilon_{i,t}, \tag{5.2}$$

where $r_{i,t}$ is the excess return of stock i in the period t and MKT_t is the excess market portfolio return over the same time (Bali et al. 2016). Harvey and Siddique (2000) tested their measure empirically and found that, indeed, it is priced in the equity market.[3]

The significance of co-skewness in predicting future returns was subsequently re-examined by Bali et al. (2016) on a substantial sample of US equities. Their outcomes, however, could be regarded as slightly disappointing. Bali et al. performed a similar exercise to the total skewness case: they sorted all the stocks in the sample on various variants of the co-skewness and formed ten decile portfolios. The mean monthly return on the long-short portfolios was long (short) in the stocks with the highest (the lowest) co-skewness. Again, the outcomes depended heavily on the implementation details. When the securities were equally weighted, only the portfolio formed on monthly co-skewness saw an average return significantly different from zero. Still, its level was low, amounting to only 0.17 percentage points with a corresponding t-statistic of 1.89. Inconsistently with this observation, for the value-weighted portfolios, none of the long-short portfolios displayed positive and significant mean returns. This leads to conclude that the influence of co-skewness on returns should be also treated with caution.

[3] See also Lambert and Hubner (2013).

Idiosyncratic Skewness The second component of the total skewness is, as mentioned it before, idiosyncratic skewness. While the last component should not include prices, and the total skewness and co-skewness are most commonly employed metrics, Boyer et al. (2010) took an alternative approach. They argued and documented that that measurement of idiosyncratic skewness based on historical returns could be improved when a number of firm-specific variables are controlled, including momentum, turnover, size, industry, and whether the firm trades on the NASDAQ exchange. The researchers indicated that the expectation of future idiosyncratic skewness, which is theoretically the most relevant variable for predicting future returns, could be better estimated as a function of historical idiosyncratic skewness and additional company characteristics. Also, some alternative techniques use measures of idiosyncratic skewness based purely on historical return data. This includes Bali et al. (2016), who justified this decision twofold: First, as Boyer et al. (2010) demonstrated some persistence in idiosyncratic skewness measured purely from historical data, measuring idiosyncratic skewness from only historical data enabled to examine this persistence empirically. Second, by using only historical data, Bali et al. (2016) alleviated the risk of the relation between these firm characteristics and future stock returns driving the apparent relation between expected idiosyncratic skewness and future stock returns documented by Boyer et al. (2010). In other words, they tried to mitigate the risk of other factors to drive the skewness-return relationship. In consequence, Bali et al. (2016) defined the idiosyncratic skewness as the sample skewness of the residuals from a Fama and French (1993) three-factor model:

$$IdioSkew_i = \frac{\frac{1}{n}\sum_{i=1}^{n} \varepsilon_{i,t}^{3}}{\left(\frac{1}{n}\sum_{i=1}^{n} \varepsilon_{i,t}^{2}\right)^{\frac{3}{2}}}, \tag{5.3}$$

where $\varepsilon_{i,t}$ is the residual from the regression corresponding to the three-factor model.

$$r_{i,t} = \alpha_i + \beta_{MKT,i} MKT_t + \beta_{SMB,i} SMB_t + \beta_{HML,i} HML_t + \varepsilon_{FF,i,t} \tag{5.4}$$

where SMB_t and HML_t are factor returns corresponding with size and value effects in month t, respectively; α_i, $\beta_{MKT,i}$, $\beta_{SMB,i}$, and $\beta_{HML,i}$ are the model's parameters; and $\varepsilon_{i,t}$ is the residual from the model. The SMB_t is the return on a diversified long-short portfolio which is long (short) in the small (large) countries, industries, or companies, and the HML_t return is based on long-short portfolios which are long (short) in the high (low) book-to-market (abbreviated as BM) portfolios.

One might wonder why would idiosyncratic skewness matter. After all, as we have already observed, it could be easily diversified away and, thus, should not play any important role. Nonetheless, there are some theoretical models that are a bit more optimistic about this issue. For example, Kane (1982) argues that the total proportion of wealth that is allocated to risky securities is influenced by portfolio skewness and that skewness preference may lead investors to form not fully diversified portfolios. Simkowitz and Beedles (1978) and Conine and Tamarkin (1981) suggest that when investors do not completely diversify, idiosyncratic skewness may play some role in asset pricing. Mitton and Vorkink (2007) propose a model, which assumes that heterogeneous skewness preference causes investors to underdiversify. Also, they document that idiosyncratic skewness effects equilibrium prices. Notably, these results match also the findings of Barberis and Huang (2008), who demonstrated that the cumulative prospect theory of Tversky and Kahneman (1992) determined the negative correlation between expected returns and individual stock's skewness.

Idiosyncratic skewness has been repeatedly tested in various countries, confirming, in general, its usefulness for predicting returns in the cross-section not only in the biggest US market.[4] How then the strategies based on idiosyncratic skewness work in comparison with the total skewness or co-skewness? Let us once again look at the results obtained by Bali et al. (2016). Again, the procedure of portfolio formation remained unchanged: all the stocks in the US equity market were sorted each month on the idiosyncratic volatility from the three-factor model of Fama and French (1992, 1993). Subsequently, equal- and value-weighted portfolios were formed, and the top and bottom portfolios were used to build a long-short portfolio that was long in the stocks with the highest idiosyncratic volatility and short in the securities with the lowest idiosyncratic volatility.

[4] See, for example, Boyer et al. (2010), Ghysel et al. (2011), de Mendonca et al. (2012), Conrad et al. (2013), Cao (2015b), Sehgal and Garg (2016), and Almeida et al. (2016).

The examinations of Bali et al. (2016) revealed a few interesting insights. Again, the results appeared highly sensitive to the implementation details, like the portfolio weighting scheme or the sorting period. The equal-weighted long-short portfolio displayed predominantly negative returns, showing that the stocks with very low idiosyncratic volatility outperform stocks with high-idiosyncratic risk. Nonetheless, the mean of returns was significant only for a very short formation period of one month. It reached −0.31% with the corresponding *t*-statistic of −2.44. Interestingly, when the portfolio components were weighted according to their capitalization, the picture changed drastically: turning it into a portfolio of high-idiosyncratic volatility stocks that overperformed. The average return on the long-short portfolio changed from negative to positive and amounted to 0.36% (*t*-stat equals 3.60).

Importantly, idiosyncratic skewness does not need to be measured based on the three-factor model. For example, Hou et al. (2017), who replicated a broad range of equity anomalies in the US stock market, implemented the strategies based on idiosyncratic volatility, with the CAPM and their own *q*-model. They found that the results were similar and independent of the particular model employed. Also Zaremba and Umutlu (2018) who extended this list with the four-factor model of Carhart (1997) and the five-factor model of Fama and French (2015), documented that the outcomes were similar for many models used.

Interestingly, the direct skewness-based measures—the total realized skewness, idiosyncratic skewness, or systematic skewness—are not the only measures possible to approximate the moments of the return distribution.

Maximum Daily Return In 2010, Bali, Cakici, and Whitelaw examined the cross-section of returns in the US stock market for years 1962–2005 with a novel measure of skewness. Initially, they supported their assumption that investors had lottery-like preferences grounded in a range of various empirical evidence: popularity of lotteries and gambling despite negative expected payoffs, long-shot bias in betting, and financial market data referring to, for example, IPOs, and the disappointing long-term performance of small growth stocks. The team devised a new measure capturing lottery-like characteristics for stocks: an exceptionally high recent daily return. Thus, they ranked all of the securities in the market on their maximum daily return over previous month. The decile of stocks with the highest daily return vividly underperformed the decile of stocks with the lowest previous-month maximum daily return. The difference was significant, robust to a battery of robustness checks, and amounted to about 1% per month. Importantly, the equities with the high maximum daily return were the ones that displayed strong positive skewness, so the results confirmed the basic concept of investors' preference for lottery-like equities. Additionally, the authors stressed the hockey-stick-like pattern emerging from the equity returns as the stocks with the highest maximum daily returns are usually small illiquid stocks with high-idiosyncratic volatility. Also, the maximum daily return, or MAX, effect was found out to subsume skewness and idiosyncratic volatility, meaning that when we control for the maximum daily returns, the other anomalies become irrelevant. Furthermore, the maximum daily return phenomenon remains valid even after controlling for other well-known return patterns, including size, value, momentum, long-run reversal, or liquidity.

Importantly, the MAX effect works well not only in the USA but also internationally. Subsequent studies of Annaert et al. (2013), Walkshausl (2014b), and Lin and Liu (2017) have extended the approach of Bali et al. (2011) to the US and European markets while Nartea et al. (2014), Zhong and Gray (2016), and Aboulamer and Kryzanowski (2016) investigated the MAX effect in South Korean, Australian, and Canadian markets, correspondingly. The MAX anomaly is present also in emerging markets, including China and India (Aziz and Ansari 2017). Furthermore, Fong and Toh (2014) have also documented that the maximum daily return phenomenon is dependent upon investor sentiment which sheds light on the behavioral underpinnings of the MAX effect. Finally, Cheon and Lee (2017) have conducted what is, perhaps, the most comprehensive international examination. They researched the MAX effect at an international level in 44 markets and reported a negative risk premium for sorting on the maximum daily return in 26 out of 44 markets. In their subsequent study, Umutlu and Bengitöz (2017) confirmed that the effect work not only in individual stock returns but also in country and sector indices.

Interestingly, the MAX variable could be also extended to the MIN variable, focusing on the minimum daily return over the last month. A theoretical foundation for that has been laid by the cumulative prospect theory of Barberis and Huang (2008), which predicts that the effect of MIN should be symmetric to the MAX effect. In essence, when small probability events become overweighted, then the securities with high absolute minimum daily returns should be avoided by investors, in consequence driving prices down and the expected returns up. In other words, equity market participants may look for a discount for high MIN securities, resulting in an undervaluation of these stocks and high subsequent payoffs. This effect was also positively verified by Umutlu and Bengitöz (2017).

Options Market As already noted, the measurement of skewness, and expected skewness in particular, may pose significant challenges and become highly vulnerable to methodological details. Therefore, some researchers have decided to derive the estimation of expected skewness directly from the option markets. Strictly speaking, there are two major strains of this type of research: (1) seeking skewness-related patterns *within* the option market and (2) predicting equity returns *based* on skewness derived from the option markets.

In general, the empirical evidence from stock options is consistent with the results for equities, documenting the hockey-stick shape of the cross-sectional return distribution. For example, Ni (2008), who investigated single-stock call option portfolios, found that in-the-money and at-the-money call options yielded on average delicately positive returns, approximating 2% per month for the three lowest quintiles of option "moneyness" whereas the portfolios of out-the-money options with high strikes and high-skew, so the options displaying the lottery ticket-properties, delivered striking negative returns, amounting to as much as −28% per month on average in the top "moneyness" quantile. A later study of Doran et al. (2012) added some seasonal flavor by documenting that the richness of out-the-money calls relative to at-the-money calls was particularly high in January, and so in the same month when lottery preferences manifest the strongest.

The second area of research focuses on the use of the option skew data in predicting the returns on underlying equities. The results in these regards remain somewhat mixed. Cremers and Weinbaum (2010), for example, having studied the deviations from put-call parity have shown that, indeed, it is able to predict future returns, but in a way inconsistent with the phenomenon of negative skewness premium. In particular, stocks for which the associated at-the-money call options are relatively expensive outperform by about 0.5 percentage points per week the equities for which the associated at-the-money put options are relatively expensive.

What does it mean? In essence, securities for which investors expect particularly elevated upside volatility (expressed in expensive calls) display tendency to subsequently overperform. On the other hand, the securities for which the market expects high downside volatility (reflected in expensive puts) tend to underperform. From the theoretical standpoint, the authors link these observations to the gradual dissemination of information suggesting that the option market incorporates information quicker than equities, leading to the option pricing having already discounted some information which is not fully included in the stock prices. Insightful investors may try to take advantage of this phenomenon, predicting the near-term stocks moves based on available option pricing data. This return forecasting ability should be particularly strong for firms that operate in an asymmetric information environment. Also, Ilmanen (2011) argues that this "apparent underreaction in stock prices to option market information" may partly reflect some insider trading: perhaps the owners of a superior information prefer to use the leverage available in the option market in order to maximize their profits.

Another interesting piece of evidence was provided by Doran and Krieger (2010). The authors have examined a few different measures of option skew and their abilities to forecast the cross-section of equity returns, confirming in general the findings of Cremers and Weinbaum (2010) stating that future payoffs remain higher for stocks who's at-the-money calls display higher volatilities than the respective at-the-money puts. Nonetheless, once they examined the option volatilities across different strike prices, they also found negative skew tendency to predict better future equity performance. In other words, equities with higher implied volatility of out-the-money puts rather than of at-the-money puts produce higher future payoffs, consistently with the hypothesis of negative skewness premium.

A short review of other option-based studies of skewness has been provided by, for example, Bali et al. (2016), who have also admitted that the results are generally mixed. Conrad et al. (2013) and Bali and Murray (2013) accentuate the negative relationship between the implied skewness and future returns. Consistent evidence has been also delivered by Amaya et al. (2015), who focused on intraday data, as well by Boyer and Vorkink (2014), who showed that options with implied skewness deliver lower future returns. Interestingly, Xing et al. (2010) have documented positive relationship between skewness and future returns. This positive link matches also the demand-based option pricing models by Bollen and Whaley (2004) and Garleanu et al. (2009). The concept of demand-based option pricing implies that investors who expect positive returns gain exposure to stocks by buying call options and selling puts. Analogously, investors anticipating negative returns establish exposure by buying puts and selling calls. By doing so, they exert price pressure, which increases or decreases relative prices, resulting in higher values of implied skewness for the stocks that investors expect to increase in value and lower values of skewness for the equities whose decrease they assess more likely.

Empirical Test of Strategies Based on Skewness

In the universe of strategies using historical return distribution, we analyzed two individual strategies: (1) *total skewness* and (2) *maximum daily return*, or MAX.

Under the *total skewness* strategy, we followed the most fundamental approach (Table 5.1) and sorted the equities on the total skewness calculated as the standardized third moment of the return distribution. We therefore used 60-month trailing returns, and we relied only on monthly data and subsequently ranked the stocks from the lowest to the highest skewness variable. When forming the long-short portfolios, we assumed the long position in the quintile portfolio with the lowest skewness and the short position in the portfolio with the highest skewness. The results for all the countries within the sample are reported in Table 5.1.

Regrettably, the sorting portfolios on the total skewness proved only moderately successful. Although some of the markets indeed exhibited some profitability, the overall performance remained rather mediocre. The alphas on the long-short portfolios were both positive and significant in ten countries, namely Canada, France, Germany, Greece, Hong Kong, Italy, Japan, Norway, Singapore, and Sweden. We, nonetheless, observed no apparent profitability in the majority of other markets.

The global long-short portfolio proved profitable with the countries weighted either equally or on stock market capitalization. The global portfolios weighted equally slightly outperformed the capitalization-weighted strategies. Their cumulative returns are detailed in Figs. 5.2 and 5.3. The streak of profits proved fairly stable but, alas, quite modest. The mean monthly returns on the equally weighted (value-weighted) strategies equaled 0.38% (0.30%) with the corresponding standard deviation of 2.05%

Table 5.1 The Performance of portfolios formed on skewness

Country	*Top portfolio mean return*	*Bottom portfolio mean return*	*Average number of firms*	*T-B portfolio*		*Standard deviation*	*Sharpe ratio*	*Beta*	*Alpha*	
				Mean return	*t-stat*				*Value*	*t-stat*
Australia	0.87	0.52	41	0.36	*(1.41)*	4.14	0.30	0.00	0.35	*(1.39)*
Austria	0.89	0.52	7	0.36	*(1.09)*	5.44	0.23	0.10	0.31	*(0.94)*
Belgium	0.98	0.98	11	0.00	*(−0.01)*	4.74	0.00	−0.04	0.02	*(0.09)*
Canada	1.07	0.49	91	0.58*	*(1.94)*	4.89	0.41	−0.10	0.65**	*(2.18)*
Denmark	1.19	1.01	11	0.18	*(0.72)*	4.14	0.15	0.01	0.17	*(0.68)*
Finland	1.35	1.12	11	0.23	*(0.71)*	5.33	0.15	−0.06	0.29	*(0.89)*
France	1.12	0.74	47	0.39*	*(1.83)*	3.48	0.39	0.00	0.39*	*(1.83)*
Germany	0.95	0.58	41	0.37*	*(1.77)*	3.48	0.37	−0.08	0.42**	*(1.99)*
Greece	1.08	−0.29	13	1.37**	*(2.11)*	10.65	0.44	0.01	1.37**	*(2.10)*
Hong Kong	0.66	−0.93	22	1.59***	*(4.12)*	6.35	0.87	−0.15	1.70***	*(4.45)*
Ireland	0.78	1.10	4	−0.31	*(−0.43)*	12.06	−0.09	0.03	−0.33	*(−0.45)*
Israel	1.14	1.13	15	0.00	*(0.01)*	5.03	0.00	0.03	0.00	*(−0.01)*
Italy	0.82	0.37	28	0.46**	*(2.33)*	3.21	0.49	0.03	0.44**	*(2.26)*
Japan	0.57	−0.02	323	0.59***	*(3.42)*	2.84	0.72	−0.07	0.59***	*(3.45)*
The Netherlands	0.90	1.07	18	−0.16	*(−0.62)*	4.33	−0.13	−0.05	−0.13	*(−0.49)*
New Zealand	0.79	1.02	5	−0.24	*(−0.59)*	6.58	−0.12	0.03	−0.26	*(−0.65)*

Norway	1.22	0.48	15	0.75**	*(2.11)*	5.81	0.44	−0.05	0.78**	*(2.20)*
Portugal	0.50	0.17	4	0.33	*(0.89)*	6.13	0.19	−0.04	0.35	*(0.93)*
Singapore	0.82	−0.19	12	1.01***	*(3.12)*	5.33	0.66	0.07	0.97***	*(2.99)*
Spain	0.90	0.61	18	0.29	*(1.24)*	3.80	0.26	0.02	0.27	*(1.18)*
Sweden	1.63	0.96	26	0.67**	*(2.31)*	4.77	0.49	−0.06	0.73**	*(2.49)*
Switzerland	1.11	1.05	29	0.06	*(0.32)*	3.13	0.07	0.01	0.05	*(0.28)*
UK	0.81	0.68	117	0.13	*(0.60)*	3.55	0.13	−0.01	0.13	*(0.62)*
USA	1.29	1.22	630	0.06	*(0.27)*	3.84	0.06	−0.03	0.08	*(0.36)*
World (EW)	0.98	0.60	1538	0.38***	*(3.04)*	2.05	0.64	−0.02	0.39***	*(3.09)*
World (VW)	1.00	0.70	1538	0.30*	*(1.78)*	2.77	0.38	−0.04	0.32*	*(1.88)*

Note: The table reports the monthly returns on the portfolios from sorts on skewness of return distribution over the trailing 60-month returns. The calculations were made based on monthly observations. "Average number of firms" is the mean monthly number of companies in the quintile portfolios. *Top portfolio* and *bottom portfolio* are quintile portfolios including the stocks with the lowest and highest skewness of the return distribution, respectively. *T-B portfolio* is the portfolio long in the top portfolio and short in the bottom portfolio. The Sharpe ratio is expressed on an annualized basis. The alpha and beta are derived from the CAPM. Mean returns, standard deviations, and alphas are expressed in percentage. Asterisks *, **, and *** indicate values significantly different from zero at the 10%, 5%, and 1% levels, respectively

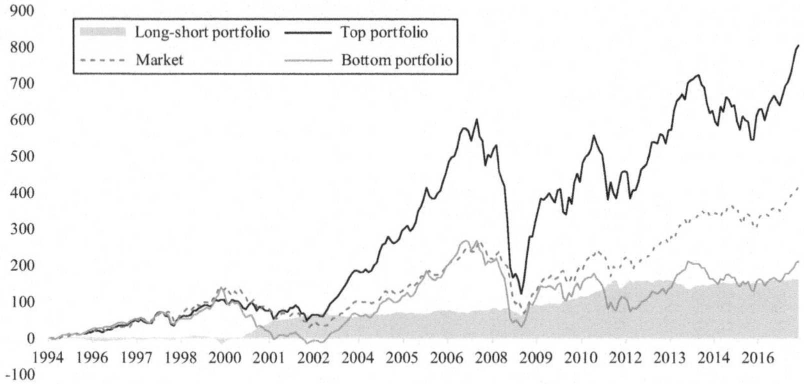

Fig. 5.2 Cumulative return on equal-weighted portfolios formed on skewness. (Note: The figure displays the cumulative return on the equal-weighted quantile of the portfolios from sorts on skewness of return distribution over the trailing 60-month returns. The calculations were made based on monthly *observations. Top portfolio* and *bottom portfolio* are quintile portfolios including the stocks with the lowest and highest skewness of the return distribution, respectively. *T-B portfolio* is the portfolio long in the top portfolio and short in the bottom portfolio. Market is the value-weighted portfolio of all the country equity markets considered. All the returns are expressed in percentage)

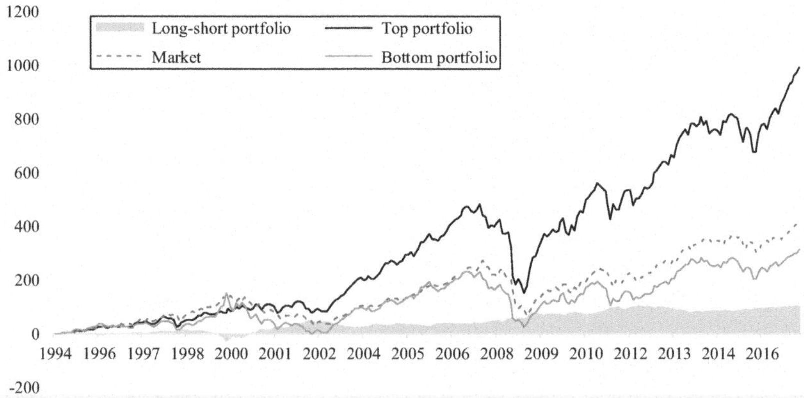

Fig. 5.3 Cumulative return on value-weighted portfolios formed on skewness. (Note: The figure displays the cumulative return on the value-weighted quantile of the portfolios from sorts on skewness of return distribution over the trailing 60-month returns. The calculations were made based on monthly observations. *Top portfolio* and *bottom portfolio* are quintile portfolios including the stocks with the lowest and highest skewness of the return distribution, respectively. *T-B portfolio* is long in the Top portfolio and short in the Bottom portfolio. Market is the value-weighted portfolio of all the country equity markets considered. All the returns are expressed in percentage)

(2.77%). Thus, the annualized Shape ratio reached 0.64 (0.38), a way lower than, for instance, the momentum-based stock-picking techniques.

The second strategy we tested was the ***maximum daily return approach*** or the *MAX*. In this case, we closely followed Bali et al. (2011) and sorted stocks on the maximum daily return over 30 preceding days. In particular, we assumed the stocks with the lowest (highest) maximum daily return to outperform (underperform) and sorted stocks into quintiles following this simple approach.

Table 5.2 presents the performance of the portfolios formed on the maximum daily return.

Interestingly, having examined international equity markets within the quintile portfolios, the MAX strategy proved insignificantly profitable when implemented with the long-short equal-weighted portfolios across the majority of the countries. Admittedly, in the USA, the long-short portfolio displayed a remarkable alpha of 1.11% per month. Nonetheless, in the 16 other countries, the alphas were indifferentiable from zero with the only notable exceptions including Canada, Greece, Hong Kong, Italy, Portugal, Spain, Sweden, and the UK.

Importantly, due to the large capitalization and robust payoffs in these countries, the global long-short MAX portfolio performed very well when weighted either on capitalization or equally. Nevertheless, the mean Sharpe ratio appeared minuscule compared to the momentum-related strategies reaching only 0.40 (0.42) in the equal-weighted approach (capitalization-weighted approach).

Figures 5.4 and 5.5 provide additional insights by presenting the cumulative returns on the global MAX portfolios. Clearly, the low MAX quintiles underperformed the high MAX quintiles, although the difference proved smaller than, for example, for momentum. Noticeably, due to the powerful MAX pattern in the large equity markets, including the USA or the UK, the cumulative returns on the low-maximum daily return stocks became particularly pronounced for the capitalization-weighted countries.

As we have shown here, not only historical average returns and their standard deviation impact the results but importantly the third moment of the return distribution. Considering thus skewness, regardless of the measurement method, can become a profitable technique in designing the investment portfolio. Another valuable insight is applying seasonal patterns.

Table 5.2 The performance of portfolios formed on maximum daily returns

Country	*Top portfolio mean return*	*Bottom portfolio mean return*	*Average number of firms*	*T-B portfolio*		*Standard deviation*	*Sharpe ratio*	*Beta*	*Alpha*	
				Mean return	*t-stat*				*Value*	*t-stat*
Australia	0.94	0.66	46	0.27	*(0.90)*	4.98	0.19	−0.03	0.30	*(0.98)*
Austria	0.62	0.83	7	−0.21	*(−0.42)*	8.25	−0.09	−0.07	−0.17	*(−0.35)*
Belgium	1.08	0.74	12	0.35	*(0.93)*	6.15	0.20	−0.25	0.53	*(1.43)*
Canada	1.31	0.25	95	1.05**	*(2.42)*	7.15	0.51	−0.09	1.12**	*(2.55)*
Denmark	1.08	1.01	12	0.07	*(0.22)*	5.24	0.05	−0.13	0.19	*(0.59)*
Finland	1.40	1.15	11	0.25	*(0.67)*	6.09	0.14	−0.12	0.37	*(0.99)*
France	1.21	0.78	47	0.43	*(1.09)*	6.45	0.23	−0.06	0.46	*(1.18)*
Germany	0.96	0.47	43	0.49	*(1.08)*	7.54	0.23	−0.14	0.57	*(1.25)*
Greece	1.36	−0.51	14	1.88***	*(3.22)*	9.57	0.68	−0.09	1.89***	*(3.24)*
Hong Kong	0.51	−0.60	23	1.11**	*(2.03)*	8.93	0.43	−0.15	1.22**	*(2.24)*
Ireland	1.21	0.74	4	0.46	*(0.60)*	12.77	0.13	0.01	0.45	*(0.58)*
Israel	1.02	0.88	15	0.14	*(0.31)*	7.31	0.07	0.06	0.12	*(0.27)*
Italy	0.92	0.36	28	0.55*	*(1.78)*	5.10	0.38	−0.03	0.57*	*(1.82)*
Japan	0.51	0.14	325	0.37	*(1.24)*	4.89	0.26	−0.19	0.38	*(1.30)*
The Netherlands	1.26	0.66	19	0.60	*(1.52)*	6.50	0.32	−0.04	0.62	*(1.56)*
New Zealand	1.11	1.11	5	0.00	*(0.01)*	5.93	0.00	0.00	0.00	*(0.01)*

Norway	0.73	0.34	15	0.39	*(0.84)*	7.69	0.18	−0.07	0.45	*(0.95)*
Portugal	0.67	−0.02	4	0.69	*(1.63)*	6.93	0.34	−0.19	0.75*	*(1.81)*
Singapore	0.40	0.09	12	0.31	*(0.75)*	6.91	0.16	0.04	0.29	*(0.69)*
Spain	0.92	0.24	18	0.68**	*(2.18)*	5.11	0.46	−0.05	0.72**	*(2.29)*
Sweden	1.69	0.88	26	0.82**	*(2.08)*	6.45	0.44	−0.10	0.91**	*(2.30)*
Switzerland	1.03	0.97	29	0.06	*(0.17)*	5.58	0.04	−0.17	0.18	*(0.52)*
UK	0.61	0.64	118	−0.03	*(−0.11)*	4.85	−0.02	−0.09	0.01	*(0.03)*
USA	1.43	0.51	716	0.92*	*(1.87)*	8.07	0.39	−0.27	1.11**	*(2.25)*
World (EW)	1.00	0.51	1645	0.49*	*(1.92)*	4.16	0.40	−0.17	0.57**	*(2.27)*
World (VW)	1.06	0.36	1645	0.71**	*(2.01)*	5.78	0.42	−0.22	0.82**	*(2.36)*

Note: The table reports monthly returns on the portfolios from sorts on the maximum daily return over the last 30 days. The calculations were made based on daily observations. "Average number of firms" is the mean monthly number of companies in the quintile portfolios. ***Top portfolio*** and ***bottom portfolio*** are quintile portfolios including the stocks with the lowest and highest maximum daily return, respectively. ***T-B portfolio*** is long in the top portfolio and short in the bottom portfolio. The Sharpe ratio is expressed on an annualized basis. The alpha and beta are derived from the CAPM. Mean returns, standard deviations, and alphas are expressed in percentage. Asterisks *, **, and *** indicate values significantly different from zero at the 10%, 5%, and 1% levels, respectively

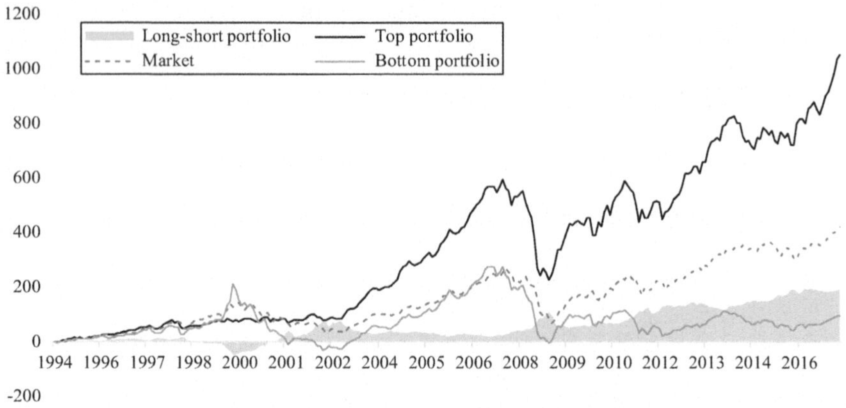

Fig. 5.4 Cumulative return on equal-weighted portfolios formed on maximum daily returns. (Note: The figure displays the cumulative return on the equal-weighted quantile of the portfolios from sorts on the maximum daily return in the last 30 days. The calculations were made based on daily observations. *Top portfolio* and *bottom portfolio* are quintile portfolios including the stocks with the lowest and highest maximum daily return, respectively. Market is the value-weighted portfolio of all the country equity markets considered. All the returns are expressed in percentage)

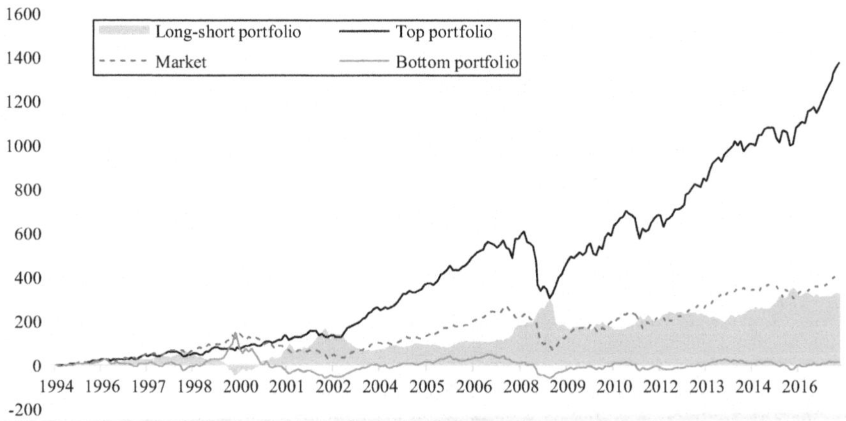

Fig. 5.5 Cumulative return on value-weighted portfolios formed on maximum daily returns. (Note: The figure displays the cumulative return on the value-weighted quantile of the portfolios from sorts on the maximum daily return over the last 30 days. The calculations were made based on daily observations. *Top portfolio* and *bottom portfolio* are quintile portfolios including the stocks with the lowest and highest maximum daily return, respectively. Market is the value-weighted portfolio of all the country equity markets considered. All the returns are expressed in percentage)

References

Aboulamer, A., & Kryzanowski, L. (2016). Are idiosyncratic volatility and MAX priced in the Canadian market? *Journal of Empirical Finance, 37*, 20–36. https://doi.org/10.1016/j.jempfin.2016.02.005.

Alemida, C., Ricca, B., & Tessari, C. (2016). Idiosyncratic moments and the cross-section of returns in Brazil. *Brazilian Review of Econometrics, 36*(2), 255–286. https://doi.org/10.12660/bre.v99n992016.18544.

Amaya, D., Christoffersen, P., Jacobs, K., & Vasquez, A. (2015). Does realized skewness predict the cross-section of equity returns? *Journal of Financial Economics, 118*(1), 135–167.

Annaert, J., De Ceuster, M., & Verstegen, K. (2013). Are extreme returns priced in the stock market? European evidence. *Journal of Banking and Finance, 37*(9), 3401–3411. https://doi.org/10.1016/j.jbankfin.2013.05.015.

Arditti, F. D. (1967). Risk and the required return on equity. *Journal of Finance, 22*(1), 19–36.

Arditti, F. D. (1971). Another look at mutual fund performance. *Journal of Financial and Quantitative Analysis, 6*(3), 909–912.

Aziz, T., & Ansari, V. A. (2017, in press). Are extreme negative returns priced in the Indian stock market? *Borsa Istanbul Review*. https://doi.org/10.1016/j.bir.2017.09.002.

Bali, T. G., & Murray, S. (2013). Does risk-neutral skewness predict the cross-section of equity option portfolio returns? *Journal of Financial and Quantitative Analysis, 48*(04), 1145–1171.

Bali, T., Cakici, N., & Whitelaw, R. F. (2011). Maxing out: Stocks as lotteries and the cross-section of expected returns. *Journal of Financial Economics, 99*(2), 427–446.

Bali, T. G., Engle, R. F., & Murray, S. (2016). *Empirical asset pricing: The cross section of stock returns*. Hoboken: Wiley.

Barberis, N., & Huang, M. (2008). Stocks as lotteries: The implications of probability weighting for security prices. *American Economic Review, 98*(5), 2066–2100.

Barberis, N., Mukherjee, A., & Wang, B. (2016). Prospect theory and stock returns: An empirical test. *Review of Financial Studies, 29*(11), 3068–3107.

Bollen, N. P. B., & Whaley, R. E. (2004). Does net buying pressure affect the shape of implied volatility functions. *Journal of Finance, 59*(2), 711–753.

Boyer, H. B., & Vorkink, K. (2014). Stock options as lotteries. *Journal of Finance, 69*(4), 1485–1527. https://doi.org/10.1111/jofi.12152.

Boyer, B., Mitton, T., & Vorkink, K. (2010). Expected idiosyncratic skewness. *Review of Financial Studies, 23*(1), 169–202.

Cao, X. (2015b). *Are idiosyncratic skewness and idiosyncratic kurtosis priced?* (Brock University working paper). Available at https://dr.library.brocku.ca/handle/10464/6426. Accessed 14 Oct 2017.

Carhart, M. M. (1997). On persistence in mutual fund performance. *Journal of Finance, 52*(1), 57–82.

Chen, L., Li, S., & Wang, J. (2011). Liquidity, skewness and stock returns: Evidence from Chinese stock market. *Asia-Pacific Financial Markets, 18*, 405–427.

Cheon, Y.-H., & Lee, K.-H. (2017, in press). Maxing out globally: Individualism, investor attention, and the cross section of expected stock returns. *Management Science*. https://doi.org/10.1287/mnsc.2017.2830.

Conine, T. E., & Tamarkin, M. J. (1981). On diversification given asymmetry in returns. *Journal of Finance, 36*(5), 1143–1155.

Conrad, J., Dittmar, R. F., & Ghysels, E. (2013). Ex ante skewness and expected returns. *Journal of Finance, 68*(1), 85–124. https://doi.org/10.1111/j.1540-6261.2012.01795.x.

Cornell, B. (2009). The pricing of volatility and skewness: A new interpretation. *Journal of Investing, 18*(3), 27–30.

Cremers, M., & Weinbaum, D. (2010). Deviations from put-call parity and stock return predictability. *Journal of Financial and Quantitative Analysis, 45*(2), 335–367.

de Mendonca, F. P., Klotzle, M. C., Pinto, A. C. F., & da Silva Montezano, R. M. (2012). The relationship between idiosyncratic risk and returns in the Brazilian stock market. *Revista Contabilidade & Finanças, 23*(60). Available online at: http://www.scielo.br/scielo.php?pid=S1519-70772012000300009&script=sci_arttext&tlng=en. Accessed 14 Oct 2017.

Dittmar, R. F. (2002). Nonlinear pricing kernels, kurtosis preference, and evidence from the cross section of equity returns. *Journal of Finance, 57*(1), 369–403.

Doran, J. S., & Krieger, K. (2010). Implications for asset returns in the implied volatility skew. *Financial Analyst Journal, 66*(1), 65–76.

Doran, J. S., Jiang, D., & Peterson, D. R. (2012). Gambling preferences and the new year effect of assets with lottery features. *Review of Finance, 16*(3), 685–731. https://doi.org/10.1093/rof/rfr006.

Fama, E. F., & French, K. R. (1992). The cross-section of expected returns. *Journal of Finance, 47*, 427–466.

Fama, E. F., & French, K. R. (1993). Common risk factors in the returns on stocks and bonds. *Journal of Financial Economics, 33*, 3–56. https://doi.org/10.1016/0304-405X(93)90023-5.

Fama, E. F., & French, K. R. (2015). A five-factor asset pricing model. *Journal of Financial Economics, 116*(1), 1–22. https://doi.org/10.1016/j.jfineco.2014.10.010.

Fernandez-Perez, A., Frijns, B., Fuertes, A.-M., & Miffre, J. (2017, forthcoming). The skewness of commodity futures returns. *Journal of Banking and Finance*. Available at SSRN: https://ssrn.com/abstract=2671165 or https://doi.org/10.2139/ssrn.2671165. Accessed 13 Oct 2017.

Fong, W. M., & Toh, B. (2014). Investor sentiment and the MAX effect. *Journal of Banking and Finance, 46*(1), 190–201. https://doi.org/10.1016/j.jbankfin.2014.05.006.

Garleanu, N., Pedersen, L. H., & Poteshman, A. M. (2009). Demand-based option pricing. *Review of Financial Studies, 22*(10), 4259–4299.

Ghysel, E., Plazzi, A., & Valkanov, R. (2011). *Conditional skewness of stock market returns in developed and emerging markets and its economic fundamentals* (Working paper). Available at http://www.unc.edu/~eghysels/papers/GPV_Oct_6_2011_EG.pdf. Accessed 14 Oct 2017.

Harvey, C. (2000). The drivers of expected returns in international markets. *Emerging Markets Quarterly,* 32–49. Available at SSRN: https://ssrn.com/abstract=795385 or https://doi.org/10.2139/ssrn.795385. Accessed 13 Oct 2017.

Harvey, C., & Siddique, A. (2000). Conditional skewness in asset pricing tests. *Journal of Finance, 55,* 1263–1296.

Hou, K., Xue, C., & Zhang, L. (2017). *Replicating anomalies* (Fisher College of Business working paper No. 2017-03-010; Charles A. Dice Center working paper No. 2017-10). Available at SSRN: https://ssrn.com/abstract=2961979 or https://doi.org/10.2139/ssrn.2961979. Accessed 30 Sept 2017.

Ilmanen, A. (2011). *Expected returns: An investor's guide to harvesting market rewards.* Hoboken: Wiley.

Kane, A. (1982). Skewness preference and portfolio choice. *Journal of Financial and Quantitative Analysis, 17*(1), 15–25.

Kapadia, N. (2006). *The next Microsoft? Skewness, idiosyncratic volatility, and expected returns.* Available at SSRN: http://ssrn.com/abstract=970120 or https://doi.org/10.2139/ssrn.970120. Accessed 28 Oct 2015.

Kimball, M. S. (1993). Standard risk aversion. *Econometrica, 61*(3), 589–611.

Kraus, A., & Litzenberger, R. H. (1976). Skewness preference and the valuation of risk assets. *Journal of Finance, 31*(4), 1085–1100.

Kumar, A. (2009). Who gambles in the stock market? *Journal of Finance, 64*(4), 1889–1933.

Kumar, A., Page, J. K., & Spalt, O. G. (2011). Religious beliefs, gambling attitudes, and financial market outcomes. *Journal of Financial Economics, 102*(3), 671–708.

Lambert, M., & Hubner, G. (2013). Comoment risk and stock returns. *Journal of Empirical Finance, 23,* 191–205. https://doi.org/10.1016/j.jempfin.2013.07.001.

Lin, T.-C., & Liu, X. (2017, forthcoming). Skewness, individual investor preference, and the cross-section of stock returns. *Review of Finance.* Available at SSRN: https://ssrn.com/abstract=2676633 or https://doi.org/10.2139/ssrn.2676633. Accessed 23 Oct 2017.

Lintner, J. (1965a). The valuation of risk assets and the selection of risky investments in stock portfolios and capital budgets. *Review of Economics and Statistics, 47*(1), 13–37.

Lintner, J. (1965b). Security prices, risk and maximal gains from diversification. *Journal of Finance, 20*(4), 587–615.

Mitton, T., & Vorkink, K. (2007). Equilibrium underdiversification and the preference for skewness. *Review of Financial Studies, 20*(4), 1255–1288.

Narayan, P. K., & Agmed, H. A. (2014). Importance of skewness in decision making: Evidence from the Indian stock exchange. *Global Finance Journal, 25*(3), 260–269.

Nartea, G. V., Wu, J., & Liu, H. T. (2014). Extreme returns in emerging stock markets: Evidence of a MAX effect in South Korea. *Applied Financial Economics, 24*(6), 425–435. https://doi.org/10.1080/09603107.2014.884696.

Ni, S. X. (2008). *Stock option returns: A puzzle*. Available at SSRN: https://ssrn.com/abstract=1340767 or https://doi.org/10.2139/ssrn.1340767. Accessed 23 Oct 2017.

Scott, R. C., & Horvath, P. A. (1980). On the direction of preference for moments of higher order than the variance. *Journal of Finance, 35*(4), 915–919.

Sehgal, S., & Garg, V. (2016). Cross sectional moments and portfolio returns: Evidence for select emerging markets. *IIMB Management Review, 28*(3), 147–159.

Sharpe, W. F. (1964). Capital asset prices: A theory of market equilibrium under conditions of risk. *Journal of Finance, 19*(3), 425–442.

Simkowitz, M. A., & Beedles, W. L. (1978). Diversification in a three-moment world. *Journal of Financial and Quantitative Analysis, 13*(5), 927–941.

Stevenson, R. W. (1999, January 29). Asked about internet issues, the Fed Chairman Shrugs. *The New York Times*. Available at http://www.nytimes.com/1999/01/29/business/the-markets-asked-about-internet-issues-the-fed-chairman-shrugs.html. Accessed 11 Oct 2017.

Teplova, T., & Mikova, E. (2011). A Higher moment downside framework for conditional and unconditional CAPM in the Russian stock market. *Eurasian Economic Review, 1*, 157–178.

Tversky, A., & Kahneman, D. (1992). Advances in prospect theory: Cumulative representation of uncertainty. *Journal of Risk and Uncertainty, 5*(4), 297–323.

Umutlu, M., & Bengitöz, P. (2017). *The cross-section of expected index returns in international stock markets*. Working paper presented at the 2017 Infiniti Conference in Valencia, Spain.

Walkshausl, C. (2014b). The MAX effect: European evidence. *Journal of Banking and Finance, 42*(1), 1–10. https://doi.org/10.1016/j.jbankfin.2014.01.020.

Xing, Y., Zhang, X., & Zhao, R. (2010). What does the individual option volatility smirk tell us about future equity returns? *Journal of Financial Quantitative Analysis, 45*(3), 641–662.

Yang, J., Zjou, Y., & Wang, Z. (2010). Conditional co-skewness in stock and bond markets: Time series evidence. *Management Science, 56*(11), 2031–2049.
Zaremba, A., & Nowak, A. (2015). Skewness preference across countries. *Business and Economic Horizons, 11*(2), 115–130.
Zaremba, A., & Andreu Sánchez, L. (2017). *Paper profits or real money? Trading costs and stock market anomalies in country equity indices.* Available at https://doi.org/10.2139/ssrn.3038514
Zaremba, A., & Umutlu, M. (2018, in press). Strategies can be expensive too! The value spread and asset allocation in global equity markets. *Applied Economics.*
Zhong, A., & Gray, P. (2016). The MAX effect: An exploration of risk and mispricing explanations. *Journal of Banking and Finance, 65*(1), 76–90.

CHAPTER 6

Januaries, Mays, and Lunar Cycles: Stock Selection with Seasonal Anomalies

Do stocks behave similarly in all months? Do they yield the same returns across the weekdays? The ever-growing empirical evidence suggests that they don't. Financial markets display a full array of calendar patterns and seasonal anomalies that more or less powerfully impact the returns. While most patterns have been known for a very long time, a few have just been proved to predict the cross-section of returns and create over performing investment portfolios.

Here we will concentrate on the seasonal patterns emerging in the stock market and translate them into efficient investment strategies. While the sources and explanations of these patterns may differ, from an investor's perspective they are all purely price based. In order to implement the seasonality strategies, the investor needs no extensive knowledge of the fundamentals or macroeconomic situation: the only useful input is the price and the knowledge of the calendar.

Seasonal Effects in Equity Markets

Let us begin the investigation of the seasonal patterns with a quick review of various seasonal and calendar effects ruling the equity markets.

A. Zaremba, J. "Koby" Shemer, *Price-Based Investment Strategies*,
https://doi.org/10.1007/978-3-319-91530-2_6

January Effect The January effect, or in other words, the turn-of-the-year effect, is a tendency of stocks to outperform in January. Since its first observation made by Wachtel in 1942, it has been frequently researched.[1]

Interestingly, the January effect emerges not only among the raw stock returns but also across the most popular strategies. Perhaps, the most well recognized is its relationship with the size effect: the January effect becomes the strongest in small stocks (Keim 1983; Rogalski and Tinic 1986). In other words, in January small companies markedly outperform the larger enterprises. It also has implications for other return factors. The value strategies are thought to underperform in December while outperforming in the beginning of the year. Considering the momentum effect, investors are perceived to stick to the winning companies at the end of the year and then switch to the value stocks in January. In other words, the momentum anomaly delivers high returns in the last month of the year but at the same time a rather poor performance in January. The empirical evidence seems to be generally supportive of such reasoning. Davis (1994) and Loughran (1997) have confirmed that the stock-level value premium to be particularly high in January, while Yao (2012) and Novy-Marx (2012) indicated the momentum returns to be the highest in December and the lowest in January. Finally, the January effect exerts influence on these strategies not only at a stock level but also at the country or industry level (Zaremba 2015; Zaremba and Umutlu 2018).[2]

Perhaps the most comprehensive study of the January effect in the US equity market was conducted by Haug and Hirschey in 2006. The authors have contributed to the evidence digging out returns dating back even to 1802 and found the January effect consistent with small-capitalization stocks. Also, Haug and Hirschey have identified the seasonal pattern in monthly returns using portfolios based on size and book-to-market factors. They have also documented a persistently negative January effect for momentum stocks. Overall, the authors concluded that the January effect is a real and continuing anomaly in small-cap stock returns, and one that is still defying an easy explanation even after over 30 years of its discovery.

[1] For classical literature, see, for example, Rozeff and Kinney (1976), French (1980), Gibbons and Hess (1981), Lakonishok and Levi (1982), Roll (1983), Keim (1983), Reinganum (1983), Ariel (1987), and Haugen and Lakonishok (1988).

[2] An investigation of analogous patterns in government bond markets by Zaremba and Schabek (2017) found no similar evidence.

The most comprehensive international study was conducted by Zhang and Jacobsen (2013). This looked at over 300 years of monthly data on the UK stock market, starting in 1693, using the longest time-series available and thus providing the authors with a relatively fresh data set, not directly linked to the US equity market.

Jacobsen and Zhang found the performance of different months varying over time with no single month—not even January—markedly outperforming the market in all their 50- and 100-year subsamples. Surprisingly, throughout the first 150 years, January, instead of excelling, ranked below the average. Furthermore, before 1830 they observed a strong positive December effect, which weakened as the January effect grew in strength. The authors finally concluded that the January effect could not have been imported from the US market as during the period the January returns in the USA remained negative.

Sell-in-May-and-Go-Away Effect The "sell-in-May-and-go-away" effect (in short, "sell-in-May", also referred to as the Halloween indicator) manifests itself in the outperformance of stocks from November to April relative to the remainder of the year. This phenomenon, originally identified by Bouman and Jacobsen (2002) across 36 equity markets, has been since confirmed in broader and longer samples by Castro and Schabek (2014) or Jacobsen and Zhang (2014) whose latest study has delivered markedly comprehensive results. The authors have used all available stock market indices for all 108 stock markets across all time periods, incorporating in total 55,425 monthly observations spanning over 319 years. The amassed evidence showed that winter returns—November to April—amount to 4.52% (t-value 9.69) and exceed the remaining summer returns. Interestingly, the effect has been gaining momentum with the average difference between November–April and May–October returns reaching 6.25% over the past 50 years. Jacobsen and Zhang (2014) have documented the sell-in-May trading strategy to beat the market more than eight out of ten times over the five-year time period.

The effect of the Halloween indicator is usually explained by mood fluctuations in equity markets. Kamstra et al. (2003) pointed to the so-called seasonal affective disorder (SAD) in the seasonal time-variation of stock market returns. As the authors point out, "SAD is an extensively documented medical condition whereby the shortness of the days in fall and winter leads to depression for many people. Experimental research in psychology and economics indicates that depression, in turn, causes heightened risk aversion." Consequently, the authors provide convincing evidence that the stock returns are significantly linked to the amount of daylight in fall and winter. More interestingly, this pattern emerges slightly different at different latitudes and in different hemispheres: the higher latitude markets show more pronounced SAD effects, and the results in the Southern Hemisphere remain six months out of phase, as are their seasons.

The "sell-in-May-and-go-away" phenomenon is particularly visible in equity indices, which helps to predict which countries will overperform in the forthcoming months. Many papers have also offered some simple trading strategies based on the Halloween indicator.[3]

The Other January Effect In 2006, Cooper et al. came up with another January-related phenomenon: the so-called the other January effect. The researchers argued that the performance of stock returns in January emerges as a predictor of the stock returns in the rest of the year. In other words, if January return is positive, then the rest of the year should also be positive and vice versa. Having investigated the data spanning from 1825 to 2003, the authors found satisfactory evidence to support the effectiveness of the "other January effect".

Why would this effect work? Cooper et al. have proposed three possible explanations related to (a) business conditions, (b) presidential cycles, and (c) the investor sentiment. None of them, however, have been supported by data. Stivers et al. (2009) have also suggested further explanations attributing it to internationally priced risk factors, a ubiquitous behavioral bias, or simply dismissing it as a temporal anomaly. In other words, it could be a statistical aberration with no underlying economic explanation, or simply tied to a specific period in a history (see, also, Schwert 2003).

The latest evidence seems to point to the latter explanation with Marshall and Visaltanachoti (2010) showing that a simple strategy based on the other January effect in fact underperforms a simple buy-and-hold strategy before and after the risk adjustment. Also, Bohl and Salm (2010), who having researched the effect across 19 international markets, found

[3] For further examinations, see Jacobsen et al. (2005), Hong and Yu (2007), Doeswijk (2008), Dumitriu et al. (2012), Sum (2013), Okada and Yamasaki (2014), Dichtl and Drobetz (2015), Dzhabarov and Ziemba (2016), Kamstra et al. (2017), Hirshleifer et al. (2017), and Zaremba and Schabek (2017).

no supportive evidence documenting only 2 out of 19 countries exhibiting a robust Other January Effect. In the light of this evidence, Bohl and Salm (2010) concluded that the other January effect can't be an international phenomenon.[4]

Ramadan Effect Ramadan fasting is one of the most well-known and celebrated religious rituals around the world. Could it also influence the performance of equity markets? Although astonishing, a recent study by Białkowski et al. (2012) revealed that in countries with a majority of Muslim population, the stock market companies display markedly more favorable behavior in the time of Ramadan than in other periods of the year.[5] Not only were the stock market returns nine times higher in Ramadan as compared to the other months, but they also saw a decrease in market volatility. This surprising phenomenon has been documented in a sample of 14 predominantly Muslim countries over the years 1989–2007.

How is it possible that the equity markets perform that well during Ramadan? According to Białkowski et al. (2012), Ramadan seem to affect investors' psychology, encouraging feelings of solidarity and social identity across Muslims communities, boosting their optimistic beliefs which then extend to their investment decisions. While other researchers asserted that "as indicated by research in positive psychology, religion provides a valuable form of social support, encourages optimistic beliefs, and contributes to the believers' happiness" (Beit-Hallahmi and Argyle 1997), some even suggested that fasting in itself can exert positive impact on investors' minds: "Clinical research shows that the Ramadan fasting generally makes people less tense and anxious (Daradkeh, 1992) and that it may also induce mild states of euphoria (Knerr and Pearl, 2008)."

The study of Białkowski et al. (2012) piqued interest in the Ramadan effect, spinning off a number of further studies from which most confirmed the existence of the phenomenon, casting, nonetheless, some doubt on the persistence of the anomaly.[6]

[4] Nighter pooled investigations of multiple anomalies in developed, emerging, and frontier markets produced supportive evidence of the "other January effect" (Zaremba and Szyszka 2016; Zaremba 2017; Zaremba and Andreu Sánchez 2017).

[5] While the study of Białkowski et al. (2012) is usually considered seminal, Husain (1998) and Seyyed et al. (2005) delivered some earlier evidence on the Ramadan seasonality.

[6] For further evidence, see Mustafa (2011), Ariss et al. (2011), Alumdhaf (2012), Nai-Chiek (2013), Alatiyat (2014), Białkowski et al. (2013), Al-Khazali (2014), Weber and Nickol (2016), Sonjaya and Wahyudi (2016), and Ali et al. (2017).

Daily Anomalies Apart from the above anomalies based on monthly analysis, other return regularities can be detected only when using higher-frequency time-series: weekly, daily, or even intraday time frames. The "weekend effect", or "Monday effect", predicts visibly lower equity returns on Mondays than on other weekdays, in particular dipping below the level of the preceding Friday. The weekend effect is usually explained by the tendency to disclose bad corporate news on Friday after the market closure, which in turn depresses the prices on Monday. Other theories link the Monday effect to short selling, as it frequently affects equities with high short-interest positions, or to investor sentiment fading over the weekend with some researchers also arguing that it may all be a result of data mining.[7]

Another daily phenomenon is the Holiday effect. This term has been used to describe a surge in stock prices, usually attributed to an increase in buying activity by traders immediately before holidays. Historically, equity prices have advanced significantly higher, as a percentage, on pre-holiday trading days. This phenomenon, explained usually by investor sentiment and behavioral biases, refers to a broad array of different holidays, including Christmas Day, New Year's Day, Martin Luther King Jr. Day, Good Friday, President's Day, Memorial Day, Independence Day, Labor Day, Thanksgiving Day, and Election Day. Investors may capitalize on this anomaly by staying in cash during other trading days and leveraging equity exposure before holidays. The return pattern is not only limited to the American equity market but appears to work well also in other countries.[8]

Focusing on the weekly effects, the intra-month effect predicts existence of positive returns only in the first half of the month whereas its variant, *the turn-of-the-month effect*, implies that the last day of the month and the subsequent three days are to be particularly elevated.[9]

[7] For references on the weekend effect, see French (1980), Gibbons and Hess (1981), Keim and Stambaugh (1984), Jaffe and Westerfield (1985), Harris (1986), Connolly (1989), Aggarwal and Rivoli (1989), Lakonishok and Maberly (1990), Abraham and Ikenberry (1994), Sias and Starks (1995), Dubois and Louvet (1996), Choudhry (2000), Rubinstein (2001), Steeley (2001), and Sullivan et al. (2001).

[8] For evidence, see Ariel (1990), Cadsby and Ratner (1992), Bhana (1994), Kim and Park (1994), Arsad and Coutts (1997), Meneu and Pardo (2004), Marrett and Worthington (2009), Ciao et al. (2009), Tiakas (2010), Gama and Viera (2013), Alagidede (2013), and Carchano and Pardo (2015).

[9] For evidence, see, for example, Ogden (1990), Cadsby and Ratner (1992), Hensel and Ziemba (1996), Kunkel et al. (2003), or Ziemba (1991).

In summary, financial literature documents a range of different calendar regularities across equity markets, which to some extent naturally overlap. As January resides within the period November–May, it may equally feed into the "sell-in-May" anomaly, driving the returns up throughout the three months. Aiming to disentangle these various calendar effects, Swinkels and van Vliet (2012) have conducted an interesting analysis by considering a range of different regularities jointly. They have examined the interactions between five broadly acknowledged seasonal anomalies, namely the Halloween effect, January effect, turn-of-the month effect, weekend effect, and holiday effect. The researchers have identified the Halloween and turn-of-the month effect as the strongest, asserting that controlling for them makes all the other calendar effects irrelevant. Although when accounted for the effects, the equity premium amounted to 7.2%, once the effects were excluded, the premium fell to −2.8%. The findings proved robust under a number of different considerations, including transactions costs, across different samples, market segments, and international stock markets. Summing up, Swinkels and van Vliet shrink the number of anomalies to only two, leaving them even more puzzling for the academic community.

Calendar Anomalies in the Cross-Section of Returns

As equity markets exhibit a range of different, to some extent intertwined, anomalies, can we employ them for equity selection? Can they help us predict which stocks will perform better in the nearest future? Yes—with the help of "seasonality" momentum.

Seasonality momentum was initially discovered by Heston and Sadka (2008, 2010) and later expanded and extensively documented by Keloharju et al. (2016). The latter research team investigated whether stocks with good returns in one calendar month are also likely to outperform in the same calendar month in the following year.

To capitalize on this return pattern, Keloharju, Linnainmaa, and Nyberg crafted a simple investment strategy. Having sorted equities on the average stock return in the same calendar month in the past, the researchers went long (short) on the equities with the highest (lowest) same-month return. A strategy based on the sorts of the same-month return delivered on average 13% per year within the US equity market in the period 1963–2011. Importantly, the strategy of sorting on the same calendar month produced a mean monthly return of 1.19%, while ranking on the other-month calendar returns displayed a negative mean monthly return of −0.96%. In consequence, the long-short same-other portfolio exhibited as much as 2.16% per month, with the corresponding *t*-statistic of 7.94. This size of abnormal returns is rarely encountered even among the best-established and most profitable equity anomalies.

The elevated payoffs on the "seasonality momentum" may be surprising, especially given the astonishing simplicity of the strategy. Moreover, Keloharju, Linnainmaa, and Nyberg showed that the profitability of their strategy is truly ubiquitous, having also researched country equity indices and commodities focusing not only on the monthly frequency but also on the daily data. The seasonality momentum strategy has been also identified in equity anomalies both within the USA and across a broad sample of international markets. Without doubt, the cross-sectional seasonality seems to belong to the narrow circle of the most reliable equity anomalies ever discovered.

Empirical Tests of Cross-Sectional Seasonality Strategies

So how have seasonality strategies performed globally over the last two decades? Examining this question empirically, let us zoom in on the *cross-sectional seasonality strategy* by Keloharju et al. (2016). Replicating it, we monthly ranked all the stocks based on their average return in the same calendar month over the previous 20 years. For example, to calculate the strategy's return in February, we sorted the equities on the average February returns over the last 20 years. Next, we formed the usual quintile portfolios. For the long-short portfolio, we assumed a long position in the securities with the highest average return and the short position in equities of the lowest return. The results of the strategy across both individual portfolios and globally are presented in Table 6.1.

The seasonality strategy worked fairly well in our sample representing international markets. The long seasonality portfolios outperformed the short portfolios in 15 out of 24 markets considered. Looking at the exceptionally high outperformance, the long-short portfolios in Japan delivered a monthly alpha of 0.87% (*t*-stat = 6.07) while in the UK the alpha amounted to 0.89% per month (*t* = stat = 0.89). All global long-short portfolios saw a monthly mean return (alpha) of 0.54% (0.52%) when equal-weighted, and 0.65% (0.64%) with the individual markets weighted

Table 6.1 The performance of international seasonality portfolios

Country	*Top portfolio mean return*	*Bottom portfolio mean return*	*Average number of firms*	*T-B portfolio*		*Standard deviation*	*Sharpe ratio*	*Beta*	*Alpha*	
				Mean return	*t-stat*				*Value*	*t-stat*
Australia	1.04	0.40	35	0.64***	*(3.21)*	3.27	0.68	0.00	0.64***	*(3.18)*
Austria	0.89	0.82	5	0.07	*(0.22)*	5.26	0.05	0.07	0.03	*(0.10)*
Belgium	0.99	0.92	9	0.07	*(0.26)*	4.28	0.05	0.11	−0.01	*(−0.05)*
Canada	1.05	0.41	71	0.64***	*(2.78)*	3.77	0.59	−0.04	0.67***	*(2.89)*
Denmark	1.47	0.99	10	0.48*	*(1.71)*	4.63	0.36	0.02	0.46	*(1.60)*
Finland	1.80	1.02	9	0.78***	*(2.59)*	4.98	0.55	0.08	0.71**	*(2.33)*
France	1.47	0.59	38	0.89***	*(4.45)*	3.27	0.94	−0.06	0.92***	*(4.63)*
Germany	1.28	0.56	32	0.72***	*(3.47)*	3.41	0.73	−0.01	0.73***	*(3.49)*
Greece	0.81	0.40	9	0.41	*(0.88)*	7.67	0.19	0.03	0.41	*(0.88)*
Hong Kong	−0.21	−0.08	17	−0.12	*(−0.34)*	5.95	−0.07	0.03	−0.14	*(−0.39)*
Ireland	1.10	1.47	3	−0.36	*(−0.65)*	9.20	−0.14	−0.03	−0.34	*(−0.61)*
Israel	0.55	0.63	11	−0.09	*(−0.16)*	8.54	−0.03	0.04	−0.10	*(−0.19)*
Italy	1.24	0.43	21	0.82***	*(3.62)*	3.71	0.76	−0.03	0.83***	*(3.66)*
Japan	0.78	−0.09	282	0.87***	*(6.08)*	2.35	1.28	0.00	0.87***	*(6.07)*
The Netherlands	1.39	0.65	15	0.74***	*(3.24)*	3.76	0.68	−0.05	0.78***	*(3.37)*
New Zealand	1.59	0.35	3	1.24**	*(2.49)*	8.17	0.53	0.21	1.08**	*(2.17)*
Norway	1.06	0.76	10	0.29	*(0.82)*	5.88	0.17	−0.02	0.31	*(0.87)*
Portugal	0.78	0.21	3	0.58	*(1.34)*	7.08	0.28	0.15	0.52	*(1.22)*
Singapore	0.52	0.07	10	0.45	*(1.26)*	5.81	0.27	0.02	0.43	*(1.22)*
Spain	1.09	0.46	15	0.63***	*(2.69)*	3.85	0.57	−0.05	0.67***	*(2.84)*
Sweden	1.74	0.76	19	0.98***	*(3.65)*	4.40	0.77	−0.02	1.00***	*(3.69)*
Switzerland	1.56	0.82	24	0.74***	*(3.94)*	3.07	0.83	−0.07	0.79***	*(4.20)*

(*continued*)

Table 6.1 (continued)

Country	*Top portfolio mean return*	*Bottom portfolio mean return*	*Average number of firms*	*T-B portfolio*		*Standard deviation*	*Sharpe ratio*	*Beta*	*Alpha*	
				Mean return	*t-stat*				*Value*	*t-stat*
UK	1.33	0.43	90	0.90***	*(6.87)*	2.15	1.45	0.01	0.89***	*(6.78)*
USA	1.25	0.68	528	0.57***	*(3.63)*	2.59	0.77	0.03	0.55***	*(3.47)*
World (EW)	1.11	0.57	1270	0.54***	*(6.28)*	1.41	1.32	0.03	0.52***	*(6.07)*
World (VW)	1.07	0.43	1270	0.65***	*(6.13)*	1.73	1.29	0.01	0.64***	*(6.02)*

Note: The table reports the monthly returns on the portfolios from sorts on the average monthly return in the same calendar month over the past 20 years. The calculations were made on the basis of monthly observations. ***Top portfolio*** and ***bottom portfolio*** are quintile portfolios including stocks with the highest and lowest average monthly returns, respectively. ***T-B portfolio*** is the portfolio long the ***top*** portfolio and short the ***bottom*** portfolio. The Sharpe ratio is expressed on an annualized basis. The alpha and beta are derived from the CAPM. Mean returns, standard deviations, and alphas are expressed in percentage. Asterisks *, **, and *** indicate values significantly different from zero at the 10%, 5%, and 1% levels, respectively by capitalization. Importantly, the global seasonality portfolios displayed very low levels of volatility: not only their betas were close to zero, but also their standard deviation stayed as low as 1.41% and 1.73% monthly for the equally weighted and value-weighted strategies, respectively. In consequence, the Sharpe ratios rose impressively high reaching 1.32 and 1.29, correspondingly.

The times-series of cumulative returns on the global seasonality, displayed in Figs. 6.1 and 6.2, confirm the stability of the strategy profits. Both under the equal-weighting (Fig. 6.1) and value-weighting (Fig. 6.2) approaches, the strategies recorded no major visible drawdown during the entire 20-year period, showing a great promise for the future reliability of this stock picking technique.

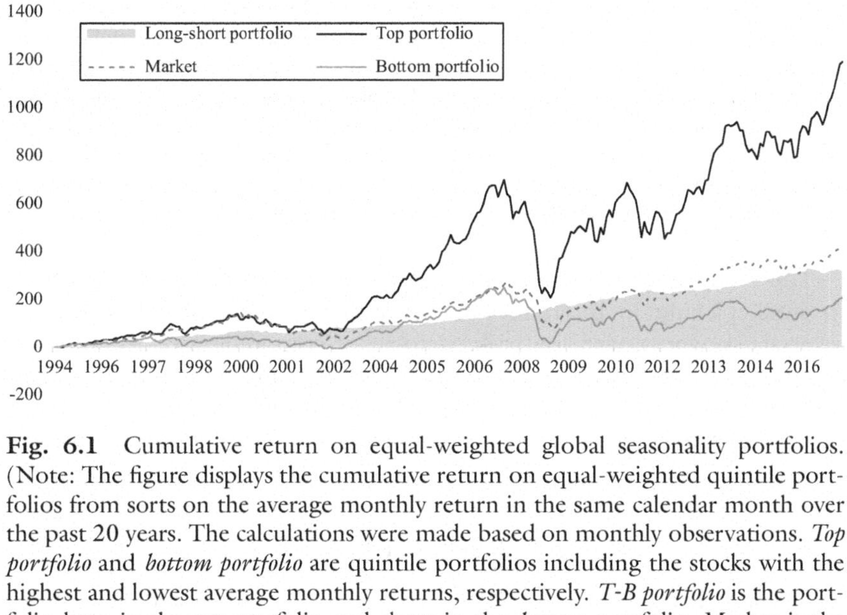

Fig. 6.1 Cumulative return on equal-weighted global seasonality portfolios. (Note: The figure displays the cumulative return on equal-weighted quintile portfolios from sorts on the average monthly return in the same calendar month over the past 20 years. The calculations were made based on monthly observations. *Top portfolio* and *bottom portfolio* are quintile portfolios including the stocks with the highest and lowest average monthly returns, respectively. *T-B portfolio* is the portfolio long in the *top* portfolio and short in the *bottom* portfolio. Market is the value weighted portfolio of all the country equity markets considered. All the returns are expressed in percentage)

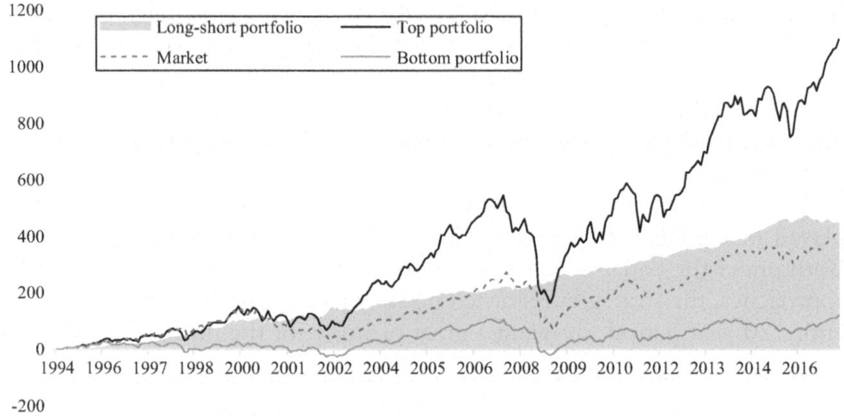

Fig. 6.2 Cumulative return on value-weighted global seasonality portfolios. (Note: The figure displays the cumulative return on value-weighted quintile portfolios from sorts on the average monthly return in the same calendar month over the past 20 years. The calculations were made based on monthly observations. *Top portfolio* and *bottom portfolio* are quintile portfolios including the stocks with the highest and lowest average monthly returns, respectively. *T-B portfolio* is the portfolio long in the *top* portfolio and short in the *bottom* portfolio. Market is the value-weighted portfolio of all the country equity markets considered. All the returns are expressed in percentage)

The cross-sectional seasonality emerges as another effective approach to stock picking in international markets. Together with momentum, reversal, skewness, and low risk, it forms a comprehensive toolbox for every quantitative investor. Importantly, all the strategies uniquely transform prices to generate the return predictive signals. Could the raw price be also used to forecast future performance? We will find out in the next chapter.

References

Abraham, A., & Ikenberry, D. L. (1994). The individual investor and the weekend effect. *Journal of Financial and Quantitative Analysis, 29*(2), 263–277.

Aggarwal, R., & Rivoli, P. (1989). Seasonal and day-of-the-week effects in four emerging stock markets. *Financial Review, 24*(4), 541–550.

Alagidede, P. (2013). Month of the year and pre-holiday effects in African stock markets. *South African Journal of Economic and Management Sciences, 16*(1). Available at http://www.scielo.org.za/scielo.php?script=sci_arttext&pid=S2222-34362013000100006

Alatiyat, M. (2014). *Ramadan effect on UAE stock market – Banks sector*. Available at SSRN: https://ssrn.com/abstract=2449967 or https://doi.org/10.2139/ssrn.2449967. Accessed 24 Oct 2017.

Ali, I., Akhter, W., & Ashraf, N. (2017). Impact of Muslim Holy Days on Asian stock markets: An empirical evidence. *Cogent Economics & Finance, 5*(1). https://doi.org/10.1080/23322039.2017.1311096.

Al-Khazali, O. (2014). Revisiting fast profit investor sentiment and stock returns during Ramadan. *International Review of Financial Analysis, 33*, 158–170. https://doi.org/10.1016/j.irfa.2014.02.003.

Alumdhaf, F. (2012). The Islamic calendar effects: Evidence from twelve stock markets. *International Research Journal of Finance and Economics, 87*, 187–191.

Ariel, R. A. (1987). A monthly effect in stock returns. *Journal of Financial Economics, 18*, 161–174.

Ariel, R. A. (1990). High stock returns before holidays: Existence and evidence on possible causes. *Journal of Finance, 45*(5), 1611–1626.

Ariss, R. T., Rezwanian, R., & Mehdian, S. M. (2011). Calendar anomalies in the Gulf Cooperation Council stock markets. *Emerging Markets Review, 12*(3), 293–307. https://doi.org/10.1016/j.ememar.2011.04.002.

Arsad, Z., & Coutts, J. A. (1997). Security price anomalies in the London international stock exchange: A 60 year perspective. *Applied Financial Economics, 7*(5), 455–464.

Beit-Hallahmi, B., & Argyle, M. (1997). *The psychology of religious behaviour, belief and experience*. London: Routledge.

Bhana, N. (1994). Public holiday share price behavior on the Johannesburg Stock Exchange. *Investment Analysts Journal, 23*(39), 45–49.

Białkowski, J., Etebari, A., & Wiśniewski, T. (2012). Fast profits: Investor sentiment and stock returns during Ramadan. *Journal of Banking and Finance, 36*(3), 835–845.

Białkowski, H., Bohl, M. T., Kaufmann, P., & Wiśniewski, T. P. (2013). Do mutual fund managers exploit the Ramadan anomaly? Evidence from Turkey. *Emerging Markets Review, 15*, 211–232.

Bohl, M. T., & Salm, C. A. (2010). The other January effect: International evidence. *European Journal of Finance, 16*, 173–182. https://doi.org/10.1080/13518470903037953.

Bouman, S., & Jacobsen, B. (2002). The Halloween indicator, "Sell in May and go away": Another puzzle. *American Economic Review, 92*(5), 1618–1635. https://doi.org/10.1257/000282802762024674.

Cadsby, C. B., & Ratner, M. (1992). Turn-of-month and pre-holiday effects on stock returns: Some international evidence. *Journal of Banking & Finance, 16*(3), 497–509.

Carchano, O., & Pardo, A. (2015). The pan-European holiday effect. *Spanish Journal of Finance and Accounting, 44*(2), 134–145. https://doi.org/10.1080/02102412.2015.1016716.

Castro, F. H., & Schabek, T. (2014). *Sell not only in May. Seasonal effects in emerging and developed markets.* Available at SSRN: http://ssrn.com/abstract=2458515 or https://doi.org/10.2139/ssrn.2458515. Accessed 23 Oct 2017.

Choudhry, T. (2000). Day of the week effect in emerging Asian stock markets: Evidence from the GARCH model. *Applied Financial Economics, 10*(3), 235–242.

Ciao, X., Premachandra, I. M., & Bhabra, G. S. (2009). Firm size and the pre-holiday effect in New Zealand. *International Research Journal of Finance and Economics, 32*, 171–187. ISSN: 1450-2887.

Connolly, R. A. (1989). An examination of the robustness of the weekend effect. *Journal of Financial and Quantitative Analysis, 24*(2), 133–169.

Daradkeh, T. K. (1992). Parasuicide during Ramadan in Jordan. *Acta Psychiatrica Scandinavica, 86*(3), 253–254.

Davis, J. (1994). The cross-section of realized stock returns: The pre-COMPUSTAT evidence. *Journal of Finance, 49*, 1579–1593. https://doi.org/10.1111/j.1540-6261.1994.tb04773.x.

Dichtl, H., & Drobetz, W. (2015). Sell in May and go away: Still good advice for investors? *International Review of Financial Analysis, 38*, 29–43. https://doi.org/10.1016/j.irfa.2014.09.007.

Doeswijk, R. Q. (2008, June). The optimism cycle: Sell in May. *De Economist, 156*, 175. https://doi.org/10.1007/s10645-008-9088-z.

Dubois, M., & Louvet, P. (1996). The day-of-the-week effect: The international evidence. *Journal of Banking and Finance, 20*(9), 1463–1484.

Dumitriu, R., Stefanescu, R., & Nistor, C. (2012). *The Halloween effect during quiet and turbulent times.* Available at SSRN: https://ssrn.com/abstract=2043757 or https://doi.org/10.2139/ssrn.2043757. Accessed 23 Oct 2017.

Dzhabarov, C. S., & Ziemba, W. T. (2016). *Sell in May and go away in the equity index futures markets.* Available at SSRN: https://ssrn.com/abstract=2721068 or https://doi.org/10.2139/ssrn.2721068. Accessed 23 Oct 2017.

French, K. R. (1980). Stock returns and the weekend effect. *Journal of Financial Economics, 8*(1), 55–69.

Gama, P. M., & Viera, E. F. S. (2013). Another look at the holiday effect. *Applied Financial Economics, 23*(20), 1623–1633. https://doi.org/10.1080/09603107.2013.8426384.

Gibbons, M. R., & Hess, P. (1981). Day of the week effects and asset returns. *Journal of Business, 54*(4), 579–596.

Harris, L. (1986). A transaction data study of weekly and intradaily patterns in stock returns. *Journal of Financial Economics, 16*(1), 99–117.

Haug, M., & Hirschey, M. (2006). The January effect. *Financial Analyst Journal, 62*(5), 78–88.

Haugen, R. A., & Lakonishok, J. (1988). *The incredible January effect: The stock market's unsolved mystery*. Homewood: Dow Jones-Irwin.

Hensel, C. R., & Ziemba, W. T. (1996). Investment results from exploiting turn-of-the-month effects. *Journal of Portfolio Management, 22*(3), 17–23.

Heston, S. L., & Sadka, R. (2008). Seasonality in the cross-section of stock returns. *Journal of Financial Economics, 87*(2), 418–445. https://doi.org/10.1016/j.jfineco.2007.02.003.

Heston, S. L., & Sadka, R. (2010). Seasonality in the cross-section of stock returns: The international evidence. *Journal of Financial and Quantitative Analysis, 45*(5), 1133–1160.

Hirshleifer, D. A., Jiang, D., & Men, Y. (2017). *Mood beta and seasonalities in stock returns*. Available at SSRN: https://ssrn.com/abstract=2880257. Accessed 23 Oct 2017.

Hong, H. G., & Yu, J. (2007). *Gone fishin': Seasonality in trading activity and asset prices*. Available at SSRN: https://ssrn.com/abstract=676743 or https://doi.org/10.2139/ssrn.676743. Accessed 23 Oct 2017.

Husain, F. (1998). A seasonality in the Pakistani equity market: The Ramadhan effect. *Pakistani Development Review, 37*(1), 77–81.

Jacobsen, B., & Zhang, C. Y. (2014). *The Halloween indicator, 'Sell in May and go away': An even bigger puzzle*. Available at SSRN: http://ssrn.com/abstract=2154873 or https://doi.org/10.2139/ssrn.2154873. Accessed 23 Oct 2017.

Jacobsen, B., Mamun, A., & Visaltanachoti, N. (2005). *Seasonal, size and value anomalies*. Available at SSRN: https://ssrn.com/abstract=784186 or https://doi.org/10.2139/ssrn.784186. Accessed 23 Oct 2017.

Jaffe, J., & Westerfield, R. (1985). The week-end effect in common stock returns: The international evidence. *Journal of Finance, 40*(2), 433–454.

Kamstra, M. J., Kramer, L. A., & Levi, M. D. (2003). *Winter blues: A SAD stock market cycle* (Federal Reserve Bank of Atlanta working paper No. 2002-13a; Sauder School of Business working paper). Available at SSRN: https://ssrn.com/abstract=208622 or https://doi.org/10.2139/ssrn.208622. Accessed 23 Oct 2017.

Kamstra, M. J., Kramer, L. A., Levi, M. D., & Wermers, R. (2017). Seasonal asset allocation: Evidence from mutual fund flows. *Journal of Financial and Quantitative Analysis, 52*(1), 71–109. https://doi.org/10.1017/S002210901600082X.

Keim, D. (1983). Size-related anomalies and stock return seasonality: Further empirical evidence. *Journal of Financial Economics, 12*, 13–32.

Keim, D. B., & Stambaugh, R. F. (1984). A further investigation of the weekend effect in stock returns. *Journal of Finance, 39*(3), 819–835.

Keloharju, M., Linnainmaa, J. T., & Nyberg, P. (2016). Return seasonalities. *Journal of Finance, 71*(4), 1557–1590.

Kim, C.-W., & Park, J. (1994). Holiday effects and stock returns: Further evidence. *Journal of Financial and Quantitative Analysis, 29*(1), 145–157.

Knerr, I., & Pearl, P. L. (2008). Ketogenic diet: Stoking energy stores and still posing questions. *Experimental Neurology, 11*, 11–13.

Kunkel, R. A., Compton, W. S., & Beyer, S. (2003). The turn-of-the-month effect still lives. *International Review of Financial Analysis, 12*(2), 207–221.

Lakonishok, J., & Levi, M. (1982). Weekend effects on stock returns: A note. *Journal of Finance, 37*(3), 883–889.

Lakonishok, J., & Maberly, E. (1990). The weekend effect: Trading patterns of individual and institutional investors. *Journal of Finance, 45*(1), 231–243.

Loughran, T. (1997). Book-to-market across firm size, exchange, and seasonality: Is there an effect? *Journal of Financial and Quantitative Analysis, 30*, 607–618. https://doi.org/10.2307/2331199.

Marrett, G. J., & Worthington, A. C. (2009). An empirical note on the holiday effect in the Australian stock market, 1996–2006. *Applied Economic Letters, 16*(17), 1769–1772.

Marshall, B. R., & Visaltanachoti, N. (2010). The other January effect: Evidence against market efficiency? *Journal of Banking & Finance, 34*(10), 2413–2424. https://doi.org/10.1016/j.jbankfin.2010.03.019.

Meneu, V., & Pardo, A. (2004). Pre-holiday effect, large trades and small investor behavior. *Journal of Empirical Finance, 11*(2), 231–246. https://doi.org/10.1016/j.jempfin.2003.01.002.

Mustafa, K. (2011). The Islamic calendar effect on Karachi stock market. *Global Business Review, 13*(3), 562–574.

Nai-Chiek, A. (2013). Seasonality in Southeast Asian stock markets: The Ramadan effect. *The IUP Journal of Applied Finance, 19*(3), 75–92.

Novy-Marx, R. (2012). Is momentum really momentum? *Journal of Financial Economics, 103*, 429–453.

Ogden, J. P. (1990). Turn-of-month evaluations of liquid profits and stock returns: A common explanation for the monthly and January effects. *Journal of Finance, 45*(4), 1259–1272.

Okada, K., & Yamasaki, T. (2014). *Investor sentiment in news and the calendar anomaly – New evidence from a large textual data*. Available at SSRN: https://ssrn.com/abstract=2394008 or https://doi.org/10.2139/ssrn.2394008. Accessed 23 Oct 2017.

Reinganum, M. R. (1983). The anomalous stock market behavior of small firms in January – Empirical tests for tax-loss selling effects. *Journal of Financial Economics, 12*, 89–104.

Rogalski, R. J., & Tinic, S. M. (1986). The January size effect: Anomaly or risk measurement? *Financial Analysts Journal, 42*(6), 63–70.

Roll, R. (1983). Vas ist das? The turn-of-the-year effect and the return premia of small firms. *Journal of Portfolio Management, 9*(Winter), 18–28.

Rozeff, M. S., & Kinney, W. R. (1976). Capital market seasonality: The case of stock returns. *Journal of Financial Economics, 3*, 379–4012.

Rubinstein, M. (2001). Rational markets: Yes or no? The affirmative case. *Financial Analysts Journal, 57*(3), 15–29.

Schwert, G. W. (2003). Anomalies and market efficiency. In G. Constantinides, M. Harris, & R. Stulz (Eds.), *Handbook of the economics of finance*. Amsterdam: North Holland.

Seyyed, F., Abraham, A., & Al-Hajji, M. (2005). Seasonality in stock returns and volatility. The Ramadan effect. *Research in International Business and Finance, 19*(3), 374–383.

Sias, R. W., & Starks, L. T. (1995). The day-of-the-week anomaly: The role of institutional investors. *Financial Analysts Journal, 51*(3), 58–67.

Sonjaya, A. R., & Wahyudi, I. (2016). The Ramadan effect: Illusion or reality? *Arab Economic and Business Journal, 11*(1), 55–71. https://doi.org/10.1016/j.aebj.2016.03.001.

Steeley, J. M. (2001). A note on information seasonality and the disappearance of the weekend effect in the UK stock market. *Journal of Banking and Finance, 25*(1), 1941–1956.

Stivers, C., Sun, L., & Sun, Y. (2009). The other January effect: International, style, and subperiod evidence. *Journal of Financial Markets, 12*, 521–546.

Sullivan, R., Timmermann, A., & White, H. (2001). Dangers of data mining: The case of calendar effects in stock returns. *Journal of Econometrics, 105*(1), 249–286.

Sum, V. (2013). *Stock market performance: High and low months*. Available at SSRN: https://ssrn.com/abstract=2275061 or https://doi.org/10.2139/ssrn.2275061. Accessed 23 Oct 2017.

Swinkels, L., & van Vliet, P. (2012). An anatomy of calendar effects. *Journal of Asset Management, 13*(4), 271–286.

Tiakas, I. (2010). The economic gains of trading stocks around holidays. *Journal of Financial Research, 33*(1), 1–26. https://doi.org/10.1111/j.1475-6803.2009.01260.x.

Weber, C., & Nickol, P. (2016). More on calendar effects on Islamic stock markets. *Review of Middle East Economics and Finance, 12*(1), 65–113. https://doi.org/10.1515/rmeef-2015-0039.

Yao, Y. (2012). Momentum, contrarian, and the January seasonality. *Journal of Banking and Finance, 36*, 2757–2769. https://doi.org/10.1016/j.jbankfin.2011.12.004.

Zaremba, A. (2015). The January seasonality and the performance of country-level value and momentum strategies. *Copernican Journal of Finance & Accounting, 2*, 195–209. http://apcz.pl/czasopisma/index.php/CJFA/article/view/CJFA.2015.024

Zaremba, A. (2017). *Performance persistence in anomaly returns: Evidence from frontier markets*. Available at SSRN: https://ssrn.com/abstract=3060876. Accessed 31 Oct 2017.

Zaremba, A., & Szyszka, A. (2016). Is there momentum in equity anomalies? Evidence from the Polish emerging market. *Research in International Business and Finance, 38*, 546–564. https://doi.org/10.1016/j.ribaf.2016.07.004.

Zaremba, A., & Andreu Sánchez, L. (2017). *Paper profits or real money? Trading costs and stock market anomalies in country equity indices*. Available at https://doi.org/10.2139/ssrn.3038514

Zaremba, A., & Schabek, T. (2017). Seasonality in government bond returns and factor premia. *Research in International Business and Finance, 41*, 292–302. https://doi.org/10.1016/j.ribaf.2017.04.036.

Zaremba, A., & Umutlu, M. (2018, in press). Strategies can be expensive too! The value spread and asset allocation in global equity markets. *Applied Economics*.

Zhang, C. Y., & Jacobsen, B. (2013). Are monthly seasonals real? A three century perspective. *Review of Finance, 17*(5), 1743–1785.

Ziemba, W. T. (1991). Japanese security market regularities: Monthly, turn of the month and year, holiday and golden week effects. *Japan and the World Economy, 3*, 119–146.

CHAPTER 7

Predicting Prices Based on… Prices? The Role of Nominal Prices

As we know, both fundamental and technical analyses investigate a broad range of various sophisticated variables to predict future returns. What would happen then if we zoomed in on the simplest possible variable, the price itself? Theoretically, the price should have zero impact on the future returns, being merely a "technical number" with no real reference to the fundamental data. In practice, however, the price does play a role.

The Role of Raw Prices

Interestingly, the evidence on the precise direction of the price impact on future returns remains to a large extent confusing.[1] The early research had pointed to something called the "low-price effect" which, in essence, is a stock anomaly of low-priced shares significantly outperforming high-priced shares on a risk-adjusted return basis. The phenomenon was first discovered by Fritzmeier (1936) researching the US stock market. Fritzmeier proved that low-priced stocks yield higher returns but at the same time entail higher risk. Clenderin (1951) and Allison and Heins (1966) identified price risk as related rather to the low "quality" of stocks perceived by investors rather than low prices. In the following research, Blume and Husic (1973) confirmed the initial observations of Fritzmeier (1936) and scrutinized beta variability. Bachrach and Galai (1979) found that systematic risk did not fully explain the superior returns of cheaper stocks. Later,

[1] This section is based on and partially sourced from Zaremba et al. (2016).

A. Zaremba, J. "Koby" Shemer, *Price-Based Investment Strategies*,
https://doi.org/10.1007/978-3-319-91530-2_7

similar investigations were conducted by Christie (1982) and Dubofsky and French (1988), who decided to apply different risk measures. The superior performance of low-priced stocks was further confirmed by Goodman and Peavy (1986) while Branch and Chang (1990) associated the low-price effect with the seasonal patterns on the stock market.[2] Finally, the effect was tested in a number of international markets: Kenya (Muthoni 2014), South Africa (Waelkens and Ward 2015), Poland (Zaremba and Żmudziński 2014), and Eastern Europe (Zaremba et al. 2016).

One of the most recent studies in support of the low-price effect was authored by Hwang and Lu (2008). The authors investigated returns in the US equity market within the years 1926–2006 proving that the share price per se is indeed relevant to the future equity returns. Based on the share price at the beginning of the research period, the authors sorted the stocks into the following five quintiles: less than \$5, \$5–\$10, \$10–\$15, \$15–\$20, and more than \$20. While within the time frame the shares with the lowest prices delivered on average 1.84% per month, the shares with the highest price only 1%. The difference amounting to 0.83% per month was significant (*t*-stat exceeding 3.2) and robust to many considerations. The profitability of this strategy turned out to be robust in the presence of other effects such as size, liquidity, book-to-market equity, earning/price ratio, and past performance. Interestingly, the payoffs were still highly seasonal: the price-based strategy returns were generated almost solely in January with the remaining months yielding insignificant returns.

Why then would the low-price effect work? In behavioral finance, the relative performance and valuation of low-priced stocks are usually linked with the phenomenon of share splits. First Bar-Yosef and Brown (1979), and later Strong (1983), observed that the low-price effect was valid for companies which split their shares. This was explained by the catering theory of nominal stock prices. According to Baker et al. (2009), the theory predicts that when investors place higher valuations on low-priced firms, managers respond by supplying shares at lower price levels, and vice versa. The theory assumes that managers believe nominal prices matter to investors and gain motivation from evidence that key return characteristics are affected by the nominal price. The splits become more frequent when the valuations of low-priced firms appear attractive relative to high-priced firms. The catering theory predicts splits to lower prices when the lower price shares are favored.

[2] The low-price anomaly was also examined by Pinches and Simon (1972), Strong (1983), and Edminster and Green (1980).

A closely related topic is stock splits. In his well-known research paper Benartzi et al. (2006) revealed that since the Great Depression the average nominal share price in the USA remained constant at around $30, despite the inflation, owing to none other than stock splits. Why then firms are so motivated to continue to split their shares? In principle, there are at least three credible attempts to answer this question. The first idea is "signaling", according to which firms keep their share prices low to signal that their higher quality status (Brennan and Copeland 1988; Ikenberry et al. 1996). The second hypothesis—sometimes referred to as "optimal trading range hypothesis"—points to the ownership base of the firm. It implies that management needs to keep the prices in a certain range to increase their ownership base. Although admittedly this is one of the most widely acknowledged explanations (Baker and Gallagher 1980), the supporting empirical evidence seems rather disappointing, examining, for example, the studies of Lamoureux and Poon (1987) and Mukherji et al. (1997). While Lamoureux and Poon (1987) did find a number of shareholders increase after the stock split, Mukherji et al. (1997) indicated that the proportion of institutional ownership remains afterward unchanged. The third hypothesis points to liquidity conditions. Theoretically, after the split the firm should be able to attract more individual investors, and thus the liquidity should improve (see, e.g., Baker and Gallagher 1980; Muscarella and Vetsuypens 1996; Schultz 2000). Interestingly, having examined the three theories jointly, Weld et al. (2009) concluded that neither is able to explain stock splits satisfactorily. As summarized by Hwang and Lu (2008), the jury is out.

By no means all researchers agree that the low-priced stocks perform that well. In 2015 Jason Birru and Baolian Wang identified a hole in the earlier reasoning for the low-price effect indicating that any model of equity prices, whether based on discounted dividends or cash flows, assumes an inverse link between the prices and expected returns, namely the lower the prices, the higher the future returns. Why? If a stock is risky, then the future payoffs will be discounted with higher discount rate, implying higher expected returns but also a lower future price. In consequence, if we sort the companies based on raw share prices, the groups will include two countervailing components: the first, a mechanical discount effect, implying that low-priced stocks should yield higher future returns, and the second, the so-called nominal price effect, predicting low-priced stocks to underperform.

To test this concept, the authors utilized a range of variables from financial statements: assets per share, book value per share, earnings per share, and dividends per share, which clearly correlate with the fundamental situation of the company. Thus controlling the variables, Birru and Wang could examine the pure low-price effects within a sample of US stocks for years 1968–2013 and discover that the fitter prices positively predict returns: the strategy of a going position in high "fitted" price stocks and a short in low "fitted" price stocks delivered a four-factor alpha of more than 0.85% per month. The authors argued that the profits stem mainly from behavioral mispricing, confirming that the payoffs are stronger both in the short and in the long leg of the long-short portfolio. In particular, the short-leg profits earned on average −0.78% per month, while the long leg an insignificant 0.08%.

Summing up, the effect of share prices on future returns still remains to some extent controversial. The results are mixed; new studies bring more surprising results, and the discussion continues.

Reverse Splits

While analyzing the influence of prices on future returns, we should also consider the reverse splits. This phenomenon is purely price-based and bears international implications in the cross-section of returns.

A reverse stock split is an operation by which company stocks are effectively merged to form a smaller number of proportionally higher priced stocks.[3] This process is relatively less known than the regular stock splits, which result in splitting a stock into less valuable stocks. The regular splits have been rigorously researched across a plethora of periods and equity markets, with the first studies dating back to the famous paper of Fama et al. (1969). The reverse splits—forming one strain of the stock split phenomena—have attracted little interest from the academic community.

In theory, share consolidations should have no impact on the stock's price. Yet, given how many companies conduct reverse splits only to find themselves again in serious financial trouble, some investors regard reverse splits as a capital punishment to the company's prospects. Indeed, the long-run performance following reverse splits appears anomalous, but whether the subsequent abnormal returns are positive or negative remains debatable.

[3] The issues discussed in this section were also described in Zaremba et al. (2016).

The theoretical argumentation supports both the positive and negative subsequent long-term returns. On the one hand, increasing nominal share price creates conditions for better pricing. To this effect Hwang et al. (2012) argued reverse splits reduce the transaction costs and help investors buy the stocks on margin, moving the share price closer to the desired range, and thus improving marketability. Additionally, Han (1995) documented reverse splits to enhance the liquidity of the stock and increase its trading volume, whereas Koski (2007) showed volatility to drop 25% as a consequence of a reverse split. On the other hand, Kim et al. (2008) suggested that "reverse stock splits are a strong indicator the company is going to be a significant underperformer in the near future," blaming the subsequent poor returns on the investors' underreaction. Further, Spudeck and Moyer (1985) argued that "reverse splits appear to be better characterized as a strong signal to the marketplace of management's lack of confidence in future stock price increases resulting from earnings improvement."

Interestingly, not only theoretical but also empirical evidence sheds little light on the long-run post-split performance. Desai and Jain (1997) as well as Kim et al. (2008) found that the firms which consolidated their shares significantly underperformed throughout the three-year period following the event. On the contrary, Hwang et al. (2012), who investigated the same stock market, observed significant positive returns in the three-year post-reverse split period. These astonishing discrepancies have never been explained, thus the long-term underperformance and overperformance still remain puzzling and unexplored phenomena in financial literature.

Perhaps the most comprehensive study of reverse splits was conducted by Zaremba et al. (2016). Their examinations provided both comprehensive and international evidence on the long-run performance following reverse splits. The authors used a sample of over 5000 reverse splits across 24 developed equity markets from three major global regions—North America, Europe, and Pacific—within the years 1990–2016. The study was largely out-of-sample, in both geographic and temporal terms. On the one hand, Zaremba et al. (2016) investigated markets where the performance following reverse splits had never been tested. On the other hand, their study started in the year when the seminal research of Desai and Jain (1997) ended.

The authors used an investor-friendly methodology, that is, the calendar-time portfolio approach. In essence, they formed portfolios of stocks with reverse splits and evaluated their performance using asset pricing models which allowed to gain a practical perspective of the investor on the phenomenon of reverse splits.

As a result, Zaremba et al. (2016) provided convincing evidence for the long-run performance following reverse splits. The negative abnormal returns continued for 18 months after the splits and remained significant in all the global regions: North America, Europe, and Pacific. In the broadest global sample, the four-factor model alpha amounted to almost −1% per month. Finally, any apparent positive abnormal returns appeared driven solely by the anomalous performance of very small companies, which are usually overrepresented among the firms consolidating their shares. Summing it up in one slogan, investors, stay away from the companies consolidating their shares![4]

Empirical Test of the Strategies Based on Raw Price

As we have pointed it out, the relation between the stock market price and future returns in the cross-section is to some extent controversial. Let us then empirically test whether these are low-price or high-price portfolios that overperform. To investigate it directly, we replicated a price-based security selection technique across the 24 countries in our sample. Specifically, each month we ranked the securities on their nominal price at the end of the previous month. Subsequently, we went long the quintile of stocks with the lowest price and short the securities with the highest price. The performance of the price-based strategies is reported in Table 7.1.

In general, our quick analysis supports the view that these are the low-priced stocks that overperform, rather than the high-priced stocks. In 12 out of 24 countries, the low-priced securities significantly outperformed the high-priced firms. The significant averages of returns (alphas) on the long-short portfolios spanned from 0.44% (0.55%) in the UK to as much as 2.45% (2.56%) in Hong Kong. Interestingly, the strategy did not work in the biggest equity markets in our sample, namely the USA and Japan, which may to some extent explain why some US-oriented studies showed such a poor performance. Importantly, in none of the investigated markets the high-priced companies delivered significantly higher returns than the low-priced companies.

[4] Further investigations of the role of reverse splits could also be found in Klein et al. (2006), Martell and Webb (2008), Maberly and Pierce (2011), Chung and Yang (2014), and Neuhauser and Thompson (2014, 2016).

Table 7.1 The performance of international portfolios from sorts on price

Country	*Top portfolio mean return*	*Bottom portfolio mean return*	*Average number of firms*	*T-B portfolio*		*Standard deviation*	*Sharpe ratio*	*Beta*	*Alpha*	
				Mean return	*t-stat*				*Value*	*t-stat*
Australia	1.16	0.23	47	0.93***	*(4.21)*	3.65	0.89	−0.15	1.05***	*(4.84)*
Austria	0.97	0.57	7	0.40	*(1.08)*	6.07	0.23	−0.11	0.46	*(1.24)*
Belgium	1.21	0.46	11	0.74*	*(1.95)*	6.25	0.41	−0.23	0.90**	*(2.40)*
Canada	1.14	0.40	95	0.74**	*(2.00)*	6.06	0.42	−0.09	0.81**	*(2.17)*
Denmark	1.28	0.62	12	0.66**	*(2.27)*	4.79	0.48	−0.12	0.77***	*(2.62)*
Finland	1.41	0.82	11	0.59**	*(2.15)*	4.55	0.45	−0.03	0.63**	*(2.25)*
France	1.14	0.63	47	0.52	*(1.51)*	5.62	0.32	−0.14	0.61*	*(1.78)*
Germany	0.97	0.33	43	0.64*	*(1.91)*	5.53	0.40	−0.01	0.65*	*(1.92)*
Greece	1.21	−0.46	13	1.67**	*(2.25)*	12.18	0.47	−0.04	1.67**	*(2.26)*
Hong Kong	0.96	−1.49	23	2.45***	*(4.85)*	8.29	1.02	−0.15	2.56***	*(5.08)*
Ireland	1.47	1.14	4	0.33	*(0.39)*	14.26	0.08	−0.04	0.36	*(0.41)*
Israel	1.14	1.03	15	0.11	*(0.34)*	5.17	0.07	−0.05	0.12	*(0.38)*
Italy	0.71	0.46	28	0.24	*(0.90)*	4.46	0.19	−0.06	0.27	*(1.00)*
Japan	0.30	0.58	325	−0.27	*(−0.76)*	5.94	−0.16	0.10	−0.28	*(−0.78)*
The Netherlands	1.11	0.76	19	0.35	*(1.02)*	5.62	0.22	−0.16	0.45	*(1.31)*
New Zealand	1.31	0.77	5	0.53	*(1.49)*	5.91	0.31	−0.01	0.54	*(1.48)*
Norway	0.97	0.15	15	0.82**	*(2.05)*	6.56	0.43	−0.09	0.90**	*(2.23)*
Portugal	0.66	0.16	4	0.50	*(1.06)*	7.67	0.22	−0.14	0.55	*(1.18)*
Singapore	0.66	−0.73	12	1.39***	*(3.59)*	6.34	0.76	0.08	1.34***	*(3.47)*
Spain	1.08	0.57	18	0.51	*(1.51)*	5.56	0.32	−0.07	0.56*	*(1.66)*
Sweden	1.44	0.84	26	0.59*	*(1.85)*	5.27	0.39	−0.10	0.69**	*(2.13)*
Switzerland	1.24	0.85	29	0.40	*(1.57)*	4.13	0.33	−0.09	0.46*	*(1.80)*

(*continued*)

Table 7.1 (continued)

Country	*Top portfolio mean return*	*Bottom portfolio mean return*	*Average number of firms*	*T-B portfolio*		*Standard deviation*	*Sharpe ratio*	*Beta*	*Alpha*	
				Mean return	*t-stat*				*Value*	*t-stat*
UK	0.94	0.50	118	0.44**	*(2.03)*	3.59	0.43	−0.23	0.55***	*(2.62)*
USA	0.93	0.97	717	−0.04	*(−0.11)*	6.06	−0.02	−0.31	0.17	*(0.47)*
World (EW)	1.06	0.42	1646	0.64***	*(3.70)*	2.82	0.78	−0.13	0.70***	*(4.12)*
World (VW)	0.82	0.59	1646	0.23	*(0.92)*	4.05	0.19	−0.21	0.34	*(1.39)*

Note: The table reports the monthly returns on the portfolios from sorts on the stock market price at the end of the previous month. The calculations were made on the basis of monthly observations. ***Top portfolio*** and ***bottom portfolio*** are quintile portfolio including the stocks with the lowest and highest average monthly returns, respectively. ***T-B portfolio*** is the portfolio that goes long the ***top*** portfolio and short the ***bottom*** portfolio. The Sharpe ratio is expressed on an annualized basis. The alpha and beta are derived from the CAPM. Mean returns, standard deviations, and alphas are expressed in percentage. Asterisks *, **, and *** indicate values significantly different from zero at the 10%, 5%, and 1% levels, respectively

At the global level, only the equal-weighted long-short portfolio exhibited positive and significant alpha, which equaled 0.70%. The disappointing performance of the value-weighted global portfolio could be intuitively understood, given that in the largest equity markets—the USA or Japan—we observe no cross-sectional relation between prices and future returns.

Another drawback of the price-based strategy is its volatility. It can be also seen in the Figs. 7.1 and 7.2 reporting the long-run cumulative returns on the global portfolios from sorts on prices. The standard deviation of monthly returns was 2.82% and 4.05% for the equal-weighted and value-weighted returns, respectively. In consequence, the Sharpe ratios are not very high amount to 0.78 and 0.19, when calculated for the equal-weighted and value-weighted returns.

The strategy assuming forming portfolios on the basis of past price is not ideal. Although it seems to work in multiple markets, it turned out unprofitable in the largest of them. Furthermore, it is characterized by relatively high volatility, negatively impacting the Sharpe ratios.

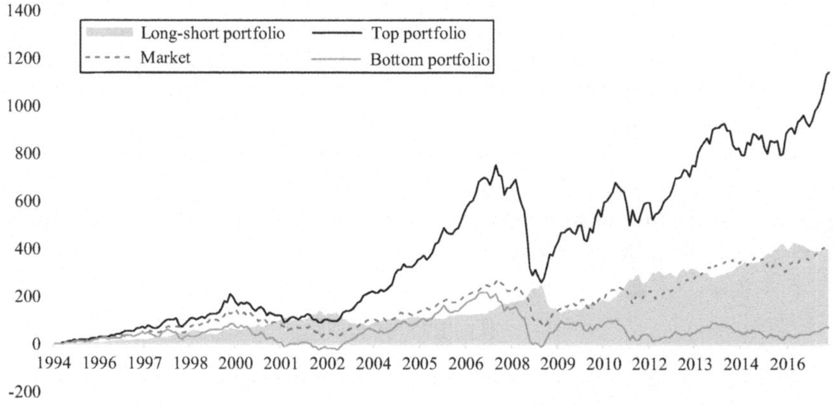

Fig. 7.1 Cumulative return on international equal-weighted portfolios from sorts on price. (Note: The figure displays the cumulative return on equal-weighted quantile the portfolios from sorts on the stock market price at the end of the previous month. The calculations were made on the basis of monthly observations. *Top portfolio* and *bottom portfolio* are quintile portfolio including the stocks with the highest and lowest prices, respectively. *T-B portfolio* is the portfolio that goes long the *top* portfolio and short the *bottom* portfolio. Market is the value-weighted portfolio of all of the country equity markets considered. All the returns are expressed in percentage)

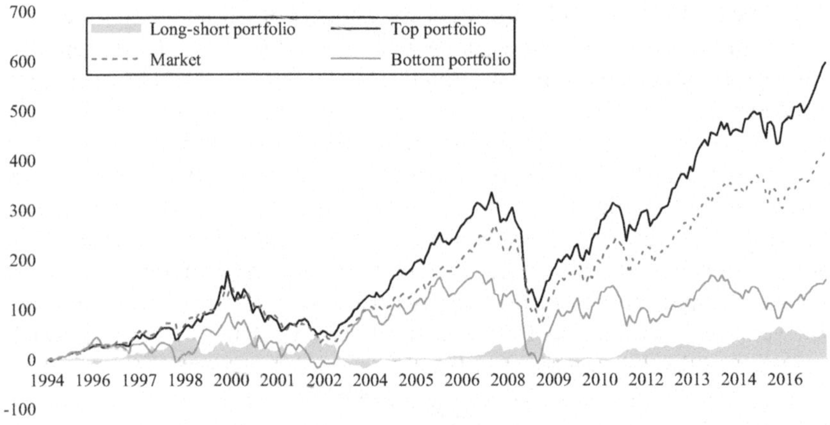

Fig. 7.2 Cumulative return on international value-weighted portfolios from sorts on price. (Note: The figure displays the cumulative return on value-weighted quantile the portfolios from sorts on the stock market price at the end of the previous month. The calculations were made on the basis of monthly observations. *Top portfolio* and *bottom portfolio* are quintile portfolio including the stocks with the lowest and the highest prices, respectively. *T-B portfolio* is the portfolio that goes long the *top* portfolio and short the *bottom* portfolio. Market is the value-weighted portfolio of all of the country equity markets considered. All the returns are expressed in percentage)

Nevertheless, the price-based technique globally still produces nice payoffs and, hence, maybe it could be a good component of a multi-strategy portfolio including more than one quantitative technique. We will research this question explicitly in the next chapter.

References

Alison, S. L., & Heins, A. J. (1966). Some factors affecting stock price variability. *Journal of Business, 39*(1), 19–23.

Bachrach, B., & Galai, D. (1979). The risk-return relationship and stock prices. *Journal of Financial and Quantitative Analysis, 14*(2), 421–441.

Baker, H. K., & Gallagher, P. L. (1980). Management's view of stock splits. *Financial Management, 9*, 73–77.

Baker, M., Greenwood, R., & Wurgler, J. (2009). Catering through nominal share prices. *Journal of Finance, 64*(6), 2559–2590.

Bar-Yosef, S., & Brown, L. D. (1979). Share price levels and beta. *Financial Management, 8*(1), 60–63.

Benartzi, S., Michaely, R., Thaler, R. H., & Weld, W. C. (2006). *The nominal price puzzle*. AFA 2007 conference paper. Available at: http://www.econ.yale.edu/~shiller/behfin/2007_03/michaely.pdf

Blume, M. E., & Husic, F. (1973). Price, beta and exchange listing. *Journal of Finance, 28*(2), 283–299.

Branch, B., & Chang, K. (1990). Low price stocks and the January effect. *Quarterly Journal of Business and Economics, 29*(3), 90–118.

Brennan, M., & Copeland, T. E. (1988). Stock splits, stock prices, and transaction costs. *Journal of Financial Economics, 22*, 83–101.

Christie, A. A. (1982). The stochastic behaviour of common stock variances – Value, leverage and interest rate effects. *Journal of Financial Economics, 10*(4), 407–432.

Chung, K. H., & Yang, S. (2014). Reverse stock splits, institutional holdings, and share value. *Financial Management, 44*, 177–216. https://doi.org/10.1111/fima.12077.

Clenderin, J. C. (1951). Quality versus price as factors influencing common stock price fluctuations. *Journal of Finance, 6*(4), 398–405.

Desai, H., & Jain, C. P. (1997). Long-run common stock returns following stock splits and reverse splits. *Journal of Business, 70*(3), 409–433. http://www.jstor.org/stable/10.1086/209724

Dubofsky, D. A., & French, D. W. (1988). Share price level and risk: Implications for financial management. *Managerial Finance, 14*(1), 6–9.

Edminster, R. O., & Greene, J. B. (1980). Performance of super-low-price stocks. *Journal of Portfolio Analysis, 7*(1), 36–41.

Fama, E. F., Fisher, L., Jensen, M. C., & Roll, R. (1969). The adjustment of stock prices to new information. *International Economic Review, 10*(1), 1–21. https://doi.org/10.2307/2525569.

Fritzmeier, L. H. (1936). Relative price fluctuations of industrial stocks in different price groups. *Journal of Business, 9*(2), 133–154.

Goodman, D. A., & Peavy, J. W., III. (1986). The low price effect: Relationship with other stock market anomalies. *Review of Business and Economics Research, 22*(1), 18–37.

Han, K. C. (1995). The effects of reverse splits on the liquidity of the stock. *Journal of Financial and Quantitative Analysis, 30*(1), 159–169. https://doi.org/10.2307/2331258.

Hwang, S., & Lu, C. (2008). *Is share price relevant?* (Working paper). Available at SSRN: https://ssrn.com/abstract=1341790 or https://doi.org/10.2139/ssrn.1341790. Accessed 18 Oct 2017.

Hwang, J.-K., Dimkpah, Y., & Ogwu, A. I. (2012). Do reverse stock splits benefit long-term shareholders. *International Advances in Economic Research, 18*(4), 439–449. https://doi.org/10.1007/s11294-012-9370-3.

Ikenberry, D., Rankine, G., & Stice, E. (1996). What do stock split really signal? *Journal of Financial and Quantitative Analysis, 31*, 357–337.

Kim, S., Klein, A., & Rosenfeld, J. (2008). Return performance surrounding reverse stock splits: Can investors profit? *Financial Management, 37*(2), 173–192. https://doi.org/10.1111/j.1755-053x.2008.00009.x.

Klein, A., Rosenfeld, J., & Tucker, X. J. (2006). *Return performance surrounding reverse stock splits: Can investors profit?* http://www.efmaefm.org/0EFMAMEETINGS/EFMA%20ANNUAL%20MEETINGS/2006-Madrid/papers/568563_full.pdf

Koski, J. (2007). Does volatility decrease after reverse stock splits? *Journal of Financial Research, 30*(2), 217–235.

Lamoureux, C., & Poon, P. (1987). The market reaction to splits. *Journal of Finance, 62*, 1347–1370.

Maberly, E. D., & Pierce, R. M. (2011). *Reconciling theory with post-reverse split return patterns: Empirical findings based on recent events.* Available at SSRN: http://ssrn.com/abstract=1825505 or https://doi.org/10.2139/ssrn.1825505. Accessed 23 Oct 2017.

Martell, T. F., & Webb, G. P. (2008). The performance of stocks that are reverse splits. *Review of Quantitative Finance and Accounting, 30*(3), 253–279. https://doi.org/10.1007/s11156-007-0052-9.

Mukherji, S., Kim, Y., & Walker, M. (1997). The effect of stock splits on the ownership structure of firms. *Journal of Corporate Finance, 3*, 167–188.

Muscarella, C., & Vetsuypens, M. (1996). Stock splits: Signalling or liquidity? The case of ADR 'solo-splits'. *Journal of Financial Economics, 42*, 3–26.

Muthoni, H. L. (2014). *Testing the existence of low price effect on stock returns at the Nairobi Securities Exchange* (Master thesis). Available at http://chss.uonbi.ac.ke/sites/default/files/chss/Huku%20L,%20D63-63781-3013,%-20MSc%20Finance.pdf. Accessed 18 Oct 2017.

Neuhauser, K. L., & Thompson, T. H. (2014). An examination of the survivability of reverse stock splits. *International Journal of Managerial Finance, 10*(3), 293–311.

Neuhauser, K. L., & Thompson, T. H. (2016). Survivability following reverse stock splits: What determines the fate of non-surviving firms? *Journal of Economics and Business, 83*, 1–22. https://doi.org/10.1016/j.jeconbus.2015.11.003.

Pinches, G. E., & Simon, G. M. (1972). An analysis of portfolio accumulation strategies employing low-priced common stock. *Journal of Financial and Quantitative Analysis, 7*(3), 1773–1796.

Schultz, P. (2000). Stock splits, tick size and sponsorship. *Journal of Finance, 55*, 429–450.

Spudeck, R. E., & Moyer, C. R. (1985). Reverse splits and shareholder wealth: The impact of commissions. *Financial Management, 14*, 52–56.

Strong, R. A. (1983). Do share price and stock splits matter? *Journal of Portfolio Management, 10*(1), 58–64.

Waelkens, K., & Ward, M. (2015). The low price effect on the Johannesburg Stock Exchange. *Investment Analysts Journal, 26*(45), 35.

Weld, W. C., Michaely, R., Thaler, R. H., & Benartzi, S. (2009). The nominal share price puzzle. *Journal of Economic Perspectives, 23*(2), 121–142.

Zaremba, A., & Żmudziński, R. (2014). The low price effect on the Polish market. *e-Finanse, 10*(1), 69–85. Available at http://yadda.icm.edu.pl/yadda/element/bwmeta1.element.ekon-element-000171278151

Zaremba, A., Konieczka, P., Okoń, S., & Nowak, A. (2016). The low price anomaly and the intriguing case of the Polish stock market. Inzinerine Ekonomika-Engineering Economics, 27(2), 163–174. https://doi.org/10.5755/j01.ee.27.2.13490.

CHAPTER 8

To Time or Not to Time? Tactical Allocation Across Strategies

The previous chapters offered a lot of different price-based strategies. Their foundations were based on various underlying concepts and economic intuitions, exhibited different risk-return profiles, and performed differently at various times. Existing finance literature proposes a lot of technical trading strategies. Essentially, they could be used as building blocks to form efficient portfolios. Thus, the critical question for every investor is how to select the right strategies and blend them together within a portfolio.

There are two essential ways an investor can improve the risk-return profile of the portfolio implementing the price-based strategies. First, the investor can diversify his portfolio across various strategies which, stemming from different philosophies, might also be more loosely correlated with each other. Thus, blending many strategies can decrease the risk within the entire portfolio. Second, the investor can dynamically change the allocation to various strategies. The aim, in this case, would be to capture the periods of strong performance and avoid the times of low returns on some anomalies. This, in turn, would still demand appropriate tools that could help forecast the future performance of particular anomalies.

These two—to some extent contradictive—approaches have their pros and cons. This chapter reviews and tests some basic ideas about how to mix a number of different strategies in order to improve the overall performance of a portfolio. We will begin by depicting the basic benefits of

A. Zaremba, J. "Koby" Shemer, *Price-Based Investment Strategies*,
https://doi.org/10.1007/978-3-319-91530-2_8

diversification and then continue with various more active approaches to factor allocation. And all of that, naturally, based only on prices and past returns.

Diversification Across Price-Based Strategies

Since Markowitz (1952) deployed his groundbreaking paper "Portfolio Selection", we have been aware that risk of the portfolio springs from two elementary sources. The first essential is the volatility of each portfolio component. Clearly, the more volatile the individual stocks are, the riskier the entire portfolio is. The second element is how the returns on individual portfolio components correlate with each other: where low correlation may evoke rapid risk reduction within the portfolio.

A very neat summary of the benefits of diversification across different strategies was provided by Ilmanen and Kizer in their paper titled "The Death of Diversification Has Been Greatly Exaggerated" published in 2012. In this research, the authors compared the effectiveness of dynamic factor diversification relative to diversification across asset classes. They provided convincing proofs that diversifying across multiple strategies is much more effective than diversifying across asset classes alone.

Ilmanen and Kizer formed two alternative portfolios: an asset-class-diversified portfolio and a factor-diversified portfolio. The first of these portfolios assumed an equal-weighted allocation to various traditional asset classes, including US stocks, non-US developed market equities, global government bonds, global non-government bonds, and emerging market stocks, small-cap stocks, commodities futures, and property. On the other hand, the factor-based portfolio comprised of a few factor strategies implemented via long-short approach. These were five equal-weighted elements, beginning with four style premia components: momentum stock style, global value stock style, global carry style, and trend style. The final two styles are representative of liquid macro-asset trading using forwards and futures for equity, fixed income, currencies, and commodities. Eventually, the fifth and final component of the factor portfolio is US large-cap equity, which was employed as a proxy for the equity premium factor (Sule 2012).

Having formed the portfolios, the authors evaluated them with standard measures, like Sharpe ratios. Ilmanen and Kizer showed the performance and risk statistics for popular US asset classes (US equity, Treasury bonds, and corporate bonds) and factor premiums (size, value, and momentum) for the period of 1927–2010. The results confirmed that the cross-factor diversification is much more efficient than cross-asset diversification. This is particularly thanks to low or even negative correlation between various strategies. In consequence, the volatility of the asset-only diversification amounted to 9.14% per month, while for the style-based portfolios only 4.36%. The differences in Sharpe ratios were also tremendous, equaling 0.48 and 1.77, respectively. Truly, diversification across strategies works.

Importantly, one of the additional insights provided by Ilmanen and Kizer (2012) was that these benefits of diversification stem largely because of the negative correlation between the returns on value and momentum strategies. Interestingly, this issue was later pursued also by Asness et al. (2013), who frequently proxied "value" with the long-run return. Thus, they proved that even in the universe of price-based strategies the risk-return profile could be greatly improved.

To sum up, the lesson that comes from these pieces of research is plain and simple. If you want to improve the performance of your portfolio, mix multiple strategies. Weight them even as simple as equally, but use many of them. The low correlation will give your portfolio a boost, improving the risk-return profile. And it could work for the price-based strategies as well!

Momentum Across Anomalies

Equal weights are straightforward. But could we use some slightly more sophisticated weights to further improve the performance? Let us take an example of momentum. Could the momentum effect be used to efficiently allocate funds across many strategies?

Oh yes, it could! As we have already documented in one of the chapters, the momentum effect is one of the most robust and pervasive stock market anomalies ever discovered. It has been documented across many stock markets (Chui et al. 2010) and asset classes (Asness et al. 2013). It is a strategy that has worked well for over two centuries. While Chabot et al. (2008) proved that momentum was profitable even in the Victorian age, Geczy and Samonov (2016) have made a tremendous research effort to demonstrate that momentum has been present in the US equity market since 1800.

Interestingly, multiple studies have also demonstrated that the momentum phenomenon is present at the meta-level, that is, in the returns on investment strategies. In other words, the momentum effect could be utilized to select the best performing strategies for the future: their historical returns are indicative of future payoffs. A number of recent research papers argue that it is possible to apply momentum strategies to successfully rotate among investment styles (Chen and De Bondt 2004; Teo and Woo 2004; Tibbs et al. 2008; Clare et al. 2010; Chen et al. 2012). Kim (2012) and Chao et al. (2012) have also proved that this is not only an equity market phenomenon, but that style momentum is present across many asset classes. Avramov et al. (2017) were the first to apply the concept of momentum to stock market anomalies. Zaremba and Szyszka (2016) and Zaremba (2017a) provided an out-of-sample confirmation of this effect in the Polish emerging market and in frontier equity markets, respectively. Finally, Zaremba (2015) delivered evidence that the momentum phenomenon drives the returns on cross-sectional strategies at the country level as well as at the stock level.

Despite this research, there is no single, broadly accepted explanation for the momentum found across investment strategies. Barberis and Shleifer (2003) have suggested that some investors categorize risky assets into different styles and allocate funds based on relative past performance. Thus, the investors move into styles that have provided good returns in the past and finance this shift by withdrawing funds from styles that have underperformed. Barberis and Shleifer (2003) have also assumed that these fund flows affect prices and imply an autocorrelation in style returns. Peng and Xiong (2006) have argued that due to limited attention, investors tend to focus more on market-level and sector-level information than on firm-specific information, while Teo and Woo (2004) have attributed style momentum to performance chasing. On the other hand, Kim (2012) has interpreted the style momentum as consistent with underreaction models. Avramov et al. (2017) have indicated that due to investors' learning as well as improvement in liquidity, the profitability of investment strategies may decline over time. Thus, the momentum strategy might be used as a tool to select the most robust cross-sectional patterns. Eventually, Zaremba and Shemer (2017) have shown that it might be at least partly driven by the stock-level momentum.

Summing up, there is a reasonable amount of evidence that the momentum could form an efficient basis for cross-factor allocation. It appears that overweighting the strategies with good past performance and underweighting these with poor results could further improve the efficiency. We will test this idea directly in this chapter.

The Role of Long-Term Returns

Momentum—also across the anomalies—usually concentrates on a short-run or long-run autocorrelation. For instance, Avramov et al. (2017) examined persistence based on 1-month returns, and Zaremba and Szyszka (2016) considered 12-month trailing returns. What about the longer term? In this case, the results are a bit mixed. Arnott et al. (2016) argue that the quantitative strategies also display a long-run reversal in returns. They indicate that long-run elevated returns may lead to an overvaluation of certain strategies. This idea corresponds with the concept of value spread, implying the difference in valuation ratios of various sides of the long-short anomaly portfolio helps to predict future returns.[1]

On the other hand, there are a handful of papers that suggest that the long-run performance could also reveal positive correlation with future returns. The basic idea behind this concept is that by measuring the long-run returns one might capture the cross-sectional variation in long-run return. In other words, you may see what is the long-run average return on the anomaly and thus allocate money to the best strategies. This idea was tested by Zaremba (2017a) in frontier markets, who also showed that the short-run momentum and long-run persistence are two separate drivers of returns, which could be combined to further improve the risk-return profile. The positive long-run correlation in returns was also identified in government bond markets (Zaremba 2017a).

To sum up, the predictive power of the long-run anomaly returns is a complicated issue. In this book, we will test to what extent it could be used.

Cross-Sectional Seasonality

One of the earlier chapters described a strategy called "seasonality momentum" or cross-sectional seasonality (Keloharju et al. 2016). It assumed sorting stocks based on their past returns in the same calendar month in the past: securities with the high (low) average return in the same calendar month tended to overperform (underperform) in the future. Interestingly, the authors showed that this strategy works also within the universe of popular equity anomalies. In other words, you can pick up the strategies

[1] For examinations of the value spread, see Asness et al. (2000), Cohen et al. (2003), Liu and Zhang (2008a, b), Michou (2009), Ilmanen et al. (2015), and Zaremba and Umutlu (2018).

on the bases of their past performance in the same calendar month in the past. Could this approach be used to rotate among the price-based strategies? We will check it.[2]

Empirical Test of Timing the Strategies

Let us now see how we can efficiently combine the portfolios of price-based strategies. We will start this review with the simplest possible approach: to equally weight all of the strategies in all portfolios. To conduct this exercise, we consider the ten strategies that we have already replicated in the earlier chapters of this book, assuming sorting on ten different price-derived variables: relative momentum, moving average, time-series momentum, long-run reversal, idiosyncratic risk, VaR, skewness, maximum daily return, cross-sectional seasonality, and stock market price. In each of the countries we consider we equally weight all of the strategies, rebalancing them monthly. We do this experiment for both long sides and short sides of the strategies, in other words with the stocks with the highest and the lowest expected returns, respectively. Eventually, we compute also the long-short portfolio, going long the equally weighted portfolio of all the long sides of the strategies and short all of the short sides of the strategies. The results of this analysis are reported in Table 8.1.

Table 8.1 presents the power of diversification across different strategies. The performance of the blended strategies was clearly more stable than of the individual strategies. For example, when we take a look at the long-short portfolios, it turns out that the average standard deviation of the returns is really low. The volatility of the equally weighted global portfolio amounts to only 2.13. In consequence, the as many as 20 of the portfolios are significantly profitable. Moreover, the Sharpe ratios rise remarkably, and in the case of the long-short global portfolio, it amounts to as much as 1.05.

The simple equal weighting of the strategy portfolios is a powerful tool. Indeed, it blends as much as 240 largely uncorrelated portfolios, so the benefits must be considerable. However, can we improve it somehow further? Oh, yes, we can. Below, we will try three different strategies based on momentum concept. We will examine whether we can use the historical returns to further improve the performance of portfolios of strategies.

[2] The effect was also tested and confirmed in factor portfolios by Zaremba (2017b).

Table 8.1 Performance of equal-weighted portfolios of strategies

	Long portfolios				*Short portfolios*				*Long-short portfolios*			
	Average	*t-stat*	*Volatility*	*Sharpe ratio*	*Average*	*t-stat*	*Volatility*	*Sharpe ratio*	*Average*	*t-stat*	*Volatility*	*Sharpe ratio*
Australia	1.14***	*(2.66)*	6.38	0.62	0.20	*(0.27)*	8.15	0.08	0.94***	*(6.82)*	2.67	1.22
Austria	0.90**	*(2.26)*	5.73	0.54	0.65	*(1.32)*	7.18	0.31	0.25	*(1.47)*	3.14	0.27
Belgium	1.20***	*(3.77)*	4.68	0.89	0.66	*(1.42)*	6.81	0.34	0.54**	*(2.57)*	3.25	0.58
Canada	1.22***	*(3.34)*	5.84	0.72	0.25	*(0.37)*	8.57	0.10	0.97***	*(5.17)*	3.68	0.91
Denmark	1.41***	*(4.01)*	5.27	0.93	0.78*	*(1.73)*	6.72	0.40	0.63***	*(4.17)*	2.74	0.80
Finland	1.44***	*(3.73)*	5.99	0.83	0.96**	*(2.04)*	7.05	0.47	0.47***	*(2.97)*	2.87	0.57
France	1.26***	*(3.66)*	5.34	0.81	0.65	*(1.24)*	7.70	0.29	0.60***	*(3.05)*	3.43	0.61
Germany	1.09***	*(3.09)*	5.32	0.71	0.32	*(0.45)*	7.90	0.14	0.77***	*(3.50)*	3.77	0.71
Greece	1.09**	*(2.04)*	10.24	0.37	−0.28	*(−0.29)*	13.86	−0.07	1.38***	*(3.64)*	6.19	0.77
Hong Kong	0.46	*(0.97)*	6.86	0.23	−0.72	*(−1.29)*	9.56	−0.26	1.18***	*(5.28)*	4.03	1.01
Ireland	1.06***	*(2.65)*	6.22	0.59	0.98	*(1.47)*	11.04	0.31	0.08	*(0.10)*	6.99	0.04
Israel	1.15***	*(2.95)*	6.93	0.57	0.80*	*(1.66)*	8.24	0.34	0.34**	*(2.06)*	3.12	0.38
Italy	0.91**	*(2.21)*	6.16	0.51	0.34	*(0.61)*	7.77	0.15	0.57***	*(3.90)*	2.35	0.84
Japan	0.55	*(1.57)*	5.31	0.36	0.11	*(0.02)*	6.86	0.05	0.44***	*(3.27)*	2.36	0.65
Netherlands	1.18***	*(3.35)*	5.38	0.76	0.68	*(1.31)*	7.40	0.32	0.51***	*(2.95)*	3.19	0.55
New Zealand	1.05***	*(2.64)*	5.66	0.64	0.70	*(1.44)*	6.89	0.35	0.35**	*(2.13)*	2.69	0.45
Norway	1.08***	*(2.62)*	6.66	0.56	0.25	*(0.35)*	8.94	0.10	0.83***	*(3.66)*	3.75	0.76
Portugal	0.72**	*(2.02)*	6.29	0.40	−0.01	*(−0.03)*	7.42	0.00	0.73***	*(3.45)*	3.15	0.81
Singapore	0.51	*(1.09)*	6.50	0.27	−0.31	*(−0.79)*	8.37	−0.13	0.82***	*(5.20)*	2.93	0.97
Spain	1.06***	*(2.61)*	5.60	0.66	0.36	*(0.63)*	7.40	0.17	0.70***	*(3.84)*	2.87	0.84
Sweden	1.62***	*(3.98)*	6.27	0.90	0.79	*(1.38)*	8.32	0.33	0.84***	*(4.16)*	3.38	0.86
Switzerland	1.29***	*(4.51)*	4.55	0.98	0.81**	*(2.08)*	6.29	0.44	0.48***	*(3.07)*	2.73	0.61

(*continued*)

Table 8.1 (continued)

	Long portfolios				*Short portfolios*				*Long-short portfolios*			
	Average	*t-stat*	*Volatility*	*Sharpe ratio*	*Average*	*t-stat*	*Volatility*	*Sharpe ratio*	*Average*	*t-stat*	*Volatility*	*Sharpe ratio*
UK	1.00***	*(3.34)*	4.93	0.70	0.40	*(0.96)*	6.50	0.21	0.60***	*(4.68)*	2.29	0.91
USA	1.26***	*(4.01)*	4.66	0.93	0.79	*(1.48)*	7.67	0.36	0.46**	*(2.36)*	3.77	0.42
World (EW)	1.07***	*(3.37)*	4.83	0.77	0.42	*(0.93)*	6.38	0.23	0.65***	*(5.06)*	2.13	1.05

Note: The table presents the performance characteristics of the equally weighted portfolios of ten different price-based strategies examined in this book: relative momentum, moving average, time-series momentum, long-run reversal, idiosyncratic risk, VaR, skewness, maximum daily return, cross-sectional seasonality, and stock market price. The world portfolio equally weights all of the strategies in 24 different countries (240 portfolios in total). All the computations are based on monthly returns. We calculate the averages separately for long and short sides of the strategies. The long-short portfolio is a differential portfolio going long (short) the equally weighted long (short) sides of the strategies. Mean returns and standard deviations are expressed in percentage. The Sharpe ratio is expressed on annualized basis. Asterisks *, **, and *** indicate values significantly different from zero at the 10%, 5%, and 1% levels, respectively

To build our momentum-based portfolios of strategies, we first sort all of the considered strategies in all of the 10 countries (240 strategies) based on the historical performance. We use three different indicators of the historical performance: (1) the trailing 1-month return, (2) the trailing 12-month return with the most recent month skipped, and (3) the trailing 60-month return with the most recent 12 months skipped. In other words, we rank the strategies on the average returns in the months (1) $t-1$, (2) $t-12$ to $t-2$, and (3) $t-60$ to $t-13$. We then measure short-term, medium-term, and long-term performance, respectively. Importantly, the measures were designed in the way so that they do not overlap each other.

When forming the portfolios, we broadly follow the approach of Avramov et al. (2017). We apply the three indicated sorts to the long and short sides of the strategies separately. Subsequently, we select the 20% portfolios (48) with the best performance and 20% portfolios with the worst performance, and equally weight them to obtain *winner* and *loser* portfolios. As we apply this exercise separately to the long and short sides of the price-based strategies, in consequence, we obtain four different portfolios: *Long winners* and *Long losers*—the best and the worst performers among the long portfolios—and *Short winners* and *Short losers*—the best and the worst performers among the short portfolios. Also, we form long-short portfolios which go long the best winners and shorts the worst losers. In other words, we assume a long position in the *Long winners* and a short position in the *Short losers.*

So how are the momentum-based strategy-picking approaches doing? Firstly, let us take a look at the portfolios of strategies formed on the short-term performance, depicted in Table 8.2.

We are focusing first on the long sides of the trade. The long portfolios with highest returns in the most recent month clearly outperformed the portfolios with the poorest returns. The mean monthly returns amounted to 1.59% and 0.54% for these two groups of strategies respectively, and the corresponding alphas equaled 1.48% and 0.44%. The outperformance was also visible in the Sharpe ratios, which amounted to 1.06 and 0.34 for the losers and winners, respectively.

Also, when we concentrate on the short sides of the strategies, the winners clearly fared better than losers. The alpha on the *Short winners* strategy equaled 0.43%, while on the *Short losers* only 0.15%.

Not surprising, the long-short portfolio, which capitalized on the superior performance of long winners and the disappointing returns on the

Table 8.2 Returns on portfolios of strategies from sorts on short-term performance

	Long side		*Short side*		*Long winners–short losers*	*Benchmark: all strategies equally weighted*
	Long winners	*Long losers*	*Short winners*	*Short losers*		
Mean	1.59***	0.54	0.57	0.29	1.30***	0.65***
	(4.70)	(1.48)	(1.31)	(0.64)	(5.55)	(5.06)
Volatility	5.17	5.59	6.40	6.75	3.78	2.13
Sharpe ratio	1.06	0.34	0.31	0.15	1.19	1.05
Worst month	−18.94	−29.81	−24.87	−32.99	−12.17	−9.29
Best month	17.69	14.63	18.50	26.43	14.31	7.66
Skewness	−0.42	−1.04	−0.44	−0.48	−0.10	−0.58
Kurtosis	1.41	3.82	1.38	3.32	2.02	3.63
Alpha	1.48***	0.44	0.43	0.15	1.32***	0.69***
	(4.27)	(1.16)	(0.98)	(0.34)	(4.94)	(4.43)
Beta	0.22**	0.20	0.28**	0.28*	−0.06	−0.09
	(2.48)	(1.61)	(2.57)	(1.92)	(−0.71)	(−2.65)

Note: The table presents the performance of portfolios of price-based strategies from sorts on the one-month performance. Each month, we sort 240 long and short portfolios (relative momentum, moving average, time-series momentum, long-run reversal, idiosyncratic risk, VaR, skewness, maximum daily return, cross-sectional seasonality, and stock market price in 24 countries) on their return in the most recent month. The *Long winners (Long losers)* are 20% of the long sides of the strategies with the best (worst) performance. The *Short winners (Short losers)* are 20% of the short sides of the strategies with the best (worst) performance. The portfolio "Long winners–short losers" is a long-short portfolio going long the *Long winners* and short the *Short losers*. We also report the performance of a benchmark portfolio equally weighting all the ten considered strategies in 24 countries. All the computations are based on monthly returns. Alpha and beta come from the CAPM. Mean returns, standard deviations, best and worst months, and alphas are expressed in percentage. The Sharpe ratio is expressed on annualized basis. Asterisks *, **, and *** indicate values significantly different from zero at the 10%, 5%, and 1% levels, respectively

short losers, delivered extraordinary profits. The mean return amounted to 1.30% per month, and the corresponding alpha 1.32%. These values nearly double the analogous measures for the benchmark equally weighting all of the strategies. Conclusion? Yes, we are able to select strategies more efficiently than simple weighting them equally. And the sorting on the last-month performance is a great example.

Tables 8.3 and 8.4 report analogous strategies but from the sorts on different periods. Importantly, our method is very robust. No matter on what historical period we sort the portfolios, the winners remain winners

Table 8.3 Returns on portfolios of strategies from sorts on medium-term performance

	Long side		*Short side*		*Long winners–short losers*	*Benchmark: all strategies equally weighted*
	Long winners	*Long losers*	*Short winners*	*Short losers*		
Mean	1.32***	0.57	0.51	0.23	1.36***	0.65***
	(3.80)	(1.45)	(1.04)	(0.42)	(5.76)	(5.06)
Volatility	5.29	5.76	6.68	7.39	3.99	2.13
Sharpe ratio	0.86	0.34	0.26	0.11	1.18	1.05
Worst month	−21.50	−27.94	−29.79	−31.72	−17.43	−9.29
Best month	13.77	19.35	22.06	25.96	15.40	7.66
Skewness	−0.86	−0.67	−0.63	−0.19	−0.48	−0.58
Kurtosis	1.63	2.90	1.91	2.48	3.35	3.63
Alpha	1.20***	0.46	0.35	0.08	1.40***	0.69***
	(3.45)	(1.17)	(0.79)	(0.16)	(4.54)	(4.43)
Beta	0.23**	0.22*	0.31**	0.30**	−0.07	−0.09
	(2.46)	(1.77)	(2.38)	(2.16)	(−0.98)	(−2.65)

Note: The table presents the performance of portfolios of price-based strategies from sorts on the 12-month performance with the most recent month skipped (t–12 to t–2). Each month we sort 240 long and short portfolios (relative momentum, moving average, time-series momentum, long-run reversal, idiosyncratic risk, VaR, skewness, maximum daily return, cross-sectional seasonality, and stock market price in 24 countries) on their average return in months t–12 to t–2. The ***Long winners (Long losers)*** are 20% of the long sides of the strategies with the best (worst) performance. The ***Short winners (Short losers)*** are 20% of the short sides of the strategies with the best (worst) performance. The portfolio "Long winners–short losers" is a long-short portfolio going long the ***Long winners*** and short the ***Short losers.*** We also report the performance of a benchmark portfolio equally weighting all the ten considered strategies in 24 countries. All the computations are based on monthly returns. Alpha and beta come from the CAPM. Mean returns, standard deviations, best and worst months, and alphas are expressed in percentage. The Sharpe ratio is expressed on annualized basis. Asterisks *, **, and *** indicate values significantly different from zero at the 10%, 5%, and 1% levels, respectively

and the losers continue to lag. Focusing on the portfolios from sorts on medium-term performance, the long-short portfolio yielded a mean monthly return of 1.09% and the alpha of 1.12%. Again, these values were much higher than for the benchmark.

Analogously, even when we sorted the portfolios on the long-run performance, the winners always outperformed the losers. As the results in Table 8.4 indicate, the alpha on the long-short portfolio equaled to 1.15%, while on the benchmark only 0.69% per month. The outperformance is clear.

Table 8.4 Returns on portfolios of strategies from sorts on long-term performance

	Long side		*Short side*		*Long winners–short losers*	*Benchmark: all strategies equally weighted*
	Long winners	*Long losers*	*Short winners*	*Short losers*		
Mean	0.91**	0.78*	0.18	0.11	1.12***	0.65***
	(2.19)	(1.86)	(0.30)	(0.16)	(4.64)	(5.06)
Volatility	5.65	5.44	7.26	7.19	3.48	2.13
Sharpe ratio	0.56	0.50	0.08	0.06	1.11	1.05
Worst month	−27.31	−20.73	−32.50	−26.25	−21.17	−9.29
Best month	15.89	13.08	28.90	26.19	10.54	7.66
Skewness	−1.03	−0.48	−0.47	−0.15	−1.27	−0.58
Kurtosis	3.44	0.74	3.20	1.18	7.59	3.63
Alpha	0.81*	0.70*	0.04	0.01	1.15***	0.69***
	(1.93)	(1.70)	(0.08)	(0.01)	(4.73)	(4.43)
Beta	0.25*	0.20**	0.34**	0.28**	−0.08	−0.09
	(1.89)	(2.11)	(2.12)	(2.10)	(−1.40)	(−2.65)

Note: The table presents the performance of portfolios of price-based strategies from sorts on the 60-month performance with the 12 most recent months skipped (t–60 to t–13). Each month we sort 240 long and short portfolios (relative momentum, moving average, time-series momentum, long-run reversal, idiosyncratic risk, VaR, skewness, maximum daily return, cross-sectional seasonality, and stock market price in 24 countries) on their average return in months t–60 to t–13. The ***Long winners (Long losers)*** are 20% of the long sides of the strategies with the best (worst) performance. The ***Short winners (Short losers)*** are 20% of the short sides of the strategies with the best (worst) performance. The portfolio "Long winners–short losers" is a long-short portfolio going long the ***Long winners*** and short the ***Short losers***. We also report the performance of a benchmark portfolio equally weighting all the ten considered strategies in 24 countries. All the computations are based on monthly returns. Alpha and beta come from the CAPM. Mean returns, standard deviations, best and worst months, and alphas are expressed in percentage. The Sharpe ratio is expressed on annualized basis. Asterisks *, **, and *** indicate values significantly different from zero at the 10%, 5%, and 1% levels, respectively

Let us wrap up our considerations in this chapter. The recent academic literature offers a number of different price-based strategies. Importantly, thanks to limited correlation of their returns, these techniques could be efficiently combined into portfolios. Even as simple techniques as equally weighting all of the strategies yield impressive risk-adjusted payoffs. However, some techniques as simple as sorting on historical returns could improve this profile even further. Simple long-short portfolios formed on the basis of the last-month returns produce an alpha that nearly doubles the equally weighted benchmark of all of the strategies across all of the countries that we consider.

References

Arnott, R., Beck, N., & Kalesnik, V. (2016). *Timing "smart beta" strategies? Of course! Buy low, sell high!* Research Affiliates. Available at https://www.researchaffiliates.com/en_us/publications/articles/541_timing_smart_beta_strategies_of_course_buy_low_sell_high.html. Accessed 31 Oct 2017.

Asness, C. S., Friedman, J. A., Krail, R. J., & Liew, J. M. (2000). Style timing: Value versus growth. *Journal of Portfolio Management, 26*(3), 50–60. https://doi.org/10.3905/jpm.2000.319724.

Asness, C. S., Moskowitz, T. J., & Pedersen, L. H. (2013). Value and momentum everywhere. *Journal of Finance, 68*(3), 929–985.

Avramov, D., Kaplanski, G., & Levy, H. (2017). *Talking numbers: Technical versus fundamental investment recommendations.* Available at SSRN: https://ssrn.com/abstract=2648292 or https://doi.org/10.2139/ssrn.2648292. Accessed 21 Oct 2017.

Barberis, N., & Shliefer, A. (2003). Style investing. *Journal of Financial Economics, 68*, 161–199.

Chabot, B., Ghysels, E., & Jagannathan, R. (2008). *Price momentum in stocks: Insights from Victorian age* (NBER working paper No. 14500). Available at: http://www.nber.org/papers/w14500. Accessed 20 Oct 2015.

Chao, H.-Y., Collver, C., & Limthanakom, N. (2012). Global style momentum. *Journal of Empirical Finance, 19*(3), 319–333. Available at https://doi.org/10.1016/j.jempfin.2012.02.001

Chen, H. S., & De Bondt, W. (2004). Style momentum within the S&P-500 index. *Journal of Empirical Finance, 11*, 483–507.

Chen, L. H., Jiang, G. J., & Zhu, X. (2012). Do style and sector indexes carry momentum? *Journal of Investment Strategies, 1*(3), 67–89.

Chui, A. C. W., Titman, S., & Wei, J. K. C. (2010). Individualism and momentum around the world. *Journal of Finance, 65*(1), 361–392.

Clare, A., Sapuric, S., & Todorovic, N. (2010). Quantitative or momentum-based multi-style rotation? UK experience. *Journal of Asset Management, 10*, 370–381.

Cohen, R. B., Polk, C., & Vuolteenaho, T. (2003). The value spread. *Journal of Finance, 58*(2), 609–641. https://doi.org/10.1111/1540-6261.00539.

Geczy, C., & Samonov, M. (2016). Two centuries of price-return momentum. *Financial Analysts Journal, 72*(5), 32–56. https://doi.org/10.2469/faj.v72.n5.1.

Ilmanen, A., & Kizer, J. (2012). The death of diversification has been greatly exaggerated. *Journal of Portfolio Management, 38*(3), 15–27. https://doi.org/10.2469/dig.v42.n4.3.

Ilmanen, A., Nielsen, L. N., & Chandra, S. (2015). *Are defensive stocks expensive? A closer look at value spreads* (AQR white paper). Available at https://www.aqr.com/library/aqr-publications/are-defensive-stocks-expensive-a-closer-look-at-value-spreads. Accessed 31 Oct 2017.

Keloharju, M., Linnainmaa, J. T., & Nyberg, P. (2016). Return seasonalities. *Journal of Finance, 71*(4), 1557–1590.

Kim, D. (2012). Cross-asset style momentum. *Asia-Pacific Journal of Financial Studies, 41*(5), 610–636. https://doi.org/10.1111/j.2041-6156.2012.01084.x.

Liu, L. X., & Zhang, L. (2008a). Momentum profits, factor pricing, and macroeconomic risk. *Review of Financial Studies, 21*(6), 2417–2448.

Liu, N., & Zhang, L. (2008b). Is the value spread a useful predictor of returns? *Journal of Financial Markets, 11*(3), 199–227. https://doi.org/10.1016/j.finmar.2008.01.003.

Markowitz, H. (1952). Portfolio selection. *Journal of Finance, 7*(1), 77–91. https://doi.org/10.1111/j.1540-6261.1952.tb01525.x.

Michou, M. (2009). Is the value spread a good predictor of stock returns? UK evidence. *Journal of Business, Finance, & Accounting, 36*(7–8), 925–950. https://doi.org/10.1111/j.1468-5957.2009.02148.x.

Peng, L., & Xiong, W. (2006). Investor attention, overconfidence and category learning. *Journal of Financial Economics, 80*(3), 563–602.

Sule, A. (2012). The death of diversification has been greatly exaggerated (Digest summary). *CFA Digest, 42*(4). Available at http://www.cfapubs.org/doi/full/10.2469/dig.v42.n4.3

Teo, M., & Woo, S.-J. (2004). Style effects in the cross-section of stock returns. *Journal of Financial Economics, 74*(2), 367–398. Available at https://doi.org/10.1016/j.jfineco.2003.10.003

Tibbs, S. L., Eakins, S. G., & DeShurko, W. (2008). Using style momentum to generate alpha. *Journal of Technical Analysis, 65*, 50–56.

Zaremba, A. (2015). *The momentum effect in country-level stock market anomalies*. Available at SSRN: https://ssrn.com/abstract=2621236 or https://doi.org/10.2139/ssrn.2621236. Accessed 23 Oct 2017.

Zaremba, A. (2017a). *Performance persistence in anomaly returns: Evidence from frontier markets*. Available at SSRN: https://ssrn.com/abstract=3060876. Accessed 31 Oct 2017.

Zaremba, A. (2017b). Seasonality in the cross section of factor premia. *Investment Analysts Journal*, (3), 165–199. https://doi.org/10.1080/10293523.2017.1326219.

Zaremba, A., & Szyszka, A. (2016). Is there momentum in equity anomalies? Evidence from the Polish emerging market. *Research in International Business and Finance, 38*, 546–564. https://doi.org/10.1016/j.ribaf.2016.07.004.

Zaremba, A., & Shemer, K. (2017, in press). Is there momentum in factor premia? Evidence from international equity markets. *Research in International Business and Finance*. https://doi.org/10.1016/j.ribaf.2017.12.002
Zaremba, A., & Umutlu, M. (2018, in press). Strategies can be expensive too! The value spread and asset allocation in global equity markets. *Applied Economics*.

CHAPTER 9

Conclusions

Recent academic research has rekindled the interest in studying investment techniques based purely on prices. These modern approaches could be broadly described as a new perspective on technical analysis. They offer investors a number of quantitative tools helping to select the best performing securities. In this book we have collected, reviewed, and replicated investment strategies based on the simplest possible variable: price. All of them could be effectively employed across multiple equity markets.

The first category, the momentum approach, which is a multi-asset phenomenon, assumes past winners to outperform and past losers to deliver poor returns. Momentum strategies have successfully performed across numerous asset classes so can be widely applied using different approaches. Irrespective of the particular approach, we prove the trend-following tactic to remain a successful tool for equity selection.

While the momentum strategy assumes the continuation of the price movement, the reversal strategies rely on a contrary assumption: predicting the price trend to revert. How can both the phenomena coexist? The solution is the investment horizon. While the momentum effect arises in the mid-term, the reversal occurs either in the short term or in the long term. The long-run reversal, albeit an interesting technique, fails to work in every single market.

Also, we have researched the low-volatility anomaly—a counter-intuitive phenomenon—which implies low-volatility assets outperform assets of high volatility. Although it could be approached using various risk measures, for

A. Zaremba, J. "Koby" Shemer, *Price-Based Investment Strategies*,
https://doi.org/10.1007/978-3-319-91530-2_9

example, total volatility, idiosyncratic volatility and beta, and the anomaly works across numerous asset classes, including stocks or corporate bonds, the effect might be considered controversial, as different indicators imply different relation to risk. We have reviewed two such measures, idiosyncratic volatility and VaR, and examined their performance in international markets.

Some studies have shown that not only the dispersion of the returns but also the shape of return distributions can predict future returns. The right-skewed distributions, displaying a large chance of exceptionally high returns, tend to perform poorly in the end. The impact of skewness can be measured in many ways: from very sophisticated measures, like co-skewness or idiosyncratic skewness, to plain and simple ones, like maximum daily return over the previous month. We have tested two of these measures, showing most promise to be used as predictors of future performance.

We have also discussed the concept of cross-sectional seasonality. The search for calendar effects has intrigued equity analyst for ever. The phenomena like the January seasonality or "sell in May and go away" are patterns known to virtually any stock market investor. We have focused on the cross-sectional seasonality effect which aggregates many seasonal anomalies. Essentially, the cross-sectional seasonality is a tendency of stocks which in the same calendar month in the past performed well (poorly) on average to continue to outperform (underperform) in the following year. We have re-examined its performance and found it relatively reliable.

Eventually, we asked the question whether we can predict returns based on … raw prices? Does the nominal price forecast future performance? We have documented that simple sorting on the raw stock market price can also help to produce stable equity returns.

All these strategies might be further implemented in a single portfolio to enhance performance. Combining a few strategies in a single portfolio, even adopting as simple approach as equal weighting, leads to a substantial risk reduction. Importantly, one can additionally apply other tactical asset allocation tools to time these various strategies. In particular, as the price-based strategies display momentum behavior, the best performing strategies over the recent months tend to continue to outperform. Only this simple approach allows to reach higher alphas than with a diversified portfolio of various long-short strategies.

Our book offers lessons for portfolio managers, individual investors, and asset allocators with a national or global investment mandate. We have shown that very simple techniques based on historical price performance allow to design reliable and profitable strategies. We have documented a powerful information content regarding the stock market price. Both technical analysis and the art of investing based on price behavior, once regarded as a voodoo-science, are far from being antiquated. To the contrary, being more alive than ever and backed up by solid academic evidence, they can once again prove helpful for equity investors.

References

Abel, A. B. (1990). Asset prices under habit formation and catching up with the Joneses. *American Economic Review, 80*(2), 38–42.

Aboulamer, A., & Kryzanowski, L. (2016). Are idiosyncratic volatility and MAX priced in the Canadian market? *Journal of Empirical Finance, 37*, 20–36. https://doi.org/10.1016/j.jempfin.2016.02.005.

Abraham, A., & Ikenberry, D. L. (1994). The individual investor and the weekend effect. *Journal of Financial and Quantitative Analysis, 29*(2), 263–277.

Accominotti, O., & Chambers, D. (2014). *Out-of-sample evidence on the returns to currency trading*. Available at SSRN: https://ssrn.com/abstract=2293684 or https://doi.org/10.2139/ssrn.2293684. Accessed 21 Oct 2015.

Achour, D., Harvey, C., Hopkins, G., & Lang, C. (1998). Stock selection in emerging markets: Portfolio strategies in Malaysia, Mexico, and South Africa. *Emerging Markets Quarterly, 2*, 38–91.

Aczel, A. D. (2012). *Complete business statistics* (8th ed.). Morristown: Wohl Publishing.

Aggarwal, R., & Rivoli, P. (1989). Seasonal and day-of-the-week effects in four emerging stock markets. *Financial Review, 24*(4), 541–550.

Ahmad, Z., & Hussain, S. (2001). KLSE long run overreaction and the Chinese New Year effect. *Journal of Business, Finance, and Accounting, 28*(1–2), 63–112.

Ahn, D.-H., Conrad, J., & Dittmar, R. (2003). Risk adjustment and trading strategies. *Review of Financial Studies, 16*(2), 459–485.

Akermann, C. A., & Keller, W. E. (1977). Relative strength does persist! *Journal of Portfolio Management, 4*(1), 38–45.

A. Zaremba, J. "Koby" Shemer, *Price-Based Investment Strategies*,
https://doi.org/10.1007/978-3-319-91530-2

Alagidede, P. (2013). Month of the year and pre-holiday effects in African stock markets. *South African Journal of Economic and Management Sciences, 16*(1). Available at http://www.scielo.org.za/scielo.php?script=sci_arttext&pid=S2222-34362013000100006

Alatiyat, M. (2014). *Ramadan effect on UAE stock market – Banks sector*. Available at SSRN: https://ssrn.com/abstract=2449967 or https://doi.org/10.2139/ssrn.2449967. Accessed 24 Oct 2017.

Alemida, C., Ricca, B., & Tessari, C. (2016). Idiosyncratic moments and the cross-section of returns in Brazil. *Brazilian Review of Econometrics, 36*(2), 255–286. https://doi.org/10.12660/bre.v99n992016.18544.

Alexeev, V. V., & Tapon, F. (2012). *Equity portfolio diversification: How many stocks are enough? Evidence from five developed markets* (FIRN research paper). Available at SSRN: http://ssrn.com/abstract=2182295 or https://doi.org/10.2139/ssrn.2182295. Accessed 26 Oct 2015.

Ali, N., Nassair, A. M., Hassan, T., & Abidin, S. Z. (2011). Stock overreaction behaviour in Bursa Malaysia: Does the length of formation period matter? *British Journal of Economics Finance and Management Sciences, 2*(2), 42–56.

Ali, I., Akhter, W., & Ashraf, N. (2017). Impact of Muslim Holy Days on Asian stock markets: An empirical evidence. *Cogent Economics & Finance, 5*(1). https://doi.org/10.1080/23322039.2017.1311096.

Alison, S. L., & Heins, A. J. (1966). Some factors affecting stock price variability. *Journal of Business, 39*(1), 19–23.

Al-Khazali, O. (2014). Revisiting fast profit investor sentiment and stock returns during Ramadan. *International Review of Financial Analysis, 33*, 158–170. https://doi.org/10.1016/j.irfa.2014.02.003.

Alonso, A., & Rubio, G. (1990). Overreaction in the Spanish equity market. *Journal of Banking and Finance, 14*, 469–481.

Alpert, M., & Raiffa, H. (1982). A progress report on the training of probability assessors. In D. Kahneman, P. Slovic, & A. Tversky (Eds.), *Judgment under uncertainty: Heuristics and biases* (pp. 294–305). New York/Cambridge: Cambridge University Press.

Alumdhaf, F. (2012). The Islamic calendar effects: Evidence from twelve stock markets. *International Research Journal of Finance and Economics, 87*, 187–191.

Alwathainani, A. M. (2012). Consistent winners and losers. *International Review of Economics and Finance, 21*, 210–220.

Amaya, D., Christoffersen, P., Jacobs, K., & Vasquez, A. (2015). Does realized skewness predict the cross-section of equity returns? *Journal of Financial Economics, 118*(1), 135–167.

Amen, S. (2013). *Beta'em up: What is market beta in FX?* Available at SSRN: http://ssrn.com/abstract=2439854 or https://doi.org/10.2139/ssrn.2439854. Accessed 21 Oct 2015.

Amenc, N., & Le Sourd, V. (2003). *Portfolio theory and performance analysis*. Hoboken: John Wiley & Sons.

Amenc, N., Goltz, F., & Lodh, A. (2012). Choose your betas: Benchmarking alternative equity strategies. *Journal of Portfolio Management, 39*(1), 88–111.

Andersen, J. V., Gluzman, S., & Sornette, D. (2000). Fundamental framework for technical analysis. *European Physical Journal B, 14*, 579–601. http://xxx.lanl.gov/abs/cond-mat/9910047

Anderson, C. W., & Garcia-Feijoo, L. (2006). Empirical evidence on capital investment, growth options, and security returns. *Journal of Finance, 61*, 171–194.

Andersson, H. (2007). Are commodity prices mean reverting? *Applied Financial Economics, 17*(10), 769–783. https://doi.org/10.1080/09603100600749204.

Andrade, S. C. (2009). A model of asset pricing under country risk. *Journal of International Money and Finance, 28*(4), 671–695.

Andreu, L., Swinkels, L., & Tjong-A-Tjoe, L. (2013). Can exchange traded funds be used to exploit industry and country momentum? *Financial Markets and Portfolio Management, 27*(2), 127–148.

Andrikopoulos, P., Daynes, A., Latimer, D., & Pagas, P. (2006). The value premium and methodological biases: Evidence from the UK equity market. *Investment Management and Financial Innovation, 3*(1), 40–59.

Ang, A. (2014). *Asset management: A systematic approach to factor investing*. New York: Oxford University Press.

Ang, A., Chen, J., & Xing, Y. (2006a). Downside risk. *Review of Financial Studies, 19*, 1191–1239.

Ang, A., Chen, J., & Xing, Y. (2006b). The cross-section of volatility and expected returns. *Journal of Finance, 61*, 259–299.

Ang, A., Hodrick, R., Xing, Y., & Zhang, X. (2009). High idiosyncratic volatility and low returns: International and further U.S. evidence. *Journal of Financial Economics, 91*, 1–23.

Anghel, A., Dumitrescu, D., & Tudor, C. (2015). Modeling portfolio returns on Bucharest Stock exchange using the Fama-French multifactor model. *Romanian Journal of Economic Forecasting, 17*(1), 22–46.

Annaert, J., De Ceuster, M., & Verstegen, K. (2013). Are extreme returns priced in the stock market? European evidence. *Journal of Banking and Finance, 37*(9), 3401–3411. https://doi.org/10.1016/j.jbankfin.2013.05.015.

Antonacci, G. (2013). *Absolute momentum: A simple rule-based strategy and universal trend-following overlay* (Research paper). Available at SSRN: http://ssrn.com/abstract=2244633 or https://doi.org/10.2139/ssrn.2244633. Accessed 18 Oct 2015.

Antonacci, G. (2015). *Dual momentum investing: An innovative strategy for higher returns with lower risk*. New York: McGraw Hill Education.

Ardila, D., Forrò, Z., & Sornette, D. (2015). *The acceleration effect and gamma factor in asset pricing* (Swiss Finance Institute research paper No. 15-30). Available at SSRN: https://ssrn.com/abstract=2645882 or https://doi.org/10.2139/ssrn.2645882. Accessed 21 Oct 2017.

Arditti, F. D. (1967). Risk and the required return on equity. *Journal of Finance, 22*(1), 19–36.

Arditti, F. D. (1971). Another look at mutual fund performance. *Journal of Financial and Quantitative Analysis, 6*(3), 909–912.

Ariel, R. A. (1987). A monthly effect in stock returns. *Journal of Financial Economics, 18*, 161–174.

Ariel, R. A. (1990). High stock returns before holidays: Existence and evidence on possible causes. *Journal of Finance, 45*(5), 1611–1626.

Ariss, R. T., Rezwanian, R., & Mehdian, S. M. (2011). Calendar anomalies in the Gulf Cooperation Council stock markets. *Emerging Markets Review, 12*(3), 293–307. https://doi.org/10.1016/j.ememar.2011.04.002.

Arnott, R. D., Hsu, J., & Moore, P. (2005). Fundamental indexation. *Financial Analyst Journal, 61*(2), 83–99.

Arnott, R., Beck, N., & Kalesnik, V. (2016). *Timing "smart beta" strategies? Of course! Buy low, sell high!* Research Affiliates. Available at https://www.researchaffiliates.com/en_us/publications/articles/541_timing_smart_beta_strategies_of_course_buy_low_sell_high.html. Accessed 31 Oct 2017.

Arsad, Z., & Coutts, J. A. (1997). Security price anomalies in the London international stock exchange: A 60 year perspective. *Applied Financial Economics, 7*(5), 455–464.

Asness, C. (2012). Momentum in Japan: The exception that proves the rule. *Journal of Portfolio Management, 37*(4), 67–75. https://doi.org/10.2469/dig.v42.n1.21.

Asness, C. S., Liew, J. M., & Stevens, R. L. (1997). Parallels between the cross-sectional predictability of stock and country returns. *Journal of Portfolio Management, 6*, 79–86.

Asness, C. S., Friedman, J. A., Krail, R. J., & Liew, J. M. (2000). Style timing: Value versus growth. *Journal of Portfolio Management, 26*(3), 50–60. https://doi.org/10.3905/jpm.2000.319724.

Asness, C. S., Moskowitz, T. J., & Pedersen, L. H. (2013). Value and momentum everywhere. *Journal of Finance, 68*(3), 929–985.

Asness, C. S., Frazzini, A., & Pedersen, L. H. (2014). Low-risk investing without industry bets. *Financial Analyst Journal, 70*(4), 24–41.

Asness, C. S., Frazzini, A., & Pedersen, L. H. (2017). *Quality minus junk.* Available at SSRN: https://ssrn.com/abstract=2312432 or https://doi.org/10.2139/ssrn.2312432. Accessed 23 Oct 2017.

Avramov, D., & Chordia, T. (2006). Asset pricing models and financial market anomalies. *Review of Financial Studies, 19*(3), 1001–1040.

Avramov, D., Chordia, T., & Goyal, A. (2006a). Liquidity and autocorrelations in individual stock returns. *Journal of Finance, 61*, 2365–2394.

Avramov, D., Chordia, T., & Goyal, A. (2006b). The impact of trades on daily volatility. *Review of Financial Studies, 19*(4), 1241–1277.

Avramov, D., Chordia, T., Jostova, G., & Philipov, A. (2007). Momentum and credit rating. *Journal of Finance, 62*, 2503–2520.

Avramov, D., Chordia, T., Jostova, G., & Philipov, A. (2013). Anomalies and financial distress. *Journal of Financial Economics, 108*(1), 139–159.

Avramov, D., Cheng, S., & Hameed, A. (2016a). Time-varying liquidity and momentum profits. *Journal of Financial and Quantitative Analysis, 51*(6), 1897–1923. https://doi.org/10.1017/S0022109016000764.

Avramov, D., Cheng, S., Schreiber, A., & Shemer, K. (2016b, in press). Scaling up market anomalies. *Journal of Investing*. Available at SSRN: https://ssrn.com/abstract=2709178 or https://doi.org/10.2139/ssrn.2709178. Accessed 23 Oct 2017.

Avramov, D., Kaplanski, G., & Levy, H. (2017). *Talking numbers: Technical versus fundamental investment recommendations*. Available at SSRN: https://ssrn.com/abstract=2648292 or https://doi.org/10.2139/ssrn.2648292. Accessed 21 Oct 2017.

Aziz, T., & Ansari, V. A. (2017, in press). Are extreme negative returns priced in the Indian stock market? *Borsa Istanbul Review*. https://doi.org/10.1016/j.bir.2017.09.002.

Bachrach, B., & Galai, D. (1979). The risk-return relationship and stock prices. *Journal of Financial and Quantitative Analysis, 14*(2), 421–441.

Bacmann, J. F., & Dubois, M. (1998). *Contrarian strategies and cross-autocorrelations in stock returns: Evidence from France*. Available at SSRN: https://ssrn.com/abstract=138176 or https://doi.org/10.2139/ssrn.138176. Accessed 23 Oct 2017.

Baker, H. K., & Gallagher, P. L. (1980). Management's view of stock splits. *Financial Management, 9*, 73–77.

Baker, N. L., & Haugen, R. A. (2012). *Low risk stocks outperform within all observable markets of the world* (Working paper). Available at SSRN: https://doi.org/10.2139/ssrn.2055431. Accessed 25 Oct 2015.

Baker, M., Greenwood, R., & Wurgler, J. (2009). Catering through nominal share prices. *Journal of Finance, 64*(6), 2559–2590.

Baker, M., Bradley, B., & Wurgler, J. (2011). Benchmarks as limits to arbitrage: Understanding the low-volatility anomaly. *Financial Analyst Journal, 67*(1), 40–54.

Balakrishnan, K., Bartov, E., & Faurel, L. (2010). Post loss/profit announcement drift. *Journal of Accounting and Economics, 50*, 20–41.

Bali, T. G., & Cakici, N. (2004). Value at risk and expected stock returns. *Financial Analyst Journal, 60*(2), 57–73.

Bali, T. G., & Cakici, N. (2008). Idiosyncratic volatility and the cross section of expected returns. *Journal of Financial and Quantitative Analysis, 43*(1), 29–58.

Bali, C., & Cakici, N. (2010). World market risk, country-specific risk and expected returns in international stock markets. *Journal of Banking and Finance, 34*, 1152–1165.

Bali, T. G., & Murray, S. (2013). Does risk-neutral skewness predict the cross-section of equity option portfolio returns? *Journal of Financial and Quantitative Analysis, 48*(04), 1145–1171.

Bali, T. G., Cakici, N., Yan, X., & Zhang, Z. (2005). Does idiosyncratic risk really matter? *Journal of Finance, 60*(2), 905–929.

Bali, T. G., Gokcan, S., & Liang, B. (2007). Value at risk and the cross-section of hedge fund returns. *Journal of Banking & Finance, 31*(4), 1135–1166.

Bali, T., Cakici, N., & Whitelaw, R. F. (2011). Maxing out: Stocks as lotteries and the cross-section of expected returns. *Journal of Financial Economics, 99*(2), 427–446.

Bali, T. G., Cakici, N., & Fabozzi, F. J. (2013). Book-to-market and the cross-section of expected returns in international stock markets. *Journal of Portfolio Management, 39*(2), 101–115.

Bali, T. G., Engle, R. F., & Murray, S. (2016). *Empirical asset pricing: The cross section of stock returns.* Hoboken: Wiley.

Bali, T. G., Subrahmanyam, A., & Wen, Q. (2017a). *Return-based factors for corporate bonds.* Available at SSRN: https://ssrn.com/abstract=2978861 or https://doi.org/10.2139/ssrn.2978861. Accessed 23 Oct 2017.

Bali, T. G., Brown, S. J., Murray, S., & Tang, Y. (2017b). A lottery-demand-based explanation of the beta anomaly. *Journal of Financial and Quantitative Analysis, 52*(6), 2369–2397. https://doi.org/10.1017/S0022109017000928.

Ball, R., & Kothari, S. (1989). Non stationary expected returns: Implications for test of market efficiency and serial correlation in returns. *Journal of Financial Economics, 25*, 51–74.

Ball, R., Kothari, S., & Shanken, J. (1995a). Problems in measuring portfolio performance: An application to contrarian investment strategies. *Journal of Financial Economics, 38*, 79–107.

Ball, R., Kothari, S. P., & Wasley, C. E. (1995b). Can we implement research on stock trading rules? *Journal of Portfolio Management, 21*(2), 54–65.

Baltas, A.-N., & Kosowski, R. (2012a). Momentum strategies in futures markets and trend-following funds. *SSRN Electronic Journal.* https://doi.org/10.2139/ssrn.1968996. Accessed 23 Oct 2017.

Baltas, A.-N., & Kosowski, R. (2012b). Improving time-series momentum strategies: The role of trading signals and volatility estimators. *SSRN Electronic Journal.* https://doi.org/10.2139/ssrn.2140091. Accessed 23 Oct 2017.

Balvers, R. J., & Wu, Y. (2006). Momentum and mean reversion across national equity markets. *Journal of Empirical Finance, 13*, 24–48.

Balvers, R., Wu, Y., & Gililand, E. (2000). Mean reversion across national stock markets and parametric contrarian investment strategies. *Journal of Finance, 55*(2), 745–772. https://doi.org/10.1111/0022-1082.00225.

Bange, M. M. (2000). Do the portfolios of small investors reflect positive feedback trading? *Journal of Financial and Quantitative Analysis, 35*, 239–255.

Bansal, R., Dittmar, R. F., & Lundblad, C. T. (2005). Consumption, dividends, and cross section of equity returns. *Journal of Finance, 60*(4), 1639–1672.

Banz, R. W. (1981). The relationship between return and market value of common stocks. *Journal of Financial Economics, 9*, 3–18.

Banz, R., & Breen, W. (1986). Sample dependent results using accounting and market data: Some evidence. *Journal of Finance, 41*(4), 779–793.

Barber, B. M., & Odean, T. (2000). Trading is hazardous to your wealth: The common stock investment performance of individual investors. *Journal of Finance, 55*(2), 773–806.

Barber, B. M., & Odean, T. (2004). Are individual investors tax savvy? Evidence from retail and discount brokerage accounts. *Journal of Public Economics, 88*(1–2), 419–442.

Barber, B., & Odean, T. (2008). All that glitters: The effect of attention on the buying behavior of individual and institutional investors. *Review of Financial Studies, 21*(2), 785–818.

Barberis, N., & Huang, M. (2001). Mental accounting, loss aversion, and individual stock returns. *Journal of Finance, 56*(4), 1247–1292.

Barberis, N., & Huang, M. (2008). Stocks as lotteries: The implications of probability weighting for security prices. *American Economic Review, 98*(5), 2066–2100.

Barberis, N., & Shliefer, A. (2003). Style investing. *Journal of Financial Economics, 68*, 161–199.

Barberis, N., & Xiong, W. (2009). What drives the disposition effect? An analysis of a long-standing preference-based explanation. *Journal of Finance, 64*(2), 751–784.

Barberis, N., Shleifer, A., & Vishny, R. (1998). A model of investor sentiment. *Journal of Financial Economics, 49*, 307–343.

Barberis, N., Mukherjee, A., & Wang, B. (2016). Prospect theory and stock returns: An empirical test. *Review of Financial Studies, 29*(11), 3068–3107.

Barroso, P., & Santa-Clara, P. (2015). Momentum has its moments. *Journal of Financial Economics, 116*(1), 111–120. https://doi.org/10.1016/j.jfineco.2014.11.010.

Barry, C., Goldreyer, E., Lockwood, L., & Rodriguez, M. (2002). Robustness of size and value effects in emerging equity markets, 1985–2000. *Emerging Markets Review, 3*, 1–30.

Barth, F., Scholz, H., & Stegmeier, M. (2017). *Momentum in the European corporate bond market: The role of characteristics-adjusted returns.* Available at SSRN: https://ssrn.com/abstract=2664491 or https://doi.org/10.2139/ssrn.2664491. Accessed 23 Oct 2017.

Bar-Yosef, S., & Brown, L. D. (1979). Share price levels and beta. *Financial Management, 8*(1), 60–63.

Basu, S. (1983). The relationship between earnings yield, market value and return for NYSE common stocks: Further evidence. *Journal of Financial Economics, 12*, 129–156.

Bauman, W. S., Conover, C. M., & Miller, R. E. (1998). Growth versus value and large-cap versus small-cap stocks in international markets. *Financial Analyst Journal, 54*(2), 75–89.

Baytas, A., & Cakici, N. (1999). Do markets overreact: International evidence. *Journal of Banking and Finance, 23*, 1121–1144.

Baz, J., Granger, N. M., Harvey, C. R., Le Roux, N., & Rattray, S. (2015). *Dissecting investment strategies in the cross section and time series.* Available at SSRN: https://ssrn.com/abstract=2695101 or https://doi.org/10.2139/ssrn.2695101. Accessed 23 Oct 2017.

Beit-Hallahmi, B., & Argyle, M. (1997). *The psychology of religious behaviour, belief and experience.* London: Routledge.

Bekaert, G., Erb, C. B., Harvey, C. R., & Viskanta, T. E. (1996). *The cross-sectional determinants of emerging equity market returns.* Retrieved from https://www0.gsb.columbia.edu/faculty/gbekaert/PDF_Papers/The_cross-sectional_determinants.pdf. Accessed 21 Sept 2015.

Bekaert, G., Harvey, C., & Lundblad, C. (2007). Liquidity and expected returns: Lessons from emerging markets. *Review of Financial Studies, 20*, 1783–1831.

Bekaert, G., Hodrick, R. J., & Zhang, X. (2012). Aggregate idiosyncratic volatility. *Journal of Financial and Quantitative Analysis, 47*(6), 1155–1185.

Beracha, E., & Skiba, H. (2011). Momentum in residential real estate. *Journal of Real Estate Finance and Economics, 43*(3), 299–320.

Bernard, S., Leippold, M., & Lohre, H. (2013). *Risk-based commodity investing* (Working paper). Available at http://viessmanncentre.ca/wp-content/uploads/2014/05/Bernardi_Leiphold_Lohre1.pdf. Accessed 24 Oct 2015.

Bhana, N. (1994). Public holiday share price behavior on the Johannesburg Stock Exchange. *Investment Analysts Journal, 23*(39), 45–49.

Bhanot, K. (2005). What causes mean reversion in corporate bond index spreads? The impact of survival. *Journal of Banking and Finance, 29*(6), 1385–1403. https://doi.org/10.1016/j.jbankfin.2004.04.003.

Bhansali, V., Davis, J., Dorsten, M. P., & Rennison, G. (2015). *Carry and trend in lots of places.* Available at SSRN: https://ssrn.com/abstract=2579089 or https://doi.org/10.2139/ssrn.2579089. Accessed 23 Oct 2017.

Bhojraj, S., & Swaminathan, B. (2006). Macromomentum: Returns predictability in international equity indices. *Journal of Business, 79*(1), 429–451.

Bhootra, A., & Hur, J. (2013). The timing of 52-week high price and momentum. *Journal of Banking & Finance, 37*(10), 3773–3782. https://doi.org/10.1016/j.jbankfin.2013.05.025.

Bhushan, R. (1989). Firm characteristics and analyst following. *Journal of Accounting and Economics, 11*(2–3), 255–274.

Białkowski, J., Etebari, A., & Wiśniewski, T. (2012). Fast profits: Investor sentiment and stock returns during Ramadan. *Journal of Banking and Finance, 36*(3), 835–845.

Białkowski, H., Bohl, M. T., Kaufmann, P., & Wiśniewski, T. P. (2013). Do mutual fund managers exploit the Ramadan anomaly? Evidence from Turkey. *Emerging Markets Review, 15*, 211–232.

Bianchi, R. J., Drew, M. E., & Polichronis, J. (2005). A test of momentum trading strategies in foreign exchange markets: Evidence from the G7. *Global Business and Economic Review, 7*(2/3), 155–179.

Bikhchandani, S., Hirshleifer, D., & Welch, I. (1992). A theory of fads, fashion, custom, and cultural change as informational cascades. *Journal of Political Economy, 100*(5), 992–1026.

Bildik, R., & Gulay, G. (2007). Profitability of contrarian strategy: Evidence from the Istanbul stock exchange. *International Review of Finance, 7*(1–2), 61–87.

Birru, J., & Wang, B. (2015). *The Nominal price premium* (Charles A. Dice Center working paper No. 2015-15). Available at SSRN: https://ssrn.com/abstract=2646775 or https://doi.org/10.2139/ssrn.2646775. Accessed 18 Oct 2017.

Black, F. (1972). Capital market equilibrium with restricted borrowing. *Journal of Business, 45*, 44–455.

Black, F. (1986). Noise. *Journal of Finance, 41*, 529–543.

Black, F. (1993). Beta and returns. *Journal of Portfolio Management, 20*(1), 8–18.

Blackburn, D. W., & Cakici, N. (2017). Overreaction and the cross-section of returns: International evidence. *Journal of Empirical Finance, 42*, 1–14. https://doi.org/10.1016/j.jempfin.2017.02.001.

Blitz, D., & de Groot, W. (2014). Strategic allocation to commodity factor premiums. *Journal of Alternative Investments, 17*(2), 103–115.

Blitz, D. C., & van Vliet, P. (2007). The volatility effect: Lower risk without lower return. *Journal of Portfolio Management, 34*(1), 102–113. https://doi.org/10.3905/jpm.2007.698039.

Blitz, D. C., & van Vliet, P. (2008). Global tactical cross-asset allocation: Applying value and momentum across asset classes. *Journal of Portfolio Management, 35*(1), 23–38. https://doi.org/10.3905/JPM.2008.35.1.23.

Blitz, D., Huij, J., & Martens, M. (2011). Residual momentum. *Journal of Empirical Finance, 18*(3), 506–521. https://doi.org/10.1016/j.jempfin.2011.01.003.

Blitz, D., Huij, J., Lansdorp, S., & Verbeek, M. (2013a). Short-term residual reversal. *Journal of Financial Markets, 16*, 477–504.

Blitz, D., Pang, J., & van Vliet, P. (2013b). The volatility effect in emerging markets. *Emerging Markets Review, 16*, 31–45.

Blitz, D., Falkenstein, E., & van Vliet, P. (2014a). Explanations for the volatility effect: An overview based on the CAPM assumptions. *Journal of Portfolio Management, 40*(3), 61–76.

Blitz, D., van der Grient, B., & Hanauer, M. (2014b). *What drives the value premium?* (White paper). Robeco. Available at https://www.robeco.com/images/20141016-what-drives-the-value-premium-june-2014.pdf. Accessed 13 Oct 2015.

Blitz, D., Hanauer, M. X., & Vidojevic, M. (2017). *The idiosyncratic momentum anomaly*. Available at SSRN: https://ssrn.com/abstract=2947044. Accessed 23 Oct 2017.

Blume, M. E. (1970). Portfolio theory: A step towards its practical application. *Journal of Business, 43*(2), 152–174.

Blume, M. E., & Friend, I. (1973). A new look at the capital asset pricing model. *Journal of Finance, 28*(1), 19–34.

Blume, M. E., & Husic, F. (1973). Price, beta and exchange listing. *Journal of Finance, 28*(2), 283–299.

Blume, L., Easley, D., & O'Hara, M. (1994). Market statistics and technical analysis: The role of volume. *Journal of Finance, 49*, 153–181.

Bohan, J. (1981). Relative strength: Further positive evidence. *Journal of Portfolio Management, 8*(1), 36–39.

Bohl, M. T., & Salm, C. A. (2010). The other January effect: International evidence. *European Journal of Finance, 16*, 173–182. https://doi.org/10.1080/13518470903037953.

Bollen, N. P. B., & Whaley, R. E. (2004). Does net buying pressure affect the shape of implied volatility functions. *Journal of Finance, 59*(2), 711–753.

Bolognesi, E., & Pividori, M. (2016). Fundamental indexation in Europe: New evidence. *Journal of Financial Management, Markets and Institutions, 4*(2), 103–128.

Bornholt, G., Gharaibeh, O., & Malin, M. (2015). Industry long-term return reversal. *Journal of International Financial Markets, Institutions and Money, 38*, 65–78. https://doi.org/10.1016/j.intfin.2015.05.013.

Bouman, S., & Jacobsen, B. (2002). The Halloween indicator, "Sell in May and go away": Another puzzle. *American Economic Review, 92*(5), 1618–1635. https://doi.org/10.1257/000282802762024.

Boussaidi, R. (2013). Representativeness heuristic, investor sentiment and overreaction to accounting earnings: The case of the Tunisian stock market. *Procedia – Social and Behavioral Sciences, 81*, 9–21.

Bowden, M. P. (2015). A model of information flows and confirmatory bias in financial markets. *Decisions in Economics and Finance, 38*(2), 197–215.

Boyer, H. B., & Vorkink, K. (2014). Stock options as lotteries. *Journal of Finance, 69*(4), 1485–1527. https://doi.org/10.1111/jofi.12152.

Boyer, B., Mitton, T., & Vorkink, K. (2010). Expected idiosyncratic skewness. *Review of Financial Studies, 23*(1), 169–202.

Brailsford, T. (1992). A test for the winner-loser anomaly in the Australian equity market: 1958–87. *Journal of Business Finance and Accounting, 19*(2), 225–241.

Branch, B., & Chang, K. (1990). Low price stocks and the January effect. *Quarterly Journal of Business and Economics, 29*(3), 90–118.

Brav, A., Geczy, C., & Gompers, P. (2000). Is the abnormal return following equity issuance anomalous. *Journal of Financial Economics, 56*, 209–249.

Brennan, M. J. (1970). Taxes, market valuation and corporate financial policy. *National Tax Journal, 25*, 417–427.

Brennan, M., & Copeland, T. E. (1988). Stock splits, stock prices, and transaction costs. *Journal of Financial Economics, 22*, 83–101.

Brennan, M. J., Cheng, X., & Li, F. (2012). Agency and institutional investment. *European Financial Management, 18*(1), 1–27.

Brown, D. P., & Jennings, R. H. (1989). On technical analysis. *Review of Financial Studies, 2*, 527–551.

Brown, A., Du, D. Y., Rhee, S. G., & Zhang, L. (2008). The returns to value and momentum in Asian markets. *Emerging Markets Review, 9*, 79–88.

Brush, J. S., & Bowles, K. E. (1983). The predictive power in relative strength and CAPM. *Journal of Portfolio Management, 9*(4), 20–23.

Burnside, A. C., Eichenbaum, M., & Rebelo, S. T. (2011). Carry trade and momentum in currency markets. *Annual Review of Financial Economics, 3*, 511–535.

Cadsby, C. B., & Ratner, M. (1992). Turn-of-month and pre-holiday effects on stock returns: Some international evidence. *Journal of Banking & Finance, 16*(3), 497–509.

Cakici, N., Fabozzi, F. J., & Tan, S. (2013). Size, value, and momentum in emerging market stock returns. *Emerging Markets Review, 16*, 46–65.

Calvet, L. E., Lakonishok, J., & LeBaron, B. (1992). Simple technical trading rules and the stochastic properties of stock returns. *Journal of Finance, 47*(5), 1731–1764.

Campbell, J. Y., & Cochrane, J. H. (1999). By fore of habit: A Consumption-based explanation of aggregate stock market behavior. *Journal of Political Economy, 107*(2), 205–251.

Campbell, K., & Limmack, R. J. (1997). Long term overreaction in the UK stock market and size adjustments. *Applied Financial Economics, 7*, 537–548.

Campbell, J. Y., & Thompson, S. (2008). Predicting the equity premium out of sample: Can anything beat the historical average? *Review of Financial Studies, 21*(4), 1509–1531.

Campbell, J., Grossman, S. J., & Wang, J. (1993). Trading volume and serial correlation in stock returns. *Quarterly Journal of Economics, 108*(4), 905–939.

Campbell, J. Y., Lo, A. W., & MacKinlay, A. C. (1997). *The econometrics of financial markets*. Princeton: Princeton University Press.

Campbell, C. J., Rhee, S. G., Du, Y., & Tang, N. (2008). *Market sentiment, IPO underpricing, and valuation* (Working paper). Available at SSRN: http://ssrn.com/abstract=1108540 or https://doi.org/10.2139/ssrn.1108540. Accessed 22 Nov 2015.

Cao, V. N. (2015a). What explains the value premium? The case of adjustment costs, operating leverage and financial leverage. *Journal of Banking & Finance, 59*, 350–366.

Cao, X. (2015b). *Are idiosyncratic skewness and idiosyncratic kurtosis priced?* (Brock University working paper). Available at https://dr.library.brocku.ca/handle/10464/6426. Accessed 14 Oct 2017.

Carchano, O., & Pardo, A. (2015). The pan-European holiday effect. *Spanish Journal of Finance and Accounting, 44*(2), 134–145. https://doi.org/10.1080/02102412.2015.1016716.

Carhart, M. M. (1997). On persistence in mutual fund performance. *Journal of Finance, 52*(1), 57–82.

Carlson, M., Fisher, A., & Giammarino, R. (2004). Corporate investment and asset price dynamics: Implications for the cross section of returns. *Journal of Finance, 59*(6), 2577–2603.

Carpenter, J. N., & Lynch, A. W. (1999). Survivorship bias and attrition effects in measures of performance persistence. *Journal of Financial Economics, 54*, 337–374.

Castro, F. H., & Schabek, T. (2014). *Sell not only in May. Seasonal effects in emerging and developed markets*. Available at SSRN: http://ssrn.com/abstract=2458515 or https://doi.org/10.2139/ssrn.2458515. Accessed 23 Oct 2017.

Chabot, B., Ghysels, E., & Jagannathan, R. (2008). *Price momentum in stocks: Insights from Victorian age* (NBER working paper No. 14500). Available at: http://www.nber.org/papers/w14500. Accessed 20 Oct 2015.

Chan, K. (1988). On the contrarian investment strategy. *Journal of Business, 61*, 147–163.

Chan, E. P. (2013). Mean reversion of currencies and futures. In *Algorithmic trading: Winning strategies and their rationale*. Hoboken: John Wiley & Sons, Inc. https://doi.org/10.1002/9781118676998.ch5.

Chan, L. K. C., Jegadeesh, N., & Lakonishok, J. (1995). Evaluating the performance of value versus glamour stocks: The impact of selection bias. *Journal of Financial Economics, 38*(3), 269–296.

Chan, L., Karceski, J., & Lakonishok, J. (1998). The risk and return from factors. *Journal of Financial and Quantitative Analysis, 33*, 159–188.

Chan, L., Karceski, J., & Lakonishok, J. (1999). On portfolio optimization: Forecasting covariances and choosing the risk model. *Review of Financial Studies, 12*, 937–974.

Chan, K., Hameed, A., & Tong, W. (2000). Profitability of momentum strategies in the international equity markets. *Journal of Financial and Quantitative Analysis, 35*(2), 153–172.

Chan, L. K., Lakonishok, J., & Sougiannis, T. (2001). The stock market valuation of research and development expenditures. *Journal of Finance, 56*, 2431–2456.

Chan, L. K. C., Jegadeesh, N., & Lakonishok, J. (2012). Momentum strategies. *Journal of Finance, 51*(5), 1681–1713.

Chang, R. P., Ko, K.-C., Nakano, S., & Rhee, S. G. (2018). Residual momentum in Japan. *Journal of Empirical Finance, 45*, 283–299. https://doi.org/10.1016/j.jempfin.2017.11.005.

Chao, H.-Y., Collver, C., & Limthanakom, N. (2012). Global style momentum. *Journal of Empirical Finance, 19*(3), 319–333. Available at https://doi.org/10.1016/j.jempfin.2012.02.001

Chaves, D. B. (2012). *Eureka! A momentum strategy that also works in Japan*. Available at SSRN: https://ssrn.com/abstract=1982100 or https://doi.org/10.2139/ssrn.1982100. Accessed 23 Oct 2017.

Chaves, D. B., & Viswanathan, V. (2016). Momentum and mean-reversion in commodity spot and futures markets. *Journal of Commodity Markets, 3*(1), 39–53.

Chaves, D. B., Hsu, J. C., Kalesnik, V., & Shim, Y. (2012). *What drives the value effect? Risk versus mispricing: Evidence from international markets* (Working paper). Available at SSRN: http://ssrn.com/abstract=1940504 or https://doi.org/10.2139/ssrn.1940504. Accessed 23 Oct 2017.

Cheema, M. A., Nartea, G. V., & Man, Y. (2017, in press). Cross-sectional and time series momentum returns and market states. *International Review of Finance*. https://doi.org/10.1111/irfi.12148.

Chen, H. S., & De Bondt, W. (2004). Style momentum within the S&P-500 index. *Journal of Empirical Finance, 11*, 483–507.

Chen, S.-N., & Jeon, K. (1998). Mean reversion behavior of the returns on currency assets. *International Review of Economics & Finance, 7*(2), 185–200. https://doi.org/10.1016/S1059-0560(98)90039-9.

Chen, A.-S., & Yang, W. (2016). Echo effects and the returns from 52-week high strategies. *Finance Research Letters, 16*, 38–46. https://doi.org/10.1016/j.frl.2015.10.015.

Chen, J., Hong, H., & Stein, J. C. (2002). Breadth of ownership and stock returns. *Journal of Financial Economics, 66*, 171–205.

Chen, L., Li, S., & Wang, J. (2011a). Liquidity, skewness and stock returns: Evidence from Chinese stock market. *Asia-Pacific Financial Markets, 18*, 405–427.

Chen, L., Novy-Marx, R., & Zhang, L. (2011b). *An alternative three-factor model*. Retrieved from SSRN: http://ssrn.com/abstract=1418117 or https://doi.org/10.2139/ssrn.1418117. Accessed 4 Nov 2015.

Chen, L. H., Jiang, G. J., & Zhu, X. (2012). Do style and sector indexes carry momentum? *Journal of Investment Strategies, 1*(3), 67–89.

Chen, D.-H., Chen, C. D., & Wu, S. C. (2014). VaR and the cross-section of expected stock returns: An emerging market evidence. *Journal of Business Economics and Management, 15*(3), 441–459.

Chen, L.-W., Yu, H.-Y., & Wang, W.-K. (2017a, in press). Evolution of historical prices in momentum investing. *Journal of Financial Markets*. Available at SSRN: https://ssrn.com/abstract=3009059. Accessed 21 Oct 2017.

Chen, Z., Li, J., & Wang, H. (2017b). *Decomposing the size premium*. Available at SSRN: https://ssrn.com/abstract=2899944 or https://doi.org/10.2139/ssrn.2899944. Accessed 23 Oct 2017.

Cheon, Y.-H., & Lee, K.-H. (2017, in press). Maxing out globally: Individualism, investor attention, and the cross section of expected stock returns. *Management Science*. https://doi.org/10.1287/mnsc.2017.2830.

Chestnutt, G. A. (1961). *Stock market analysis: Facts and principles*. Larchmont: American Investors Service.

Choi, J. (2013). What drives the value premium? The role of asset risk and leverage. *Review of Financial Studies, 26*(11), 2845–2875.

Chopra, N., Lakonishok, J., & Ritter, J. (1992). Measuring abnormal performance. *Journal of Financial Economics, 31*, 235–268.

Chordia, T., & Shivakumar, L. (2002). Momentum, business cycle, and time varying expected returns. *Journal of Finance, 57*(2), 985–1019.

Choudhry, T. (2000). Day of the week effect in emerging Asian stock markets: Evidence from the GARCH model. *Applied Financial Economics, 10*(3), 235–242.

Chow, T., Hsu, J. C., Kalesnik, V., & Little, B. (2011). A survey of alternative equity index strategies. *Financial Analysts Journal, 67*(5), 37–57.

Christie, A. A. (1982). The stochastic behaviour of common stock variances – Value, leverage and interest rate effects. *Journal of Financial Economics, 10*(4), 407–432.

Christopherson, J. A., Ferson, W. E., & Turner, A. L. (1999). Performance evaluation using conditional alphas and betas. *Journal of Portfolio Management, 26*(1), 59–72.

Chui, A. C. W., Titman, S., & Wei, J. K. C. (2010). Individualism and momentum around the world. *Journal of Finance, 65*(1), 361–392.

Chui, A. C. W., Wei, J. K. C., & Xie, F. (2013). *Explaining the value premium around the world: Risk or mispricing?* (Working paper). Available at http://repository.ust.hk/ir/Record/1783.1-66583

Chung, K. H., & Yang, S. (2014). Reverse stock splits, institutional holdings, and share value. *Financial Management, 44*, 177–216. https://doi.org/10.1111/fima.12077.

Ciao, X., Premachandra, I. M., & Bhabra, G. S. (2009). Firm size and the pre-holiday effect in New Zealand. *International Research Journal of Finance and Economics, 32*, 171–187. ISSN: 1450-2887.

Clare, A., & Thomas, S. (1995, October). The overreaction hypothesis and the UK stock market. *Journal of Business & Accounting, 22*(7), 961–973.

Clare, A., Sapuric, S., & Todorovic, N. (2010). Quantitative or momentum-based multi-style rotation? UK experience. *Journal of Asset Management, 10*, 370–381.

Clare, A., Seaton, J., Smith, P. N., & Thomas, S. (2016). The trend is our friend: Risk parity, momentum and trend following in global asset allocation. *Journal of Behavioral and Experimental Finance, 9*, 63–80. https://doi.org/10.1016/j.jbef.2016.01.002.

Clark, A., & Oswald, A. (1996). Satisfaction and comparison income. *Journal of Public Economics, 61*(3), 359–381.

Clarke, R., de Silva, H., & Thorley, S. (2006). Minimum-variance portfolios in the US equity market. *Journal of Portfolio Management, 33*(1), 10–24.

Clarke, R., de Silva, H., & Thorley, S. (2010). Know your VMS exposure. *Journal of Portfolio Management, 36*(2), 52–59.

Clenderin, J. C. (1951). Quality versus price as factors influencing common stock price fluctuations. *Journal of Finance, 6*(4), 398–405.

Clyde, W. C., & Osler, C. L. (1997). Charting: Chaos theory in disguise? *Journal of Futures Markets, 17*, 489–514.

Cochrane, J. H. (1991). Production-based asset pricing and the link between stock returns and economic fluctuations. *Journal of Finance, 46*, 209–237.

Cochrane, J. H. (1996). A cross-sectional test of an investment-based asset pricing model. *Journal of Political Economy, 104*, 572–621.

Cochrane, J. H. (2005). *Asset pricing*. Princeton: Princeton University Press.

Cohen, R. B., Polk, C., & Vuolteenaho, T. (2003). The value spread. *Journal of Finance, 58*(2), 609–641. https://doi.org/10.1111/1540-6261.00539.

Conine, T. E., & Tamarkin, M. J. (1981). On diversification given asymmetry in returns. *Journal of Finance, 36*(5), 1143–1155.

Connolly, R. A. (1989). An examination of the robustness of the weekend effect. *Journal of Financial and Quantitative Analysis, 24*(2), 133–169.

Conrad, J., & Kaul, G. (1993). Long-term market overreaction or biases in computer returns? *Journal of Finance, 48*(1), 39–63.

Conrad, J., Gultekin, M. N., & Kaul, G. (1997). Profitability of short-term contrarian strategies: Implications for market efficiency. *Journal of Business & Economic Statistics, 15*(3), 379–386. https://doi.org/10.2307/1392341.

Conrad, J., Dittmar, R. F., & Ghysels, E. (2013). Ex ante skewness and expected returns. *Journal of Finance, 68*(1), 85–124. https://doi.org/10.1111/j.1540-6261.2012.01795.x.

Cooper, M. J., Gutierrez, R. C., Jr., & Hameed, A. (2004). Market states and momentum. *Journal of Finance, 59*(3), 1345–1365. https://doi.org/10.1111/j.1540-6261.2004.00665.x.

Cooper, M., McConnell, J., & Ovtchinnikov, A. (2006). The other January effect. *Journal of Financial Economics, 82*, 315–341.

Cooper, M. J., Gulen, H., & Schill, M. J. (2008). Asset growth and the cross-section of stock returns. *Journal of Finance, 63*, 1609–1651.

Cooper, H., Mitrache, A., & Priestley, R. (2017). *A global macroeconomic risk model for value, momentum, and other asset classes.* Available at SSRN: https://ssrn.com/abstract=2768040. Accessed 23 Oct 2017.

Cornell, B. (2009). The pricing of volatility and skewness: A new interpretation. *Journal of Investing, 18*(3), 27–30.

Covel, M. W. (2007). *The complete turtle trader: How 23 novice investors became overnight millionaires.* New York: HarperCollins Publishers.

Covel, M. W. (2009). *Trend following: Learn to make millions in up or down markets.* London: FT Press.

Cowles, A., III, & Jones, H. E. (1937). Some a posteriori probabilities in stock market criteria. *Econometrica, 5*(3), 280–294.

Cremers, M., & Weinbaum, D. (2010). Deviations from put-call parity and stock return predictability. *Journal of Financial and Quantitative Analysis, 45*(2), 335–367.

Cutler, D. M., Poterba, J. M., & Summers, L. H. (1990). Speculative dynamics and the role of feedback traders. *American Economic Review, 80*, 63–68.

Da Costa, N. C. (1994). Overreaction in the Brazilian stock market. *Journal of Banking and Finance, 18*, 633–642.

Da, Z., & Schaumburg, E. (2007). *Target prices, relative valuations and the premium for liquidity provision* (AFA 2007 Chicago meetings paper). University of Notre Dame.

Da, Z., Liu, Q., & Schaumburg, E. (2011). *Decomposing short-term return reversal* (Federal Reserve Bank of New York staff report No. 513). Available at https://www.newyorkfed.org/medialibrary/media/research/staff_reports/sr513.pdf. Accessed 9 Oct 2017.

Da, Z., Liu, Q., & Schaumburg, E. (2014a). A closer look at the short-term return reversal. *Management Science, 60*, 658–674.

Da, Z., Gurun, U., & Warachka, M. (2014b). Frog in the pan: Continuous information and momentum. *Review of Financial Studies, 27*, 2171–2218.

Dahlquist, M., & Bansal, R. (2002a). *Expropriation risk and return in global equity markets* (EFA 2002 Berlin meetings presented paper). Available at SSRN: http://ssrn.com/abstract=298180 or https://doi.org/10.2139/ssrn.298180. Accessed 21 Sept 2015.

Daniel, K. D., & Moskowitz, T. J. (2013). *Momentum crashes* (Swiss Finance Institute research paper No. 13-61; Columbia Business School research paper No. 14-6; Fama-Miller working paper). Available at SSRN: http://ssrn.com/abstract=2371227 or https://doi.org/10.2139/ssrn.2371227. Accessed 17 Nov 2015.

Daniel, K., & Titman, S. (1999). Market efficiency in an irrational world. *Financial Analysts Journal, 55*, 28–40.

Daniel, K., Hirshleifer, D., & Subrahmanyam, A. (1998). A theory of overconfidence, selfattribution, and security market under- and over-reactions. *Journal of Finance, 53*, 1839–1885.

Daradkeh, T. K. (1992). Parasuicide during Ramadan in Jordan. *Acta Psychiatrica Scandinavica, 86*(3), 253–254.

Darvas, N. (1960). *How I made $2,000,000 in the stock market.* Larchmont: American Research Council.

Davis, J. (1994). The cross-section of realized stock returns: The pre-COMPUSTAT evidence. *Journal of Finance, 49*, 1579–1593. https://doi.org/10.1111/j.1540-6261.1994.tb04773.x.

de Bondt, W. E. M. (1993). Betting on trends: Intuitive forecasts of financial risk and return. *International Journal of Forecasting, 9*, 355–371.

de Carvalho, R. L., Dugnolle, P., Lu, X., & Moulin, P. (2014). Low-risk anomalies in global fixed income: Evidence from major broad markets. *Journal of Fixed Income, 23*(4), 51–70. https://doi.org/10.3905/jfi.2014.23.4.051.

de Giorgi, E. G., Post, T., & Yalcin, A. (2013). *A concave security market line.* Available at SSRN: http://ssrn.com/abstract=1800229 or https://doi.org/10.2139/ssrn.1800229. Accessed 25 Sept 2017.

de Groot, W., & Huij, J. (2011). *Are the Fama-French factors really compensations for distress risk?* (Working paper). Available at SSRN: http://ssrn.com/abstract=1840551 or https://doi.org/10.2139/ssrn.1840551. Accessed 12 Oct 2015.

de Groot, W., Huij, J., & Zhou, W. (2012a). Another look at trading costs and short-term reversal profits. *Journal of Banking and Finance, 36*(2), 371–382. https://doi.org/10.1016/j.jbankfin.2011.07.015.

de Groot, W., Pang, J., & Swinkels, L. A. P. (2012b). The cross-section of stock returns in frontier emerging markets. *Journal of Empirical Finance, 19*(5), 796–818.

de Groot, W., Karstansje, D., & Zhou, W. (2014). Exploiting commodity momentum along the futures curves. *Journal of Banking & Finance, 48*, 79–93.

de Long, B. J., Shleifer, A., Summers, L. H., & Waldmann, R. J. (1990a). Noise trader risk in financial markets. *Journal of Political Economy, 98*, 703–738.

de Long, J. B., Shleifer, A., Summers, L. H., & Waldmann, R. J. (1990b). Positive feedback investment strategies and destabilizing rational speculation. *Journal of Finance, 45*(2), 379–395.

de Mendonca, F. P., Klotzle, M. C., Pinto, A. C. F., & da Silva Montezano, R. M. (2012). The relationship between idiosyncratic risk and returns in the Brazilian stock market. *Revista Contabilidade & Finanças, 23*(60). Available online at: http://www.scielo.br/scielo.php?pid=S1519-70772012000300009&script=sci_arttext&tlng=en. Accessed 14 Oct 2017.

De Moor, L., & Sercu, P. (2013a). The smallest stocks are not just smaller: Global evidence. *European Journal of Finance, 21*(2), 51–70.

De Moor, L., & Sercu, P. (2013b). The smallest firm effect: An international study. *Journal of International Money and Finance, 32*, 129–155.

De Bondt, W. F. M., & Thaler, R. (1985). Does the stock market overreact? *Journal of Finance, 40*(3), 793–805.

De Bondt, F., & Thaler.R. (1987). Further evidence on the investor overreaction and stock market seasonality. *Journal of Finance, 42*, 557–581.

DeMarzo, P., Kaniel, R., & Kremer, I. (2004). Diversification as a public good: Community effects in portfolio choice. *Journal of Finance, 59*(4), 1677–1715.

Desai, H., & Jain, C. P. (1997). Long-run common stock returns following stock splits and reverse splits. *Journal of Business, 70*(3), 409–433. http://www.jstor.org/stable/10.1086/209724

Dhouib, F. H., & Abaoub, E. (2007). Does the Tunisian stock market overreact? *Asian Academy of Management Journal of Accounting and Finance, 3*(2), 83–107.

Diacogiannis, G., & Kyriazis, D. (2007). Testing the performance of value strategies in the Athens Stock Exchange. *Applied Financial Economics, 17*, 1511–1528.

Dichev, I. D. (1998). Is the risk of bankruptcy a systematic risk? *Journal of Finance, 53*(3), 1131–1147.

Dichtl, H., & Drobetz, W. (2015). Sell in May and go away: Still good advice for investors? *International Review of Financial Analysis, 38*, 29–43. https://doi.org/10.1016/j.irfa.2014.09.007.

Dimitriou, D., & Simos, T. (2011). The relationship between stock returns and volatility in the seventeen largest international stock markets: A semi-parametric approach. *Modern Economy, 2*, 1–8.

Dimson, E., & Marsh, P. (1999). Murphy's law and market anomalies. *Journal of Portfolio Management, 25*(2), 53–69.

Dissanaike, G. (1997). Do stock market investors overreact? *Journal of Business and Accounting, 24*, 27–49.

Dittmar, R. F. (2002). Nonlinear pricing kernels, kurtosis preference, and evidence from the cross section of equity returns. *Journal of Finance, 57*(1), 369–403.

Doeswijk, R. Q. (2008, June). The optimism cycle: Sell in May. *De Economist, 156*, 175. https://doi.org/10.1007/s10645-008-9088-z.

Doran, J. S., & Krieger, K. (2010). Implications for asset returns in the implied volatility skew. *Financial Analyst Journal, 66*(1), 65–76.

Doran, J. S., Jiang, D., & Peterson, D. R. (2012). Gambling preferences and the new year effect of assets with lottery features. *Review of Finance, 16*(3), 685–731. https://doi.org/10.1093/rof/rfr006.

Dowd, K. (2000). Adjusting for risk: An improved Sharpe ratio. *International Review of Economics and Finance, 9*(3), 209–222.

Du, D. (2011). Value premium and investor sentiment. *Advances in Behavioral Finance & Economics: The Journal of the Academy of Behavioral Finance, 1*(2), 87–101.

Dubofsky, D. A., & French, D. W. (1988). Share price level and risk: Implications for financial management. *Managerial Finance, 14*(1), 6–9.

Dubois, M., & Louvet, P. (1996). The day-of-the-week effect: The international evidence. *Journal of Banking and Finance, 20*(9), 1463–1484.

Dudler, M., Gmuer, B., & Malamud, S. (2014). *Risk adjusted time series momentum* (Swiss Finance Institute research paper No. 14-71). Available at SSRN: https://ssrn.com/abstract=2457647 or https://doi.org/10.2139/ssrn.2457647. Accessed 23 Oct 2017.

Dudler, M., Gmur, B., & Malamud, S. (2015). Momentum and risk adjustment. *Journal of Alternative Investment, 18*(2), 91–103. https://doi.org/10.3905/jai.2015.18.2.091.

Dumitriu, R., Stefanescu, R., & Nistor, C. (2012). *The Halloween effect during quiet and turbulent times.* Available at SSRN: https://ssrn.com/abstract=2043757 or https://doi.org/10.2139/ssrn.2043757. Accessed 23 Oct 2017.

Durham, J. B. (2013). *Momentum and the term structure of interest rates* (FRB of New York staff report No. 657). Available at SSRN: http://ssrn.com/abstract=2377379 or https://doi.org/10.2139/ssrn.2377379. Accessed 20 Oct 2015.

Duyvesteyn, J., & Martens, M. (2014). Emerging government bond market timing. *Journal of Fixed Income, 23*(3), 36–49.

Dzhabarov, C. S., & Ziemba, W. T. (2016). *Sell in May and go away in the equity index futures markets.* Available at SSRN: https://ssrn.com/abstract=2721068 or https://doi.org/10.2139/ssrn.2721068. Accessed 23 Oct 2017.

Easterday, K. E., Sen, P. K., & Stephan, J. (2009). The persistence of the small firm/January effect: Is it consistent with investors' learning and arbitrage efforts? *Quarterly Review of Economics and Finance, 49*(3), 1172–1193.

Easterlin, R. (1995). Will raising the incomes of all raise the happiness of all? *Journal of Economic Behavior and Organization, 27*, 35–47.

Eberhardt, A. C., Maxwell, W. F., & Siddique, A. R. (2004). An examination of long-term abnormal stock returns and operating performance following R&D increases. *Journal of Finance, 59*, 623–650.

Edwards, W. (1983). Human cognitive capabilities, representativeness, and ground rules for research. In P. Humphreys, O. Svenson, & A. Vari (Eds.), *Analysing and aiding decision processes* (pp. 507–513). Amsterdam: North-Holland.

Ehsani, S. (2017). *Factor momentum and the momentum factor*. Available at SSRN: https://ssrn.com/abstract=3014521. Accessed 23 Oct 2017.

Elgammal, M. M., & McMillan, D. G. (2014). Value premium and default risk. *Journal of Asset Management, 15*, 48–61.

Elton, E. J., & Gruber, M. J. (1995). *Modern portfolio theory and investment analysis*. Hoboken: John Wiley & Sons.

Elton, E. J., Gruber, M. J., Das, S., & Hlavka, M. (1993). Efficiency with costly information: A reinterpretation of evidence from managed portfolios. *Review of Financial Studies, 6*(1), 1–22.

Erb, C. B., Harvey, C. R., & Viskanta, T. E. (1995). Country risk and global equity selection. *Journal of Portfolio Management, 21*(2), 74–83.

Erb, C. B., Harvey, C. R., & Viskanta, T. E. (1996a). Expected returns and volatility in 135 countries. *Journal of Portfolio Management, 22*(3), 46–58.

Erb, C. B., Harvey, C. R., & Viskanta, T. E. (1996b). Political risk, economic risk, and financial risk. *Financial Analyst Journal, 52*(6), 29–46.

Estrada, J. (2008). Fundamental indexation and international diversification. *Journal of Portfolio Management, 34*(3), 93–109.

Evans, A., & Schmitz, C. (2015). *Value, size and momentum on equity indices – A likely example of selection bias* (WINTON Global Investment Management working paper). Available at https://www.wintoncapital.com/assets/documents/research-papers/ValueSizeMomentumonEquityIndices2015-09-07.pdf. Accessed 11 Nov 2015.

Faber, M. T. (2010). *Relative strength strategies for investing*. Available at SSRN: http://ssrn.com/abstract=1585517 or https://doi.org/10.2139/ssrn.1585517. Accessed 21 Oct 2015.

Fairfield, P. M. (2003). Accrued earnings and growth: Implications for future profitability and market mispricing. *Accounting Review, 58*, 353–371.

Falkenstein, E. G. (1994). *Mutual funds, idiosyncratic variance, and asset returns* (PhD thesis). Northwestern University. Available at http://www.researchgate.net/publication/269698051. Accessed 25 Oct 2015.

Falkenstein, E. (1996). Preferences for stock characteristics as revealed by mutual fund portfolio holdings. *Journal of Finance, 51*(1), 111–135.

Falkenstein, E. G. (2009). *Risk and return in general: Theory and evidence*. Available at SSRN: http://ssrn.com/abstract=1420356 or https://doi.org/10.2139/ssrn.1420356. Accessed 28 Oct 2015.

Falkenstein, E. G. (2012). *The missing risk premium: Why low volatility investing works*. CreateSpace Independent Publishing Platform.

Fama, E. F. (1970). Efficient capital markets: A review of theory and empirical work. *Journal of Finance, 25*(2), 383–417.

Fama, E. F., & Blume, M. E. (1966). Filter rules and stock market trading. *Journal of Business, 39*(1), 226–241.

Fama, E. F., & French, K. R. (1992). The cross-section of expected returns. *Journal of Finance, 47*, 427–466.

Fama, E. F., & French, K. R. (1993). Common risk factors in the returns on stocks and bonds. *Journal of Financial Economics, 33*, 3–56. https://doi.org/10.1016/0304-405X(93)90023-5.

Fama, E. F., & French, K. R. (1996). Multifactor explanations of asset pricing anomalies. *Journal of Finance, 51*(1), 55–84.

Fama, E. F., & French, K. R. (1998). Value versus growth: The international evidence. *Journal of Finance, 53*(6), 1975–1999.

Fama, E. F., & French, K. R. (2006). Profitability, investment and average returns. *Journal of Financial Economics, 82*, 491–518.

Fama, E. F., & French, K. R. (2008). Dissecting anomalies. *Journal of Finance, 63*(4), 1653–1678.

Fama, E. F., & French, K. R. (2012). Size, value, and momentum in international stock returns. *Journal of Financial Economics, 105*(3), 457–472.

Fama, E. F., & French, K. R. (2015). A five-factor asset pricing model. *Journal of Financial Economics, 116*(1), 1–22. https://doi.org/10.1016/j.jfineco.2014.10.010.

Fama, E. F., & MacBeth, J. D. (1973). Risk, return and equilibrium: Empirical tests. *Journal of Political Economy, 81*(3), 607–636.

Fama, E. F., Fisher, L., Jensen, M. C., & Roll, R. (1969). The adjustment of stock prices to new information. *International Economic Review, 10*(1), 1–21. https://doi.org/10.2307/2525569.

Fan, S., Opsal, S., & Yu, L. (2015). Equity anomalies and idiosyncratic risk around the world. *Multinational Finance Journal, 19*(1), 33–75.

Feng, Z., Price, S. M., & Sirmans, C. F. (2014). The relation between momentum and drift: Industry-level evidence from equity Real Estate Investment Trusts (REITs). *Journal of Real Estate Research, 36*(3), 407.

Fernandez-Perez, A., Fuertes, A.-M., & Miffre, J. (2014). *Is idiosyncratic volatility priced in commodity futures markets?* Available at SSRN: http://ssrn.com/abstract=2120587 or https://doi.org/10.2139/ssrn.2120587. Accessed 24 Oct 2015.

Fernandez-Perez, A., Frijns, B., Fuertes, A.-M., & Miffre, J. (2017, forthcoming). The skewness of commodity futures returns. *Journal of Banking and Finance*. Available at SSRN: https://ssrn.com/abstract=2671165 or https://doi.org/10.2139/ssrn.2671165. Accessed 13 Oct 2017.

Ferrer-i-Carbonell, A. (2005). Income and well-being: An empirical analysis of the comparison income effect. *Journal of Public Economics, 89*(5–6), 997–1019.

Ferson, W. E., & Harvey, C. R. (1994). Sources of risk and expected returns in global equity markets. *Journal of Banking and Finance, 18*, 775–803.

Ferson, W. E., & Schadt, R. W. (1996). Measuring fund strategy and performance in changing economic conditions. *Journal of Finance, 51*(2), 425–461.

Fink, J., Fink, K., & He, H. (2010). Idiosyncratic volatility measures and expected return. *Financial Management, 41*(3), 519–553.

Fischhoff, B., Slovic, P., & Lichtenstein, S. (1977). Knowing with certainty: The appropriateness of extreme confidence. *Journal of Experimental Psychology: Human Perception and Performance, 3*(4), 552–564.

Fong, W. M., & Toh, B. (2014). Investor sentiment and the MAX effect. *Journal of Banking and Finance, 46*(1), 190–201. https://doi.org/10.1016/j.jbankfin.2014.05.006.

Forner, C., & Marhuenda, J. (2003). Contrarian and momentum strategies in the Spanish stock market. *European Financial Management, 9*(1), 67–88.

Forsythe, R., Nelson, F., Neumann, G., & Wright, J. (1992). Anatomy of an experimental stock market. *American Economic Review, 82*, 1142–1161.

Francis, J. C. (1990). *Investments: Analysis and management*. New York: McGraw Hill Higher Education.

Frank, R. H. (2011). *The Darwin economy: Liberty, competition, and the common good*. Princeton: Princeton University Press.

Frazzini, A. (2006). The disposition effect and underreaction to news. *Journal of Finance, 61*(4), 2017–2046.

Frazzini, A., & Pedersen, L. H. (2014). Betting against beta. *Journal of Financial Economics, 111*, 1–25. https://doi.org/10.1016/j.jfineco.2013.10.005.

French, K. R. (1980). Stock returns and the weekend effect. *Journal of Financial Economics, 8*(1), 55–69.

French, C. W. (2003). The treynor capital asset pricing model. *Journal of Investment Management, 1*(2), 60–72.

Frieder, L. (2008). Investor and price response to patterns in earnings surprises. *Journal of Financial Markets, 11*, 259–283.

Friend, I., & Blume, M. (1970). Measurement of portfolio performance under uncertainty. *American Economic Review, 60*, 561–575.

Fritzmeier, L. H. (1936). Relative price fluctuations of industrial stocks in different price groups. *Journal of Business, 9*(2), 133–154.

Fu, F. (2009). Idiosyncratic risk and the cross-section of expected returns. *Journal of Financial Economics, 91*(1), 24–37.

Fuertes, A. M., Miffre, J., & Rallis, G. (2010). Tactical allocation in commodity futures markets: Combining momentum and term structure signals. *Journal of Banking and Finance, 34*, 2530–2548.

Fuertes, A. M., Miffre, J., & Fernández-Pérez, A. (2015). Commodity strategies based on momentum, term structure and idiosyncratic volatility. *Journal of Futures Markets, 35*(3), 274–297.

Fung, W., & Hsieh, D. A. (1997). Survivorship bias and investment style in the returns of CTAs. *Journal of Portfolio Management, 24*(1), 30–41.

Gali, J. (1994). Keeping up with the Joneses: Consumption externalities, portfolio choice, and asset prices. *Journal of Money, Credit and Banking, 26*(1), 1–8.

Gama, P. M., & Viera, E. F. S. (2013). Another look at the holiday effect. *Applied Financial Economics, 23*(20), 1623–1633. https://doi.org/10.1080/09603107.2013.8426384.

Garcia, R., Mantilla-Garcia, D., & Martellini, L. (2014). A model-free measure of aggregate idiosyncratic volatility and the prediction of market returns. *Quantitative Analysis, 49*(5–6), 1133–1165. https://doi.org/10.1017/S0022109014000489.

Garlappi, L., & Song, Z. (2013). *Can investment shocks explain value premium and momentum profits?* (Working paper). Available at http://finance.sauder.ubc.ca/~garlappi/Papers/IShockReturn_Dec_10.pdf. Accessed 13 Oct 2015.

Garleanu, N., & Pedersen, L. H. (2007). Liquidity and risk management. *American Economic Review, 97*, 193–197.

Garleanu, N., Pedersen, L. H., & Poteshman, A. M. (2009). Demand-based option pricing. *Review of Financial Studies, 22*(10), 4259–4299.

Gartley, H. M. (1935). *Profits in the stock market.* Pomeroy: Lambert Gann Publishing.

Gartley, H. M. (1945). Relative velocity statistics: Their application in portfolio analysis. *Financial Analyst Journal, 51*(1), 18–20.

Gebhardt, W. R., Hvidkjaer, S., & Swaminathan, B. (2005). Stock and bond market interaction: Does momentum spill over? *Journal of Financial Economics, 75*(3), 651–690.

Geczy, C., & Samonov, M. (2016). Two centuries of price-return momentum. *Financial Analysts Journal, 72*(5), 32–56. https://doi.org/10.2469/faj.v72.n5.1.

George, T. J., & Hwang, C.-Y. (2004). The 52-week high and momentum investing. *Journal of Finance, 59*, 2145–2176.

George, T. J., & Hwang, C.-Y. (2007). Long-term return reversals: Overreaction or taxes? *Journal of Finance, 62*(6), 2865–2896.

George, T. J., & Hwang, C. Y. (2010). A resolution of the distress risk and leverage puzzles in the cross section of stock returns. *Journal of Financial Economics, 96*, 56–79.

Georgopoulou, A., & Wang, G. J. (2016, in press). The trend is your friend: Time-series momentum strategies across equity and commodity markets. *Review of Finance*. Available at SSRN: http://ssrn.com/abstract=2618243. Accessed 11 Sept 2017.

Gharaibeh, O. K. (2015). Long-term contrarian profits in the Middle East market indices. *Research Journal of Finance and Accounting, 6*(16). Available at SSRN: https://ssrn.com/abstract=2684807. Accessed 23 Oct 2017.

Ghysel, E., Plazzi, A., & Valkanov, R. (2011). *Conditional skewness of stock market returns in developed and emerging markets and its economic fundamentals* (Working paper). Available at http://www.unc.edu/~eghysels/papers/GPV_Oct_6_2011_EG.pdf. Accessed 14 Oct 2017.

Gibbons, M. R., & Hess, P. (1981). Day of the week effects and asset returns. *Journal of Business, 54*(4), 579–596.

Gilovich, T., Vallone, R., & Tversky, A. (1985). The hot hand in basketball: On the misperception of random sequences. *Cognitive Psychology, 17*, 295–314.

Goebel, P. R., Harrison, D. M., Mercer, J. M., & Whitby, R. J. (2012). REIT momentum and characteristic-related REIT Returns. *Journal of Real Estate Finance and Economics, 47*(3), 564–581.

Goetzman, W., & Kumar, A. (2008). Equity portfolio diversification. *Review of Finance, 12*(3), 433–463. https://doi.org/10.1093/rof/rfn005.

Goodman, D. A., & Peavy, J. W., III. (1986). The low price effect: Relationship with other stock market anomalies. *Review of Business and Economics Research, 22*(1), 18–37.

Gorton, G. B., Hayashi, F., & Rouwenhorst, K. G. (2013). The fundamentals of commodity futures returns. *Review of Finance, 17*, 35–105.

Goyal, A., & Jegadeesh, N. (2017). *Cross-sectional and time-series tests of return predictability: What is the difference?* (Swiss Finance Institute research paper No. 15-13). Available at SSRN: https://ssrn.com/abstract=2610288 or https://doi.org/10.2139/ssrn.2610288. Accessed 23 Oct 2017.

Goyal, A., & Santa-Clara, P. (2003). Idiosyncratic risk matters! *Journal of Finance, 58*(3), 975–1008.

Goyal, A., & Wahal, S. (2015). Is momentum and echo? *Journal of Financial and Quantitative Analysis, 50*(6), 1237–1267. https://doi.org/10.1017/S0022109015000575.

Graham, J. R. (1999). Herding among investment newsletters: Theory and evidence. *Journal of Finance, 54*(1), 237–268.

Green, J., Hand, J. R. M., & Zhang, F. (2016). *The characteristics that provide independent information about average U.S. monthly stock returns*. Available at SSRN: https://ssrn.com/abstract=2262374 or https://doi.org/10.2139/ssrn.2262374. Accessed 23 Oct 2017.

Griffin, J. M. (2002). Are the Fama and French factors global or country specific? *Review of Financial Studies, 15*, 783–803.

Griffin, J. M., & Lemmon, M. L. (2002). Book-to-market equity, distress risk, and stock returns. *Journal of Finance, 57*, 2317–2336.

Griffin, J. M., Ji, X., & Martin, S. J. (2003). Momentum investing and business cycle risk: Evidence from pole to pole. *Journal of Finance, 58*(6), 2515–2547.

Griffin, J., Ji, X., & Martin, S. J. (2005). Global momentum strategies: A portfolio perspective. *Journal of Portfolio Management, 31*(2), 23–39.

Grinblatt, M., & Keloharju, M. (2000). The investment behavior and preference of various investor types: A study of Finland's unique data set. *Journal of Financial Economics, 55*(1), 43–67.

Grinblatt, M., & Keloharju, M. (2001). What makes investors trade? *Journal of Finance, 56*(2), 589–616.

Grinblatt, M., & Moskowitz, T. M. (2004). Predicting stock price movements from past returns: The role of consistency and tax-loss selling. *Journal of Financial Economics, 71*, 541–579.

Grinblatt, M., & Titman, S. (1989). Portfolio performance evaluation: Old issues and new insights. *Review of Financial Studies, 2*, 393–421.

Grobys, K. (2015, forthcoming). Another look at momentum crashes: Momentum in the European monetary union. *Applied Economics*. Available at SSRN: http://ssrn.com/abstract=2564488 or https://doi.org/10.2139/ssrn.2564488. Accessed 11 Nov 2015.

Grobys, K. (2016). Another look at momentum crashes: Momentum in the European monetary union. *Applied Economics, 48*(19), 1759–1766.

Grobys, K., Heinonen, J.-P., & Kolari, J. W. (2016). *Is currency momentum driven by global economic risk?* Available at SSRN: http://ssrn.com/abstract=2619146 or https://doi.org/10.2139/ssrn.2619146. Accessed 28 Aug 2015.

Grossman, S., & Miller, M. H. (1988). Liquidity and market structure. *Journal of Finance, 43*, 617–633.

Grossman, S. J., & Stiglitz, J. E. (1976). Information and competitive price systems. *American Economic Review, 66*, 246–253.

Grossman, S. J., & Stiglitz, J. E. (1980). On the impossibility of informationally efficient markets. *American Economic Review, 70*, 393–408.

Grundy, B. D., & Martin, J. S. (2001). Understanding the nature of the risks and the sources of the rewards to momentum investing. *Review of Financial Studies, 14*(1), 29–78.

Gu, F. (2005). Innovation, future earnings, and market efficiency. *Journal of Accounting, Auditing and Finance, 20*, 385–418.

Guilmin, G. (2015). *The effective combination of risk-based strategies with momentum and trend following*. Available at SSRN: http://ssrn.com/abstract=2556747 or https://doi.org/10.2139/ssrn.2556747. Accessed 11 Oct 2015.

Hahn, J., & Lee, H. (2009). Financial constraints, debt capacity, and the cross-section of stock returns. *Journal of Finance, 64*, 891–921.

Haller, G. (1965). *The Haller theory of stock market trends.* West Palm Beach: Gilber Haller.

Hambusch, G., Hong, K. J., & Webster, E. (2015). Enhancing risk-adjusted return using time series momentum in sovereign bonds. *Journal of Fixed Income, 25*(1), 96–111. https://doi.org/10.3905/jfi.2015.25.1.096.

Hameed, A., & Mian, G. M. (2015). Industries and stock return reversals. *Journal of Financial and Quantitative Analysis, 50*(1–2), 89–117.

Han, K. C. (1995). The effects of reverse splits on the liquidity of the stock. *Journal of Financial and Quantitative Analysis, 30*(1), 159–169. https://doi.org/10.2307/2331258.

Han, Y., & Lesmond, D. (2011). Liquidity biases and the pricing of cross-sectional idiosyncratic volatility. *Review of Financial Studies, 24*, 1590–1629.

Hanauer, M. (2014). Is Japan different? Evidence on momentum and market dynamics. *International Review of Finance, 14*(1), 141–160.

Hansson, B. (2004). Human capital and stock returns: Is the value premium an approximation for return on human capital? *Journal of Business Finance & Accounting, 31*(3–4), 333–358.

Hao, Y., Chu, H.-H., Ho, K.-Y., & Ko, K.-C. (2016). The 52-week high and momentum in the Taiwan stock market: Anchoring or recency biases? *International Review of Economics & Finance, 43*, 121–138. https://doi.org/10.1016/j.iref.2015.10.035.

Harris, L. (1986). A transaction data study of weekly and intradaily patterns in stock returns. *Journal of Financial Economics, 16*(1), 99–117.

Harvey, C. (2000). The drivers of expected returns in international markets. *Emerging Markets Quarterly*, 32–49. Available at SSRN: https://ssrn.com/abstract=795385 or https://doi.org/10.2139/ssrn.795385. Accessed 13 Oct 2017.

Harvey, C. R. (2004). Country risk components, the cost of capital, and returns in emerging markets. In S. Wilkin (ed.), *Country and political risk: Practical insights for global finance* (pp. 71–102). London: Risk Books. Available at SSRN: http://ssrn.com/abstract=620710 or https://doi.org/10.2139/ssrn.620710. Accessed 21 Sept 2015.

Harvey, C. R., Liu, Y., & Zhu, H. (2016). … and the cross-section of expected returns. *Review of Financial Studies, 29*(1), 5–68. https://doi.org/10.1093/rfs/hhv059.

Haug, M., & Hirschey, M. (2006). The January effect. *Financial Analyst Journal, 62*(5), 78–88.

Haugen, R. A., & Baker, N. (1991). The efficient market inefficiency of capitalization-weighted stock portfolios. *Journal of Portfolio Management, 17*(1), 35–40.

Haugen, R. A., & Baker, N. L. (1996). Commonality in the determinants of expected stock returns. *Journal of Financial Economics, 41*(3), 401–439.

Haugen, R. A., & Heins, A. J. (1975). Risk and the rate of return on financial assets: Some old wine in new bottles. *Journal of Financial and Quantitative Analysis, 10*(5), 775–784.

Haugen, R. A., & Lakonishok, J. (1988). *The incredible January effect: The stock market's unsolved mystery*. Homewood: Dow Jones-Irwin.

Heaton, J. C., & Lucas, D. J. (2000). Portfolio choice and asset prices: The importance of entrepreneurial risk. *Journal of Finance, 55*(3), 1163–1198.

Heisler, J. (1994). Loss aversion in a futures market: An empirical test. *Review of Futures Markets, 13*(3), 793–822.

Hellwig, M. (1982). Rational expectations equilibrium with conditioning on past prices: A mean-variance example. *Journal of Economic Theory, 26*, 279–312.

Henriksson, R. D. (1984). Market timing and mutual fund performance: An empirical investigation. *Journal of Business, 57*(1), 73–96.

Henriksson, R. D., & Merton, R. C. (1981). On market timing and investment performance II: Statistical procedures for evaluating forecasting skills. *Journal of Business, 54*(4), 513–533.

Hensel, C. R., & Ziemba, W. T. (1996). Investment results from exploiting turn-of-the-month effects. *Journal of Portfolio Management, 22*(3), 17–23.

Heston, S. L., & Sadka, R. (2008). Seasonality in the cross-section of stock returns. *Journal of Financial Economics, 87*(2), 418–445. https://doi.org/10.1016/j.jfineco.2007.02.003.

Heston, S. L., & Sadka, R. (2010). Seasonality in the cross-section of stock returns: The international evidence. *Journal of Financial and Quantitative Analysis, 45*(5), 1133–1160.

Hirshleifer, D., Hsu, P.-H., & Li, D. (2013). Innovative efficiency and stock returns. *Journal of Financial Economics, 107*, 632–654.

Hirshleifer, D. A., Jiang, D., & Men, Y. (2017). *Mood beta and seasonalities in stock returns*. Available at SSRN: https://ssrn.com/abstract=2880257. Accessed 23 Oct 2017.

Ho, H. G., & Sraer, D. A. (2015, forthcoming). Speculative betas. *Journal of Finance*. Available at SSRN: https://ssrn.com/abstract=1967462 or https://doi.org/10.2139/ssrn.1967462. Accessed 23 Oct 2017.

Hong, H., & Stein, J. (1999). A unified theory of underreaction, momentum trading, and overreaction in asset markets. *Journal of Finance, 54*(6), 2143–2184.

Hong, H. G., & Yu, J. (2007). *Gone fishin': Seasonality in trading activity and asset prices*. Available at SSRN: https://ssrn.com/abstract=676743 or https://doi.org/10.2139/ssrn.676743. Accessed 23 Oct 2017.

Hong, H., Lim, T., & Stein, J. C. (2000). Bad news travels slowly: Size, analyst coverage, and the profitability of momentum strategies. *Journal of Finance, 55*(1), 265–295.

Hou, K., & Loh, R. (2016). Have we solved the idiosyncratic volatility puzzle? *Journal of Financial Economics, 121*(1), 167–194. https://doi.org/10.1016/j.jfineco.2016.02.013.

Hou, K., Peng, L., & Xiong, W. (2006). *R^2 and price inefficiency* (Research in Financial Economics in its series working paper series with number 2006-23). Available at http://www.cob.ohio-state.edu/fin/dice/papers/2006/2006-23.pdf. Accessed 9 Sept 2017.

Hou, K., Karolyi, G. A., & Kho, B. C. (2011). What factors drive global stock returns? *Review of Financial Studies, 24*(8), 2527–2574. https://doi.org/10.1093/rfs/hhr013.

Hou, K., Xue, C., & Zhang, L. (2015). Digesting anomalies: An investment approach. *Review of Financial Studies, 28*(3), 650–705. https://doi.org/10.1093/rfs/hhu068.

Hou, K., Xue, C., & Zhang, L. (2017). *Replicating anomalies* (Fisher College of Business working paper No. 2017-03-010; Charles A. Dice Center working paper No. 2017-10). Available at SSRN: https://ssrn.com/abstract=2961979 or https://doi.org/10.2139/ssrn.2961979. Accessed 30 Sept 2017.

Houweling, P., & van Zundert, J. (2014). *Factor investing in the corporate bond market.* Available at SSRN: http://ssrn.com/abstract=2516322 or https://doi.org/10.2139/ssrn.2516322. Accessed 25 Oct 2015.

Houweling, P., & van Zundert, J. (2017). Factor investing in the corporate bond market. *Financial Analysts Journal, 73*(2), 100–115. https://doi.org/10.2469/faj.v73.n2.1.

Houweling, P., Beekhuizen, P., Bus, S., Haesen, D., Kwaak, P., Verberk, V., & Wang, R. (2012). *The low risk anomaly in credits* (Robeco Research note). Available at https://www.robeco.com/images/the-low-risk-anomaly-in-credits.pdf. Accessed 24 Oct 2015.

Hsieh, H.-H., & Hodnett, K. (2011). Tests of overreaction hypothesis and the timing of mean reversals on the JSE Securities Exchange (JSE): The case of South Africa. *Journal of Applied Finance and Banking, 1*(1), 107–130.

Hsu, J. C., & Campolo, C. (2006). New frontiers in index investing: An examination of fundamental indexation. *Journal of Indexes, 58*, 32–37.

Huang, D., & Miao, J. (2016). *Oil prices and the cross-section of stock returns.* Available at SSRN: https://ssrn.com/abstract=2847514. Accessed 23 Oct 2017.

Huang, W., Liu, Q., Rhee, S. G., & Zhang, L. (2010). Return reversals, idiosyncratic risk, and expected returns. *Review of Financial Studies, 23*, 147–168.

Hueng, C. J., & Yau, R. (2013). Country-specific idiosyncratic risk and global equity index returns. *International Review of Economics & Finance, 25*, 325–337.

Hühn, H. L., & Scholz, H. (2017). *Alpha momentum and price momentum.* Available at SSRN: https://ssrn.com/abstract=2287848 or https://doi.org/10.2139/ssrn.2287848. Accessed 23 Oct 2017.

Hung, K., & Glascock, J. L. (2010). Volatilities and momentum returns in real estate investment trusts. *Journal of Real Estate Finance and Economics, 41*(2), 126–149. https://doi.org/10.1007/s11146-008-9165-8.

Hurst, B. K., Ooi, Y. H., & Pedersen, L. H. (2013). Demystifying managed futures. *Journal of Investment Management, 11*(3), 42–58.

Hurst, B., Ooi, Y. H., & Pedersen, L. H. (2017). *A century of evidence on trend-following investing*. Available at SSRN: https://ssrn.com/abstract=2993026. Accessed 23 Oct 2017.

Husain, F. (1998). A seasonality in the Pakistani equity market: The Ramadhan effect. *Pakistani Development Review, 37*(1), 77–81.

Hwang, S., & Lu, C. (2008). *Is share price relevant?* (Working paper). Available at SSRN: https://ssrn.com/abstract=1341790 or https://doi.org/10.2139/ssrn.1341790. Accessed 18 Oct 2017.

Hwang, J.-K., Dimkpah, Y., & Ogwu, A. I. (2012). Do reverse stock splits benefit long-term shareholders. *International Advances in Economic Research, 18*(4), 439–449. https://doi.org/10.1007/s11294-012-9370-3.

Ikenberry, D., Rankine, G., & Stice, E. (1996). What do stock split really signal? *Journal of Financial and Quantitative Analysis, 31*, 357–337.

Ilmanen, A. (2011). *Expected returns: An investor's guide to harvesting market rewards*. Hoboken: Wiley.

Ilmanen, A., & Kizer, J. (2012). The death of diversification has been greatly exaggerated. *Journal of Portfolio Management, 38*(3), 15–27. https://doi.org/10.2469/dig.v42.n4.3.

Ilmanen, A., Nielsen, L. N., & Chandra, S. (2015). *Are defensive stocks expensive? A closer look at value spreads* (AQR white paper). Available at https://www.aqr.com/library/aqr-publications/are-defensive-stocks-expensive-a-closer-look-at-value-spreads. Accessed 31 Oct 2017.

Iqbal, J., & Azher, S. (2014). Value-at-risk and expected stock returns: Evidence from Pakistan. *Lahore Journal of Economics, 19*(2), 71–100.

Iqbal, J., Azher, S., & Ijaz, A. (2013). Predictive ability of value-at-risk methods: Evidence from the Karachi Stock Exchange-100 Index. *IUP Journal of Financial Risk Management, 10*(1), 26–40.

Irwin, S. H., & Park, C. H. (2008). The profitability of technical analysis in commodity markets. In F. J. Fabozzi, R. Fus, & D. G. Kaiser (Eds.), *The handbook of commodity investing*. Hoboken: John Wiley & Sons.

Irwin, S. H., Zulauf, C. R., & Jackson, T. E. (1996). Monte Carlo analysis of mean reversion in commodity futures prices. *American Journal of Agricultural Economics, 78*(2), 387–399.

Ismail, E. (2012). Do momentum and contrarian profits exist in the Egyptian stock market? *International Research Journal of Finance and Economics, 87*, 48–72.

Israel, R., & Moskowitz, T. J. (2013). The role of shorting, firm size, and time on market anomalies. *Journal of Financial Economics, 108*(2), 275–301.

Israel, R., Palhares, D., & Richardson, S. A. (2016). *Common factors in corporate bond and bond fund returns*. Available at SSRN: https://ssrn.com/abstract=2576784 or https://doi.org/10.2139/ssrn.2576784. Accessed 23 Oct 2017.

Israelsen, C. L. (2005). A refinement to the Sharpe ratio and information ratio. *Journal of Asset Management, 5*(6), 423–427.

Ivkovic, Z., & Weisbenner, S. (2009). Individual investor mutual fund flows. *Journal of Financial Economics, 92*(2), 223–237.

Jacobs, H. (2015). What explains the dynamics of 100 anomalies? *Journal of Banking & Finance, 57*, 65–85. https://doi.org/10.1016/j.jbankfin.2015.03.006.

Jacobs, H. (2016). Market maturity and mispricing. *Journal of Financial Economics, 122*(2), 270–287. https://doi.org/10.1016/j.jfineco.2016.01.030.

Jacobs, H., & Müller, S. (2017a). *Anomalies across the globe: Once public, no longer existent?* Available at SSRN: https://ssrn.com/abstract=2816490 or https://doi.org/10.2139/ssrn.2816490. Accessed 23 Oct 2017.

Jacobs, H., & Müller, S. (2017b). *...and nothing else matters? On the dimensionality and predictability of international stock returns*. Available at SSRN: https://ssrn.com/abstract=2845306 or https://doi.org/10.2139/ssrn.2845306. Accessed 23 Oct 2017.

Jacobs, H., Regele, T., & Weber, M. (2016). *Expected skewness and momentum*. Available at SSRN: https://ssrn.com/abstract=2600014 or https://doi.org/10.2139/ssrn.2600014. Accessed 11 Sept 2017.

Jacobsen, B., & Zhang, C. Y. (2014). *The Halloween indicator, 'Sell in May and go away': An even bigger puzzle*. Available at SSRN: http://ssrn.com/abstract=2154873 or https://doi.org/10.2139/ssrn.2154873. Accessed 23 Oct 2017.

Jacobsen, B., Mamun, A., & Visaltanachoti, N. (2005). *Seasonal, size and value anomalies*. Available at SSRN: https://ssrn.com/abstract=784186 or https://doi.org/10.2139/ssrn.784186. Accessed 23 Oct 2017.

Jaffarian, E. (2009). Managed futures. In K. Wilkens-Christopher (Ed.), *CAIA level II. Advanced core topics in alternative investments*. Hoboken: John Wiley & Sons.

Jaffe, J., & Westerfield, R. (1985). The week-end effect in common stock returns: The international evidence. *Journal of Finance, 40*(2), 433–454.

Jagannathan, R., & Ma, T. (2003). Risk reduction in large portfolios: Why imposing the wrong constrains helps. *Journal of Finance, 58*(4), 1651–1684.

Jank, S. (2014). *Specialized human capital, unemployment risk, and the value premium* (Working paper). Available at SSRN: http://ssrn.com/abstract=2526119 or https://doi.org/10.2139/ssrn.2526119. Accessed 15 Sept 2017.

Janssen, L. (2014). *The effect of credit risk on stock returns.* Available at http://arno.uvt.nl/show.cgi?fid=135567. Accessed 15 Sept 2015.

Jegadeesh, N. (1990). Evidence of predictable behavior of security returns. *Journal of Finance, 45*, 881–898.

Jegadeesh, N. (1991). Seasonality in stock price mean reversion: Evidence from U.S. and the U.K. *Journal of Finance, 46*(4), 1427–1444. https://doi.org/10.1111/j.1540-6261.1991.tb04624.x.

Jegadeesh, N., & Titman, S. (1993). Returns to buying winners and selling losers: Implications for stock market efficiency. *Journal of Finance, 48*, 65–91.

Jegadeesh, N., & Titman, S. (1995). Short-horizon return reversals and the bid-ask spread. *Journal of Financial Intermediation, 4*, 116–132.

Jegadeesh, N., & Titman, S. (2001). Profitability of momentum strategies: An evaluation of alternative explanations. *Journal of Finance, 56*(2), 599–720.

Jegadeesh, N., Kim, J., Krische, S., & Lee, C. M. C. (2004). Analyzing the analysts: When do recommendations add value? *Journal of Finance, 59*(3), 1083–1124.

Jensen, M. C. (1978). Some anomalous evidence regarding market efficiency. *Journal of Financial Economics, 6*(2–3), 95–101.

Jensen, M. C., & Benington, G. A. (1970). Random walks and technical theories: Some additional evidence. *Journal of Finance, 25*(2), 469–482.

Jensen, M. C., Black, F., & Scholes, M. S. (1972). The capital asset pricing model: Some empirical tests. In M. C. Jensen (Ed.), *Studies in the theory of capital markets.* New York: Praeger Publishers.

Ji, X., Martin, S., & Yao, Y. (2017, in press). Macroeconomic risk and seasonality in momentum profits. *Journal of Financial Markets.* https://doi.org/10.1016/j.finmar.2017.04.002.

Jiang, G., Lee, C. M., & Zhang, Y. (2005). Information uncertainty and expected returns. *Review of Accounting Studies, 10*, 185–221.

Jones, S. (1993). Another look at time varying risk and return in a long horizon contrarian trading strategy. *Journal of Financial Economics, 33*, 67–93.

Jostova, G., Nikolova, S., Philipov, A., & Stahel, C. W. (2013). Momentum in corporate bond returns. *Review of Financial Studies, 26*(7), 1649–1693.

Kaestner, M. (2006). Anomalous price behaviour following earnings surprises: Does representativeness cause overreaction? *Revue de l'Association Francaise de Finance, 27*, 5–31.

Kahneman, D. (2013). *Thinking, fast and slow.* New York: Farrar, Straus and Giroux.

Kahneman, D., & Tversky, A. (1972). Subjective probability: A judgment of representativeness. *Cognitive Psychology, 3*, 430–454.

Kalesnik, V. (2013). *Smart beta and the pendulum of mispricing* (Research affiliates white paper). Available at https://www.researchaffiliates.com/en_us/publications/articles/s_2013_09_smart-beta-and-the-pendulum-of-mispricing.html

Kamstra, M. J., Kramer, L. A., & Levi, M. D. (2003). *Winter blues: A SAD stock market cycle* (Federal Reserve Bank of Atlanta working paper No. 2002-13a; Sauder School of Business working paper). Available at SSRN: https://ssrn.com/abstract=208622 or https://doi.org/10.2139/ssrn.208622. Accessed 23 Oct 2017.

Kamstra, M. J., Kramer, L. A., Levi, M. D., & Wermers, R. (2017). Seasonal asset allocation: Evidence from mutual fund flows. *Journal of Financial and Quantitative Analysis, 52*(1), 71–109. https://doi.org/10.1017/S002210901600082X.

Kane, A. (1982). Skewness preference and portfolio choice. *Journal of Financial and Quantitative Analysis, 17*(1), 15–25.

Kang, C. O., & Kang, H. G. (2009). The effect of credit risk on stock returns. *Journal of Economic Research, 14*, 49–67.

Kapadia, N. (2006). *The next Microsoft? Skewness, idiosyncratic volatility, and expected returns.* Available at SSRN: http://ssrn.com/abstract=970120 or https://doi.org/10.2139/ssrn.970120. Accessed 28 Oct 2015.

Kaul, G., & Nimalendrum, M. (1990). Price reversals: Bid-ask errors or market overreaction. *Journal of Financial Economics, 28*, 67–93.

Kaustia, M. (2010). Disposition effect. In H. K. Baker & J. R. Nofsinger (Eds.), *Behavioral finance.* Hoboken: John Wiley & Sons, chapter 10.

Keim, D. (1983a). Size-related anomalies and stock return seasonality: Further empirical evidence. *Journal of Financial Economics, 12*, 13–32.

Keim, D. (1983b). Stock return seasonality and the size effect. *Journal of Financial Economics, 12*, 13–32.

Keim, D. B., & Stambaugh, R. F. (1984). A further investigation of the weekend effect in stock returns. *Journal of Finance, 39*(3), 819–835.

Keloharju, M., Linnainmaa, J. T., & Nyberg, P. (2016). Return seasonalities. *Journal of Finance, 71*(4), 1557–1590.

Khang, K., & King, T. D. (2004). Return reversals in the bond market: Evidence and causes. *Journal of Banking and Finance, 28*(3), 569–593.

Kim, D. (2012). Cross-asset style momentum. *Asia-Pacific Journal of Financial Studies, 41*(5), 610–636. https://doi.org/10.1111/j.2041-6156.2012.01084.x.

Kim, J., & Lee, C. (2017). *Idiosyncratic volatility and stock return predictability: Evidence from the Korean stock market.* Available at http://www.kafo.or.kr/board_common/file_download.asp?Board_Key=144&File_Key=226&flag=2. Accessed 6 Sept 2017.

Kim, C.-W., & Park, J. (1994). Holiday effects and stock returns: Further evidence. *Journal of Financial and Quantitative Analysis, 29*(1), 145–157.

Kim, M. J., Nelson, C. R., & Startz, R. (1991). Mean reversion in stock prices? A reappraisal of the empirical evidence. *Review of Economic Studies, 58*, 515–528.

Kim, S., Klein, A., & Rosenfeld, J. (2008). Return performance surrounding reverse stock splits: Can investors profit? *Financial Management, 37*(2), 173–192. https://doi.org/10.1111/j.1755-053x.2008.00009.x.

Kim, H., Arvind, M., & Petkevich, A. (2012). *Sources of momentum in bonds* (Mays Business School research paper No. 2012-40). Available at SSRN: http://ssrn.com/abstract=2054711 or https://doi.org/10.2139/ssrn.2054711. Accessed 20 Oct 2015.

Kim, A. Y., Tse, Y., & Wald, J. K. (2016). Time series momentum and volatility scaling. *Journal of Financial Markets, 30*, 103–124. https://doi.org/10.1016/j.finmar.2016.05.003.

Kimball, M. S. (1993). Standard risk aversion. *Econometrica, 61*(3), 589–611.

Klein, A., Rosenfeld, J., & Tucker, X. J. (2006). *Return performance surrounding reverse stock splits: Can investors profit?* http://www.efmaefm.org/0EFMAMEETINGS/EFMA%20ANNUAL%20MEETINGS/2006-Madrid/papers/568563_full.pdf

Knerr, I., & Pearl, P. L. (2008). Ketogenic diet: Stoking energy stores and still posing questions. *Experimental Neurology, 11*, 11–13.

Knight, J., Song, L., & Gunatilaka, R. (2009). Subjective well-being and its determinants in rural China. *China Economic Review, 20*(4), 635–649.

Kogan, L., & Papanikolaou, D. (2013). Firm characteristics and stock returns: The role of investment specific shocks. *Review of Financial Studies, 25*, 2718–2759.

Koski, J. (2007). Does volatility decrease after reverse stock splits? *Journal of Financial Research, 30*(2), 217–235.

Kothari, S. P., Shanken, J., & Sloan, R. (1995). Another look at the cross-section of expected stock returns. *Journal of Finance, 50*(1), 185–224.

Kraus, A., & Litzenberger, R. H. (1976). Skewness preference and the valuation of risk assets. *Journal of Finance, 31*(4), 1085–1100.

Kroencke, T. A., Schindler, F., & Schrimpf, A. (2013). International diversification benefits with foreign exchange investment styles. *Review of Finance, 18*(5), 1847–1883.

Kryzanowski, L., & Zhang, H. (1992). The contrarian investment strategy does not work in Canadian markets. *Journal of Financial and Quantitative Analysis, 27*(3), 383–395.

Kumar, A. (2009). Who gambles in the stock market? *Journal of Finance, 64*(4), 1889–1933.

Kumar, P. (2014). *Need for mean reversion in forecasting emerging market exchange rates*. Available at SSRN: https://ssrn.com/abstract=2547451 or https://doi.org/10.2139/ssrn.2547451. Accessed 23 Oct 2017.

Kumar, A., Page, J. K., & Spalt, O. G. (2011). Religious beliefs, gambling attitudes, and financial market outcomes. *Journal of Financial Economics, 102*(3), 671–708.

Kunkel, R. A., Compton, W. S., & Beyer, S. (2003). The turn-of-the-month effect still lives. *International Review of Financial Analysis, 12*(2), 207–221.

La Porta, R. (1996). Expectations and the cross-section of stock returns. *Journal of Finance, 51*(5), 1715–1742.

La Porta, R., Lakonishok, J., Shleifer, A., & Vishny, R. (1997). Good news for value stocks: Further evidence on market efficiency. *Journal of Finance, 52*(2), 859–874.

Lakonishok, J., & Maberly, E. (1990). The weekend effect: Trading patterns of individual and institutional investors. *Journal of Finance, 45*(1), 231–243.

Lakonishok, J., & Smidt, J. (1988). Are seasonal anomalies real? A ninety-year perspective. *Review of Financial Studies, 1*, 403–425.

Lakonishok, J., Schleifer, A., & Vishny, R. W. (1994). Contrarian investment, extrapolation, and risk. *Journal of Finance, 49*(5), 1541–1578.

Lambert, M., & Hubner, G. (2013). Comoment risk and stock returns. *Journal of Empirical Finance, 23*, 191–205. https://doi.org/10.1016/j.jempfin.2013.07.001.

Lamoureux, C., & Poon, P. (1987). The market reaction to splits. *Journal of Finance, 62*, 1347–1370.

Le Sourd, V. (2007). *Performance measurement for traditional investments. Literature survey* (Research paper). DHEC Risk and Asset Management Research Centre. Available online: http://www.edhec-risk.com/performance_and_style_analysis/perf_measurement/index_html/attachments/EDHEC%20Publi%20performance%20measurement%20for%20traditional%20investment.pdf. Accessed 16 Oct 2017.

Lee, J. B. T. (2008). *Higher idiosyncratic moments and the cross-section of expected stock returns* (Ph.D. thesis). University of Washington. Available at http://hdl.handle.net/2292/16213. Accessed 14 Oct 2017.

Lee, E., & Piqueira, N. (2017). Short selling around the 52-week and historical highs. *Journal of Financial Markets, 33*, 75–101. https://doi.org/10.1016/j.finmar.2016.03.001.

Lee, C. M., & Swaminathan, B. (2000). Price momentum and trading volume. *Journal of Finance, 55*, 2017–2069.

Lefevre, E. (2010). *Reminiscences of a stock operator: With new commentary and insights on the life and times of Jesse Livermore*. Hoboken: John Wiley & Sons.

Lehmann, B. N. (1990). Fads, martingales, and market efficiency. *Quarterly Journal of Economics, 105*(1), 1–28.

Lettau, M., & Ludvigson, S. (2001). Consumption, aggregate wealth, and expected stock returns. *Journal of Finance, 56*(3), 815–849.

Levine, A., & Pedersen, L. H. (2016). Which trend is your friend? *Financial Analysts Journal, 72*(3), 51–66. https://doi.org/10.2469/faj.v72.n3.3.

Levy, R. A. (1967). Relative strength as a criterion for investment selection. *Journal of Finance, 22*(4), 595–610.

Levy, R. A. (1968). *The relative strength concept of common stock price forecasting*. Larchmont: Investors Intelligence.

Levy, H. (1978). Equilibrium in an imperfect market: A constraint on the number of securities in the portfolio. *American Economic Review, 68*, 643–658.

Lhabitant, F. S. (2008). Commodity trading strategies: Examples of trading rules and signals from the CTA sector. In F. J. Fabozzi, R. Fuss, & D. G. Kaiser (Eds.), *The handbook of commodity investing*. Hoboken: John Wiley & Sons.

Li, F. W., & Wei, J. K. C. (2015). Momentum life cycle around the world: The roles of individualism and limits to arbitrage. In *Asian Finance Association (AsianFA) 2015 Conference Paper*. Available at SSRN: http://ssrn.com/abstract=2565305 or https://doi.org/10.2139/ssrn.2565305. Accessed 20 Oct 2015.

Liang, S. X., & Wei, K. C. J (2016). Volatility risk factors and stock returns around the world: Implications for multinational corporations. In *Asian Finance Association (AsFA) 2013 Conference*. Available at SSRN: https://ssrn.com/abstract=2217622 or https://doi.org/10.2139/ssrn.2217622. Accessed 23 Oct 2017.

Liew, J., & Vassalou, M. (2000). Can book-to-market, size and momentum be risk factors that predict economic growth? *Journal of Financial Economics, 57*, 221–245.

Lin, T.-C., & Liu, X. (2017, forthcoming). Skewness, individual investor preference, and the cross-section of stock returns. *Review of Finance*. Available at SSRN: https://ssrn.com/abstract=2676633 or https://doi.org/10.2139/ssrn.2676633. Accessed 23 Oct 2017.

Lin, H., Wu, C., & Zhou, G. (2017). *Does momentum exist in bonds of different ratings?* Available at SSRN: https://ssrn.com/abstract=2872382 or https://doi.org/10.2139/ssrn.2872382. Accessed 23 Oct 2017.

Lintner, J. (1965a). The valuation of risk assets and the selection of risky investments in stock portfolios and capital budgets. *Review of Economics and Statistics, 47*(1), 13–37.

Lintner, J. (1965b). Security prices, risk and maximal gains from diversification. *Journal of Finance, 20*(4), 587–615.

Liu, L. X., & Zhang, L. (2008a). Momentum profits, factor pricing, and macroeconomic risk. *Review of Financial Studies, 21*(6), 2417–2448.

Liu, N., & Zhang, L. (2008b). Is the value spread a useful predictor of returns? *Journal of Financial Markets, 11*(3), 199–227. https://doi.org/10.1016/j.finmar.2008.01.003.

Liu, M., Liu, Q., & Ma, T. (2011). The 52-week high momentum strategy in international stock markets. *Journal of International Money and Finance, 30*, 180–204.

Lo, A., & MacKinlay, C. (1990). Data-snooping biases in tests of financial asset pricing models. *Review of Financial Studies, 3*(3), 431–467.

Locke, P. R., & Mann, S. C. (2005). Professional trader discipline and trade disposition. *Journal of Financial Economics, 76*(2), 401–444.

Lord, C., Ross, L., & Lepper, M. (1979). Biased assimilation and attitude polarization: The effects of prior theories on subsequently considered evidence. *Journal of Personality and Social Psychology, 37*, 2098–2109.

Lou, D. (2014). Attracting investor attention through advertising. *Review of Financial Studies, 27*, 1797–1829.

Loughran, T. (1997). Book-to-market across firm size, exchange, and seasonality: Is there an effect? *Journal of Financial and Quantitative Analysis, 30*, 607–618. https://doi.org/10.2307/2331199.

Loughran, T., & Ritter, J. R. (1996). Long-term market overreaction: The effect of low-priced stocks. *Journal of Finance, 51*(5), 1959–1970. https://doi.org/10.1111/j.1540-6261.1996.tb05234.x.

Lu, Z., & Murray, S. (2017, in press). Bear beta. *Journal of Financial Economics*. Available at SSRN: https://ssrn.com/abstract=2871737 or https://doi.org/10.2139/ssrn.2871737. Accessed 25 Feb 2018.

Lubnau, T., & Todorova, N. (2015). Trading on mean-reversion in energy futures markets. *Energy Economics, 51*, 312–319. https://doi.org/10.1016/j.eneco.2015.06.018.

Lukac, L. P., Brorsen, B. W., & Irwin, S. H. (1988). A test of futures market disequilibrium using twelve different technical trading systems. *Applied Economics, 20*(5), 523–639.

Luttmer, E. (2005). Neighbors as negatives: Relative earnings and well-being. *Quarterly Journal of Economics, 120*(3), 963–1002.

Luu, B. V., & Yu, P. (2012). Momentum in government-bond markets. *Journal of Fixed Income., 22*(2), 72–79.

Maberly, E. D., & Pierce, R. M. (2011). *Reconciling theory with post-reverse split return patterns: Empirical findings based on recent events*. Available at SSRN: http://ssrn.com/abstract=1825505 or https://doi.org/10.2139/ssrn.1825505. Accessed 23 Oct 2017.

Maheshwari, S., & Dhankar, R. S. (2015). The long-run return reversal effect: A re-examination in the Indian stock market. *Journal of Business Inquiry, 14*(2). Available at https://uvu.edu/woodbury/docs/jbi-09-15-208.pdf

Malin, M., & Bornholt, G. (2013). Long-term return reversal: Evidence from international market indices. *Journal of International Financial Markets, Institutions and Money, 25*, 1–17. https://doi.org/10.1016/j.intfin.2013.01.002.

Malkiel, B., & Xu, Y. (1997). Risk and return revisited. *Journal of Portfolio Management, 23*(3), 9–14. https://doi.org/10.3905/jpm.1997.409608.

Malkiel, B., & Xu, Y. (2004). *Idiosyncratic risk and security returns* (AFA 2001 New Orleans meetings). Available at SSRN: http://ssrn.com/abstract=255303 or https://doi.org/10.2139/ssrn.255303. Accessed 25 Oct 2015.

Markowitz, H. (1952). Portfolio selection. *Journal of Finance, 7*(1), 77–91. https://doi.org/10.1111/j.1540-6261.1952.tb01525.x.

Marrett, G. J., & Worthington, A. C. (2009). An empirical note on the holiday effect in the Australian stock market, 1996–2006. *Applied Economic Letters, 16*(17), 1769–1772.

Marshall, B. R., & Visaltanachoti, N. (2010). The other January effect: Evidence against market efficiency? *Journal of Banking & Finance, 34*(10), 2413–2424. https://doi.org/10.1016/j.jbankfin.2010.03.019.

Martell, T. F., & Webb, G. P. (2008). The performance of stocks that are reverse splits. *Review of Quantitative Finance and Accounting, 30*(3), 253–279. https://doi.org/10.1007/s11156-007-0052-9.

Martellini, L. (2008). Toward the design of better equity benchmarks: Rehabilitating the tangency portfolio from modern portfolio theory. *Journal of Portfolio Management, 34*(4), 34–41.

Maymin, P. Z., Maymin, Z. G., & Fisher, G. S. (2014). Momentum's hidden sensitivity to the starting day. *Journal of Investing, 23*(2), 114–123. https://doi.org/10.3905/joi.2014.23.2.114.

McDonald, J. (1973). French mutual fund performance: Evaluation of internationally diversified portfolios. *Journal of Finance, 28*(5), 1161–1180.

McLean, R. D. (2010). Idiosyncratic risk, long-term reversal, and momentum. *Journal of Financial and Quantitative Analysis, 45*, 883–906.

McLean, D., & Pontiff, J. (2016). Does academic research destroy stock return predictability? *Journal of Finance, 71*(1), 5–32. https://doi.org/10.1111/jofi.12365.

Meneu, V., & Pardo, A. (2004). Pre-holiday effect, large trades and small investor behavior. *Journal of Empirical Finance, 11*(2), 231–246. https://doi.org/10.1016/j.jempfin.2003.01.002.

Menkoff, L., Sarno, L., Schmeling, M., & Schrimpf, A.(2011). *Currency momentum strategies*. Available at SSRN: http://ssrn.com/abstract=1809776 or https://doi.org/10.2139/ssrn.1809776. Accessed 21 Oct 2015.

Merton, R. C. (1981). On market timing and investment performance: An equilibrium theory of value for market forecasts. *Journal of Business, 54*(3), 363–406.

Merton, R. (1987). A simple model of capital market equilibrium with incomplete information. *Journal of Finance, 42*, 483–510.

Michou, M. (2009). Is the value spread a good predictor of stock returns? UK evidence. *Journal of Business, Finance, & Accounting, 36*(7–8), 925–950. https://doi.org/10.1111/j.1468-5957.2009.02148.x.

Miffre, J., & Rallis, G. (2007). Momentum strategies in commodity futures markets. *Journal of Banking & Finance, 31*(6), 1863–1886. https://doi.org/10.1016/j.jbankfin.2006.12.005.

Miller, E. M. (1977). Risk, uncertainty, and divergence of opinion. *Journal of Finance, 32*(4), 1151–1168.

Miller, M. H., & Scholes, M. (1972). Rates of return in relation to risk: A reexamination of some recent findings. In M. C. Jensen (Ed.), *Studies in the theory of capital markets*. New York: Praeger.

Mitton, T., & Vorkink, K. (2007). Equilibrium underdiversification and the preference for skewness. *Review of Financial Studies, 20*(4), 1255–1288.

Mohanram, P. (2005). Separating winners from losers among low book-to-market stocks using financial statement analysis. *Review of Accounting Studies, 10*, 133–170.

Monoyios, M., & Sarno, L. (2002). Mean reversion in stock index futures markets: A nonlinear analysis. *Journal of Futures Markets, 22*(4), 285–314. https://doi.org/10.1002/fut.10008.

Moskowitz, T. J., & Grinblatt, M. (1999). Do industries explain momentum? *Journal of Finance, 54*(4), 1249–1290.

Moskowitz, T. J., Ooi, Y. H., & Pedersen, L. H. (2012). Time series momentum. *Journal of Financial Economics, 104*(2), 228–250.

Moss, A., Clare, A., Thomas, S. H., & Seaton, J. (2015). Trend following and momentum strategies for global REITs. *Journal of Real Estate Portfolio Management, 21*(1), 21–31.

Mossin, J. (1966). Equilibrium in a capital asset market. *Econometrica, 35*(4), 768–783.

Mukherji, S., Kim, Y., & Walker, M. (1997). The effect of stock splits on the ownership structure of firms. *Journal of Corporate Finance, 3*, 167–188.

Muller, C., & Ward, M. (2010). Momentum effects in country equity indices. *Journal for Studies in Economics and Econometrics, 34*(1), 111–127.

Muscarella, C., & Vetsuypens, M. (1996). Stock splits: Signalling or liquidity? The case of ADR 'solo-splits'. *Journal of Financial Economics, 42*, 3–26.

Mustafa, K. (2011). The Islamic calendar effect on Karachi stock market. *Global Business Review, 13*(3), 562–574.

Muthoni, H. L. (2014). *Testing the existence of low price effect on stock returns at the Nairobi Securities Exchange* (Master thesis). Available at http://chss.uonbi.ac.ke/sites/default/files/chss/Huku%20L,%20D63-63781-3013,%20MSc%20Finance.pdf. Accessed 18 Oct 2017.

Nagel, S. (2012). Evaporating liquidity. *Review of Financial Studies, 25*(7), 2005–2039. https://doi.org/10.1093/rfs/hhs066.

Nai-Chiek, A. (2013). Seasonality in Southeast Asian stock markets: The Ramadan effect. *The IUP Journal of Applied Finance, 19*(3), 75–92.

Narang, R. K. (2013). *Inside the black box: A simple guide to quantitative and high frequency trading*. Hoboken: Wiley.

Narayan, P. K., & Agmed, H. A. (2014). Importance of skewness in decision making: Evidence from the Indian stock exchange. *Global Finance Journal, 25*(3), 260–269.

Nartea, G. V., Wu, J., & Liu, H. T. (2014). Extreme returns in emerging stock markets: Evidence of a MAX effect in South Korea. *Applied Financial Economics, 24*(6), 425–435. https://doi.org/10.1080/09603107.2014.884696.

Neuhauser, K. L., & Thompson, T. H. (2016). Survivability following reverse stock splits: What determines the fate of non-surviving firms? *Journal of Economics and Business, 83*, 1–22. https://doi.org/10.1016/j.jeconbus.2015.11.003.

Ng, K. Y., & Phelps, B. D. (2015). The hunt for a low-risk anomaly in the USD corporate bond market. *Journal of Portfolio Management, 42*(1) 63–84.

Ni, S. X. (2008). *Stock option returns: A puzzle*. Available at SSRN: https://ssrn.com/abstract=1340767 or https://doi.org/10.2139/ssrn.1340767. Accessed 23 Oct 2017.

Northcraft, G. B., & Neale, M. (1987). Experts, amateurs, and real estate: An anchoring-and-adjustment perspective on property pricing decisions. *Organizational Behavior and Human Decision Processes, 39*, 84–97.

Nosfinger, J. R., & Sias, R. W. (1999). Herding and feedback trading by institutional and individual investors. *Journal of Finance, 54*(6), 2263–2295.

Novy-Marx, R. (2012). Is momentum really momentum? *Journal of Financial Economics, 103*, 429–453.

Novy-Marx, R. (2013). The other side of value: The gross profitability premium. *Journal of Financial Economics, 108*, 1–28.

Novy-Marx, R., & Velikov, M. (2016). A taxonomy of anomalies and their trading costs. *Review of Financial Studies, 29*(1), 104–147. https://doi.org/10.1093/rfs/hhv063.

O'Neil, W. (2009). *How to make money in stocks: A winning system in good times and bad* (4th ed.). New York: McGraw Hill Education.

Odean, T. (1998a). Are investors reluctant to realize their losses? *Journal of Finance, 53*(5), 1775–1798.

Odean, T. (1998b). Volume, volatility, price, and profit when all traders are above average. *Journal of Finance, 53*(6), 1887–1934.

Ogden, J. P. (1990). Turn-of-month evaluations of liquid profits and stock returns: A common explanation for the monthly and January effects. *Journal of Finance, 45*(4), 1259–1272.

Okada, K., & Yamasaki, T. (2014). *Investor sentiment in news and the calendar anomaly – New evidence from a large textual data*. Available at SSRN: https://ssrn.com/abstract=2394008 or https://doi.org/10.2139/ssrn.2394008. Accessed 23 Oct 2017.

Okunev, J., & White, D. (2000). Do momentum based strategies still work in foreign currency markets. *Journal of Financial and Quantitative Markets, 38*(2), 422–457.

Olszewski, F., & Zhou, G. (2014). Strategy diversification: Combining momentum and carry strategies within a foreign exchange portfolio. *Journal of Derivatives & Hedge Funds, 19*(4), 311–320.

Osler, C. L. (2000). Support for resistance: Technical analysis and intraday exchange rates. *Economic Policy Review, 6*, 53–65.

Ozdagli, A. K. (2012). Financial leverage, corporate investment, and stock returns. *Review of Financial Studies, 25*, 1033–1069.

Page, M., & Way, C. (1992). Stock market overreaction: The South African evidence. *Investment Analysts Journal, 21*, 35–49.

Palazzo, B. (2012). Cash holdings, risk, and expected returns. *Journal of Financial Economics, 104*, 162–185.

Pan, M. S., Liano, K., & Huang, G.-C. (2004). Industry momentum strategies and autocorrelations in stock returns. *Journal of Empirical Finance, 11*(2), 185–202.

Park, C.-H., & Irwin, S. H. (2007). What do we know about the profitability of technical analysis? *Journal of Economic Surveys, 21*(4), 786–826.

Park, K.-I., & Kim, D. (2013). Sources of momentum profits in international stock markets. *Accounting and Finance, 54*(2), 567–589.

Park, T. H., & Switzer, L. N. (1996). Mean reversion of interest-rate term premiums and profits from trading strategies with treasury futures spreads. *Journal of Futures Markets, 16*(3), 331–352. https://doi.org/10.1002/(SICI)1096-9934(199605)16:3<331::AID-FUT5>3.0.CO;2-K.

Pastor, L., & Stambaugh, R. F. (2003). Liquidity risk and expected stock returns. *Journal of Political Economy, 111*(3), 642–685.

Peng, L., & Xiong, W. (2006). Investor attention, overconfidence and category learning. *Journal of Financial Economics, 80*(3), 563–602.

Penman, S., Richardson, S., & Tuna, I. (2007). The book-to-price effect in stock returns: Accounting for leverage. *Journal of Accounting Research, 45*, 427–467.

Pepelas, A. (2008). *Testing the overreaction hypothesis in the UK Stock market by using inter & intra industry contrarian strategies*. Available at SSRN: https://ssrn.com/abstract=1282776 or https://doi.org/10.2139/ssrn.1282776. Accessed 23 Oct 2017.

Pettengill, G., & Jordan, B. (1990). The overreaction hypothesis, firm size and stock market seasonality. *Journal of Portfolio Management, 16*(3), 60–64.

Phalippou, L. (2004). *What drives the value premium* (INSEAD working paper). Available at http://www3.nd.edu/~pschultz/Phalippou.pdf. Accessed 13 Oct 2015.

Piotroski, J. D. (2000). Value investing: The use of historical financial statement information to separate winners from losers. *Journal of Accounting Research, 38*, 1–52.

Pirrong, C. (2005). *Momentum in futures markets* (EFA 2005 Moscow meetings paper). Available at SSRN: http://ssrn.com/abstract=671841 or https://doi.org/10.2139/ssrn.671841. Accessed 21 Oct 2015.

Plessis, J., & Hallerbach, W. G. (2016). Volatility-weighting applied to momentum strategies. *Journal of Alternative Investments*. https://doi.org/10.3905/jai.2016.2016.1.050.

Pogue, G., Solnik, B., & Rousselin, A. (1974). *International diversification: A study of the French mutual funds* (Working paper). Sloan School of Management. Available at http://dspace.mit.edu/handle/1721.1/48147. Accessed 17 Oct 2015.

Pojarliev, M., & Levich, R. M. (2013). *A new look at currency investing*. CFA Institute Research Foundation Monograph. Available at SSRN: http://ssrn.com/abstract=2571391. Accessed 20 Oct 2015.

Pospisil, L., & Zhang, J. (2010). Momentum and reversal effects in corporate bond prices and credit cycles. *Journal of Fixed Income, 20*(2), 101–115.

Pouget, S., & Villeneuve, S. (2008). *Price formation with confirmation bias*. Available at http://www.creedexperiment.nl/enable2008/pouget.pdf. Accessed 24 Oct 2015.

Pouget, S., & Villeneuve, S. (2012). *A mind is a terrible thing to change: Confirmation bias in financial markets* (IDEI working papers 720). Toulouse: Institut d'Économie Industrielle (IDEI). Available at http://idei.fr/sites/default/files/medias/doc/wp/2012/wp_idei_720.pdf. Accessed 24 Oct 2015.

Rabin, M., & Schrag, J. (1999). First impressions matter: A model of confirmatory bias. *Quarterly Journal of Economics, 114*, 37–82.

Reidpath, D. D., & Diamond, M. R. (1995). A nonexperimental demonstration of anchoring bias. *Psychological Reports, 76*, 800–802.

Reinganum, M. R. (1983). The anomalous stock market behavior of small firms in January – Empirical tests for tax-loss selling effects. *Journal of Financial Economics, 12*, 89–104.

Rhea, R. (1932). *The Dow theory*. New York: Barrons.

Richards, A. J. (1997). Winner-loser reversals in national stock market indices: Can they be explained? *Journal of Finance, 52*(5), 2129–2144. https://doi.org/10.1111/j.1540-6261.1997.tb02755.x.

Richardson, S., Sloan, R. G., Soliman, M., & Tuna, I. (2005). Accrual reliability, earnings persistence and stock prices. *Journal of Accounting and Economics, 39*, 437–485.

Ro, S. H., & Gallimore, P. (2013). Real estate mutual funds: Herding, momentum trading and performance. *Real Estate Economics, 42*(1), 190–222.

Roberts, H. (1967). *Statistical versus clinical prediction of the stock market* (Unpublished manuscript).

Roberts, M. C. (2005). Technical analysis and genetic programming: Construction and testing a commodity portfolio. *Journal of Futures Markets, 25*(7), 643–660.

Rogalski, R. J., & Tinic, S. M. (1986). The January size effect: Anomaly or risk measurement? *Financial Analysts Journal, 42*(6), 63–70.

Roll, R. (1983). Vas ist das? The turn-of-the-year effect and the return premia of small firms. *Journal of Portfolio Management, 9*(Winter), 18–28.

Roll, R. (1984). A simple implicit measure of the effective bid-ask spread in an efficient market. *Journal of Finance, 39*, 1127–1139.

Roll, R. (1992). A mean/variance analysis of tracking error. *Journal of Portfolio Management, 18*(4), 13–22.

Rosenberg, B., Reid, K., & Lanstein, R. (1985). Persuasive evidence of market inefficiency. *Journal of Portfolio Management, 11*, 9–17.

Roussanov, N. (2010). Diversification and its discontents: Idiosyncratic and entrepreneurial risk in the quest for social status. *Journal of Finance, 65*(5), 1755–1788.

Rouwenhorst, G. K. (1998). International momentum strategies. *Journal of Finance, 53*(1), 267–284.

Rouwenhorst, G. K. (1999). Local return factors and turnover in emerging stock markets. *Journal of Finance, 54*, 1439–1464.

Rozeff, M. S., & Kinney, W. R. (1976). Capital market seasonality: The case of stock returns. *Journal of Financial Economics, 3*, 379–4012.

Rubinstein, M. (2001). Rational markets: Yes or no? The affirmative case. *Financial Analysts Journal, 57*(3), 15–29.

Sagi, J., & Seasholes, M. (2007). Firm-specific attributes and the cross section of momentum. *Journal of Financial Economics, 84*(2), 389–434.

Saleh, W. (2007). Overreaction: The sensitivity of defining the duration of formation period. *Applied Financial Economics, 17*, 45–61.

Saleh, W., & Al Sabbagh, O. (2010). Short-term stock price momentum, long-term stock price reversal and the effect of information uncertainty. *International Journal of Accounting and Finance, 2*(1), 1–48.

Samuelson, P. A. (1965). Proof that properly anticipated prices fluctuate randomly. *Industrial Management Review, 6*, 41–49.

Santos, T., & Veronesi, P. (2006). Labor income and predictable stock returns. *Review of Financial Studies, 19*(1), 1–44.

Schmidt, P. S., von Arx, U., Schrimpf, A., Wagner, A. F., & Ziegler, A. (2015). *Size and momentum profitability in international stock markets* (Swiss Finance Institute Research paper No. 15-29). Available at SSRN: http://ssrn.com/abstract=2642185 or https://doi.org/10.2139/ssrn.2642185. Accessed 20 Oct 2015.

Schneider, P., Wagner, C., & Zechner, J. (2016). *Low risk anomalies?* (CFS WP No. 550). Available at SSRN: https://ssrn.com/abstract=2858933. Accessed 23 Oct 2017.

Schultz, P. (2000). Stock splits, tick size and sponsorship. *Journal of Finance, 55*, 429–450.

Schwager, J. D. (1994). *The new market wizards: Conversations with America's top traders*. New York: HarperCollins.

Schwager, J. D. (2003). *Stock market wizards: Interviews with America's top stock traders*. New York: HarperBusiness.

Schwager, J. D. (2012a). *Hedge fund market wizards: How winning traders win?* Hoboken: John Wiley & Sons.

Schwager, J. D. (2012b). *Market wizards, updated: Interviews with top traders.* Hoboken: John Wiley & Sons.

Schwert, G. W. (2003). Anomalies and market efficiency. In G. Constantinides, M. Harris, & R. Stulz (Eds.), *Handbook of the economics of finance.* Amsterdam: North Holland.

Seamans, G. (1939). *The seven pillars of stock market success.* Brightwaters: Windsor Books.

Sehgal, S., & Garg, V. (2016). Cross sectional moments and portfolio returns: Evidence for select emerging markets. *IIMB Management Review, 28*(3), 147–159.

Sekuła, P. (2015). Nadreaktywność GPW w Warszawie – analiza empiryczna. *Zeszyty Naukowe Uniwersytetu Szczecińskiego nr 855, "Finanse, Rynki Finansowe, Ubezpieczenia", 74*(1), 171–180.

Sensoy, B. (2009). Performance evaluation and self designated benchmark indexes in the mutual fund management industry. *Journal of Financial Economics, 92*(1), 25–39.

Serban, A. F. (2010). Combining mean reversion and momentum trading strategies in foreign exchange markets. *Journal of Banking & Finance, 34*(11), 2720–2727. https://doi.org/10.1016/j.jbankfin.2010.05.011.

Seyyed, F., Abraham, A., & Al-Hajji, M. (2005). Seasonality in stock returns and volatility. The Ramadan effect. *Research in International Business and Finance, 19*(3), 374–383.

Shaik, R. (2011). *Risk-adjusted momentum: A superior approach to momentum investing* (White paper). Bridgeway Capital Management. Available at http://www.dorseywright.com/downloads/hrs_research/Momentum%20White%20Paper%202011%20Fall.pdf

Sharpe, W. F. (1964). Capital asset prices: A theory of market equilibrium under conditions of risk. *Journal of Finance, 19*(3), 425–442.

Sharpe, W. F. (1966). Mutual fund performance. *Journal of Business, 39*(January), 119–138.

Sharpe, W. F. (1981). Decentralized investment management. *Journal of Finance, 36*(2), 217–234.

Sharpe, W. F. (1992). Asset allocation: Management style and performance measurement. *Journal of Portfolio Management, 18*, 7–19.

Shefrin, H., & Statman, M. (1985). The disposition to sell winners too early and ride losers too long: Theory and evidence. *Journal of Finance, 40*(3). Papers and Proceedings of the Forty-Third Annual Meeting American Finance Association, Dallas, Texas, December 28–30, pp. 777–790.

Shiller, R. J. (1984). *Stock prices and social dynamics* (Cowles Foundation Paper #616, pp. 457–510). Available at http://www.econ.yale.edu/~shiller/pubs/p0616.pdf. Accessed 9 Oct 2017.

Shiller, R. J. (1988). Portfolio insurance and other investor fashions as factors in the 1987 stock market crash. *NBER Macroeconomic Annual, 3*, 287–296.

Shleifer, A. (2000). *Inefficient markets: An introduction to behavioral finance*. Oxford: Oxford University Press.

Shleifer, A., & Vishny, R. W. (1997). The limits of arbitrage. *Journal of Finance, 52*(1), 35–55.

Shon, J., & Zhou, P. (2010). Do divergent opinions explain the value premium? *Journal of Investing, 19*(2), 53–62.

Sias, R. (2007). Causes and seasonality of momentum profits. *Financial Analysts Journal, 63*(2), 48–54.

Sias, R. W., & Starks, L. T. (1995). The day-of-the-week anomaly: The role of institutional investors. *Financial Analysts Journal, 51*(3), 58–67.

Silber, W. L. (1994). Technical trading: When it works and when it doesn't. *Journal of Derivatives, 1*, 39–44.

Simkowitz, M. A., & Beedles, W. L. (1978). Diversification in a three-moment world. *Journal of Financial and Quantitative Analysis, 13*(5), 927–941.

Sloan, R. G. (1996). Do stock prices reflect information in accruals and cash flows about future earnings? *Accounting Review, 71*, 289–315.

Slovic, P., & Lichtenstein, S. (1971). Comparison of Bayesian and regression approaches to the study of information processing in judgement. *Organizational Behavior and Human Performance, 6*, 649–744.

Smith, D. M., & Pantilei, V. S. (2013, forthcoming). Do 'dogs of the world' bark or bite? Evidence from single-country ETFs. *Journal of Investing*. Available at SSRN: https://ssrn.com/abstract=2279246 or https://doi.org/10.2139/ssrn.2279246. Accessed 23 Oct 2017.

Sonjaya, A. R., & Wahyudi, I. (2016). The Ramadan effect: Illusion or reality? *Arab Economic and Business Journal, 11*(1), 55–71. https://doi.org/10.1016/j.aebj.2016.03.001.

Soros, G. (2003). *The alchemy of finance*. Hoboken: John Wiley & Sons.

Spierdijk, L., Bikker, J. A., & van den Hoek, P. (2012). Mean reversion in international stock markets: An empirical analysis of the 20th century. *Journal of International Money and Finance, 31*(2), 228–249. https://doi.org/10.1016/j.jimonfin.2011.11.008.

Spudeck, R. E., & Moyer, C. R. (1985). Reverse splits and shareholder wealth: The impact of commissions. *Financial Management, 14*, 52–56.

Stambaugh, R. F., Yu, J., & Yuan, Y. (2012). The short of it: Investor sentiment and anomalies. *Journal of Financial Economics, 104*(2), 288–302. https://doi.org/10.1016/j.jfineco.2011.12.001.

Steeley, J. M. (2001). A note on information seasonality and the disappearance of the weekend effect in the UK stock market. *Journal of Banking and Finance, 25*(1), 1941–1956.

Stevenson, R. W. (1999, January 29). Asked about internet issues, the Fed Chairman Shrugs. *The New York Times.* Available at http://www.nytimes.com/1999/01/29/business/the-markets-asked-about-internet-issues-the-fed-chairman-shrugs.html. Accessed 11 Oct 2017.

Stiglitz, J. E. (1989). Using tax policy to curb speculative trading. *Journal of Financial Services, 3,* 101–115.

Stivers, C., Sun, L., & Sun, Y. (2009). The other January effect: International, style, and subperiod evidence. *Journal of Financial Markets, 12,* 521–546.

Stock, D. (1990). Winner and loser anomalies in the German stock market. *Journal of Institutional and theoretical Economics, 146*(3), 518–529.

Stockopedia. (2012). *What is a momentum crash and why does it happen?* Available at http://www.businessinsider.com/what-is-a-momentum-crash-and-why-does-it-happen--2012-11. Accessed 10 Sept 2017.

Subrahmanyam, A. (2005). Distinguishing between rationales for short-horizon predictability of stock returns. *Financial Review, 40,* 11–35.

Sule, A. (2012). The death of diversification has been greatly exaggerated (Digest summary). *CFA Digest, 42*(4). Available at http://www.cfapubs.org/doi/full/10.2469/dig.v42.n4.3

Sullivan, R., Timmermann, A., & White, H. (2001). Dangers of data mining: The case of calendar effects in stock returns. *Journal of Econometrics, 105*(1), 249–286.

Sum, V. (2013). *Stock market performance: High and low months.* Available at SSRN: https://ssrn.com/abstract=2275061 or https://doi.org/10.2139/ssrn.2275061. Accessed 23 Oct 2017.

Summers, L. H., & Summers, V. P. (1989). When financial markets work too well: A cautious case for a securities transactions tax. *Journal of Financial Services, 3,* 261–286.

Svenson, O. (1981). Are we all less risky and more skillful than our fellow drivers? *Acta Psychologica, 47*(2), 143–148.

Swallow, S., & Fox, M. A. (1998). *Long run overreaction on the New Zealand Stock Exchange* (Commerce Division discussion paper, 48). Available at http://citeseerx.ist.psu.edu/viewdoc/download?doi=10.1.1.568.515&rep=rep1&type=pdf

Sweeney, R. J. (2006). Mean reversion in G-10 nominal exchange rates. *Journal of Financial and Quantitative Analysis, 41*(3), 685–708 http://www.jstor.org/stable/27647266.

Swinkels, L., & van Vliet, P. (2012). An anatomy of calendar effects. *Journal of Asset Management, 13*(4), 271–286.

Sylvain, S. (2014). *Does human capital risk explain the value premium puzzle?* (Working paper). Available at SSRN: http://ssrn.com/abstract=2400593 or https://doi.org/10.2139/ssrn.2400593. Accessed 30 Sept 2017.

Szakmary, A. C., & Zhou, X. (2015). Industry momentum in an earlier time: Evidence from the Cowles data. *Journal of Financial Research, 38*(3), 319–347.

Szymanowska, M., de Roon, F., Nijman, T., & van den Goorbergh, R. (2014). An anatomy of commodity futures risk premia. *Journal of Finance, 69*(1), 453–482.

Szyszka, A. (2013). *Behavioral finance and capital markets: How psychology influences investors and corporation.* New York: Palgrave Macmillan.

Taleb, N. N. (2005). *Fooled by randomness: The hidden role of chance in life and in the markets.* New York: Random House.

Taleb, N. N. (2006). *The black swan: The impact of the highly improbable.* New York: Random House.

Tamura, H., & Shimizu, Y. (2005). *Fundamental indices. Do they outperform market-cap weighted indices on a global basis?* Tokyo: Global Quantitative Research, Nomura Securities.

Teo, M., & Woo, S.-J. (2004). Style effects in the cross-section of stock returns. *Journal of Financial Economics, 74*(2), 367–398. Available at https://doi.org/10.1016/j.jfineco.2003.10.003

Teplova, T., & Mikova, E. (2011). A Higher moment downside framework for conditional and unconditional CAPM in the Russian stock market. *Eurasian Economic Review, 1*, 157–178.

Teplova, T., & Mikova, E. (2015). New evidence on determinants of price momentum in the Japanese stock market. *Research in International Business and Finance, 34*, 84–109.

Tiakas, I. (2010). The economic gains of trading stocks around holidays. *Journal of Financial Research, 33*(1), 1–26. https://doi.org/10.1111/j.1475-6803.2009.01260.x.

Tibbs, S. L., Eakins, S. G., & DeShurko, W. (2008). Using style momentum to generate alpha. *Journal of Technical Analysis, 65*, 50–56.

Tinic, S. M., & West, R. R. (1986). Risk, return and equilibrium: A revisit. *Journal of Political Economy, 94*, 126–147.

Titman, S., Wei, K. J., & Xie, F. (2004). Capital investments and stock returns. *Journal of Financial and Quantitative Analysis, 39*, 677–700.

Treynor, J. L (1962). *Toward a theory of market value of risky assets* (Unpublished manuscript). Final version in *Asset Pricing and Portfolio Performance* (pp. 15–22), 1999, Robert A. Korajczyk (ed.). London: Risk Books. Available also at SSRN: http://ssrn.com/abstract=628187 or https://doi.org/10.2139/ssrn.628187. Accessed 17 Oct 2015.

Treynor, J., & Mazuy, K. (1966). Can mutual funds outguess the market? *Harvard Business Review, 44*, 131–136.

Tripathi, V., & Aggarwal, S. (2009). The overreaction effect in Indian stock market. *Asian Journal of Business and Accounting, 2*(1–2), 93–114.

Tversky, A., & Kahneman, D. (1971). Belief in the law of small numbers. *Psychological Bulletin, 2*, 105–110.

Tversky, A., & Kahneman, D. (1974). Judgement under uncertainty: Heuristics and biases. *Science, 185*, 1124–1131.

Tversky, A., & Kahneman, D. (1982). Judgments of and by representativeness. In D. Kahneman, P. Slovic, & A. Tversky (Eds.), *Judgment under uncertainty: Heuristics and biases* (pp. 84–98). Cambridge: Cambridge University Press.

Tversky, A., & Kahneman, D. (1992). Advances in prospect theory: Cumulative representation of uncertainty. *Journal of Risk and Uncertainty, 5*(4), 297–323.

Umutlu, M. (2015). Idiosyncratic volatility and expected returns at the global level. *Financial Analysts Journal, 71*(6), 58–71.

Umutlu, M., & Bengitöz, P. (2017). *The cross-section of expected index returns in international stock markets.* Working paper presented at the 2017 Infiniti Conference in Valencia, Spain.

van Horne, J. C., & Parker, G. G. C. (1967). The random-walk theory: An empirical test. *Financial Analyst Journal, 23*(6), 87–92.

van Horne, J. C., & Parker, G. G. C. (1968). Technical trading rules: A comment. *Financial Analyst Journal, 24*(4), 128–132.

van Vliet, P., Blitz, D., & van der Grient, B. (2011). *Is the relation between volatility and expected stock returns positive, flat or negative?* Available at SSRN: http://ssrn.com/abstract=1881503 or https://doi.org/10.2139/ssrn.1881503. Accessed 25 Oct 2015.

van Zundert, J. (2017). *A new test for cross-sectional momentum.* Available at SSRN: https://ssrn.com/abstract=2880097. Accessed 23 Oct 2017.

Verousis, T., & Voukelatos, N. (2015). *Cross-sectional dispersion and expected returns.* Available at SSRN: https://ssrn.com/abstract=2734192 or https://doi.org/10.2139/ssrn.2734192. Accessed 23 Oct 2017.

Vinod, H. D., & Morey, M. R. (1999). *A double Sharpe ratio* (Working paper). Available at SSRN: http://papers.ssrn.com/sol3/papers.cfm?abstract_id=168748. Accessed 16 Oct 2017.

Vu, J. D. (2012). Do momentum strategies generate profits in emerging stock markets? *Problems and Perspectives in Management, 10*(3), 2012.

Wachtel, S. B. (1942). Certain observations on seasonal movements in stock prices. *Journal of Business, 15*, 184–193.

Waelkens, K., & Ward, M. (2015). The low price effect on the Johannesburg Stock Exchange. *Investment Analysts Journal, 26*(45), 35.

Walkshausl, C. (2014a). International low-risk investing. *Journal of Portfolio Management, 41*(4), 45–56.

Walkshausl, C. (2014b). The MAX effect: European evidence. *Journal of Banking and Finance, 42*(1), 1–10. https://doi.org/10.1016/j.jbankfin.2014.01.020.

Walkshausl, C., & Lobe, S. (2010). Fundamental indexing around the world. *Review of Financial Economics, 19*(3), 117–127.

Wang, M. S. (2012). Idiosyncratic volatility, illiquidity and the expected stock returns: Exploring the relationship with quantile regression. *Investment Management and Financial Innovations, 9*(4), 104–112 http://businessperspectives.org/journals_free/imfi/2012/imfi_en_2012_04_Wang.pdf.

Wang, P., & Kochard, L. (2011). *Using a Z-score approach to combine value and momentum in tactical asset allocation.* Available at SSRN: https://ssrn.com/abstract=1726443 or https://doi.org/10.2139/ssrn.1726443. Accessed 23 Oct 2017.

Wang, K. Q., & Xu, J. (2015). Market volatility and momentum. *Journal of Empirical Finance, 30*, 79–91. https://doi.org/10.1016/j.jempfin.2014.11.009.

Wang, H., & Yu, J. (2013). *Dissecting the profitability premium* (AFA 2013 San Diego meetings paper). Retrieved from SSRN: https://doi.org/10.2139/ssrn.1711856. Accessed 4 Nov 2015.

Wason, P. C. (1960). On the failure to eliminate hypotheses in a conceptual task. *Quarterly Journal of Experimental Psychology, 12*, 129–140.

Waszczuk, A. (2014a). Assembling international equity datasets – Review of studies on the cross-section of returns. *Procedia Economics and Finance: Emerging Markets Queries in Finance and Business(EMQ 2013), 15*, 1603–1612.

Waszczuk, A. (2014b). *Diversity of empirical design – Review of studies on the cross-section of common stocks* (Working paper). Available at SSRN: http://ssrn.com/abstract=2428054 or https://doi.org/10.2139/ssrn.2428054. Accessed 11 Oct 2015.

Watson, S. R., & Buede, D. M. (1987). *Decision synthesis: The principles and practice of decision analysis.* Cambridge: Cambridge University Press.

Weber, M., & Camerer, C. F. (1998). The disposition effect in securities trading: An experimental analysis. *Journal of Economic Behavior and Organization, 33*(2), 167–184.

Weber, C., & Nickol, P. (2016). More on calendar effects on Islamic stock markets. *Review of Middle East Economics and Finance, 12*(1), 65–113. https://doi.org/10.1515/rmeef-2015-0039.

Wei, J. Z. (2011). *Do momentum and reversals coexist?* Available at SSRN: https://ssrn.com/abstract=1679464 or https://doi.org/10.2139/ssrn.1679464. Accessed 10 Oct 2017.

Wei, J. Z., & Yang, L. (2012). *Short-term momentum and reversals in large stocks.* Available at SSRN: https://ssrn.com/abstract=2029984 or https://doi.org/10.2139/ssrn.20299849. Accessed 10 Oct 2017.

Welch, I. (2000). Herding among security analysts. *Journal of Financial Economics, 58*, 69–396.

Weld, W. C., Michaely, R., Thaler, R. H., & Benartzi, S. (2009). The nominal share price puzzle. *Journal of Economic Perspectives, 23*(2), 121–142.

Wilmott, P. (2008). *Paul Wilmott on quantitative finance.* Hoboken: John Wiley & Sons.

Wu, Y. (2011). Momentum trading, mean reversion and overreaction in Chinese stock market. *Review of Quantitative Finance and Accounting, 37*(3), 301–323.

Wyckoff, R. F. (1924). *How I trade in stocks and bonds: Being some methods evolved and adapted during my thirty-three years' experience in Wall Street.* New York: Magazine of Wall Street.

Xing, Y., Zhang, X., & Zhao, R. (2010). What does the individual option volatility smirk tell us about future equity returns? *Journal of Financial Quantitative Analysis, 45*(3), 641–662.

Yan, Z., & Zhao, Y. (2013). International diversification: Simple or optimization strategies? *International Journal of Finance, 25*(1), 1–33.

Yang, J., Zjou, Y., & Wang, Z. (2010). Conditional co-skewness in stock and bond markets: Time series evidence. *Management Science, 56*(11), 2031–2049.

Yao, Y. (2012). Momentum, contrarian, and the January seasonality. *Journal of Banking and Finance, 36*, 2757–2769. https://doi.org/10.1016/j.jbankfin.2011.12.004.

Yufeng, H., Guofu, Z., & Yingzi, Z. (2016). A trend factor: Any economic gains from using information over investment horizons? *Journal of Financial Economics, 122*(2), 352–375. https://doi.org/10.1016/j.jfineco.2016.01.029.

Zakamulin, V. (2015a). *A comprehensive look at the empirical performance of moving average trading strategies.* Available at SSRN: https://ssrn.com/abstract=2677212 or https://doi.org/10.2139/ssrn.2677212. Accessed 19 Oct 2017.

Zakamulin, V. (2015b). Market timing with a robust moving average. Available at SSRN: https://ssrn.com/abstract=2612307 or https://doi.org/10.2139/ssrn.2612307. Accessed 19 Oct 2017.

Zakamulin, V. (2016a). *Revisiting the profitability of market timing with moving averages.* Available at SSRN: https://ssrn.com/abstract=2743119 or https://doi.org/10.2139/ssrn.2743119. Accessed 19 Oct 2017.

Zakamulin, V. (2016b). *Market timing with moving averages: Anatomy and performance of trading rules.* Available at SSRN: https://ssrn.com/abstract=2585056 or https://doi.org/10.2139/ssrn.2585056. Accessed 19 Oct 2017.

Zaremba, A. (2015a). *The momentum effect in country-level stock market anomalies.* Available at SSRN: https://ssrn.com/abstract=2621236 or https://doi.org/10.2139/ssrn.2621236. Accessed 23 Oct 2017.

Zaremba, A. (2015b, forthcoming). Investor sentiment, limits on arbitrage, and the performance of cross-country market anomalies. *Journal of Behavioral and Experimental Finance*, 9, 136–163. http://dx.doi.org/10.1016/j.jbef.2015.11.007

Zaremba, A. (2015c). *The financialization of commodity markets: Investing during times of transition.* New York: Palgrave Macmillan.

Zaremba, A. (2015d, forthcoming). Is there low-risk anomaly across countries? *Eurasian Economic Review.* 69(1), 45–65.

Zaremba, A. (2015e). The January seasonality and the performance of country-level value and momentum strategies. *Copernican Journal of Finance & Accounting, 2*, 195–209. http://apcz.pl/czasopisma/index.php/CJFA/article/view/CJFA.2015.024

Zaremba, A. (2015f). Country selection strategies based on value, size and momentum. *Investment Analyst Journal, 44*(3), 171–198.

Zaremba, A. (2016a). Strategies based on momentum and term structure in financialized -commodity markets. *Business and Economics Research Journal, 7*(1), 31–46.

Zaremba, A. (2016b). Risk-based explanation for the country-level size and value effects. *Finance Research Letters, 18*, 226–233. https://doi.org/10.1016/j.frl.2016.04.020.

Zaremba, A. (2016c). Has the long-term reversal reversed? Evidence from country equity indices. *Romanian Journal of Economic Forecasting, 19*(1), 88–103. http://www.ipe.ro/rjef/rjefl_16/rjefl_2016p88-103.pdf

Zaremba, A. (2016d). *Country risk and expected returns across global equity markets.* Available at SSRN: https://ssrn.com/abstract=2778061. Accessed 23 Jan 2018.

Zaremba, A. (2017a). Performance persistence of government bond factor premia. *Finance Research Letters, 22*, 182–189. https://doi.org/10.1016/j.frl.2016.12.022.

Zaremba, A. (2017b). *Performance persistence in anomaly returns: Evidence from frontier markets.* Available at SSRN: https://ssrn.com/abstract=3060876. Accessed 31 Oct 2017.

Zaremba, A. (2017c). Combining country equity selection strategies. *Contemporary Economics, 11*(1), 107–126. https://doi.org/10.5709/ce.1897-9254.231.

Zaremba, A. (2017d). Seasonality in the cross section of factor premia. *Investment Analysts Journal*, (3), 165–199. https://doi.org/10.1080/10293523.2017.1326219.

Zaremba, A., & Andreu Sánchez, L. (2017). *Paper profits or real money? Trading costs and stock market anomalies in country equity indices.* Available at https://doi.org/10.2139/ssrn.3038514

Zaremba, A., & Czapkiewicz, A. (2017a). Digesting anomalies in emerging European markets: A comparison of factor pricing models. *Emerging Markets Review, 31*, 1–15. https://doi.org/10.1016/j.ememar.2016.12.002.

Zaremba, A., & Czapkiewicz, A. (2017b, in press). The cross section of international government bond returns. *Economic Modelling.* https://doi.org/10.1016/j.econmod.2017.06.011.

Zaremba, A., & Miziołek, T. (2017a). Fundamental indexation in European emerging markets. *Romanian Journal of Economic Forecasting, 20*(1), 23–37.

Zaremba, A., & Miziołek, T. (2017b, in press). Nothing lasts forever (and everywhere): Fundamental indexation at the global level. *Journal of Index Investing*, 8(3), 6–20. https://doi.org/10.3905/jii.2017.8.3.006

Zaremba, A., & Nikorowski, J. (2017). *Trading costs, short sale constraints, and the performance of stock market anomalies in Emerging Europe*. Available at SSRN: https://ssrn.com/abstract=2778063. Accessed 23 Oct 2017.

Zaremba, A., & Nowak, A. (2015a). Skewness preference across countries. *Business and Economic Horizons*, (2), 115–130. https://doi.org/10.15208/beh.2015.09.

Zaremba, A., & Nowak, A. (2015b). Czy historyczna skośność pozwala prognozować stopy zwrotu na polskim rynku akcji? *Zeszyty Naukowe Uniwersytetu Szczecińskiego. Finanse, Rynki Finansowe, Ubezpieczenia. Ryzyko, Zarządzanie, 73*, 735–748.

Zaremba, A., & Schabek, T. (2017). Seasonality in government bond returns and factor premia. *Research in International Business and Finance, 41*, 292–302. https://doi.org/10.1016/j.ribaf.2017.04.036.

Zaremba, A., & Shemer, J. (2016a). *Country asset allocation*. New York: Palgrave Macmillan.

Zaremba, A., & Shemer, J. (2016b). Is small beautiful? Size effect in stock markets. *Country Asset Allocation*, 67–79. https://doi.org/10.1057/978-1-137-59191-3_4.

Zaremba, A., & Shemer, J. (2016c). Momentum effect across countries. *Country Asset Allocation*, 161–181. New York: Palgrave Macmillan. https://doi.org/10.1057/978-1-137-59191-3_10.

Zaremba, A., & Shemer, J. (2016d). Value versus growth: Is buying cheap always a bargain? *Country Asset Allocation*, 9–38. New York: Palgrave Macmillan. https://doi.org/10.1057/978-1-137-59191-3_2.

Zaremba, A., & Shemer, K. (2016e). *What drives the momentum in factor premia? Evidence from international equity markets*. Paper presented at the 20th EBES Conferences, September 28–30, 2016, Vienna, Austria.

Zaremba, A., & Shemer, J. (2016f). Testing the country allocation strategies. *Country Asset Allocation*, 123–136. New York: Palgrave Macmillan. https://doi.org/10.1057/978-1-137-59191-3_7

Zaremba, A., & Shemer, K. (2017, in press). Is there momentum in factor premia? Evidence from international equity markets. *Research in International Business and Finance*. https://doi.org/10.1016/j.ribaf.2017.12.002

Zaremba, A., & Szyszka, A. (2016). Is there momentum in equity anomalies? Evidence from the Polish emerging market. *Research in International Business and Finance, 38*, 546–564. https://doi.org/10.1016/j.ribaf.2016.07.004.

Zaremba, A., & Umutlu, M. (2018a, in press). Strategies can be expensive too! The value spread and asset allocation in global equity markets. *Applied Economics*.

Zaremba, A., & Umutlu, M. (2018b, in press). Less pain, more gain: Volatility-adjusted residual momentum in international equity markets. *Investment Analysts Journal*. https://doi.org/10.1080/10293523.2018.1469290.

Zaremba, A., & Umutlu, M. (2018c). Size matters everywhere: Decomposing the small country and small industry premia. *The North American Journal of Economics and Finance, 43*, 1–18. https://doi.org/10.1016/j.najef.2017.09.002.

Zaremba, A., & Umutlu, M. (2018d). *Opposites attract: Alpha momentum and alpha reversal in country and industry equity indexes* (Unpublished working paper).

Zaremba, A., & Żmudziński, R. (2014). The low price effect on the Polish market. *e-Finanse, 10*(1), 69–85. Available at http://yadda.icm.edu.pl/yadda/element/bwmeta1.element.ekon-element-000171278151

Zaremba, A., Konieczka, P., Okoń, S., & Nowak, A. (2016a). The low price anomaly and the intriguing case of the Polish stock market. *Inzinerine Ekonomika-Engineering Economics, 27*(2), 163–174. https://doi.org/10.5755/j01.ee.27.2.13490.

Zaremba, A., Okoń, S., & Asyngier, R. (2016b). *Reverse splits in international stock markets: Reconciling the evidence on long-term returns*. Available at SSRN: https://ssrn.com/abstract=2820586. Accessed 18 Oct 2017.

Zarowin, P. (1989). Does the stock market overreact to corporate earnings information? *Journal of Finance, 44*, 1385–1399.

Zarowin, P. (1990). Size, seasonality, stock market and overreaction. *Journal of Financial and quantitative Analysis, 25*, 113–125.

Zhang, X. F. (2006). Information uncertainty and stock returns. *Journal of Finance, 61*(1), 105–101.

Zhang, C. Y., & Jacobsen, B. (2013). Are monthly seasonals real? A three century perspective. *Review of Finance, 17*(5), 1743–1785.

Zhong, A., & Gray, P. (2016). The MAX effect: An exploration of risk and mispricing explanations. *Journal of Banking and Finance, 65*(1), 76–90.

Zhou, G., & Zhu, Y. (2013). *An equilibrium model of moving-average predictability and time-series momentum*. Available at SSRN. doi: https://doi.org/10.2139/ssrn.2326650. Accessed 23 Oct 2017.

Zhu, Z., & Yung, K. (2016). The interaction of short-term reversal and momentum strategies. *Journal of Portfolio Management, 42*(4), 96–107. https://doi.org/10.3905/jpm.2016.42.4.096.

Ziemba, W. T. (1991). Japanese security market regularities: Monthly, turn of the month and year, holiday and golden week effects. *Japan and the World Economy, 3*, 119–146.

Index[1]

[1] Note: Page numbers followed by 'n' refer to notes.

A. Zaremba, J. "Koby" Shemer, *Price-Based Investment Strategies*,
https://doi.org/10.1007/978-3-319-91530-2

The manufacturer's authorised representative in the EU is Springer Nature Customer Service Centre GmbH, Europaplatz 3, 69115 Heidelberg, Germany. If you have any concerns regarding our products, please contact ProductSafety@springernature.com

Printed and bound by CPI Group (UK) Ltd, Croydon, CR0 4YY
05/10/2026
02228128-0011